THE ART OF BURNING BRIDGES

THE ART OF BURNING BRIDGES
A Life of John O'Hara

GEOFFREY WOLFF

ALFRED A. KNOPF NEW YORK 2003

THIS IS A BORZOI BOOK PUBLISHED BY ALFRED A. KNOPF

Copyright © 2003 by Geoffrey Wolff

www.aaknopf.com

Knopf, Borzoi Books, and the colophon are registered trademarks of Random House, Inc.

A portion previously appeared in Vanity Fair.

Owing to limitations of space, all permissions to reprint previously published material
can be found immediately following the index.

Library of Congress Cataloging-in-Publication Data
Wolff, Geoffrey.
The art of burning bridges : a life of John O'Hara / Geoffrey Wolff.—1st ed.
p.   cm.
Includes bibliographical references (p.) and index.
ISBN 0-679-42771-6 (alk. paper)
1. O'Hara, John, 1905–1970. 2. Novelists, American—20th century—Biography. I. Title.
PS3529.H29 Z93 2003
813'.52—dc21
[B]   2002043095

Manufactured in the United States of America
First Edition

For Heidi, Megan, and Ivan

The dark street lightened, the dwellings of the rich loomed up around them, he stopped his coupé in front of the great white bulk of the Mortimer Joneses' house, somnolent, gorgeous, drenched with the splendor of the damp moonlight. Its solidity startled him. The strong walls, the steel of the girders, the breadth and beam and pomp of it were there only to bring out the contrast with the young beauty beside him. It was sturdy to accentuate her slightness—as if to show what a breeze could be generated by a butterfly's wing.

—F. SCOTT FITZGERALD, "WINTER DREAMS"

CONTENTS

ACKNOWLEDGMENTS

As one old enough to have become a "resource" for biographers meaning to write about a few of my friends and acquaintances, I have learned how much energy and consideration is demanded of people willing to be interviewed, to search for and share letters and snapshots, to dig for dates and sequences, to estimate the character and even the value of another's life. To trust a biographer with one's memories and memorabilia requires faith, often blind faith. What's in it for the source? More pertinently, what's in it for the subject? The meeting ground between sources and biographers is so strewn with misapprehension, bad faith, betrayal, and misquotation that it is a wonder that anyone consents to be exploited for any biography. But in fact almost all of John O'Hara's living friends and extended family members gave to me what they could of their memories, judgments, and documents.

Let's stipulate that selflessness is a happy mystery, but much of the generosity from which this book benefitted can be explained by the determination of O'Hara's friends and kin (and even foes, such as Brendan Gill) to redress the casual disdain triggered in some influential strangers by his very name. Moreover, all of those who helped were eager to celebrate this or that piece of O'Hara's fiction that they wanted other readers to experience.

A process of reputational rehabilitation began the year after O'Hara's death, in the form of weekly installments of "O'Hara's Roots," by Charles W. Bassett, published in the *Pottsville Republican* from March 20, 1971, to January 8, 1972. I have drawn liberally on Bassett's series for accounts of O'Hara's school days and newspaper work. The first general biography, Finis Farr's *O'Hara,* followed in 1973 and is especially valuable as a portrait composed from inside the tent, by a friend of O'Hara's and—especially—of O'Hara's friends. Two years later came *The O'Hara Concern,* Matthew J. Bruccoli's laborious excavation of the details of O'Hara's history, an investigation of the facts underlying family legends, a huge album of photos and facsimiles, a vigorous if often injudicious effort to boost O'Hara's achievement as a writer. If Bruccoli's literary judgments often seem superficial—as narrow and pugnacious as a defense counsel's—he has assembled one hell of an archive. *The O'Hara Concern* was followed in 1977 by Bruccoli's edited collection *"An Artist Is His Own Fault": John O'Hara on Writers and Writing,* followed the next year by his edition of *Selected Letters of John O'Hara* (1978), a work invaluable to the book at hand. Also published in 1978, Bruccoli's *John O'Hara: A Descriptive Bibliography* specifies chapter and verse on various editions of O'Hara's books, their critical reception and sales, the author's articles, essays, and even the blurbs he wrote. Published in 1980, Frank Mac-Shane's *The Life of John O'Hara* gives especially detailed accounts of O'Hara's Hollywood years and of his friendship with Adele Lovett.

Like Bruccoli and MacShane, I have been assisted crucially in my research by the accessibility of the John O'Hara Papers at the Pattee Library, Pennsylvania State University, whose Sandy Stelts and the late Charles Mann opened doors, shared papers in the process of being archived, and let me linger in a reconstruction of O'Hara's workplace known as the Linebrook Study. (Alexander Nehamas, current owner of Linebrook, invited me to look over the place.) Early in my research the *New Yorker* files, housed in the New York Public Library, were made available to scholars, and from these I got the magazine's perspective on O'Hara's work and behavior. The Firestone Library at Princeton let me look at Kyle Crichton's letters, and Columbia's Butler Library gave me access to Random House, Bennett Cerf, and Lionel Trilling papers. The Bryn Mawr library provided copies of Katharine White's summary of O'Hara. Marybeth Evans, of the PBS television station WVIA in Pittston, Pennsylvania, provided audio tapes of an O'Hara jamboree broadcast by its FM station over the course of 1995. Carter, Ledyard & Milburn, attorneys for the O'Hara estate, provided access to his papers stored for safe keeping at the United States Trust Company.

Among those who granted interviews and corresponded with me I'd like to thank especially Patience Outerbridge Banister, Marjorie Benchley, David Brown, Joseph M. Fox, Kate Gardiner, Peter Gates, Brendan Gill, Alexandra Isles, Janet (Barnes) Lawrence, William D'O. Lippincott, John Logan, Robert Loomis, Richard M. Ludwig, William Maxwell, John McPhee, David Outerbridge, Lorraine Rowan, and Elaine Steinbeck.

Kathleen O'Hara Fuldner, O'Hara's youngest and only surviving sibling, opened her house, kitchen, scrapbooks, and opinions to me. C. D. B. ("Courty") Bryan got me started once I decided I would write about his stepfather. He made suggestions, was articulately emphatic in his affection, argued with me when I seemed to him offtrack. Mary Leigh ("Lili") Pell Whitmer was tirelessly hospitable and helpful in remembering the years just before and after Belle Wylie O'Hara's death.

Wylie O'Hara Doughty is in a class by herself. I only wish that her father could have heard her talk about him. I heard her, and what she said—how she said what she said—shifted many emphases in this book. She involved her husband Scott and daughter Belle in the process of research; she trusted me with the most personal of letters, with unique copies of snapshots, with persistent goodwill. I can't hope that she'll say of the man I describe, "Yes, that's him." But I do know that if I got her father wrong, it isn't Wylie's fault.

Getting a biography wrong or right is a function at least as crucially of expression as it is of research and comprehension. Holding my feet to the fire—insisting that I said what I had meant to say and that what I had meant to say I had meant to be fair—a couple of friends read my first draft and brought to its details their ungoverned responses: Richard Ford insisted implacably that I be at least as hard on myself as I was on John O'Hara; Maile Meloy read wanting to love every word, and let me know not only which words she didn't love (and why) but which words she did. Her enthusiasm encouraged me, as did responses from Amanda Urban, my wife Priscilla, brother Toby, and son Justin. Several colleagues at the University of California, Irvine, read this book in progress, and spurred it on.

For his detailed attention as an editor, Gary Fisketjon is a wonder. He weighs *everything*. Believe me, to unwrap a typescript returned by Gary is to question how he ever came to accept the damned thing in the first place. Quibbles and cavils, squiggles here, there heads-put-on-tails and tails-on-heads, every sentence and thought put to the test: Is this as clear as you can get it? But his relentless interrogation is accompanied by a companion shrug: It's up to you, just think about it, whatever you decide, whatever. Gary despises effusive praise, so if you're reading this, if it hasn't been deleted, it's proof he's as good as his word, that what the writer finally wants to put in the record will go in the record.

PREFACE:

THE ONE WHO DIDN'T WIN THE NOBEL PRIZE

It would be dismal but not far-fetched to conclude that this was how John O'Hara regarded himself. During the long home stretch of his career, wiseass critics too often wrote him off as a truculent malcontent, a social climber embittered by his exclusion from the world's pickiest club. Even the briefest (or friendliest) piece about O'Hara featured some variation of his 1962 telegram to John Steinbeck: "CONGRATULATIONS. I CAN THINK OF ONLY ONE OTHER AUTHOR I'D RATHER SEE GET IT."[1]

Well, of course. O'Hara was an imaginative writer, an instrument calibrated to desire what the world wouldn't provide. More, O'Hara wanted with feral appetite what a withholding culture simply refused to give. But it's also true that Steinbeck was O'Hara's pal, and there's at least as much admiration as rue in his congratulation, but try telling that to the smirkers. And how they loved to smirk! Even O'Hara's best friends—among whom O'Hara himself cannot be numbered, however peacock-proud he may have seemed—loved to pile on. He was also celebrated as the One Who Didn't Go to Yale—witness Hemingway's snotty proposal to take up a collection dedicated to sending him to the university of his dreams. In an inventory of John O'Hara snubs, you wouldn't want to neglect the Master of the Fancied Slight, variously attributed to Robert Benchley, Bennett Cerf, Harold Ross, or . . . Joel Sayre attributes the remark to Richard Maney, "the demon Broadway press agent,"[2] while Burton Bernstein, a *New Yorker* staffer and James Thurber biographer, summarizes O'Hara as "the one everybody fought with. As [Wolcott] Gibbs said, he was master of the fancied slight."[3]

And then there was his much relished humiliation—on account of his blackthorn walking stick—at the hands (again) of Hemingway, a fine one to mock ambition or pretense. Was it not "Papa" who put himself in the boxing ring with Tolstoy and rated himself the champ or at the least the winner on points—a pugilistic handicapping that Norman Mailer was soon enough keen to join. It's an old reflex, this Boss Dog, Numero Uno syndrome, and John O'Hara was in no way unique for suffering from it, or for wanting so much, right down to a Century Association rosette for his Brooks Brothers lapel. Any Boy Scout showing off a full drape of merit badges craves what O'Hara craved, to be recognized as excellent and accomplished. Yet it is also true that few writers have shown themselves off with such humorless theatricality, as unprotected by restraint as O'Hara, or contended so nakedly and hornily for prizes and marks of distinctions. My god, he even bullied a Random House editor (unavailingly) to collect matchbooks from New York's Racquet & Tennis Club, so that he could set them about to impress visitors at his house in Princeton. But such stories, however irresistible, don't tell O'Hara's story; they wouldn't tell anyone's story.

Egregious episodes of bad judgment and cruelty marred O'Hara's life, especially when he was drinking too much; and certain of these outrages—uncontested in their hatefulness—threaten to discolor any valuation of O'Hara's nature. I can hardly deny or ignore that O'Hara punched a couple of women, or that he battled an actual midget after inquiring, down the bar at a New York nightspot, "What the fuck do you think *you're* staring at?" to someone perhaps even more sensitive than himself to offensive scrutiny. At the same time, I can imagine the effect of such facts on the impartial reader, let alone on scorners who consider that it is sufficient to know he was a big man who brutalized little men and women. These days—having been so thoroughly tutored in the reading of addiction and abuse—too many of us are lay psychologists, therapists, criminologists . . . and hanging judges.

In a *Paris Review* interview, Fran Lebowitz—an unstinting admirer of O'Hara's work—remarks that he "is an underrated writer because every single person who knew him hated him."[4] No, they didn't. "Everyone tells you stories about what a jerk he was, what an idiot, what a social climber, how awful he was." Yes, many do. "He's one of my favorite writers. . . . As soon as all the people who knew him die off, people will come to share my opinion."

My aim is to hurry this process along, to restore to John O'Hara's complicated history those human and occupational particulars that make him a writer worthy of attention and a stab at understanding, and to make such a stab while many still live who knew and loved or respected him, or were astonished by his nerve.

Any biographer who has ever been quoted or represented in print by anyone, however fastidious or friendly, should be chastened by the experience. Janet Malcolm's *The Silent Woman: Sylvia Plath & Ted Hughes*—her study of contending published portraits favoring one partner to the discredit of the other—isolates for investigation a charged moment in the poets' tempestuous marriage. Briefly: Sylvia Plath strode purposefully out of the Smith College library to discover her husband ambling, side by side with a pretty coed, from a wooded trail. She had searched for Hughes in the library (he was late for their meeting), and had emerged from the building's "cold shadow" with her "bare arms chilled." Immediately she spied her betrayer and his jezebel. She assumed an affair, and, believing the accuracy of her perception, memorialized it in her journal and later in a letter, sharing her certainty with her mother. The journal entry was strikingly designed, replete with novelistic details. Indeed, it was composed in part to serve as working notes for a would-be Jamesian novel. Plath narrates a crushing drama of faithless duplicity: "He was walking with a broad, intense smile, eyes into the uplifted doe-eyes of a strange girl with brownish hair, a large lipsticked grin, and bare thick legs in khaki Bermuda shorts. I saw this in several sharp glances, like blows. . . . [Ted's] smile became too white-hot, became fatuous, admiration-seeking. . . . The girl's eyes souped up giddy applause."[5] When Plath's putative rival realizes the adulterer's wife has spotted them, her eyes (it's too dark to see their color) start with guilt, and she flees, leaving Hughes, it seems, speechless, but Plath anything but. . . . All those forces arrayed against her: that cold, shadowed library; her bare (thin?) arms combating the bare (thick) legs of her rival, that "strange girl" with her grotesquely besotted "lipsticked grin."

Despite certain point-of-view alarms, despite the luxury of the entry's modifiers, this detailed written account lent Plath's version of the episode an evidentiary patina of validity. Biographers unfriendly to Hughes were free to report as fact what was after all autobiography, in the form of a document as reliable, say, as an income tax return. Much later, Hughes broke his silence, with calculated reluctance, and offered in testimony to his late wife's instability this very phantom of cheating. Never happened. The coed was nothing to him, merely some young woman from some nearby university who had attended his poetry classes; meeting by happenstance along the path from Paradise Pond, teacher and student had exchanged an impersonal sentence or two, and that was an end to that.

But not quite, as Malcolm observes. Hughes's version sounds right, has appropriate scale and detailing, accords with a reasonable reader's experience of unreasonable suspicions. But who knows, finally? Anne Stevenson, a biographer friendly to Hughes's position, describes Plath's jealousy as an "overreaction," and declares that the student was "in fact" merely who Hughes said she was. Malcolm is not so sure:

> The alert reader will be struck by and want to challenge Stevenson's terms "overreaction" and "in fact." . . . The questions raised by [Stevenson's interpretation] only underscore the epistemological insecurity by which the reader of biography and autobiography (and history and journalism) is always and everywhere dogged. In a work of nonfiction we almost never know the truth of what happened. The ideal of unmediated reporting is regularly achieved only in fiction, where the writer faithfully reports on what is going on in his imagination. . . . We must always take the novelist's and the playwright's and the poet's word, just as we are almost always free to doubt the biographer's or the autobiographer's or the historian's or the journalist's. In imaginative literature we are constrained from considering alternative scenarios—there are none. This is the way it *is*. Only in nonfiction does the question of what happened and how people thought and felt remain open.[6]

Ignoring fictional incompetence (a writer knowing not or caring not what her characters do), and making allowance for unreliable narrators operating within the reliable universal laws of their author's imagination, Malcolm's argument seems savvy. Yoknapatawpha County: William Faulkner, Sole Proprietor. (O'Hara ruled the Region, known also as the

O'Hara Concern.) But so deeply imprinted is the reader's well-earned suspicion of authority of any kind, even fiction's sovereigns are regularly doubted in their most unconditional declarations. See Eudora Welty's essay—"Is Phoenix Jackson Really Dead?"—in which the fiction writer articulates her resentment at the impudence of readers who have written in to ask whether "A Worn Path" has been composed intentionally to mislead the reader into believing that a dead woman "actually" lives.

How does the biographer differ, then, from the novelist? Is the biographer's thumb on the scale? Many if not most biographers—spurred by an impulse to defend, attack, or merely explain—have guessed their subject's weight before its parts have been measured. Attracted by a chimera of theoretical, psychological, or sociological consistency, they shape fictions that willfully ignore the unaccountable surprises and reversals in any life lived or remembered.

Wolcott Gibbs trots out a tale many times told about O'Hara, in so many variations that it is impossible to credit one above another, or to know that any version describes facts. The root version has O'Hara assigned by a magazine to fly over New York in an airplane. He does; it lands; he breaks a window in the cockpit; he is subdued by "authorities." In Gibbs's rendering, the *New Yorker* had made the assignment to have a report on the sight of Manhattan from aloft. Afraid of airsickness, O'Hara prepared himself for the flight by getting insensibly drunk. When the plane landed, he awoke, misapprehended that the taxiing craft had no pilot, and escaped as best he could.[7] In Nathaniel Benchley's 1941 variant, *Time* had assigned O'Hara to cover Amelia Earhart's arrival at Newark. O'Hara got drunk, missed the landing, got another pilot to fly him to Miller Field, landed, taxied and so forth, debarked, came to the drunken misapprehension that the plane was being stolen, ran alongside it, smashed the cockpit window, was flattened by a mechanic, and awoke in a ditch. This kind of yarn makes a biographer wonder if sorting lives is fit work for an adult. The versions are there, in print, with citations available. But they're baloney. Maybe John O'Hara flew over New York in an airplane, and maybe a magazine paid his fare, and probably he got drunk, and probably he passed out. You'd think a biographer's blood would run hot in the presence of such a lively canard, but mine runs cold. Knowing in my bones that this story is false, how can I be certain that anything I think I know about the exact sequences of his daily life is factual?

O'Hara, usually a determined answerer, used his story "We're Friends Again" to ask associated questions, with higher stakes: "What really can any of us know about any of us, and why must we make such a thing of loneliness when it is the final condition of us all?"

Writing as someone who has been my father's biographer, and very much a first-person narrator, I feel twice chastened. In approaching John O'Hara I assumed, eager to postulate cause from effect, that I knew what made him tick even before I had held to my ear the intricate clockwork that is any human character.

O'Hara was the son of a doctor. So was my father.

O'Hara's father, a surgeon like my grandfather, failed to consider his own mortality, made no plans for any time beyond his own time, died young with an estate in ruins. He was impetuous and—like my grandfather—imperious. He quarreled with staff: Dr. O'Hara, a Catholic, with Protestants; Dr. Wolff, a Jew, with Catholics. Both left (in protest and noisily) the hospitals at which they were chiefs of staff to establish competing hospitals. Both vacationed in Atlantic City. Both practiced in small cities satellite to the Big City (Hartford/New York for Dr. Wolff, Pottsville/Philadelphia for Dr. O'Hara).

O'Hara's father, an Irishman ambiguously poised in a culture of WASP ascendancy, seemed less alert to or troubled by clubmen's judgment of his social standing than was his son. Ditto my grandfather, the Jewish father of Duke Wolff.

O'Hara's father was extravagantly aggrieved by his child's failings, operatic in his disdain and self-pity. When O'Hara was canned from prep school for a binge on graduation eve, his "father's anger was terrible to see; his mother was once again terribly disappointed." So too Dr. Wolff, after Duke went on a bender from Roxbury. ("You may easily understand my astonishment in finding that you are repeating the great source of serious trouble you are giving both your mother and myself. . . . I am so sad about it all that I hardly know what to say to you.") I would have guessed that the fathers' over-the-top rhetoric of contempt might have had similar effects on the chastised, but in fact the lash made O'Hara surly and my father ingratiating.

O'Hara's mother was the peacemaker, warmhearted and big-bosomed, indulgent. So too Hattie Wolff.

O'Hara was mesmerized by Yale, a virtual lifelong prisoner of that institution's imagined graces and advantages. So powerful was Yale's pull on my father's affection (he owned several English bulldogs!) that it never entered his mind not to claim to have gone there.

O'Hara, like Duke, was an Anglophile; they shared reverence for things silver and leather, and would devote hours to the polishing of cigarette cases and hand-lasted field or riding boots. The Brits regarded this excessive affection with icy indifference. Waughs laughed at O'Hara; my father was described by Lord Van Sittart, whom he so admired, as "that chap always badgering one for an introduction to one's tailor."

Both were obsessed with automobiles. They both owned MG TCs, same vintage.

Both had hair-trigger tempers, extravagant responses to wounded pride.

Both were nasty drunks.

Both had their awful teeth—paradoxically awful, given exaggerated fastidiousness—pulled in order to qualify for enlistment, in both cases an unavailing sacrifice.

Both owned blackthorn walking sticks.

Both, in youth, dressed alternately like slobs or like dandies.

Both stole, in effect, memberships at New York's Racquet & Tennis Club: O'Hara pilfered playing cards and went after those matchbooks; my father on a rare visit swiped writing paper and used the club's address on his New York driver's license.

In short, from such an extraordinary—or is it?—alignment of tastes and circumstances I expected to write about a character not my father's fraternal twin, but at least a version of my father. Added to my own preoccupation—perhaps unwholesomely persistent—with accounts of revered objects and anxious manners, I expected that I was an appropriate teller of John O'Hara's tale. I know now that if I am, it is not for the reasons I suspected.

From similar circumstances and preoccupations came two characters who couldn't have endured each other's company in a crowded jazz club, let alone at a dinner table. Now, years after I began this project, I know this, but what—as a biographer, as a reader—am I to make of it? Maybe, in the way that opposites are said to attract, likenesses repel: maybe having someone's number—as O'Hara and my father would have had each other's—is not to love someone better. But any alignment I try to make between Duke Wolff and John O'Hara makes me feel like a child playing around with magnetic Scottie dogs, facing them one way to come at each other, the other to scoot away.

No: there is a solution at hand both humbling and liberating. If representative objects—a blue Brooks Brothers shirt and a Racquet & Tennis Club tie—don't wholly express or contain or summarize the character inhabiting those objects, a biographer had best scruple to let some mysteries lie where they will. The complexity of human character is beyond any formal account to complete, but not impossible to portray. Also, taking to heart the reason William Maxwell gave for talking with this stranger about his friend John O'Hara: "Good writers deserve to be remembered."

THE ART OF BURNING BRIDGES

1 . THE REGION

Downtown Pottsville, sucked dry by suburban shopping malls, scratches the eyes. The signs of municipal putrescence are everywhere. Along Centre Street, main and hardened artery, vacant stores beg for tenants with desperate red telephone numbers stenciled on plywood where windows used to be. Automobiles, peppered by coal trucks and salted by PennDOT, wait impatiently at traffic lights, eager to get out of town. Even the parking meters look cold and penniless.

—WILLIAM ECENBARGER, *PHILADELPHIA INQUIRER,* MAY 16, 1984

A decade later, the first time I visited the small city with the unmusical name of Pottsville, I was struck by a regional exhaustion awesome in its frank display. It's too easy to curl my lip, I know. Pottsville had been obliged to accustom itself to disdain and condescension enough from John O'Hara, its most famous citizen. I resolved to remember that if the Region was sooty, grim, and used-up, so were many places I'd lived and worked: Bridgeport, Providence, Waltham. But this was so scuffed as to be spooky. Maybe it was the high contrast of the scenery: green pastures abruptly corrupted by deep scars, the earth littered with mine-tailings lit by a brilliant spring sun. My approach from the west to the anthracite coal country of Schuylkill County in east-central Pennsylvania was through Shamokin (with great mounds of slag heaped like abandoned landfill), through Minersville (whose anomalous fancy restaurant, complete with awning, had long ago been boarded up), past sagging barns (billboarded with "Chew Mail Pouch Tobacco") along tapped-out collieries and the abandoned tracks of the Reading, Blue Mountain & Northern Railroad, listening to nutty right-wing syndicated vitriol coming in stronger and stronger from the Pottsville station. Skirting the western edge of Norwegian Township, across the Schuylkill River, I drove along West Market Street, reluctantly pulling to a halt at Sixth Street, my goal on that cloudless May afternoon.

So this was the eroded town that had inspired the prolonged fuss of John O'Hara's best fiction. It was difficult to imagine how such a place could have inspired anything, but that's the hocus-pocus of the creative enterprise, by which high drama can be cobbled from low stakes, inspired even by a burg where you couldn't kill an hour.

I walked along Sixth, across Norwegian Street (middle and lower-middle class in O'Hara's time, reduced from that prominence today) and uphill to Mahantongo Street. Pottsville, climbing opposed hills, was settled in the gap between shoulders of Sharp Mountain. In the eighteenth century it was a frontier trading post organized by a pioneer, John Pott. Ninety miles northwest of Philadelphia, less than half that distance northeast of Harrisburg, its considerable fortune was made by the discovery nearby of the world's richest known vein of anthracite coal.

The discovery itself is the stuff of fable, which would have you believe that a local farmer (Necho Allen) set a fire in his hearth dug into the surrounding earth and that soon the fireplace was aflame, pretty much eternally. A more candidly fictional version has this same pioneer, now rigged out in buckskins and coonskin cap, as the author of a Christmas Eve miracle, beheld from afar by a Quaker merchant from Philadelphia. Lo, in the east, at midnight, came a glow, a "strange effulgence." Encountering the amazed trader, Necho Allen explained that he had inadvertently produced the bright manifestation: sleeping in the forest, fearful of the panther that had previously mauled him, Allen had set a hearty campfire, and "several hours later I was awakened by summerlike heat. . . . Then I saw that the solid earth all about me seemed to be afire."[1]

However it got found, the fuel for sure got used. Anthracite—glossy, black, hard coal—was prized as clean-burning: harder to ignite than soft coal, it gives off less smoke and greater heat. The precise geological pressures and accidents that formed this black gold were unfairly allotted, bestowed like a longshot lottery win on one particular region: eastern Pennsylvania has 97 percent of all anthracite in the United States, but the problem in the early nineteenth century was how to get it from there to the places where people would pay to set it on fire. The Schuylkill River offered one way, and by 1815 the Schuylkill Navigation Company had opened a canal between Pottsville ("hardly more than one shabby log hut," in the evaluation of a local historian) and Pottstown, extending it to Port Carbon (a distance of more than a hundred miles) by 1825, when Pottsville's boom began. By 1830, financial trusts from Philadelphia were buying up huge tracts of anthracite-rich forests and farmlands, and by the time of the Civil War, Pottsville—the Schuylkill County seat—was the commercial and professional center of a mining bonanza. ("The best site in the anthracite," went the boosters' motto, and before houses were heated with oil and gas, hard coal was the mother lode.) Track was laid to carry the coal, and along the river they carried this black gold to the sea, the bounty flowing down to the capital's rich delta, the City of Brotherly Love. At flood tide of the surge, nine trains a day ran to Philadelphia, but sufficient wealth stuck to Pottsville's managers of mines and railroads and banks to provoke that cocky town's burghers—especially those of English and Scottish stock—to regard themselves as gentry. In John O'Hara's time there, the Philadelphia & Reading Coal & Iron Company (also called the "P&RC&I," or "the Coal & Iron") dug sixty million tons of hard coal per year; yet by 1971, a year after O'Hara's death, the tonnage was down to six million. Today no trains run from Pottsville to anywhere, and the population has stolen away from twenty-five thousand to sixteen thousand.

I was now at the downhill corner of Sixth and Mahantongo (said to be an aboriginal word boasting of "plenty of meat"), number 606, where John O'Hara was raised in a spacious townhouse. His parents were Irish and Catholic—his mother a music-loving and tennis-playing lady with finishing-school manners, his father a respected physician and surgeon—and even in the constricted society of Presbyterian and Episcopal-dominated Pottsville, Patrick and Katharine O'Hara were personages. The outward display of their consequence now stood before me, in need of paint and a carpenter. The house, set close to the sidewalk, was built in 1870 by the Yuengling family, who owned the nation's oldest brewery, and still do. (The survival of the brand is just: I commend the honey-hued lager.) John O'Hara had been born January 31, 1905, down at 125 Mahantongo, but when he was eleven his flourishing father, improving his station, bought the Yuengling house when the brewers built a grand Tudor showplace farther up Mahantongo, up, up, always up, the American direction. Patrick O'Hara kept 125 as his office, with a large porch lined with benches to serve as a waiting room and inside examination and operating rooms; out back was a stable for the horses the Doctor loved to ride and to teach his son to ride.

Before coal barons and bankers settled there, Mahantongo was the street along which Welsh and German and pious Pennsylvania Dutch farmers had brought their produce into town from the Mahantongo Valley. Now it was a street of commerce, display, and churches. The Coal & Iron headquarters—a brick edifice as squat and sturdy as a safe—was downhill near the business hub of Centre Street. Across and down Mahantongo from 606, two short blocks—called "squares" in the Region—the O'Haras' Church of St. Patrick sits right beside D. C. Yuengling & Son. Owing to the proximity of that brewery's master system of heat, water, and electricity, the Yuenglings had provided 606 with those refinements. The three-storied house had six bedrooms, formal living and dining rooms, a music room with his mother's piano. There was a tiled entry, parquet floors, Spanish crystal chandelier, German stained-glass windows. Out front had been a hitching post, where John O'Hara's beloved pony had been tethered.

Out front now—or at least the last time I visited—is a plaque confirming that O'Hara had indeed lived there. While I was studying this memorial (and checking to see that the street sign spelled Mahantongo correctly, after years of announcing Mahant*a*ngo), an elderly man approached me with an air of knowing precisely where he had come from and whither he meant to go. I suspected he might also offer direction and other useful information to an outlander lost in his neighborhood. I suspected wrong.

"What do you want?" he said.

"Nothing, thanks. Just sightseeing."

"What do you *want?*"

I crossed the street, toward the dual sanctuary of church and brewery, while he stayed on his side, the Presbyterian side, muttering balefully at me. (He recalled the fellow William Ecenbarger wrote about in 1984, "Forgetting John O'Hara: Pottsville's Revenge." This citizen, "bent in the shape of a question mark," was asked if he knew 606's most famous resident: "Yeah, I knew him, but I never had any use for him. He was a bum, and he wrote a lot of lies about this town." These sour sentries must stand watch in shifts.)[2]

I recollected an offhand observation of O'Hara's about the town he called Gibbsville, that it gave a first and last impression that the traveler would have been safer at home. Pottsville's population descends from taciturn Dutch farmers who worked the difficult soil of mountains hereabout, and from the roughneck, sullen miners who worked the spider-webbed veins where hard coal hides deep underground. Soft coal, wide-seamed near the surface, was for softies; as dispassionate a publication as *The Almanac of American Politics 1996* described Schuylkill County's citizens during O'Hara's time as "tough-talking miners and factory workers who stayed menacingly in the background unless a character stumbled into the wrong roadhouse at night or the wrong diner at dawn."

An observant friend not given to melodrama had recently journeyed through and suggested the town had been invaded by body snatchers, and surely its enterprises, if not its human occupants, had vanished. I had read that 125 was for a time a hair salon, "Cut Loose" or "Hair Today," gone now. Across the street, at the corner of Progress Avenue and Mahantongo, the Necho Allen Hotel was boarded up after a time in limbo as a roost for the homeless. Ten years ago the *Philadelphia Inquirer* had reported that "big signs at the Necho Allen Hotel promise food, spirits and rooms, but little signs say it's up for sheriff's sale."[3] It had once been Pottsville's Ritz, built in the 1920s at a cost of over a million, with a bar in the basement, the Coal Mine Taproom, got up to seem like, well, a coal mine: anthracite walls and waiters lighting their order pads with the lamps set in their miner's helmets. (Piquant pride in a local product has not been utterly dulled: at Mootz Candies, on Pottsville's Centre Street, a visitor could still buy black licorice on a string and coal candy dispensed in a miniature coal bin with a miniature coal hammer to break it.)

At the Historical Society of Schuylkill County I asked the young man on duty a question or two about the famous author's standing in his hometown, pitching these queries in a scholarly tone almost too decorous for words.

What I got for a response was a narrowing of the eyes and a thinning of the lips: "Why do you want to know?"

"I'm writing about his life. He lived here."

"So?"

When I mentioned the plaque that proclaimed John O'Hara a product of Pottsville, the young man asked if I'd seen it with my own eyes.

"Why?" I wondered. "Has it been moved?"

"You could say that," he said. "You could also say that people around here have strong feelings about the fella you're poking into here."

The nature of those feelings I could guess.

At Oxford, the actual county seat of imaginary Yoknapatawpha County ("William Faulkner, Sole Proprietor"), the writer's house—Rowan Oak—is a shrine. (O'Hara's *Pal Joey* is shelved, just as the Master left it, with some mystery stories in the bedroom bookcase.) Visit the courthouse square around which the idiot Benjy Compson was driven the wrong way and you'll find a life-size bronze Faulkner in a wide-brimmed bronze hat, seated on a bronze bench, holding a bronze pipe, looking quizzical or perhaps drunk; to make room for the goofy monument, its sponsors caused a magnolia tree to be cut down, provoking the statue's detractors to label its patrons troglodytes of the Snopes stamp. This is all to the good, a writer and his characters shaking up the place he wrote about, decades after his death. In Sauk Centre, Minnesota—Sinclair Lewis's Gopher Prairie—the high school athletes are called the "Mainstreeters," and a visitor wouldn't be allowed to leave town without visiting "The Original Main Street" or the Sinclair Lewis Boyhood Home and Museum. Sherwood Anderson's Winesburg—in fact Clyde, Ohio—has a Sherwood Anderson Memorial Park, just as Willa Cather's Red Cloud has a Willa Cather Memorial Prairie. Thomas Wolfe's hometown erected a statue in downtown Asheville, but when the writer was alive and memorializing his fellow North Carolinians, he was threatened with libel suits, not to mention lynchings. Anderson was reviled by his fellow citizens during his lifetime, as were Faulkner (by Snopesian trash and magnolia-scented debutantes alike) and Lewis (by boosters and Rotarians). Maybe the latter two were redeemed by their Nobels.

Apart from his sometimes-kidnapped plaque, O'Hara has been commemorated by Pottsville rather mordantly: John O'Hara Street—erstwhile Minersville Street—is a "short, dingy cul-de-sac" created when the town's celebrated whorehouses (one local roadhouse named itself the Pussy Café) were torn down to make space for public housing; his namesake street makes the local news largely due to the frequency and infamy of crimes reported from its address.[4]

In the spring of 1935, less than a year after the publication of *Appointment in Samarra,* O'Hara's first novel, scandalized and titillated the citizens, the author wrote a letter from Cape Cod to Walter S. Farquhar, star sports editor of the *Pottsville Journal,* from which O'Hara had been fired as a reporter. A mentor and friend, Farquhar had written asking for help getting a job with a magazine or book publisher in New York; O'Hara couldn't promise a job, but he gave plenty of free advice: "[I]f you write a movie plot I'll get you dough for it, a novel I'll help you sell it, a poem I'll help you sell it, I'll give you a send-in that will count with any publisher in New York. . . . The same with the better magazines. I'm known to them, and I will help you sell a good article or story to almost any mag you mention, if it's one of the better magazines. . . . If you're going to get out of that God awful town, for God's sake write something that will *make* you get out of it. Write something that automatically will sever your connection with the town, that will help you get rid of the bitterness you must have stored up against all those patronizing cheap bastards in that dry-fucked excrescence on Sharp Mountain."[5]

What we may read into this relationship between town and novelist is hardly a failure of communication, but how had it soured so? After all, this was the altar-boy eldest son of one of the most esteemed families in a region stingy about bestowing its esteem. Of course, the words *writer* and *alien* go together as comfortably as *privileged* and *insider.* John O'Hara, by virtue of his standing as a doctor's son, was a privileged insider as well as a self-exiled outcast. The perfect place for the fiction writer to look is from the terrace, like an F. Scott Fitzgerald character peering through the country club window at the dancers inside, judging them, perhaps mocking their airs and footwork. The imaginative writer doesn't flinch from the objectionable, courts outsider status, makes trouble, relishes gossip and scandal. In O'Hara's long story "Ninety Minutes Away" (1963), the police sergeant of such a town as Pottsville disparages such a reporter as its author—"poking his nose in where it doesn't belong"—for being "an againster."[6]

For those with a commitment to serenity, to closing the doors behind them and drawing the curtains and keeping from children the messy sights of birth and death, it must seem perverse: disturbing the peace, showing off, telling secrets, wanting more than what's been offered. And it *is* perverse reflexively to say no way, fuck you, gimme. But O'Hara had an imaginative writer's natural reflexes right from the start: he understood very well that if fiction is about any general impulse, it is about denial. Someone wants something that someone else—many someones, the great "They"—will not give. Club membership, a kind word, love, a Nobel Prize, piles of money, the presidency, a clean bill of health, a nice review, a bicycle for Christmas, sexual intimacy, a starting position on the football team, an entry in *Who's Who* or in the *Social Register.* . . . There are as many things to be denied as there are to be desired, and people to want and withhold them. If writers differ intrinsically from other people, their difference is defined by a vocational obligation to be dissatisfied. Good fiction comes of friction, so why should Pottsville, Pennsylvania, as close in its business of mining as human beings can get to the commerce and sociology of an ant colony, honor an enemy of industry, subordination, and order?

At sixty, John O'Hara troubled to write a long letter to his English literary agent asking that put-upon and patient gentleman to engage the services of a London solicitor to engage the services of another solicitor in County Mayo to run the genealogical bona fides of the O'Hara family, which its descendant bragged was "one of the eight oldest names in Ireland, going back to the ninth century."

Eighteen months earlier he had written his brother Tom an affectionate and clear-eyed biography of their family, root and branch. This letter synthesizes many of O'Hara's lifelong preoccupations with the outward manifestations and interior hunches of specialness, even of majesty:

> But I have always felt that we are something out of the usual run. The Delaney side we know about. They were pre-Revolutionary American. But I mean beyond that, on the O'Hara side. Do you remember William Wright, an old mining engineer who lived in Heckscherville and was a patient of the old man's? He had gout, was chair-ridden, and I often had the dubious pleasure of bathing his gouty foot, putting some kind of powder on it, and wrapping bandages around it. While this was going on he and the old man would talk, talk, talk. Well, he convinced the old man that the O'Haras of our line were descendants of the Ninth-century kings, and he went to the trouble of authenticating our right to the coat of arms. Our papa pretended not to care about such things, but if you look in the History of Pennsylvania biography of the old man, you will find that coat of arms right there. When [O'Hara's

third wife] Sister and I were in Dublin a few years ago my friend Geraldine Fitzgerald explained to me that the gentry were not so much in awe of me as an author as of one of "the real thing," O'Hara being one of the seven or eight ancient Irish names. Well, I believe that, if only for two reasons: whenever I am in the company of the Irish (and this has been true all my life) I instantly get a feeling of being a little bit superior to the other ones—and they in turn look at me as though whatever I had to say was going to be important. There is a kind of resentful respect to them, and I have sensed it since I was a small kid. I even got it with the late JFK, and I always had it with his father. . . . [I]t is not mere egomania. It almost has nothing to do with me, because I watched the same thing happening between Irish men and women and the old man. You never saw anyone get fresh with him. . . . And even if it exists only in my imagination, it's what I face the world with.[7]

It's all here: the conviction—a bravado as essential to any beginning imaginative writer as it is risible in maturity—of set-apartness, of predestined authority and majesty planted by fate in the genes. Here's the son's wonderment at his father's power, at the reverence of Dr. O'Hara's patients, an amazement most doctors' children will recognize. Here's O'Hara's bravura recollection of detail and process, and his willingness to detour from his core story—we are descended from kings, and what Irish family suspects it is not?—to the particulars of treating gout and the hands-on intimacy of his early apprenticeship to his father's practice. Here's O'Hara's characteristic precision of identification and location (William Wright . . . mining engineer . . . Heckscherville . . . chair-ridden). Here's the dropped name of a movie star. Here is the egomania of imagining the slain president's awed deference to Himself. And finally, here is a lucid declaration of the crazy and fierce will of that inventive power with which John O'Hara recovered and reshaped the facts of the world at whose center he—as its narrator—necessarily stood.

In his genealogical instructions to his London agent, the mission was to track his bloodline back through his paternal grandfather, Michael, to a certain James O'Hara, a captain under General George Washington and ultimately quartermaster general (no: make that "the *first* Quartermaster," he duly noted) of the Continental army. What in fact he presumed on Watson in this "investigation" was "to establish my eligibility for one of the American ancestor-worship societies . . . the Society of the

Cincinnati . . . founded by officers of Washington's army. . . . Interestingly enough, another O'Hara, Charles, was a. d. c. to Lord Cornwallis. When Cornwallis surrendered to Washington at Yorketown, he sent his sword by General Charles O'Hara. It is therefore quite possible that I was represented on both sides at Yorketown."

Possible despite the odds. What's certain is that John O'Hara's grandfather Michael, born in Ballina, County Mayo, came to America as an infant during the early 1830s. A cavalry lieutenant in the Union army, he was unaccountably (or all too accountably) known by his descendants as the "Major," and during the Civil War he happened on the Pennsylvanian town of Shenandoah in grave fulfillment of the pledge he'd made to a dying comrade personally to deliver bad news to his parents. The Major (let's grant him a field promotion) hung around to work on the railroad being built between Shenandoah and Pottsville, one component of the coal-bearing and miner-moving network lacing together the towns of Schuylkill County during those early years of easy abundance.

Now, the American client bragged to his agent that Michael was "quite a guy," "a real swashbuckler" and entrepreneur and impresario with "his finger in many pies." Peacock-pride in bloodline is commonly the enemy of honest reporting, but John O'Hara was nothing if not true to the paradoxes of character, so that he reported of the Major that "ethics never bothered him much." He was hardworking, with an eye for the main chance. He launched himself with no bankroll, only a few horses: thus a livery business. Horses could pull hearses: thus an undertaking establishment, the quick and the dead pulling happily in tandem. By dint of horses he was also in the house-moving business and part owner of the circus to which he had leased three hundred head. He built the Shenandoah Opera House, later renamed the O'Hara Theater, and associated with the actors and singers and musicians he booked to perform there. He was chief burgess of Shenandoah before it became, in his grandson's estimate, "a third-class city." Writing his brother in 1963, John O'Hara precisely calibrated that on the Schuylkill County ladder their paternal grandparents "were the top people of Shenandoah, which is top of nothing much, but top."[8]

Michael's son Patrick was born the day after Christmas, 1867, and grew up working in his father's livery, getting an education in the sweaty verities of violent acts and language, and sealing his passion for horses. Ambitious for his family of six children, the Major sent young Patrick to the Roman Catholic Niagara University, whence he entered the University of Pennsylvania medical school, graduating in 1892, at twenty-four. His brothers Michael and James also studied medicine at Penn, but failing to get degrees they became partners in an undertaking firm. "There was always money around," John O'Hara recollected, "and there were always fights about money." After feuding with his brothers—"all larceny," his son concluded: "I always suspected Jim had a bit of necrophilia in him, and I certainly suspect him of not leaving any wedding rings in the caskets"—Patrick O'Hara practiced briefly in New Orleans; when his father died in 1893, he accepted a Republican patronage appointment as surgeon to the Schuylkill County Alms House and superintendent of the Hospital for the Insane in Schuylkill Haven, six miles to the south of Pottsville. Many years later one of his sons recollected for a newspaper reporter that Patrick O'Hara despised saxophone music "because it reminded him of the wailing of the mad women after the asylum's lights were doused for the night." (Biographers hunger for such animating details, and storytelling sons are happy to relate such legends as their fathers had bequeathed them.)

Patrick O'Hara, dark-haired and handsome, presented a picture of mastery and weight. His smile was deliberate and occasional: in photographs his eyes aim unblinkingly where they mean to look, with his chin slightly tucked into his shoulder, just in case an onlooker might be foolish enough to throw a punch. He was an amateur boxer and ferocious teetotaler. His own father, according to family legend, had got rowdy from whiskey punch when celebrating his discharge from the army and—brandishing his sword—accidentally sliced a friend. The Major swore off drink eternally, and when Patrick's youngest brother, Arthur, died drunk by falling in front of a train, Patrick swore off as well.

John O'Hara's mother, Katharine Delaney, was raised in Lykens, across the Schuylkill County line to the west. Just as the Major had married a Franey, from an old Shenandoah family ("The Franeys were of the *gentle* Irish, like the Delaneys. The O'Haras were violent and spectacular"), Patrick also married up.[9]

Lykens, like Shenandoah, was a satellite of Pottsville, thirty miles distant, on the fringes of coal country. In fact, it was nearer the state capital at Harrisburg, and took its bucolic spirit from the adjacent Pennsylvania Dutch farm country. John O'Hara remembered his grandfather Joseph Delaney as "the nicest man in the world, bar none."[10]

Seven years before the 1903 wedding of Patrick O'Hara to Katharine Delaney at Our Lady Help of Christians Church in Lykens, Dr. O'Hara had left his sinecure at the alms house following a scandal involving whiskey supposedly supplied for medicinal application to patients; in reality the whiskey was applied to the thirst of the staff, in an amount considerably less than was billed to the county. The mastermind of this petty chisel was a liquor dealer with political pull and a Dickensian business card, Joseph Nichter of Mellett & Nichter, Ale & Porter. When Dr. O'Hara discovered the graft and summoned Nichter to his office, the entrepreneur arrived stinking of rye. His flamboyant tailoring and oiled hair, not to speak of his jewelry, did not make a favorable impression, and the good doctor further explained, once Nichter lit a cigar, that he'd send him to prison if he didn't adjust his manners and scruples. Nichter threatened him back, and then conspired to have him fired. Instead, word of the doctor's exotic rectitude spread to the leading citizens of Pottsville, who urged him to set up practice in their town.

Dr. O'Hara became the first resident surgeon of Pottsville Hospital in 1896, and at that time opened his practice at 125 Mahantongo Street. He frequently traveled to Philadelphia to study the procedures of his mentor, Dr. John Blair Deaver, an 1878 graduate of the University of Pennsylvania medical school and fellow Irishman who wore a waxed moustache and demonstrated his medical techniques at Lackenau Hospital while wearing leather riding boots. This was the Philadelphia of Thomas Eakins, whose painting *The Gross Clinic*—with its theatrical illumination of the bloody art and science of surgery—excited local controversy, pitting decorum against realism. For the young Dr. O'Hara, surgery must have seemed noble and bracing.

Surely he took his training as seriously as he took himself. Short-statured, his posture was so erect that friends and family recollected him as having been tall. Proud and hot-tempered, he'd lead with his chin when it suited him. He quickly earned a reputation in Pottsville for candor, heroic grudge-nursing, and an exaggerated code of honor. He also enjoyed spending the money he'd earned. He dressed expensively, favoring conservative suits, tightly knotted ties, stiff-collared shirts showing half an inch of starched and gold-linked cuffs. He lived across the street from his office in comfortable bachelor quarters at the Pottsville Club. He was put on retainer by the Philadelphia & Reading Coal & Iron Company to tend to miners injured in the collieries. These accidents frequently occurred beyond easy reach of town, out in the "patches" (as these clumps of shacks were called) near the pits and shafts. Miner's lung, gas explosions, collapses, train wrecks: business was brisk. Nationwide, twelve thousand miners were killed between 1900 and 1920. Crowded in darkness near machines that drilled and dug anthracite, chains under severe load, crackers that smashed big chunks into bits, men were the weak links. Awful head injuries were common, and Dr. O'Hara soon achieved local celebrity for his mastery of trephining, an elaboration of trepanning. The trepan, a brutal mining tool used to sink a shaft through rock, lent its name to the medical device used to bore through the skull to relieve killing fluid pressure. The trephine was a circular saw–like instrument with which to remove a disk of bone from the skull.

To the prosperous Delaneys, Patrick O'Hara must have seemed a good match for their daughter. Thirteen years younger than the doctor, Katharine had been the valedictorian of her class at Eden Hall, a convent of the Sacred Heart near Philadelphia. She was smart and gentle, good at French and at the piano, which she studied under a student of Franz Liszt. Her father, born Israel Delaney, had been a Protestant orphan raised in Lykens by a family named Blum. At fourteen he gave himself the name Joseph and converted to Roman Catholicism, and Dr. O'Hara's own impeccably Catholic credentials must have confirmed the Delaneys in their favorable impression of this rising Pottsville star.

Joseph Delaney owned rental properties, a coal business, a lumberyard, a wholesale grocery and hardware store in Lykens. The year before his daughter's marriage, Delaney made himself a local hero by extending credit to coal miners during their strike. If Schuylkill County was a region of deep ethnic and class hostility, the social fabric was repeatedly stressed and torn by depredations of mine managers. Among the county's population of a quarter million, there were enemies in abundance. Collisions were everywhere: Presbyterian Scots against Catholic Irish; Irish set themselves against Welsh laborers; and all Celts loathed their British-bred bosses. Similarly, Pottsville (management) opposed Shenandoah (workers). Lithuanians resented Italians and Germans. Swedes stood apart. Roman Catholics distrusted and despised Greek and Russian Orthodox Catholics. Miners' daughters in peasant kerchiefs high-hatted bareheaded miners' daughters, the greasy pole mobbed with climbers and backsliders. The Welsh were experienced miners (in recognition of which such bountiful veins as the Glendower bore Welsh place names), while the Irish immigrants who'd fled the potato famine were treated like chattel and put to the menial, hard-labor chores of sorting slate and cracking coal for the Welsh.

Bitterness and gall had hung over the Region even before the Molly Maguire battles began during the Civil War, a terrorist campaign by a secret society of Irish miners to protest being drafted into "a rich man's war," not to mention being underpaid and overworked. Some Irish brought to America a tradition of violently answering British oppressions. William V. Shannon explains in *The Irish in America* that these sporadic terrorists had had "no political programs or large aims. They took action on specific local grievances. If a landlord converted tilled fields into grazing lands, the Whiteboys [of Munster] maimed his cattle or burned his outbuildings. . . . If a landlord beat down wages, the land-less farm laborers and their brothers and friends among the tenants beat up the landlord's agent or burned his crops."[11]

After vicious strikes in 1842 and 1868–70, another in 1875 was brutally broken by a Pinkerton detective, James McParlan, hired by the Philadelphia & Reading Coal & Iron Company, specifically by the notorious robber baron (and Episcopalian Irishman) Franklin Gowen. McParlan infiltrated the Molly Maguires' inner circles, located in a house on Pottsville's Centre Street. (It seems fitting that the Mollies themselves had infiltrated the local chapter of the Ancient Order of Hibernians, a fraternal Irish order commonly as devoted to amiable secrecy, pietistic mumbo jumbo, winks, and handclasps as the Protestant Odd Fellows, say, or Yale's Skull and Bones.) The spy presented his evidence against many miners, and Gowen himself closed the prosecution case at Pottsville's hilltop stone fortress of a jail and courthouse. Ten men, convicted of murdering a couple dozen company superintendents and policemen from ambush, were hanged by the Commonwealth of Pennsylvania on Black Thursday, June 21, 1877, four in nearby Mauch Chunk (happily renamed Jim Thorpe, for its most famous citizen) and six in Pottsville, where it was planned to hang all six simultaneously till civic uncertainty as to the sturdiness of the gallows dictated that the condemned be strung up in pairs. Priests attended, a good crowd watched, and Pottsville was on the map. Arthur Conan Doyle made Schuylkill County the setting for his *Valley of Fear,* a novel exploiting the notorious events in which, a historian has noted, "a private corporation initiated the investigation through a private detective agency, a private police force arrested the supposed offenders, and the coal company attorneys prosecuted—the state provided only the courtroom and hangman."[12] Patrick O'Hara was ten years old. The Irish lads were buried in consecrated ground. More hangings soon followed.

Charles W. Bassett, writing about O'Hara in the *Pottsville Journal*, reports that by 1877 the P&RC&I's "Pottsville collieries were the most extensive and the deepest (1,584 feet) in the United States," and the strikes were also impressive. In 1900, a forty-two-day walkout was ended by the intervention of a couple thousand National Guardsmen. Finally, in 1902—the year before Patrick's marriage, and three before John O'Hara's birth—almost a hundred and fifty thousand striking coal miners—assisted in their negotiations by Teddy Roosevelt—won the right to an eight-hour day and a six-day workweek.

The residue of bitterness from these antagonisms can't be exaggerated. In so tight a geographical region, with such high stakes for everyone, mistrust and contempt were epidemic. To be in the position of the O'Haras and the Delaneys—Irish, educated, and wealthy—was to straddle many boundaries. That Joseph Delaney had extended credit to striking miners was in dramatic contrast to the commonplace relationship that obtained between these men and mine-company landlords and stores, a dreary process in which a miserly compensation for filthy and killing toil was then recouped by inflated rents and food prices, keeping laborers perpetually in arrears to bosses.

The society John O'Hara was born into on January 31, 1905, was superficially stable and thriving, and the economy would mature and flourish with him, peaking just before he left the Region—more or less for good—in the late 1920s. By the time (1913) Henry Ford was paying his assembly-line workers five dollars a day, a worker could earn that same fine salary in the mines. And digging coal supported many other businesses: the railroads, of course, but also lumber companies, hardware businesses, foundries, breweries. The Region had metal factories, a silk mill, shirt and dress factories. As implicated as John O'Hara's parents were in the economy and culture of Pottsville's turbocharged engine of progress and prosperity, the O'Haras—and especially the Delaney side of the family—took their habits and passions from husbandry. The Delaneys were gatherers rather than hunters, farmers and breeders rather than such profiteers as whalers or miners. These opposed responses to America's bounty—plant or excavate—were temperamental and economic choices, or collisions, central to John O'Hara's raising, and to his understanding of American manners and ambition. Writing of Melville and of Ahab's murderous reflex to ravish the sea, the critic Gavan Daws extends his meditation on whaling to landlocked exploitation, observing that "mining meant tearing up and disemboweling a new land and moving on, as against farming land in the expectation of a permanent human relationship with the earth."[13] (This distinction, in the aftermath of farm and forest ruin, has become chimerical.) The families were proud that no Franey, O'Hara, or Delaney ever dug coal from a mine, or owned a mine from which others tore coal.

When John O'Hara wrote to his brother of the "gentle" Delaneys and the "violent and spectacular" O'Haras, he remembered precisely how gentleness had showed itself as a vital force. Unlike the brooding and bickering O'Haras, the Delaneys were close-knit and jolly. In addition to his mother, the Delaney children included John's favorite uncle, Eugene, an engineer, and favorite aunt, Verna, who'd played shortstop on the Eden Hall softball team. He remembered her as outgoing and witty, and dedicated a novella to her.

Katharine Delaney O'Hara was a hit in Pottsville. She liked parties, played determined tennis and smart bridge. She practiced her French at the Cercle Française, and performed piano duets—Chopin, Mussorgski—at Pottsville's Academy of Music with Mrs. Francis X. Reilly. If it's fair to conjecture that Mrs. Reilly was Irish and Catholic, it is nevertheless true that Mrs. O'Hara did not confine her associations to fellow parishioners of St. Patrick's. Although she made it a lifelong daily practice to attend six a.m. mass, she also made close friends among co-members of the Outdoor Club, which later became the Schuylkill Country Club, in turn reconfigured by O'Hara as the Lantenengo Country Club, scene of many a class conflict in O'Hara's fiction. The O'Haras were by no means controversial members of this exclusive club dominated by those of English or—like the Yuenglings—German origins. Episcopalians, Presbyterians, and Lutherans were pleased enough to have made room for Dr. O'Hara at the Pottsville Club before he was married, and after he married Katharine Delaney—good company, refined, with pretty manners—the couple were certifiably "attractive," as the choosy choose to say.

John O'Hara's mother remained close to her kin, and the Delaneys and their daughter enacted their mutual affections by traveling back and forth between Pottsville and the Delaney farm in Lykens. Those journeys made a vivid impression; at Centre Street and Mahantongo, a short walk from the house where O'Hara had been born, mother and son would climb aboard the Minersville trolley, riding it out to the Lehigh Valley Railroad station. From there they made their slow way to Lykens via the Westwood Switch. The change of trains at the Westwood depot offered two distinct sorts of conveyance, depending on the schedule: a passenger through-train, with comfortable tufted seats and polished bright work inlaid with mother-of-pearl, or the miners' local, crowded with grimy and exhausted men seated on hard wood benches, stinking of sweat and coal oil and damp rubber boots and burned wicks from their helmet lamps, traveling mostly in sullen silence. Another change took the O'Haras to Lykens: the end of the line.

At the depot there, the O'Haras would be fetched by a horse-drawn delivery coach advertising J. I. Delaney's store. The driver, Ambrose Bupp, would let O'Hara take the team's reins going up steep hills, and release the wagon's brake at the hills' bottoms.* During these boyhood visits, O'Hara would ride shotgun for Ambrose during grocery deliveries, hauling provisions out to Polish Row and to the neighborhoods of Irish and Scots and Pennsylvania Dutch and scattered black families. They always stopped at a watering trough in front of the Exchange Hotel, at whose bar it was Ambrose Bupp's mission to take on a substantial load of rye, and sometimes—when Ambrose decided that too much whiskey was only almost enough—he'd suffer an "asthma attack," and Grandfather Delaney would fire him, a downsizing Ambrose chose to disregard, showing up for work the next morning wearing what O'Hara took to be a cowboy's Stetson, and offering the boy the reins.

Grandfather Delaney was a soft touch; he looked like Santa Claus, white-bearded and big-bellied. His wife would greet her grandchildren with musical enthusiasm: "my t-r-r-reasures."[14] But the boy also noticed the deference that was paid the Delaneys, and sweet as they were, they kept a measurable distance between their family and their customers and tenants. In his novel *Ourselves to Know* (1960), O'Hara remembers

---

*So pleasurable were O'Hara's memories of these excursions that he chose in 1968 to tell the readers of his *Holiday* essay, "Hello Hollywood Good-Bye," that the wagon, manufactured by Swab, was "considered superior to the Studebaker," and inquired, by the way: "Do you know what a chunk is?" A chunk is a workhorse of the kind that hauled his grandfather's Swab (John O'Hara, "Hello Hollywood Good-Bye," *Holiday* [May 1968]).

station: "Like all children I realized at an early age that older people did not treat each other as equals. A man and his wife were a little above you or a little below you. All the people who stopped to chat with my grand-parents were a little below them, and they could not help showing it."[15] *They* refers to the visitors rather than the grandparents, but much later O'Hara would come also to understand—and not wish to forget—that Joseph Delaney, owing to his Catholicism and want of membership in some Masonic order or other, had been excluded from the board of directors of the Lykens bank.

Ambrose was responsible for the care of the Delaneys' large stable of horses, and in this work too he included young O'Hara. Feeding, brush-ing, watering, bedding down, soaping, currying, neatsfoot-oiling the horses' hooves, saddle-soaping the leather tack—it can't be overstated how vital were horses in O'Hara's childhood, and the scrupulous instruc-tions the boy learned he passed along like a catechism to his younger sib-lings. In the same letter he wrote to Graham Watson in which he requested a check of his ancient pedigree, O'Hara closed by confessing, "I am full of small plans. I am also thinking of buying a thoroughbred in Ireland and racing him here [in Princeton, New Jersey?] next year."[16] At the age of sixty, O'Hara was obsessively regular in his passions, a sworn enemy of surprise, and to long for a racehorse is about as startling as ambitions get.

Or perhaps it isn't, in his case. The Major's livery business was big enough to lease three hundred horses to the John B. Robinson Circus, and he'd also built a racetrack—fitted out with starting equipment and judges' stand—at his farm outside Shenandoah. Dr. O'Hara used horses to visit his far-flung patients, stabling the animals out behind 125 Mahan-tongo, and later made practical use of the hitching post in front of 606. He bought Oakland Farm, a 160-acre place a bit south of Pottsville in Cressona, and he took his son to the races in Allentown and Reading, Kutztown and Lebanon. John was taught to ride by his father, but his skill was fine-tuned by troopers at the state police barracks near Pottsville. Dr. O'Hara's dream, after John's brothers were born, of an O'Hara polo team was destined to go unrealized as surely as his assump-tion that John would become a surgeon. In a 1969 interview the son recalled his father's estimation of him: "John is the best horseman in Eastern Pennsylvania, but outside of that he isn't worth a damn."[17]

Such a sour estimate came years after a childhood that was rich with adventure and objects. While visiting in Lykens, O'Hara would play at the railroad spur behind his grandfather's lumber yard, climbing on the freight cars and gondolas loaded with goods for the yard and general store; he remembered "giving hand signals to a mythical crew, and supplying my own sound effects." But it was in the store itself that lifelong preoccupations were imprinted, where young John examined and handled the stuff: bolts of Number 50 cotton, hardware, reels of thread, spice and pickles and sugar coconut and coffee and tea, Dietz lanterns, Keebler & Weyl's sweet cakes, dried figs, wood chests holding whole categories of things, ranks of items upon which was put exact values. He developed a sensual reverence for objects—their prices and provenance, their weights and measures—that became totemic, a fixation on the substantial that was irresistible in his imagination and in his prose.

By the year of John's birth, Dr. O'Hara was a personage in the Region. During the fall of 1905 he joined a delegation of ambitious American surgeons on a tour of the great European centers of medical practice: Paris, London, Berlin, Brussels, Vienna, Rome, Geneva, Dublin. His study at home was similarly systematic and passionate; he learned Italian to communicate more efficiently with those miners. Years later O'Hara would boast that his father "was the only man who could enter a certain part of town during a Black Hand war."[18] He learned sign language because it interested him, and as soon as his firstborn was old enough to comprehend anything, Johnny-boy—as he liked to call his child—understood that his father had consequence. The concept of good-better-best was an existential scale. To be a doctor's son was to experience the reflected deference paid to any educated professional, plus the reverence paid a healer who routinely saved his neighbors' lives, and those of their husbands, wives, and children. To be a doctor's son was to expect a passerby to curtsy or tip the hat.

The summer of John's twelfth year, a story in the *Pottsville Republican* proclaimed his father a hero. During a vacation in Atlantic City, while swimming at a sumptuous hotel pool, Dr. O'Hara had noticed that "a very wealthy woman of Pittsburgh, Mrs. Winstead, wife of a large manufacturer in the smoky city, in an effort to dive off one of the boards, had her foot caught between the lances and fractured her right limb."[19] She passed out from the pain and "went to the bottom of the pool." Dr. O'Hara rescued and revived her, set her bones, "and removed her to her suite at the Traymore Hotel. He was congratulated by hundreds of people including the husband of the woman." The newspaper reported with pride that the hotel physician remarked that Pottsville's own had "bandaged the injured limb better than any he had ever seen." And that was while the Doctor was taking a break. (By the way, John himself didn't learn to swim until the last year of his life.)

Compounding the young man's comprehension of his family's high estate in Schuylkill County was the atmosphere of opulence Dr. O'Hara created on behalf of his household, and there was plenty of meat indeed on Mahantongo Street. Dr. O'Hara was earning in the neighborhood of twenty-five thousand a year in 1905, very good money; and after Mary and Joseph were born in 1907 and 1909, the move up the hill to 606 must have promised an eternal progress. Big house, big farm, big family: next came brothers Martin, Thomas, James, and Eugene, and a final sibling—Kathleen—in 1920. (The eldest son, looking back on his mother's fecund efficiency, remarked a conspicuous lack of sentimental fuss in her maternal rhetoric: "She bore six sons and two daughters, and the only thing I ever heard her say about that was, Thank heavens all my children have well shaped heads.")[20]

Despite its waxing population, 606 Mahantongo had rooms and nooks enough to offer privacy; unlike his siblings, Johnny-boy had a private bedroom, on the third floor, from which he liked to shout down a speaking tube to the kitchen, or pour water down that tube into a victim's ear at the other end. When he was ten, Dr. O'Hara gave him a .22 octagonal-barrel Winchester pump, and later set up a rifle range for him in the basement. The boy dragooned his siblings into games of hide-and-seek, and especially enjoyed standing undiscovered but undisguised in the dark of a stair landing. And in the full light of day he liked to show off.

His first horse was a Shetland named Dot. Other ponies followed: Billy, Midge, Captain, Major, and Colonel. As a grown man he recalled a circus that had come to Pottsville when he was nine, remembered it parading up Centre Street from the railroad depot. O'Hara, with his lacerating instinct for mortifying detail, for the gesture ill-conceived but audaciously hounded to its mortifying end, locates himself joining that parade of flamboyant circus performers and trained exotic beasts pulling on a wagon-load of ice a dead whale. There he was, aboard a child-size Conestoga wagon—a lavish caprice custom-built to please the O'Hara children—drawn by four ponies, tricked out in a full cowpoke's outfit, hoping that he'd be mistaken for a professional circus rider. He wasn't, of course. "That's Dr. O'Hara's boy!"[21]

But to be Dr. O'Hara's boy was to be somebody. Before he reached his teens, the Doctor began taking him on his rounds. Like many another father with a passion—for fly fishing or Art Tatum or Charles Dickens or the Boston Red Sox—he wanted his to be contagious. And why shouldn't it have been? To be a doctor in Patrick O'Hara's time must have been thrilling. There was sound reason to revere science for its application of sense and method to mysterious bad luck, but when Johnny-boy accompanied his father out to the patches to tend to people stricken by accident or epidemic or congenital defect, anything could go wrong. Typhoid, malaria, pneumonia, strep, tuberculosis—these words were frequently death sentences. Before sulfa or antibiotics, before most of the surgical procedures we take for granted, it was high drama out there with Dad and his bag of tricks. Think of Ernest Hemingway's "Indian Camp," written—like O'Hara's remarkable story "The Doctor's Son"—early in the writer's career, while he was still preternaturally alert to the sensation of being more acted upon than acting, of being the center of consciousness in a busy life in which he was not the center of action. "I grew up one Christmas day," O'Hara confided to his final *New Yorker* editor and friend, William Maxwell, "stopping to pick up the priest in my governess cart so that he could take Holy Viaticum to Stink Schweikert's father, who was lying on a railway track with a leg mashed off." At twelve he went with his father to a coal train wreck at Molina Junction and held the hand of a man dying of burns, and then tried to comfort the brakeman, who died after Dr. O'Hara was forced to amputate his legs. He held their hands because "the nurses were busy." He told Maxwell that "every time the telephone rang there was a chance that death would be in on the call, especially late at night. 'He died on the table,' was a sentence I heard a hundred times—at the dinner table."[22] By a paradox of decorum, as though insisting that each of these doings, however frequent, had weight, Dr. O'Hara was outraged when his eldest son discussed at that same dinner table, and in defiance of his father's mandate of discreet silence, the recent suicide of the Necho Allen's barber.

A crucial lesson most imaginative writers learn is that a force arrives, bidden or unbidden, that capsizes a character, or threatens to. This crisis is as ruthlessly binary as an on/off setting on a light. A ditch is dug between before and after. Maybe there's a divorce, maybe someone loses a job, or a fire sweeps through the house, or bad news comes from the doctor. For a doctor's child, bad news—life-changing bad news—is as regular as healthy heartbeat, and no observant doctor's child can fail to understand this primary element of successful narrative: what happens to the character must matter to the character, decisively. In Hemingway's "Indian Camp," a masterpiece of concision and illumination, battering events blow through the narrative like a line squall: a woman, lying on the lower berth of a bunk in a dank shanty, is in labor at the bark peelers' camp, endures the screaming pain of an impassable breech delivery. Her husband, lying on the upper bunk, suffers his own agony from an infected foot he had cut three days earlier with an ax. Soon, with blinding narrative speed, Dr. Adams has performed a jackknife C-section, sewing the wound with tapered gut leader; during this messy and resolute procedure, while shrieks wrack the shanty, the woman's husband has slit his throat with a razor, and dies quietly in a pool of blood. But the story isn't principally about the Indians. It's about the doctor's son—Nick Adams's vision confused by uncertain lighting and obscured sight lines—learning for the first time that pain is routine, that healing is brutal, that people die . . . just like that, the end hidden if the observer should so much as blink. One minute you're fishing with your uncle and your dad, the next you're in a foul-smelling camp populated with strangers whose entire fate is in your father's hands. Standing in the shadows you watch your father move and choose and command and cut and sew. Before this has had a chance to register, Nick gets a good view of the sagging, wet upper bunk "when his father, the lamp in one hand, tipped the Indian's head back."[23] This is what writers mean by point of view. It's also how doctors' children come dramatically to mythologize or recoil from their parents' daily work.

The Doctor (such he was called even by his wife; he abhorred his given name, Patrick, perhaps—John-like—merely because it had been given) had dynastic ambitions. He meant to addict his son to veneration for medicine, and the wonder is how John managed to resist the pull of his father's passion, his bravura sense of resolve, speed, and verve.

John liked to tell the story of his father's rescue of a newsboy who'd been run over by a trolley car. In the fiction writer's biographical telling, Dr. O'Hara—dressed in white tie and tails for a dinner at the Pottsville Medical Club—crawled beneath the dangerous wheels to save the broken boy. Modified by his mother's recollection, the facts were even more theatrical: Mrs. O'Hara had been waiting for the Mauch Chunk trolley when she heard "the unmistakable clatter of a runaway horse." The milk wagon it drew collided with the Minersville trolley, and the dairyman's daughter was pinned between heavy milk cans and dragged beneath the wheels.[24] Dr. O'Hara vaulted a railing, shouted for a jack, freed the flayed girl, then raced her to Pottsville Hospital, where she died. (Yet another version has the Doctor formally dressed to attend a concert at the Academy of Music.) The son's version bears several of his signatures: the elegant costume, worn to a ceremonial occasion, at a club exclusive as to merit, where one doctor among many—*his* doctor—is the exemplary primus inter pares, the noblest—or most Nobelish—of all.

As Hemingway translated himself into Nick Adams, John O'Hara created the continuing character James Malloy, and was astute about Malloy's anxieties as well as his special knowledge of Gibbsville. When O'Hara was thirteen, in the autumn of 1918, the Spanish flu pandemic tore through the patches of Schuylkill County. The symptoms were awful: ague, headache, muscle pain, coughing fits, nausea. Dr. O'Hara was exposed by responsibility to a plague more dreadful in consequence than the Great War which had just preceded it. Worldwide more than twenty million died, and this strain of influenza was eccentric in its choice of victims, often selecting the healthy over the frail. It offered a graphic lesson in caprice, and young John O'Hara, like Nick Adams at the Indian camp, was made to learn it.

"The Doctor's Son" (1935) begins in James Malloy's voice not at the local commencement of this mysterious and awful scything, but in its middle: "My father came home at four o'clock one morning in the fall of 1918, and plumped down on a couch in the living room. He did not get awake until he heard the noise of us getting breakfast and getting ready to go to school, which had not yet closed down. When he got awake, he went out front and shut off the engine of the car, which had been running while he slept, and then he went to bed and stayed, sleeping for nearly two days. Up to that morning he had been going for nearly three days with no more than two hours' sleep at a stretch."[25]

The evocation of exhaustion, the aftermath of extraordinary exertion, is masterful.* The attention of the doctor's son is first captured not by his

*In *A Rage to Live* (1949), the first of O'Hara's baggy Pennsylvania family epics, its principal male character is discussing with his wife a local surgeon, Doctor O'Brien: "A good surgeon is very hard to like, Grace. Admire them, I do that. But they're something like medicine-men in an Indian tribe. They know something the rest of us don't know, and if we don't respect them they won't cast out devils or cure our pains in the belly. We're afraid of them. I had to see O'Brien tired before I began to like him" (John O'Hara, *A Rage to Live* [New York: Random House, 1997], p. 29).

father's heroic deeds but by his absolute consumption, a bowing to
fatigue so conclusive that this person of regular habits is too tired to shut
off the engine of his automobile (a resonant and fatal motif in *Appointment in Samarra,* completed shortly before this story).

"The Doctor's Son" narrates the episodic course of the epidemic—
subtly insinuated by the end of the reference to school as having "not yet
closed down"—from a privileged position. Young Malloy—taught to tip
his hat to priests and doctors—is appointed by his father to be a driver
for the medical student (unable to drive) sent to relieve him. Together
young Dr. Myers—not yet an M.D. but given the title "Doctor" by Dr.
Malloy so that he will act like one—and James Malloy travel throughout
the Region seeing to sick and dying Irish and Hungarian miners, as well
as to the family of a mine-company manager. Everywhere he goes James
is asked about his father—how is he? where is he? why do we have to settle for this second-stringer?—and everywhere he goes he notices the
way other people live and how they die. Like Nick Adams, he sees more
than a kid is conventionally meant to see; a bit older than Nick Adams,
he doesn't want to quit looking. A reader can't escape recollecting the
bad light and foul smell of the Indian camp when encountering James
Malloy's stygian journey to the lower orders in a shanty out at a Hungarian patch. Dr. Myers, like Nick Adams's father, has been begged to lend
a hand to a sick family:

> The ground around the house had a goaty odor because the wire which
> was supposed to keep them out was torn in several places. The yard was
> full of old wash boilers and rubber boots, tin cans and the framework of
> an abandoned baby carriage. . . . We walked around to the back door, as
> the front door is reserved for the use of the priest when he comes on
> sick calls. The Hunkie woman seemed happier and encouraged, and
> prattled away as we followed her into the house, the doctor carefully
> picking his way through stuff in the yard.
>
> The woman hung up her coat and hat on a couple of pegs on the
> kitchen wall, from which also hung a lunch can and a tin coffee bottle,
> the can suspended on a thick black strap, and the bottle on a braided
> black cord. A miner's cap with a safety lamp and a dozen buttons of the
> United Mine Workers of America was on another peg, and in a pile on
> the floor were dirty overalls and jumper and shirt. The woman sat down
> on a backless kitchen chair and hurriedly removed her boots, which left

her barefoot. There was an awful stink of cabbage and dirty feet in the house. . . . Finally the woman led the way to the front of the house. In one of the two front rooms was an old-fashioned bed. The windows were curtained, but when our eyes became accustomed to the darkness we could see four children lying on the bed. . . . The half-covered little girl got awake, or opened her eyes and looked at the ceiling. She had a half-sneering look about her nose and mouth, and her eyes were expressionless.[26]

That girl is about to die, of course. But the story isn't really about death. It's about James Malloy's eyes becoming "accustomed to the darkness," and opening wide, and not blinking. It's about being noticed—the doctor's son and all—and especially about noticing. The narrator notices Dr. Myers having an affair with the wife of the mine-company manager (and, not incidentally, the mother of a girl Jimmy has a crush on), but the most marvelous intensity is lavished on those objects recollected with surgical precision: the can suspended on a thick black strap, the bottle on a braided black cord, the associative vitality that connects "half-covered" with "half-sneering," linking the objective to the psychological. As a doctor's son, James Malloy got to—was obliged to—venture where children don't go: into darkened rooms, on the other (interior) side of shut curtains. When he came back out into the light, he emerged as a writer.

"Indian Camp" ends with a shuddering apprehension of mortality, like a chill breath of autumn rippling the surface of a Michigan lake. Resting in the stern of a rowboat, watching his father row them away from the awful-night-scene, trailing his hand in the summer-warmed water, young Nick "felt quite sure that he would never die."[27] Did ever a Chinese firecracker of an adverb—"quite"!—blow so deep a hole in the ground beneath the feet?

"The Doctor's Son" ends on a sour and sad note: after Dr. Myers returns to Philadelphia, but before the last of the dead bodies has been counted, and before the story jumps forward in time to reveal that James Malloy cannot remember the married name of the girl he loved that fall, Dr. Malloy, apropos of nothing especially, turns on his son and rails at him. James has been driving him to see desperate patients. Father and son are tired to the bone, and on each other's nerves. James wants his father to buy him a coonskin coat; his father mocks this ambition, and criticizes his son's driving. Every fact in this story has conspired to encourage James's reverence for his father: Dr. Malloy was the first to use this technique, the best at that procedure, the champion this, the consummate that. And here's what it comes to: "Twice I very nearly fell asleep while driving. The second time I awoke to hear my father saying: '. . . [O'Hara's ellipses] And my God! To think that a son of mine would rather rot in a dirty stinking newspaper office than to do this. Why, I do more good and make more money in twenty minutes in the operating room than you'll be able to make the first three years you're out of college. If you *go* to college. Don't drive so fast!' "[28]

John O'Hara's stories and novels have a perverse genius for emotional brutality. Nothing more sours an O'Hara character than unrequited love, and Dr. O'Hara was Dr. Malloy to the letter in his love-starved ambition for his son to become a doctor, to go to Oxford, to learn surgery at "Dublin, then Vienna."

No dice. The anti reflex was in John O'Hara's DNA, and not from his mother's side. Years later, in 1941, after his father was long dead and he himself had celebrated him many times for his greatness, he wrote a column for *Newsweek* in which his meditation on physicians argues that "outside of his own profession, the average doctor is a fairly ignorant man. . . . You can't kid me much about the docs. . . . He most always is deficient in general culture." A storm out of a blue sky no less shocking than Dr. Malloy's attack on his son, the attack is so thoughtless and coarse that it might even be construed—but isn't meant, I think—as irony.

And yet. . . . In these frictions between fathers and sons, there always comes "and yet. . . ." A couple of years before he died, O'Hara told an interviewer that he had seriously considered—after completing *Appointment in Samarra*—beginning college as a frosh, hastening through the undergraduate requirements, entering medical school, and becoming a psychiatrist! But that unreliable recollection of unsatisfied ambition or longing came later, after sweet literary success. Now, in the period during and after the flu pandemic, Dr. Patrick Henry O'Hara met in his son a match for stubborn pride, for prickly self-governance. He offered Johnny-boy a simple bribe of ten thousand dollars, to be deposited in a savings account until the twelve-year-old was mature enough to spend it as he pleased, if only he would promise to try to become a doctor. The son said no.

A potboiling novelist would make of this primal conflict a melodrama of recrimination, rewritten wills, and disownership; a Periclean or Jacobean dramatist would make a tragedy of regicide or banishment, of insurrection or exile. Surely the extravagance of Dr. O'Hara's affection for the boy as a child—a warmth expressed materially and sentimentally and by a lavish expense of time in his firstborn's company—soured into extravagant disappointment. The infant was remembered by his child-hood friends as having been given—bestest, mostest, soonest—Pottsville's first teddy bear. John's brother Thomas remembered a negative charge of "electricity between [eldest son and father], in spite of the fact that you could see they admired each other."[29] Not yet thir-teen, soon after he repudiated the bribe to become a doctor, Johnny-boy began secretly smoking, to spite his father, who he must have known would discover the evidence of Sweet Caporals, Omars, and Luckies. He was learning, precociously, to be a teenage pain in the ass. When the two of them went to Philadelphia's Franklin Field to watch the University of Pennsylvania Quakers play football, the son rooted for the opponents of his father's alma mater. But the doctor continued to indulge the doctor's son with every available substantial advantage, with dancing and boxing lessons, with expensive clothes and club memberships.

If the two lived together at 606 Mahantongo warily, on the 160-acre farm in the rolling hill country of the Panther Valley they continued to share common affections. Dr. O'Hara created a reliably money-wasting gentleman's farm, with a barn and large white farmhouse built into a hill-side and overlooking a meadow. He bought a fine herd of Jersey cows and joined the Jersey Cattle Breeders of America. In his late fifties, his son could recite from memory the estimable pedigree of their bull, Noble of St. Mary's, a son of Noble of Oaklands[30] (price tag, three thou-sand dollars). There were pigs and chickens, and the kids collected eggs for breakfast. Life at the farm was sweet; they ate much and they ate well, meat, scrapple, apple butter, shoofly pie, and vegetables raised by a tenant farmer.

Out in the country John took boxing lessons from his father's black chauffeur and groom, Arthur Woodruff, and valued his father's leg-endary shortness of temper and quickness to respond to the most hap-hazard insult with his fists. Dr. O'Hara had learned to box at the University of Pennsylvania from William Muldoon, a trainer nicknamed the Old Roman for his probity and indifference to pain. The Doctor made good use of this education: he knocked down a policeman who'd stopped him for speeding to a patient in need, and less nobly, following a traffic dispute, KO'd a milk-wagon driver who'd called him a four-eyed bastard. (To be precise, he at that moment was six-eyed, wearing at once two pairs of glasses—one pair for near vision and another for distance.) Dr. O'Hara counted among his friends a professional boxer, Philadelphia Jack O'Brien, whom he pestered into sparring with him, getting knocked silly for his impertinence.

Way back when he'd set up his first practice on New Orleans's Tchoupitoulas Street, Dr. O'Hara liked to "kill time by shooting rats on the levee."[31] He owned a small armory of shotguns, kept a .38 in his office, and carried a .32 revolver in his medical bag. Latent violence crackled in the atmosphere of his household; Dr. O'Hara was willing to spank his kids for disobeying. Later, after Johnny-boy began to drink— communion wine he snuck as an altar boy at St. Patrick's, and then hard stuff at Pat Joyce's bar when he was thirteen—his father's temper went off like a bottle rocket. Coming home one morning unexpectedly from house calls, Dr. O'Hara discovered his son still drunk from an all-nighter, and was said to have beaten him with a heavy chair until his wife interceded, and brother Joe dabbed at John's blood. This was a story told by Martin O'Hara after John's death, and it became part of the biographical record, too melodramatic to be ignored. But you have to wonder: a "heavy Tudor chair"? And the Doctor beat "his son over the head with it"? And "the damage was severe enough to keep John in bed for a number of days"?[32] I guess anything is possible, but I hear a bad short story trying to escape from the facts; still, whatever they were, I wonder whether John O'Hara's pride would ever recover from such shame, or if his father's could.* But beyond doubt, between father and son the punch and counterpunch of provocations and responses became too routine, and another brother, Tom, more plausibly recollected a time when his father "knocked John down and started to kick him and I just burst into tears." Johnny-boy got a scar out of that encounter, but Tom (in a 1970 letter to his children) was proud to speculate that "maybe I saved John a broken rib or spleen."

At the pacific sanctuary of the farm, the boy learned at thirteen to

---

*A variant version, told by Kathleen O'Hara Fuldner, has Dr. O'Hara "knock[ing] down" his son after learning that he'd stolen five dollars from a schoolmate, though in fact the thief was a different "John."

drive his father's Ford roadster, and also had access to Dr. O'Hara's two Buicks. At fourteen, while Dr. O'Hara was in Toledo on Independence Day, 1919, watching the Dempsey-Willard heavyweight championship bout, John stole the six-cylinder Buick touring car to impress an audience of friends; the joyride ended back in the hills with a snapped connecting rod and a long tow home. The Doctor's response did not fail to confirm his son's anxiety.

But the calculated purpose of these country retreats was to kindle in his family—especially his firstborn—an infatuation with horses. After his dignity outgrew the pony carts and the Shetland pony, John got a five-gaited chestnut mare, Julia, that his father had bought in Bowling Green, Kentucky. The boy taught his magnificent horse such tricks as standing on her hind legs. An ease and aptitude with horses—at that time and in that part of the country—was a ticket to ride, socially. Dr. O'Hara's dynastic dreams were not limited to a family polo team: his son's horsemanship might lead him to the ethereal reaches of the Devon Horse Show, one of Philadelphia's snottier assemblages of the privileged. Young John was caparisoned in breeches and brilliantly buffed brown knee-high leather boots, a princely fifty-five dollars from Philadelphia's Steigerwalt.

In his story "It Must Have Been Spring" (1934), O'Hara draws directly on his memory of his boyhood in Pottsville to reveal and celebrate the heart-speeding tension he felt in his father's unpredictable fire-and-ice rhythms of contempt and respect. The story is very short, confined with claustrophobic effect to the perspective of a boy setting out for the stable in his brand-new riding habit, under the stern eyes of his father, a physician. He has to pass newsboys along the way, and he's carrying, hidden in the pocket of his new corduroy habit, a set of spurs. He's learned that the spurs—more even than his polished boots and riding breeches—provoke the newsboys to yell "Cowboy-crazy!" The narrator has already lost a tooth in a fight over this ridicule: "It was not only because I hated what they called me. I hated their ignorance; I could not stop and explain to them that I was not cowboy-crazy, that I rode an English saddle and posted to the trot. I could not explain to a bunch of newsboys that Julia was a five-gaited mare, a full sister to Golden Firefly, and that she herself could have been shown if she hadn't had a blanket scald."[33]

This is at first glance a conventional narrative of first-person child-

hood oppression, in which They—cruel and arbitrary—bully the vic-
tim/speaker, Me. But the passage is complicated by its invincible expression of superiority, of power hidden in the well-tailored pocket. What
else is hidden in those pockets is a pack of Melachrino cigarettes, and
when he sees his father watching him approach, the cocksure, mare-
proud scorn leaks impotently from the son of the doctor, who is posed on
the porch of his office:

> He was standing with his legs spread apart, with his hands dug deep in
> his pockets and the skirt of his tweed coat stuck out behind like a spar-
> row's tail. He was wearing a gray soft hat with a black ribbon and with
> white piping around the edge of the brim. He was talking across the
> street to Mr. George McRoberts, the lawyer, and his teeth gleamed
> under his black mustache. He glanced in my direction and saw me and
> nodded, and put one foot up on the porch seat and went on talking until
> I got there.
>
> I moved toward him, as always, with my eyes cast down, and I felt
> my riding crop getting sticky in my hand and I changed my grip on it
> and held the bone handle. I never could tell anything by my father's
> nod, whether he was pleased with me or otherwise.[34]

The speaker's self-consciousness is infectious; reading it brings a
blush of anticipatory shame to my own cheeks. The narrator's nerves
ache at the thought that one's mere existence is an offense to one's hero,
sensing that one's presentation—dress, posture, or even odor, as the boy
fears that his father might smell smoke on his breath—is at once distort-
ingly amplified and microscopically under the scrutiny of a severe judge.
And then the tension is abruptly released:
" 'You look fine,' he said. 'You really look like something. Here.' He
gave me a five-dollar bill."
And what can the speaker say? " 'Thank you,' I said, and turned away,
because suddenly I was crying."
He walks away, afraid to put his hand to his face, adamant in his resistance to a confession of the very sentiment—a potent mixture of relief
and longing and hot anger—that the story serves to honor. It is a story
naked in its revelation of father/son tension, and of the mystery of discrimination. What must the newsboys think of me? Here's what I think
of them. What does my father—whom I see with such loving precision—

see when he looks my way? Well, I'll tell you, I "look fine." I mustn't let him—fuck him anyway!—see that I care.

There's a postscript to this nervy scene. Brendan Gill, ten years younger than O'Hara and another Irish son of a doctor, was his colleague on the *New Yorker* and, before their falling-out, his drinking and dinner companion. One night in New York, following supper at "21" and many a drink, Gill and his wife found themselves in the Upper East Side apartment of O'Hara and his second wife, Belle Wylie. O'Hara had been avuncularly lecturing him on money, lessons which fell (Gill writes in *Here at The New Yorker*) "upon deaf ears, though of course I enjoyed being worried over." The Gills finished their nightcaps and began their good-byes. "O'Hara got unsteadily to his feet, protesting that he had one last treat in store for us." Gill prepares the scene like the master after-dinner raconteur that he was: O'Hara's twenty-minute disappearance into the bedroom, the mystery building. And then the payoff: "When he emerged, he was utterly transformed. He had taken off his ordinary clothes and decked himself out in a cowboy outfit of incomparable Reno richness. He was all leather and steel and silk: a bedazzling one-man compilation of boots, spurs, chaps, holsters, and guns with nickeled butts. Above the chaps came a checked shirt and a scarf knotted about the neck, and above the big, boozy face floated a surpassingly broad, high-crowned, creamy sombrero."[35]

And so the Gills laughed. Of course they did! Who could fail to? And how wised-up that laughter, from a Yale man, my goodness a Skull and Bones tap-ee! A *New Yorker* writer born to the voice: good-natured, observant, smart and then some, with that "Reno richness" and those nickel-butted guns (if you're willing to believe in them). "Cowboy-crazy" after all! And how predictably silly was O'Hara's bristling fury! So why is it that my sympathy—indeed a feeling of full-hearted fraternity—is drawn to the ridiculous yob with the big, boozy face? Or to the bull rather than to the picador?

John O'Hara had been encouraged to develop what a teacher recognized to be his unmistakable gift; this was in eighth grade, at St. Patrick's School, and the teacher was a nun. Retroactive memories of enthusiasm always seem in hindsight prophetic, but if every parent acted on every teacher's enthusiasm for a child's promise at the fiddle or hand-eye co-ordination at the softball plate, the world would be even more sadly littered with broken dreams. O'Hara's siblings later fashioned a grand Hegelian contest from the putative battle for the boy's ambition: father pushing him this way toward medicine, nun pulling him that way toward literature. In truth, Johnny-boy was a predictable product of a household that valued books and education.

He began school at Miss Katie Carpenter's, a private academy on Norwegian Street, but near enough to the upper reaches of Mahantongo Street to suit the tastes of the mine bosses, bankers, professionals—the Episcopalian establishment of Pottsville—who sent their children there. John loved his school, the grand house where classes were taught, and the grounds' shade trees, spacious lawn, and croquet court. He loved the school cat, and he loved the school's director, to whom he dedicated *From the Terrace* (1958), his favorite among his novels: "To Miss Katie Carpenter, God bless her." His first teacher taught by the Montessori method and got her pupils reading before first grade, though O'Hara had taught himself to read before he got to Miss Katie's, puzzling out meanings by sounding out newspaper headlines. The boy learned fine penmanship and arithmetic early, and by his testimony the man became a millionaire using the austere declarative sentences Miss Katie favored. But in the end, Katherine the teacher's influence fell out of favor with Katharine the mother.

God was the problem, the wrong God, too little deference paid the pope, or too few sacraments observed. At Katie Carpenter's young John was learning High Church Episcopalian hymns; when the Delaneys came over from Lykens of a Sunday to worship with the O'Haras at St. Patrick's, they wondered why the boy wasn't up to speed with his Catholic psalmody and Glorias. An even worse apostasy, he was chanting the Lord's Prayer with the Episcopalian doxology. So his mother pulled him from this school and sent him across Mahantongo Street to St. Patrick's and the Sisters of St. Joseph, where it was to be his destiny to learn properly to serve the mass she attended every morning. "I got a cassock and surplice," O'Hara recollected, "and raised my mother's foolish hopes that she had produced a Jesuit."[36]

Parochial school might not have been John O'Hara's notion of earthly heaven, but it extended his social range and sharpened the instruments of calibration crucial to a novelist of manners. He went to St. Patrick's (the highest steeple in Pottsville, but not the town's social summit) with "the Studs Lonigans of our place and time," who dismissed him as a "ristycrat," and glancing across the street at the O'Hara townhouse, he was consoled by the illusion that they were correct. He was discouraged by his parents from bringing schoolmates home to play, a message akin to asking a child to memorize and follow two sets of contradictory regulations: You belong at school with your kind, fellow Catholics; you are to avoid the company of rough Catholic kids. (This in a town where a union between man and wife from discrete Pottsville parishes—St. Pat's and St. John's—was considered a mixed marriage.) It is not difficult to imagine how O'Hara's notorious ambivalence about class and its layerings was germinated and fertilized. Proud, but not socially aggressive; ambitious, but unwilling to be assimilated—his parents lavished opportunity on their son even as they hedged him with rigid expectations grounded on arbitrary proprieties. What was he to think? Who was he to be?

In fact, learning to read and to write, he could be any damned thing he chose: once the manipulation of words had unlocked the gates of family, home, and Pottsville, nothing could contain him. His brother Martin recollected his mother's memory of having brought home to 606 a tapestry embroidered with the Great Pyramid: "John was only a little boy then but he was so impressed by the great eye on the pyramid [maybe Mother had brought home a likeness of the backside of a dollar bill?] that he wrote a story about it."[37] At six the precocious fictioneer had been given the gift of a hand-printing set; it's safe to assume that the following day he was a published writer.

The Sisters of St. Joseph were crackerjack teachers of orthography, etymology, syntax, and geography; the lessons—learned by rote—took. In geography class, for example, O'Hara and his classmates were obliged to memorize the states, their capitals, the bodies of water—if any—on which those capitals were situated, the boundaries of each state. A nun would demand:

" 'Master O'Hara, bound Connecticut.'

" 'Connecticut. Connecticut is bounded on the north by Massachusetts, on the east by Rhode Island, on the south by Long Island Sound, on the west by New York.' "[38]

Years later he astonished Robert Benchley with the parlor trick of naming all the counties of Massachusetts. He had not learned these from the nuns, but from the nuns he had learned to scrutinize maps and atlases with ardent attention, unlike the "dull hostility" with which he faced multiplication tables. Memorization of facts and forms—fraternity rituals or the tenets of various Christian creeds—was of a piece with his fanatical loyalty to objects. Pottsville friends were impressed—and that was a significant goal of the exercise—by his power to recall song lyrics. His love of trains led him to sit by the tracks watching them pass—but anyone could passively watch; John O'Hara learned the names of those trains, the specifications of the locomotives that pulled them, and the schedules of every principal passenger train in the country.

Impressing pals comes at a price, of course. One St. Patrick's kid remembered him as having been "extremely arrogant."[39] Shy or arrogant: these modifiers are used interchangeably to describe someone indifferent to conversation with the person doing the modifying. Thus another recalled what he himself hadn't remembered: "I don't remember John ever showing a lot of interest in me. What does come to mind is that he was always late for school even though he lived just a block away."

He'd come home for noontime lunch, and so would Dr. O'Hara. If Johnny-boy beat his father home, he'd rush to the second floor and use the busybody, a kind of periscopic spyglass, to track the Doctor's approach up Mahantongo Street from his office. The Doctor's gait was vigorous, and he'd take the front steps two at a time, then pull open the unlocked oak front door and sweep into the tiled front hall. The Doctor wasn't one to make a casual, "Hi, honey, I'm home," entrance. Before the two withdrew from each other, the firstborn would greet his father at the inner door off the hallway and keep him company while they climbed the stairs to the second floor, where the Doctor would slip into a comfortable jacket, and then again as they went back down to the formal paneled basement dining room. The midday meal was a ceremonial occasion, with a trencherman's bounty prepared by the German cook. High-minded talk was the rule at the long, crowded table; gossip was discouraged, but the Doctor did expect a profitable account of his family's progress since breakfast.

That accounting would inevitably include Mrs. O'Hara's morning worship at mass, and for two years—from the ages of ten to twelve— Johnny-boy's attendance there as an altar boy. Yet there was nothing sanctimonious about his mother's manner. She was mirthful, even giggly, a notable mimic, and her musical ear for the distinctions between voices—their signature airs and irregularities—was seductive to her son's writerly reflexes. When she and John were alone together, Katharine Delaney O'Hara would narrate the social history of the

Region, playing all the parts. When her son would reciprocate with an anecdote about one character or another he'd encountered during his explorations of Pottsville, she'd gently grill him for detail: What exactly did Furry say? In what tone and cadence? With raised eyebrow? Lowered lid?

But this formal meal was not the appropriate occasion for a show of Mrs. O'Hara's wit and playfulness. Her husband's stern bearing was so vigilantly decorous that even his rebellious son caught a lifelong dose of rigidity. Patrick O'Hara liked to affect an at-ease posture so stiff in its calculation—angled just-so against the mantel, rubbing his chin in an exhibition of thoughtfulness—that it confounded spontaneity. Self-importance was congenital, father to son, as was exaggerated self-consciousness.

After lunch, and before Dr. O'Hara returned to his practice and Johnny-boy to school, the family would retire to the music room. Perhaps sister Mary would play the harp, an expensive model from Lyon and Healy. Or Mrs. O'Hara would accompany, on the Brinkerhoff upright, the Doctor's sweet tenor: *Have you ever been across the sea to Ireland. . . . ?* Later, John would play the violin (badly) for the amusement of his own daughter, and soon—for the amusement of himself and his pals—he'd play mandolin and kazoo and banjo in a rough approximation of the jazz he soaked up through the medium of his family's Victor Victrola. (He announced as a teenager that he had two ambitions: to own a Stutz Bearcat and to lead a jazz band.)[40]

A supple dancer despite his rigid posture, O'Hara could thank his mother's affection for music and his father's sense of propriety for full immersion in dancing classes. The boy was to have every social advantage, and to prepare for Pottsville's busy round of cotillions and assemblies—to learn not to bunny-hug to waltz time, or fox-trot to the polka—there were weekly instructions at the Misses Linders' School of the Dance. Young John attended in a navy blue Norfolk jacket bought by his father in Philadelphia. Carrying his patent-leather dancing pumps in a sack, he and his sister Mary were delivered with Miss Augusta Yuengling, by chauffeured Lozier. The boys held white silk handkerchiefs in their left hands, to keep their sweat to themselves. The girls wore gloves. Predictably, biographers who interviewed O'Hara's long-ago partners—these ex-kids who had carried into old age the crushes and grievances of kids who had been held tenderly, who had not been

cut in on, whose toes had been stepped on—got a turbulent range of
recollection: young John was graceful, or he was witty, or he was sarcastic, he was boring or bored, or snooty, he was shy, or he had an inferiority complex.

The classes were run by Miss Lettie and Miss Katie Linder, and to be
invited caused him to feel "a little smug and snobbish." What—given his
family's standing, spending, and ambitions—didn't conspire to aggravate
that smugness? Looking back fifteen or so years at those dancing classes,
at the invitations that arrived each autumn, O'Hara was quick to note
that not every son and daughter of Pottsville received embossed cards.
"If, for example, your father owned a saloon, you weren't invited, no
matter how much money your father possessed. And if your father was a
bank director and lived on Mahantongo Street, and had a Winton and
had given you a pony, but was Jewish, you weren't invited."[41]

Same with clubs, of course. The Pottsville Club, founded in 1888, was
the oldest, aping the furnishings and manners of a London gents' society,
even unto banning women save for two special dances a year. It is tempt-
ing to imagine what a member of White's or the Athenaeum would have
made of this show of exclusion, but all that really mattered was that
selection mattered in Pottsville, and that the O'Haras had been chosen.
They were also invited annually to the Pottsville Assembly, whose New
Year's Eve ball was the toughest ticket in town, a simulacrum of the
Philadelphia Assembly, whose members would not likely have offered
Pottsville's assemblers reciprocal privileges.

Within John's youth, the simple good fun of the Outdoor Club, with
modest food served in an unpretentious wood-framed summer cottage
and casual dances to a local trio called the Tasmanian Tinsmiths, gave
way to the haute pretenses of the Schuylkill Country Club, with formal
dances, waiters in uniform, and a membership committee with the
power to wreck lives. Indeed, it is at just such an institution, the Gibbsville Country Club, that Julian English so memorably wrecks his future
in *Appointment in Samarra* by the expedient of throwing a drink of
whiskey into the florid face of Harry Reilly, the vulgar, newly rich club
bore—an Irishman, it's worth mentioning—at that moment tailored in
monkey suit and white tie.

Of all the social complexities that spurred John O'Hara's anger, pride,
envy, squinting focus, truculence, and art, his Irishness led the charge.
Little wonder that he felt ambivalence. Even Dr. O'Hara, so ferociously

proud, was vulnerable to a kind of reflexive shame at the low standing of his people. His son Joseph remembered driving with him past a factory announcing on its door a need for laborers: "No Irish Need Apply," in the notorious language of one among so many contemporary prejudices. In a conversation with Frank MacShane, he recalled asking his father whether the notice applied to them. No, his father answered, "we are Americans," explaining that the warning was directed at recent immigrants, as though this made it reasonable. All that was necessary was that the Irish change their standing in the community's esteem, and all that was necessary to do this was that "the Irish become hardworking and sober and overcome their national weaknesses, laziness and drink."[42]

His Irishness was the obdurate wall against which John O'Hara beat his fist and the ivied, protective wall behind which he huddled with his proud clan. The social historian William V. Shannon is rough on O'Hara's ethnic self-consciousness, contrasting the "social stigmata" of the "lace-curtain Irish" from which Fitzgerald wrought marvelous dreamworlds of class and aspiration to the shaming mortification of O'Hara's micks. Shannon diminishes his fiction as displays of "bleeding wounds," and accuses the author of picking at his "Irishness like a scab. It is one of the furious impulses that agitate his work, but he has never fully confronted his own past and made peace with it. His evasiveness has impoverished his fiction."[43]

Shannon is neither fair nor sensitive to the creative value of resentment. "Furious impulses" are not enemies of energetic fiction; making "peace" is no friend to dramatic conflict. And to accuse O'Hara of a failure to confront his past is willfully to ignore a preoccupation with that past that sometimes overwhelmed his alertness to pasts dissimilar to his own.

John O'Hara's Irishness was a dumb fact which he couldn't ignore and did not wish to. For him it was a defining fact—at once debasing and special—and neither for the first time nor the last he voiced its bounds eloquently in an eruption by Jim Malloy in O'Hara's second novel, *Butterfield 8*. The outburst—in terms of that novel's needs irrelevant—is delivered in a speakeasy, and Malloy is there with a well-bred Gibbsville woman, Isabel Stannard. He abruptly turns on her, accusing her of slumming: "People like you make me mad, I mean people like you, people whose families have money and send them to good schools and belong to country clubs and have good cars—the upper crust, the swells."

She is, of course, offended by the reductive stereotyping, and interrupts Malloy, trying to knock the chip off his shoulder: "I beg your par-
don, but why are you talking about you people, you people, your kind of
people, people like you. *You* belong to a country club, you went to good
schools and your people at least *had* money—"

And at that Malloy interrupts her, and delivers a soliloquy:

> I want to tell you something about myself that will help to explain a lot
> of things about me. You might as well hear it now. First of all, I am a
> Mick. I wear Brooks clothes and I don't eat salad with a spoon and I
> probably could play five-goal polo in two years, but I am a Mick. Still
> a Mick. Now it's taken me a little time to find this out, but I have at
> last discovered that there are not two kinds of Irishmen. There's only
> one kind. I've studied enough pictures and known enough Irishmen
> personally to find that out. . . . I've looked at dozens of pictures of
> the best Irish families at the Dublin Horse Show and places like that,
> and I've put my finger over their clothes and pretended I was look-
> ing at a Knights of Columbus picnic—and by God you can't tell the
> difference.[44]

As Scott Fitzgerald memorably postulated in the opening sentences
of "The Rich Boy," the collective—Irish, say—is an enemy of character
in fiction: "Begin with an individual, and before you know it you find that
you have created a type; begin with a type, and you find that you have
created—nothing." Fitzgerald immediately forgot his own warning with
his oft-repeated: "Let me tell you about the very rich. They are different
from you and me."[45] This distinction did his story no favor, not because it
was as stupid as Hemingway snidely tried to make it sound (yeah, they
have more money) but because Fitzgerald was right the first time:
"There are no types, no plurals." The best imaginative writers concern
themselves with distinctive characters rather than case studies, with particular members rather than "the whole damned tribe," as James Baldwin said in remarking on his frustrated and futile resistance to being
typecast as the Black Jeremiah.

In Fitzgerald's "The Rich Boy," it rightly counts that Anson Hunter is
a Yale man. Yale—Tom Buchanan's university—is typed as brutal and
commercial, metropolitan and unforgiving in contrast to Princeton's
dreamy, southern charm. For Fitzgerald the choice of a college—even in

a cosmos limited to three stars, and actually only two, since Harvard was beyond telescope range—did not so much determine character as it revealed inclination, a more complex and interesting matter. But for O'Hara as for his alter ego, the Yale type gave an aura, an outward token of benediction, of having been Chosen: "Well, I am often taken for a Yale man, by Yale men," Jim Malloy tells Isabel. "That pleases me a little, because I like Yale best of all the colleges."[46]

There is something defiantly small-minded, heroically elementary, about Malloy's confusion of institutional affiliation with personal grace. O'Hara shared this reductio ad absurdum—Eli rules!—but by his apprehension of the social implications of anxious Irishness, O'Hara felt authorized to take the anxious master himself to school. His earliest located letter to Fitzgerald, written in 1933, responds to an Irish character in "More Than Just a House," a Fitzgerald story he'd recently read: "We get to the second thing you've done so well: Lawrie the climber; and I wonder why you do the climber so well. Is it the Irish in you? *Must* the Irish always have a lot of climber in them? Good God!" The Delaneys may have had some spurious kinship with Protestant gentry, but the O'Haras! Having recited his late "black Irish" father's medical achievements—"the first doctor in the U.S. to use oxygen in pneumonia . . . recognized by [Dr. John B.] Deaver as being one of the best trephiners and appendix men in the world," he continues. "I go through cheap shame when the O'Hara side gets too close for comfort."[47]

To which Fitzgerald replied that no matter if he were crowned king of Scotland after an education at Eton and Cambridge, "I would still be a parvenu."[48] Welcome to the club, I guess. It's odd that such a determined againster would want to belong to any club, but odd is what makes a story particular and not everybody's. O'Hara lets Isabel Stannard expect to find Irish gangsters in a speakeasy, then lights Jim Malloy's fuse; this setup is too clumsy to surprise the reader or to illuminate Malloy.

It would be difficult to imagine this fiction written by a John O'Hara who'd gone to St. Paul's, joined Fence Club at Yale, and been tapped by Bones. That George Orwell was schooled at Eton, Dwight Macdonald at Exeter, and Robert Lowell at St. Mark's seems merely incidental to their life's work. But like Fitzgerald and John Cheever (ditto Holden Caulfield), O'Hara was sent to a third-rate boarding school; and when he got the boot, he slipped even lower on the ladder. Pottsville liked to send its Katie Carpenter boys to the Hill in Pottstown, to the Yale-feeder Andover, or to Lawrenceville, where Dink Stover studied and triumphed on the playing fields, before his victories at Yale. John O'Hara very well knew which school was which: Owen Johnson's Lawrenceville stories about the Tennessee Shad were staples in the family's library. (So was Booth Tarkington, whose Penrod sagas encouraged in the adolescent a Tom Sawyerish appetite for inventive mischief.)

In 1920, O'Hara—having exhausted the academic and social resources of St. Patrick's, his final year spent in the ignominy of a commercial course, shorthand and bookkeeping and the like—was sent to boarding school in the Bronx, St. John's College High School of Fordham University, better known as Fordham Prep. The choice of schools was his parents': his mother still kept alight a guttering faith that her eldest son would turn with zealousness to the one true belief; his father craved for his son the intellectual rigor and general discipline of the Jesuits: "The Jebbies will knock some sense into his head," the Doctor promised himself.

Ho-ho, and fat chance. At fifteen, Johnny-boy didn't look or care to behave much like a boy anymore: taller than six feet, with a filled-out body, he brought to jaded New York from bumpkin Pottsville a refined expertise in cigarette smoking, boozing, sarcasm, and hierarchy. He spurred a fistfight his first night at school, and "got the shit beaten out of me." As a consequence, he was immediately elected president of his class by his schoolmates, mostly middle-class Irish like him, or Italian, like Tony Tessaro, who'd beaten him up. O'Hara was one of fifteen boarders among the school population of six hundred; the others he and his fellow inmates referred to as "Day Hops."

Katharine O'Hara's sister Verna McKee, married to an officer in the Immigration Service, was to keep an auntish eye on the scholar, from the security of her very domestic household in East Orange, New Jersey. The general idea was to make certain that young John's weekends were unhilarious; his free time, already shortened and tamed by six days of classes, was to have as its ruling occasion a church service in East Orange. It must have been galling to pass along the edges of Manhattan en route from one dowdy suburb to another.

The school had some years on it: founded in 1841, it was ancient by contrast to Choate, say, or Deerfield. Its gray stone walls were ivied, and the spacious lawns well tended, but Groton it was not, and who could possibly have understood this better than John O'Hara, even at fifteen— or perhaps especially at fifteen? He liked tennis and golf, but the inter-dependency of team sports predictably irritated him: "Don't go to a Jesuit school if you don't like baseball." Don't go, moreover, if you don't believe in the divinity of the Church, or the sanctity of priests, or if you're not eager to learn what Jesuits are eager to teach. He was more interested in mastering the customs of Manhattan, sneaking off to such speakeasies as the Pre Catalan, a nightclub especially popular with Yalies. While he was stuck in the Bronx, there were beer joints available to Fordham College fun-seekers, and he studied culture at local movie theaters and vaudeville houses. When he wasn't otherwise engaged, he sulked at his desks in various classrooms, drawing caricatures of his schoolmates and masters. In his second year, he flunked three of five courses (English history, algebra, and biology) and didn't set the world on fire with the two he passed, Latin (D+) and English (gentleman's C). He was "honorably dismissed," in the language of his transcript. Long after, stirred by O'Hara's worldly success, Fordham Prep's prefect of dis-cipline—Father Arthur Shea, S.J.—wrote to the no-longer poor lost lamb in an unavailing effort to call him home to the flock. Not likely: "The priests ruined it for me." (Before he got to Fordham, O'Hara—in common with probably two thirds of all students who would ever attend parochial schools—had decided he was disillusioned by what he under-stood, or believed he knew, of Pottsville's priests' platitudes, favoritism toward the well-connected, and tippling.)

All Fordham students were obliged to unite in expressions of religious ardor; like his schoolmates, he was a member of the Apostleship of Prayer and the League of the Sacred Heart, whose purpose was—among other high-minded purposes touching on good deeds and public ser-vice—"to join the great work of reparation for the outrages daily offered our Lord by sinners." This particular apostle became more zealous to compound the outrages than to atone for them, and created a notorious incident during a confession when he was asked what he planned by way of penance for a misdemeanor and replied, "Nothing, because it is not a mortal sin." To which the priest was reported to have responded: "I see we have a smart young theologian here," causing O'Hara to leave the confession booth without further comment. Attentive readers will notice that this report could only have come from one of two participants in the encounter, and that it didn't likely come from the priest, and didn't reflect ill on O'Hara's wit or nerve. If ever he was tormented by the contest between faith and rationalism for the prize of his soul, this agon went undramatized in his fiction and correspondence. Uncharacteristically, he expressed his dampened fervor temperately; he recognized his grandfather Israel Delaney, a convert to Catholicism, as "quietly devout . . . a dear and lovely man" to whom Catholicism had given "only peace, not turmoil." During World War II, and when he was hospitalized with a bleeding ulcer, O'Hara was asked to state his religious affiliation, "in the event of the last extremity," as he explained in a 1962 letter to Charles Poore, a lead book critic of the *New York Times*. "I said, 'None.' But if they had asked me 'Religious influence?' I'd have had to give a different answer."

It is surely true that his Fordham instructors believed, in defiance of what O'Hara took on faith to be solid evidence to the contrary, that they knew more than he did. The brothers in the Bronx had swallowed without salt their good press—just as Dr. and Mrs. O'Hara had—and their arrogance outbid any a student could muster. Finis Farr, O'Hara's friend, earliest biographer, and fellow Irish Catholic, warmed to this chapter of his work: "It was an item of American belief, even among Protestants, that the trained minds of the Jesuits were the keenest article in the intellectual hardware shop. Their brains were filled with learning beyond all calculation, so said the commentators in saloons, livery stables and barber shops, and they attributed to the Jesuits a special cunning manner of debate that could tie you right up, no matter what the point at issue."

Young John, however, was not impressed, and as a former teacher explained, "He thought he knew it all. When things were explained to him, he thought his way was better."[49]

Oh, was Dr. O'Hara cross when his son came home with his skeptical airs and a pink slip! Well, if Fordham wasn't a sufficient social and intellectual challenge for his exacting Johnny-boy, how about Keystone Normal School (say what?) in Kutztown, midway between Allentown and Reading in Mennonite country, where the flappers and philosophers journeyed downtown by horse and buggy, wearing black suits and ankle-length bulletproof skirts. But before banishing the downwardly mobile prep schooler to this hick practice school for a hick teachers' college, the Doctor maneuvered to get him a five-dollar-a-shift job working as a scab, stoking locomotives and waking the strike-breaking railway crews from their troubled sleep in the dorms out at Port Carbon in time to make their runs.* It was a bleak summer, enduring at home the cold rage of his father and the dismay of his mother, and at work the hatred of the picket line and the abuse of sleepy workers, whom O'Hara had to pester into signing a card that proved he had wakened them when he failed to waken them, and provoking his irate bosses to send him out to St. Clair, the largest coal-loading yard in the nation, and put him to work as a pit man greasing the locomotives. It was filthy and dangerous work, as a mining and railroad surgeon—practiced in amputations—had every reason to know. That was a summer of awful friction between the father and son. John managed not to complain, but neither was he shy about coming home to 606 grease-grimed and sweat-soaked, black with coal dust and half ruined from fatigue. Finally, the Doctor blinked when his wife told him, "I hope you understand that you're just slowly killing your son." Then the boy was given leave to take an easier job—as what he called "baggage smasher," a loader—for Railway Express. He had his eyes opened those miserable months. In years to come he'd crow that he was alone among distinguished writers in his ability to drive a locomotive, but even if the boast was true, that was the least of what he learned in the summer of 1921. Going among miners and laborers was no longer a spectator's privilege, and now he joined them as a comrade in misery out at the patches and shacks, the marshaling yards and switches and slagheaps of culm, at the settlements worn out before they'd been completed, and became accustomed to habituated terror, suspicion, and resentment. He came to this society as an Irish kid with a sorry present and a shaky future, and threw himself into desperate, furious drinking and singing and fighting and whoring at speakeasy saloons and roadhouses, the Pig and Whistle, the Burning Rag. The Amber Lantern, the Rattlesnake. And often it seemed that the only function of fun was to toss in the sad jackpot of a hangover.

You'd imagine that after such a summer Keystone Normal would seem like heaven itself, but to think this you'd have to discount the persecuting power of shame over John O'Hara. He still dreamed of Yale, kept alert to the Great Chain of Fraternal Being between DKE and Psi U or whatever. Twenty-five miles southeast of Pottsville, this teach-

*Thirty years later, writing in *Collier's,* O'Hara boasted of "having tied up the whole Sunbury Division [of the Pennsy] by failing to rout out a bunch of crews."

ing school had evolved from the Maxatawny Seminary. It was a plain place, soberly and condescendingly approved by the *Pottsville Standard* as an institution where "every man's child, whether rich or poor, may enjoy the benefits of an education which but a few years ago was given to the rich man's son alone."[50] But not, perhaps, to the child of the dark-skinned. In an aside to the letter explaining his religious history to Charles Poore, O'Hara mentioned that "several members of the [Keystone] faculty were sheet-carrying members of the Ku Klux Klan." Woe was John! Not a place you'd be eager to list as alma mater in *Who's Who*, not an institution with an abbreviation in the *Social Register.*

O'Hara warned his father and boasted to his friends that he wouldn't last long, and he didn't: less than a year. The students—mostly young women—were divided between Catholics and Pennsylvania Dutch farmers. Hard to believe, but even in such a place social scales responded to delicate weights. Philo was a literary society, the Philometheans, and O'Hara—for that school year only known as "Jack"—got in the other one, the Keystone Society. In a short story O'Hara wrote when he was fifty-nine, a character remarks, "Oh, how we hated those Keystones. . . . A Catholic couldn't get into Philo when I was there." What must he have felt, making do with the second-best literary club at Keystone Normal? This is the same man who mused forty or so years later in a letter to his stepson Courtland Bryan that the Doctor had been blackballed at Penn by DKE due to his religion, while he himself was "given a sub-freshman bid to Delta Phi, a socially much better fraternity."* This must have been offered in 1922, during his sentence at Keystone. Putting aside the sole-cism of "socially much better," there's something unsettling in the facts and syntax of O'Hara's letter to his young Yale kinsman, and he keeps pil-ing it on: in 1922 he was also offered pre-bids (how would these work, by the way?) to DKE at Amherst, and then—what the hell, list them all!—to the entire Greek alphabet at Wesleyan, Lehigh, Penn State, Lafayette, and Cornell. Then, astonishingly, he concludes: "At Yale I probably would have made Bones (and wanted Keys) on literary accomplishment, and with little or no consideration of my being a Catholic, which I was then."

Many years after leaving there, driving past Keystone in his Mercedes with a Princeton resident and friend (St. Paul's School—or "SPS," as

---

*Finis Farr, quoting this letter, discloses that there was no DKE chapter at Penn in 1890.

O'Hara and Paulies liked to put it—and Harvard), he pointed out the undistinguished campus and remarked that he had been sent there "for penance."[51] This he didn't choose to suffer in silence. Keystone schoolmates remembered him as snide or arrogant, sarcastic or opinionated, seldom right but always certain. It was agreed that he was a heavy drinker with a short-fuse temper. He picked a fistfight with a student who decided it was a good idea to wear an orange peel on his lapel to mock St. Patrick's Day—and that unlucky joker was O'Hara's friend. Imagine how Jack treated his enemies.

O'Hara was bounced from Keystone for discipline problems, principally insubordination toward the preparatory school's president, a despot named Amos C. Rothermel, a priggish sermonizer. The authorized history of what became Kutztown State College fails to translate him into a charismatic leader of students: "Principal Rothermel was a rigidly pious man, who succeeded admirably in projecting a saintly image of himself. He moved with the measured, steady and stately stride of one walking the straight and narrow path." This martinet, who according to his friendly biographer had "overlearned the art of moralizing,"[52] warned O'Hara, with unmodulated gravity, to discontinue his courtship of the daughter of a trustee. No dice. Moreover, O'Hara was guilty of general mopery, lounging about as he did in his coonskin coat, strumming the banjo in a group calling itself the "Jolly Trio," cutting up in chemistry class, flunking chemistry, trig, and Cicero. So they booted him, Rothermel evidently announcing the disgrace in chapel. Keystone Normal threw him right into the brier patch—where his father was waiting. And this time the Doctor really was pissed off!

Back in Pottsville during the rest of the academic year, O'Hara was obliged to work, variously, jerking soda at Hodgson's drugstore, reading gas meters, holding a surveying rod for a road-building company, shoveling gravel, puddling steel, pulling guard duty, and renting rowboats at Lakeside Amusement Park, at the far reach of the trolley line. He took to baggage smashing again, and more responsibly hired on as an "evaluating engineer" with a local company, traveling the Region with a crew to inspect mines and power stations for design and maintenance flaws. He lived part-time on the road, giving himself sanctuary from the Doctor's hanging-judgment, and invested his sixty-dollar monthly salary in a showoff's wardrobe.

His experience as a doctor's son, and now as a licensed and professional snoop, was tailor-made for a would-be writer. And John O'Hara was already that. "By the time I was fifteen," he told the *New York Times's* obituary writer Alden Whitman, "I knew all the rules and I certainly knew what I wanted to do. I wasn't going to be diverted by becoming a polo player (which I could have been, but I didn't have the money)* or by taking other jobs. I knew I had to be what I've become."[53]

It also helped O'Hara's imaginative reach and power of connection—the structure itself of his fiction—that Pottsville and the Region were ideally scaled to encourage a writer to explore networks of manners and economy, family and ethnic stresses, ambition and exclusion. Huge cities or tiny towns commonly throw a novelist back on the self, bobbing like a cork in a turbulent river, or sticking out like a sore thumb from a dwarfed hand. Pottsville was not too big, not too small: just right. Coincidence is never strained in such a place. It wouldn't be necessary for a character to say, You'll never guess who I ran into this morning on Mahantongo Street. Everyone ran into everyone, all the time, and because of the nature of the Region's business, all enterprise flowing into the Coal & Iron headquarters, a faux Italianate palace ("suitable for a museum or a club of millionaires," in the calculation of Finis Farr) at 325 South Centre Street, hard by Trinity Episcopal Church, a countinghouse through which circulated much of the worldly treasure from local banks and mines and railroads. Such a self-consciously purse-proud edifice was tailor-made for a fiction writer's need to centralize and mystify the striving and losing, the tactical victories and strategic routs, of a coherent society.

During the year following his expulsion from Keystone Normal, O'Hara became infatuated with the daughter of the manager of the Girard estate, a regional octopus of mining and banking and property interests. Colonel James Archbald, father of Margaretta, was an elder in the Presbyterian Church and a Yale graduate (in company with more than twenty fellow Pottsville gentlemen). The Archbalds lived way uphill from the O'Haras on Mahantongo Street, and their daughter had a remarkable smile, was popular, comely, and smart, a Bryn Mawr graduate in 1921, two years before O'Hara, at eighteen, began courting her in 1923. (Cum laude she was, but was elevated to summa whenever her beau invoked her credentials.) She was twenty-two, and the match couldn't have seemed promising, but O'Hara was—of course—

---

*This is a bit like boasting I could've been a piano player, but I didn't have fingers.

determined. This was for him that first love that is different in kind from all that come after, and he made it his business to remember how it felt. Eleven years later, writing from New York to his brother Tom, he urged him to practice his prose in a daily Pepysian diary noting objects and idiom, artifacts and fashion. He didn't keep a diary himself, he confessed, but he had kept one once, during 1922 and 1923: "That was a great year; I was home from school, between Kutztown and Niagara, and it was the first year Marg and I were in love. I haven't seen that diary for a long time, but I can remember movies, tunes, clothes, slang, parties—everything."[54]

It's a very American literary phenomenon, this intense fidelity to objects and emotions recollected from childhood and youth, an overpowering nostalgia (even when young) for a time—one's time, *the* time—perhaps still in the present tense. Because he was self-absorbed, when O'Hara looked at other people populating that just-bygone time, he imagined what they had seen when they looked at him. To be master of the fancied slight offers the consolation of being as well the master of fancy, and to be the master of fancy requires sharp-eyed and accurate-eared mastery of detail and nuance, "tunes, clothes, slang, parties—everything."

Whatever Margaretta Archbald thought of John O'Hara, it is certain that she often reciprocated his affection, and that they continued to take seriously their future together up until—and perhaps beyond—his first marriage in 1931. What Colonel Archbald thought of O'Hara is not as obvious as might be imagined. Here was an Irish Catholic wiseguy, smoking and drinking and acting up, unable to remain in good standing at boarding schools Archbald may never have heard of, or had and wished he hadn't. You'd have to cut the Colonel some slack if he was intolerant, if he doubted the prospects of the young locomotive greaser and soda jerk. But in fact there's no evidence that he forbade—or even tried to discourage—his daughter's interest in this unpromising young man, nor that Archbald minded that he was Catholic, or Irish. There's much evidence that he tried to get him jobs, and that he recommended him to Yale.

Yale again, eternally! O'Hara couldn't get it out of his head. Cole Porter's "Bingo" and "Bulldog," the Whiffenpoof's egregiously inappropriate mascots, those "poor little lambs" (meat packers' legatees was more like it), windowless stone crypts, the secret societies with parodically ominous names like Wolf's Head and Skull and Bones, theme-park Oxbridge architecture bought in wholesale quadrangled lots by newish fortunes from Whitney and Harkness and Vanderbilt, grave football heroes leaning with studied nonchalance against the Yale fence, hair parted in the middle, letter-sweatered in that big block "Y" that had—in the accurate appraisal of Finis Farr, a Princeton Tiger—"the effect of a Chinese ideogram" signifying money, worldliness, sportsmanship, pre-destined prosperity. Just ask Tom Buchanan.

During O'Hara's year in purgatory, following the mortification of Key-stone, he corresponded with his best Pottsville friend, Robert ("Fishie") Simonds, a freshman at Dartmouth. Simonds, who also lived on Mahan-tongo Street, was the son of the local school superintendent, and the two hung out in what began as a kids' gang and became, under O'Hara's enthusiastic charter, a club named by a member's father the Purity League. The other associates were Ransloe ("Beanie") Boone, the son of a doctor and cousin of a Medal of Honor recipient who became Calvin Coolidge's White House doctor; "Deacon" Deysher; Eddie Fox; and Fred Hoefel (later a victim of polio), whose father kept on hand a prodi-gal inventory of bootleg spirits. O'Hara—called Johnno or Doc by his comrades—took more seriously than his companions could quite credit the bylaws and procedures of the Purity League, which he dreamed of establishing as a drinking fraternity—to be titled Sigma Lambda Alpha—with reach far beyond eastern Pennsylvania. Dream the impos-sible dream.

The Colonel's odd hobby was the arcana of university fraternities and clubs and secret societies. Perhaps O'Hara's passionate interest in club-manship on such a literal level was a thing he and his first-love's father just happened to share like some freakily twinned DNA, or maybe the seeds of Archbald's fanatical knowledge of pins, ties, handshakes, haz-ings, secret oaths, rites, rings, songs, networks, and hierarchies fell opportunely on moist loam fertilized and turned and ready for any seed at all that wasn't planted by Dr. O'Hara. Whatever its provenance, club-manship enchanted O'Hara for life.

Without a reason in the world to imagine that he could finish high school, let alone that his father would agree to send him to any college, he mused by mail to Simonds about his future, and if he didn't spell the words New Haven, they were clearly implied. He told Simonds that he meant "to rate a good national social, a drinking club" and by the way a "minor varsity letter." And maybe he'd star in a play, and also join "the

Lit," and while he was at it he would "also like to be a political boss." Oddly, he says of his avidity to join social clubs that "the only sincerely unselfish feeling I'd have would be fraternity spirit." All other collegiate ambitions would be in service "purely for me, and not 'for the good of the college.' Frankly, I think that stuff is horseshit."[55] He managed inter alia to patronize his friend for studying at an Ivy League university beneath the salt of the Big Three: "You get to know the rich at Yale, Harvard or Princeton. Nowhere else."

Setting an upwind course for the future, O'Hara in his correspondence with Simonds tacked between the callow would-be frat boy and an apprentice novelist of manners. In response to what must have been a plea from the high-minded frosh to elevate the matter and manner of their exchanges, O'Hara assured Simonds that he had put aside his earliest childish things and moved on to adolescence: "My toy has been about everything one can imagine; the study of behavior; the change in lines of a Packard car; the loopholes in certain laws. Every damn thing imaginable has come in for a share of inspection by me."[56]

It was perhaps in response to his son's ardor for selected strata of knowledge, the inside dope, that the Doctor decided to give him a final chance to redeem himself as a student. Pulling strings at his own Niagara University, Dr. O'Hara got his son admitted to the university's prep school in the fall of 1923, for the third time selecting a secondary school attached to a college or university. This time the students' intellectual and moral and theological education was in the control of the Vincentian Fathers, less formidably learned than the Jesuits but no less sanctimonious than Principal Rothermel. Piety was institutionalized by prayer meetings and novenas, "and the college literary magazine, ominously called *The Index* (to which John did not contribute), ran to religious essays."[57]

A 1961 short story, "In the Silence," alludes to O'Hara's brief affiliation with the school; the speaker, an erstwhile newspaper reporter telling a clubmate a story from his distant past, begins with clunky exposition, which soon lifts to vivid reverie:

As you know, I didn't go to Groton. I went to a school in Niagara Falls that was older than Groton but considerably less fashionable. I probably never would have heard of the school if my father hadn't gone there. It's no longer in existence. It was an all-day train ride, or a sleeper jump, and I preferred the day train because I was young and fascinated by any travel. . . . In those days I never took a nap on a train. Too much to see.

Well, in 1924, I was on my way back to school after Easter vacation. I was rich, must have had twenty or thirty dollars in my kick, either from bridge or a crap game, and when I changed trains and got on the Buffalo Day Express, as it was called, I bought a Pullman chair. Two of my classmates from Baltimore were on the train, but riding day coach. To hell with them, I said, I'll ride the plush. . . .

So I sat in the Pullman, really luxurious they were then, too. Beautiful woodwork. Mother-of-pearl in the paneling. Big chairs. A brass spittoon. A polite porter who knew his job and had plenty of self-respect, instead of these characters that hate their jobs and hate you. Comfort and ease, and always the *people* that got on and off along the way.[58]

He kept his eyes focused and his ears tuned. For a solipsist, O'Hara was acutely attentive to the stories accompanying all those travelers— "always the *people*"—open wide to his own construction.

The year began well. According to undocumented family legend, whose source could only be the scholar-athlete himself, O'Hara—"just fooling around"—broke the school shot-put record and, having done so, never put the shot again, his ambition having been satisfied. Studying diligently, he got top honors in Spanish and in English. According to at least two biographers,* O'Hara's grade of 97 was the highest ever recorded at Niagara (an absolute that this biographer, who confesses to a lazy failure to chase down and pin facts of this nature, absolutely disbelieves).

Almost forty years later, writing to the New York city planner Robert Moses, O'Hara summarized his experience: "I had a good year there," even if "I felt I was about fifty-five years older than everyone else in the school."[59] He fell into the custom of taking a solitary walk every afternoon to nearby Lewiston. Smoking a pipe, he'd carry along a book to read, and "pause for the view from the Niagara Falls Country Club and watch the Toronto boat come in from the Lake." (Even here his prospect of choice was from the country club!) He'd sometimes visit an army sergeant based at Fort Niagara, "a wild Irishman called Foxie Cole" who'd been the Doctor's chauffeur before going off to France in World War I. He'd brought back German war souvenirs for John, and now gave him the gift of his fire-breathing lectures in opposition to smoking and

*Frank MacShane, *The Life of John O'Hara* (New York: E. P. Dutton, 1980), p. 26, and Charles Bassett, *Republican,* 10 July 1971.

drinking, in loyalty, perhaps, to his former employer. Homilies concluded, he'd light Piedmonts for the both of them and stand the boy a drink at the canteen.

In fact, drink undid O'Hara at Niagara Prep, and his sorry end was a sad comedy of self-destruction. Having taken his entrance exams for Yale (class of '28, most likely, though the record here relies on his own testimony, uncommonly—for him—unspecific), and having certainly been named class poet and valedictorian, he had prepared to deliver his 1924 graduation remarks on the subject of "The Parting of the Ways."[60] The Doctor drove his wife back to the old alma mater with imaginable pride, and arrived just in time to witness face to face his son's most flamboyant disgrace.

On the night before graduation, O'Hara and two classmates went barhopping and got themselves so drunk at a roadhouse that they were detained by a couple of state policemen, who were so entertained by O'Hara's ostentatious blarney that they joined the three students and led them "to places not even the cabbies knew about." When the five had exhausted the alcoholic resources (principally Canadian whiskey) of the county, the officers returned the boys to Niagara Prep just long enough after dawn to be paraded past the Fathers up early for their devotions following mass, walking the campus "reading their daily offices."[61] O'Hara, graduation suit muddied and ripped, slunk to his dorm room to sleep off his binge and was awakened by a faculty member in the company of Dr. O'Hara. The former reported to the drunk that he'd been stripped of all his academic honors, not to mention his diploma. The latter, having been roused with this disgraceful news in his Buffalo hotel room, unwilling to look upon his son for the duration of a motor journey to Pottsville, ordered him to return by train, alone with his shame, and let's assume not riding the plush. There was something about institutional approval that this againster simply couldn't abide.

The consequence of his self-immolation on the bond between father and son was ruinous. If Katharine's tearful dismay with her adored son was grievous, Patrick's rage was utter and unequivocal. "I'll be damned if I'll send a drunk to Yale" was a bristling promise made and kept during the first moments John opened his sticky, bloodshot eyes in his dorm room to find his father's red face hovering like a fireball above him. As far as Dr. O'Hara was concerned, his son had violated two principles sacred to a gentleman: he had dishonored the dignity of his family and he had broken his word, not to mention his own commandment against drinking. When the Doctor had agreed to give his son a final chance at a final school, he had begged Niagara Prep to take the errant student on as a personal favor to a distinguished alumnus, and had extracted from his son an oath that he would behave himself, "be good."[62]

Even before he went to Niagara, O'Hara's ties to his father had been severely strained. When an eighteen-year-old confides to a pal that his pater is pissed off with him for mischief, there's generally a surface sheen of bravado to the account, however acute the underlying pain. And while his correspondence with Bob Simonds was nothing if not blustering, by May of 1923 there was no swagger left in his report of his father's attitude:

> My father and I are off again. This time he has sufficient reason to become perturbed: someone has told him of my boozing. He told me about what he had heard and made several dire threats which aren't even interesting; he hasn't the nerve to carry them out, but nevertheless, life henceforth will be a veritable hell for me. He has made it so before and he'll use every means he can to make it hell, because of all things he hates, liquor receives double its share—he had a brother who, when drunk, fell down a flight of stairs and died from the effects of the fall. [Author's note: this is a variation on the death of Great-uncle Arthur, also said to have died beneath the wheels of a train, also when drunk.] As I told you and Lem, our relations have been anything but amicable since August 1921.[63]

Long after the commencement calamity, O'Hara told an interviewer, "Father never really spoke cordially to me after that [morning]."[64] It is difficult to imagine what tone he adopted with the Doctor. O'Haras could nurse grudges lovingly, with exquisite attention to minute fractions of tort and resentment. If the son's characteristic truculence was already well in place before he came home alone by train from Niagara, and if the father's operatic dismay was already in full baritone cry, the poisoned relationship turned even more toxic. Writing after John O'Hara's death a summary of his work and bona fides for *Scribner's Essays on American Literature,* the critic Charles Child Walcutt took eloquent note of a continuing character motif:

> The bad-tempered quarrel in which one or both parties evince a stubborn nastiness is the keynote of the O'Hara action. Stubbornness is

close to the heart of it. The quarrelers seem eager to establish an impossible line and then refuse to budge an inch from it. There is never any persuasion, any compromise, any reconciliation. They would rather take umbrage than second thought. They would rather give a blow than an inch. They will not think anything less than the worst of each other. The wounds of *amour propre* never heal. When the continuation of the action demands a working reconciliation, it has the quality of two steel rods bending a millimeter or two toward each other.[65]

It's extraordinary how otherwise intelligent and bighearted people can set up such implacable oppositions. The Doctor's father had imposed an oath against alcohol; the Doctor was Manichean in his own regulations: obey or be damned. Any parent with rudimentary observational power has learned—sooner, one hopes, than too late—that unconditional mandates and prohibitions are futile, often calamitous. It isn't the rules themselves that are unwise, or even ungovernable, but the all-or-nothing form of their declaration. Never lie to me, son, or else. Be a virgin on your wedding day, daughter, or be no daughter of mine. My way or the highway is merely the most recent dumb version of Creon's intractable ruling against the burial of Antigone's brother. The rest is Hegelian: two partial rights/wrongs, each declaring its absolute authority, collide. This, if the stakes are high enough, is called tragedy. If the stakes are lower, it is mere domestic quarrel, an eagerness "to establish an impossible line and then refuse to budge an inch from it."

The emotional charge of the Doctor's righteous shame and fury at his screwup son was better suited to Medea's response to Jason's want of gratitude, Orestes' to Clytemnestra's murderous treachery. The scale was improper, self-indulgent, and, given this histrionic wrath, it's a wonder he allowed his heir to share a house and to break bread with him. It must be assumed that Katharine O'Hara asserted her interest in this family matter. However a truce was brokered, the hard reality remains a shame and scandal, that John O'Hara's revered, capable, accomplished, and honorable father never again—in his son's estimation—spoke a cordial word to him.

Fury was replaced, evidently, by the killing frost of indifference and resignation. Dr. O'Hara, coldly facing the manifest fact of his son's failure as a student (which confirmed in his view a doom in any favored calling), undertook to drum up a job for him as a utility cub reporter for the *Pottsville Journal*. "Job" is maybe too grand a word for it. "Apprenticeship," rather, at a starting salary of no pence per week, with no raises promised, and even so Dr. O'Hara had to call in a favor from his country clubmate Harry Silliman, the paper's publisher, with whom he'd quarreled, to get his son a foot in the door. But despite the pissant wages of sin, O'Hara understood that a writing job was a shinny up the pole from his previous jobs, and from his miserable prospects.

The *Journal* was the afternoon edition of the *Pottsville Republican,* with its offices down the hill at 215 South Centre Street. O'Hara joined a cohort of thirty-five or so, and was trained by a month of wandering around the paper's editorial offices and printing department, taking in the atmosphere. He liked the casual busyness of the editorial offices, each day's final achievement punctuated by the rumble of the basement presses shaking the floors as the first edition marked the gains and losses of a Pottsville day.

O'Hara was required to study for rhetorical models Shakespeare and the King James Bible (whose narrative influence is sometimes hidden by the inverted pyramid—name, age, and address on top, pretty detail way down the column, past where the reader has quit going—mandated by conventional journalistic presentation). His first story was like something out of the Old Testament by way of *Hamlet,* a killing out in Port Carbon, a son who'd murdered his father. Near the end of "The Doctor's Son," immediately following the doctor's anguished, furious outburst in the Buick—"And my God! To think that a son of mine would rather rot in a dirty stinking newspaper office" than be a doctor—Malloy's father punches the boy on the shoulder. Malloy stops the car and takes a tire iron from the floor of the car: " 'Now just try that again,' I said."[66]

Malloy reached for a tire iron; O'Hara reached for his typewriter. As Freud articulated, the writer's alchemy is to translate bad luck into good, to sublimate—daydream—the pain of an unhappy and resentful childhood, say, into a good story.* To put it Stanley Elkin's way, writing is a

---

*Ward Just, in the title story of his first collection (1979), quoting Freud's happy calculation in Lecture Twenty-three of the General Introduction, uses "Honor, Power, Riches, Fame, and the Love of Women" to summarize the good fortune an artist may cobble from an exploitation, a formal expression, of his failed desires. Just writes: "Frustrated, he attempts to satisfy himself by making fantasies which, according to Freud, represent repressed infantile longings. The great analyst then goes on to describe the artist's 'puzzling ability' to reproduce his fantasies so persuasively that other disappointed souls are—consoled," bestowing treasure and esteem on the consoler (*Honor, Power, Riches, Fame, and the Love of Women* [New York: E. P. Dutton, 1979], p. 26).

revenge against bullies. And by the time John O'Hara began writing for the *Pottsville Journal,* he believed his father to be a bully. What life was like at 606 Mahantongo Street in these days can be imagined, and it must have come as a relief to O'Hara that his daily work was to report the distresses and thwarted ambitions of others, to be freed by necessity from the prison house of self, to listen rather than boast, to investigate troubles worse than his own. During his apprenticeship at the newspaper he briefly considered a career as a car salesman, but it's unimaginable that he would have been half as happily suited to sweet persuasion and customer-is-always-right submission than was Julian English. And how often do they award a Pulitzer in car sales? Already, writing "A Cub Tells His Story" in May of 1925 (his only *Journal* piece that survives), he was dreaming of swinging for the fences: "I have not been named as the twenty-year-old sensation for anything I have written in my brief career in journalism . . . but there is time. I have every hope of winning a Pulitzer Prize, and if I ever get to it, I intend to write The Great American Novel."[67]

But O'Hara's tropism toward reporting went beyond compulsive ambition. He had a feral appetite to know things, especially secrets. Just as fiction makes wholesome the psychopathology of lying, journalism licensed prying and gossip. If doors were barred owing to his Irishness, Catholicism, or bad reputation, a reporter for the *Pottsville Journal* carried credentials attesting to his right to knock at those doors until they were opened, or locked up tight. A reporter is by profession an outsider/insider, the spy at the keyhole, the one who knows (or likes to assume he does) the awful secret behind the freshly painted facade. In "A Cub Tells His Story," O'Hara tells that the news editor, sending him to Port Carbon to cover that murder, instructed him to "get the facts." This assumes that facts can be got, and O'Hara had absolute faith in the assumption: the cocksure young man adjudicated disputing versions on the fly, grilling "teachers, business men and the doctor who had attended Mr. DeWitt before he died." The resolution of competing accounts of the shooting required entire hours of inference: "I managed to get about three versions of the shooting but finally I heard what I thought to be the true story."[68]

A reporter is also the ur–pain in the ass. O'Hara liked to sign his *Journal* columns "Petronius," after Gaius, author of the *Satyricon,* scourge, and courtier. The culture of journalism perfectly suited O'Hara's cynicism and sentimentality, opposing emotions frequently sold by the set. In 1950, writing for the *Journal* his recollection of cub reporting, he revealed the hard-boiled sweetness that forever complicated his work— at its worst fogging it with tears and choking it with suppressed sobs. "It wasn't all fun, of course. Newspaper men and women have more fun for a very obvious reason: if they didn't, they'd go crazy. It's an old and for-gotten maxim that every piece of news hurts somebody. . . . The deeper meaning of the statement is that when an item of news is 'nice' about somebody, somebody else is hurt because it wasn't about him. But I could—and won't—tell you about covering a mining accident for The Journal. The bell rang, the signal that a car was coming up, presumably with the injured or dead. The car came up, and all that was on it was a foot, a human foot in a miner's Pac boot."

So many signatures in this brief passage: the naked confession of envy, as though every reader not only shared that venal sin but wouldn't even bother disguising the fact; the testy refusal to answer a question (Please, John, won't you tell us about covering a mining accident?) that hasn't been asked; the genius immediacy of the report he immediately retails: a ringing bell, a suspenseful wait for the tragic load, the blunt fact of a foot—conventionally such a scene's climax—trumped by the locating detail of the workboot that didn't quite protect it.

O'Hara wrote every kind of thing for the *Journal* save ads and editorials. He was a second-string sports reporter behind Walter Southall Far-quhar, ex-coach of the Pottsville high school football team and an elder social acquaintance from local club and Assembly dances. Mining com-munities in Pennsylvania have a noble history of producing determined and sturdy football players, and the Pottsville Maroons, a team of merce-nary brutes (the fearsome Hoot Flanagan was a teammate of Duke Osborn, who eschewed a helmet in favor of a felt baseball cap) in league with the Canton Bulldogs and the Green Bay Packers, won a protested 1925 National Football League championship against the Chicago Car-dinals. (The protest—a byzantine tale of fixes and treachery and resent-ments—fed Pottsville's bitterness toward all those two-bit sons of bitches east, west, north, and south of Schuylkill County.)

Farquhar was a good sportswriter, modeling his style on Grantland Rice's, but despite his subordinate's patronizing advice that his mentor quit the "dry-fucked" hinterlands, he stuck to his Pottsville post for more than fifty years. During O'Hara's first autumn at the *Journal* he covered many Maroons contests with Farquhar, notably an away game against the Providence Steamrollers that ended with the two reporters writing from the Biltmore hotel in their underwear—while their outerwear dried steaming and stinking on radiators—about a wet afternoon of play.

Farquhar believed in the cub's gift and goodwill, and tolerated his posturing excesses. He was one of only three fellow workers O'Hara knew when he joined the *Journal,* giving evidence of Pottsville's insulated stratifications of class and calling. His old friend Beanie Boone was a reporter, and Kit Bowman, a young Mount Holyoke graduate and the daughter of a mine superintendent, was the society-page editor. One cold winter morning, as the three youngsters were leaving the office to drink hot chocolate at Hodgson's before gathering news, their boss Silliman remarked: "I know one thing about this paper. I'll bet it's the only paper that has three reporters that wear 'coonskin coats.' "

His work at the *Journal*—whatever the stresses at home—was a happy progress for O'Hara, and he remembered his time there with self-deprecating affection. In 1950, by which time he was fixed in his refusal to concede error and slow to laugh at himself in print, he reported that the paper's city editor "caught me using the word protégé when I meant cortege," and recollected an afternoon when the publisher caught Kit Bowman giving Boone and O'Hara Charleston dance lessons in the office: " 'For God's sake,' said Silliman—and fled."

He liked the sardonic lingo reporters were obliged to self-censor in censorious Pottsville—"They're as immoral as flies," was a credo O'Hara picked up from his colleague Curt Sterner and took to heart, applying it not only to the citizens of Schuylkill County but to men, women, and children worldwide. He was, though, temperamentally unsuited to daily reporting. He was shy, or distant, among strangers, and by his own contemporary account in "A Cub Tells His Story," he "suffer[ed] from an inferiority complex." Like any newshound, he was frequently rebuffed by subjects resentful of his intrusions on their privacy, dignity, or misdeeds. This he hated, and to push himself to meddle, he increasingly resorted to bluster.

He enjoyed most his job as a rewrite man, reading more than a dozen newspapers a day trolling for items bizarre or scandalous to share with the citizens of Pottsville, in a daily column titled "After Four O'Clock." It was in this office-bound employment that he became familiar with "The

Conning Tower," Franklin P. Adams's column in New York's *P.M.*, a model for his own hodgepodge of bob-ended news. This granted him access to a wider world and to its hidden corners. Though no specimen columns from "After Four O'Clock" survive, it is reasonable to guess that the format trained O'Hara in the crafts of transition and juxtaposition, and daily deadlines overcame his terror of blank paper. He was always a fast writer, and as soon as he finished one story, he turned by learned habit to another.

One might imagine that O'Hara's natural curiosity, ambition, and talent would've made him a perfect news-writer, if not news-gatherer. His first *Journal* story—the patricide in Port Carbon—had run almost as written, and the news editor's report card on it was auspicious: "Pretty good—but we could have used more details."[69] An insufficiency of detail would never impoverish another O'Hara narrative, so it might be assumed that he was off to the races. But no: poor deportment and unreliability blotted his employment record to the degree that he could never be an institutional man. Still, if he wrote too fast and too much for the good of his literary art, his productivity was legendary, and the will he lavished on starting new work and seeing it through to its end—its first-draft end, more precisely—was frequently heroic. He worked despite rejection and ICU-class hangovers in hotel rooms, on whatever table or bed would support a typewriter. He didn't whine, and he didn't make excuses for missed deadlines. But he worked when he felt like working, and didn't when he didn't. He was tardy, disobedient, impetuous, usually unapologetic. He was fit only to be a free lance, thanks be.

But in the winter of 1925 the undoing of his association with the *Journal* was still in the future. The apprentice-cub had been put on the payroll, starting at six dollars per week and rising eventually to twenty-five. He had the look and the moves: hat pushed back on the head, cigarette dangling from a sneer. "In the Silence," told by a newsman, revisits, thirty-five years later, how it must have been, a variation on a doctor's— or son of a doctor's—slanted view of human experience:

> A young newspaper reporter sees so much in the first few years that he
> begins to think he's seen it all. That makes for a very unattractive wise-
> guy attitude, what I call unearned cynicism. After you've lived a good
> many years I don't see how you can be anything but cynical, since all
> any of us have a right to expect is an even break, and not many get that.
> But I thought I knew it all, and I didn't. It took me many more years to

realize that a reporter covering general news lives an abnormal life, in that he sees people every day at the highest or lowest point of their lives. Day after day, people in trouble with the law, having accidents, losing control of themselves.[70]

Even as a smoke-shrouded skeptic he relished the comfort of a uniform, and the Purity League—O'Hara's tight association of fellow scoffers that his pioneer biographer Charles W. Bassett titles the "Pottsville Wild Bunch"—maintained during the holidays the fraternal discipline of an unvarying response to all Christmas greetings: "Humbug!"[71] The Purity League would hang out at Hodgson's—pronounced approximately "Hudson's"—where O'Hara only two years earlier had jerked sodas. (One of his most appreciated *Journal* essays was a lament for the drugstore's closing a year or so later.) Pottsville coxcombs would gather daily for cocoa and cigarettes, and nonchalantly check the time of day on their pocketwatches, from which depended fraternity keys (reason enough to shun wristwatches, considered then to be effete). Those who would not or could not join a fraternity were known as "barbs," barbarians, and though you might expect such a reflexive againster as O'Hara to sympathize with outskirters, you'd be wrong. Barbs tramped in their galoshes elsewhere than Hodgson's to drink hot chocolate when the Yale, Penn, Lehigh, and Lafayette boys were in town.

In addition to fraternity lore—what *really* went on at the fugitive drinking fraternity, TNE, or within the privy chambers of Kappa Beta Phi, and why did a Kappa Bete meeting a brother mutter B. U. X?*—the common thread that tied together the Purity League and many another confederation of college returnees to Pottsville was haberdashery. There were always several straight-backed cadets from West Point or Staunton Military Academy, elegantly severe and set apart in long gray greatcoats. John O'Hara, Simonds, and Boone were known behind their backs as the "Three Horsemen" as they strutted down Mahantongo Street in their raccoon coats, and I don't want even to imagine an overheated Hodgson's boothful of snow-damp pelts. (Dr. O'Hara was forward in his opinion that the huge fur coats were appropriate to coachmen obliged to sit outside in the cold, but vulgar—and, worse, silly!—on the backs of gentlemen.) I can more happily imagine the acres of soft caramel and heather tweeds, the flannels, the Scotch-grained plain-cap shoes, but-

Bottoms Up, ten times, according to "Appointment with O'Hara," *Colliers,* December 23, 1955.

toned-down Oxford shirts, rep ties, tattersall waistcoats. The boys talked fashions as avidly as any *Vanity Fair*–reading bobbed-hair flapper got up in lipstick and stockings rolled beneath the knee. How did Pottsville's McMahon's or Doutrich's stack up against Philly's best haberdashery— Jacob Reed's—let alone New Haven's J. Press, Princeton's Langrock, New York's Tripler? Was a Norfolk suit just possibly too-too? (Nah.) How about knickerbockers on the links or in the auto? And who was the first to swan into Hodgson's in a pair of Scotch-tongued brogues? At their size-switching, fashion-tweaking ages, the Brummels necessarily wore new clothes, but the brand-new look was, of course, anathema. Finis Farr tells of O'Hara buying a hat at McMahon's, and then taking it out to the sidewalk and jumping up and down on it to prepare it for wearing. " 'Please, John,' said Mr. McMahon, 'if anybody asks you where that hat came from, don't say you got it here.' "[72]

On those bracing cold mornings—with the whole day awaiting, and their eternally youthful and ever on-and-up lives stretching amiably before them—they took the leisure to discuss the merits of competing brands of buffalo robes to warm passengers huddled together in the backseats of Mercer Raceabouts and Marmon Speedsters. At Christmas thirty years later, writing in *Collier's,* John O'Hara recollected that season vividly: The cold air was bracing, and heavy snow hid the squalor of the company houses out in the patches and bandaged the mining wounds gouged into hillsides. But driving off to a dance, that was the ticket: "It was a rare night when we could drive without chains, and at the club dances there were frequent calls for hot water for frozen radiators. . . . The sounds of chains slapping and curtains flapping are as much a part of those Christmases as the rather prettier 'Do It Again' and 'Lady of the Evening' and 'When Hearts Are Young.' "[73]

So the chums at Hodgson's talked about last night and the nights to come. Had the pater and mater kicked in with those four $2.50 gold pieces to pay for the Assembly? Had one of the Purity League boys really got lit up last night on boilo, Polish homecrafted whiskey hot out of the still?* They expressed strongly held opinions about music, girls, espe-

*In "Coalspeak," an online lexicon of the contemporary diction and locutions of the Region, "boilo" is specified as a "homemade Yuletide beverage . . . served hot in shot glasses. . . . Making boilo was a leading cause of fires in The Region, since the whiskey is added while the mixture cooks on the stovetop. If any of it splashes on the stove, look out!" (Amy and Denise McFadden et al., "Coal-Speak: Dictionary of the Coal Region," <http://www.coalregion.com/speak.htm>, 1998, accessed November 5, 1998.)

cially what the boys termed "new stuff," out-of-town visitors from Mount Holyoke and Bryn Mawr, and the new-grown little sisters home from Ethel Walker and Dobbs Ferry.

John O'Hara did not let his work at the *Journal* obstruct these mornings of social history, sensual strategy, and oratory. Consequences were for later.

Or for right now. In the late winter of 1925 the bill for the O'Haras' comfort and material extravagance was coming due, providence having a dirty trick to play on the strongest of the family. The bad news sneaked up Mahantongo Street from the barbershop where the Doctor indulged every morning in a clean shave. The barber stopped John on Centre Street and warned him that his father was failing: "I'm worried about Doctor. He wakes up slow under the towel and his skin feels slack to the razor." His complexion was pallid; razor nicks were slow to heal.[74] His sons and daughters noticed that he was even becoming slow to anger.

Patrick O'Hara had been overtaxed by the Spanish flu pandemic seven years earlier, and since 1922 he had been at the vortex of a brutal medical feud. He abraded some of his colleagues, principally because he questioned the fees they charged the Philadelphia & Reading for mining accidents. From the O'Hara side, it was assumed that his colleagues were jealous of his surgical skill, though the facts of such a matter are notoriously unavailable to biography. During 1923 he had lost half his sight owing to the rupture of a blood vessel in one eye, but he continued to cut and repair and sew despite this impediment to his precision, and continued to be blunt and tactless in his disapprovals. He believed, perhaps correctly, that a colleague at Pottsville Hospital was practicing under an assumed name, and he criticized the hospital for shielding the man from inquiry. But the deepest wound seems to have been his growing conviction that the hospital's Protestant staff showed disdain for their Catholic associates, despite the fact that Dr. O'Hara was the hospital's chief surgeon and chief of staff. His father's grievances incited in his eldest son indignation, and set in motion deep-running currents of shame. He wanted to face down the Protestant medicos who'd dared question his father's standing, to beat at them with his fists.

Instead, Patrick and some fellow-feeling colleagues (but not Dr. Boone, the father of Beanie, both Boones soon to be ex-friends of O'Hara père et fils) left Pottsville Hospital and founded Good Samaritan Hospital, one block over from Mahantongo, on East Norwegian Street.

Thus what had been mixed was now formally divided: this miserable distrust and pettiness must have been an agony for Dr. O'Hara, socially as well as professionally. He wasted his strength presiding over stormy late-night brainstorming sessions at 606 Mahantongo with his fellow defectors during which their individual and communal and ever-accumulating torts were reviewed and sullenly nursed. His deterioration was obvious, and a few weeks after the New Year, 1925, a provisional diagnosis was made by a Philadelphia internist of Bright's disease, a distress of the kidneys whose symptoms include exacerbated fatigue.

A rest in Florida was prescribed. When he told his wife that he wanted to vacation alone in the sun, she said, "Doctor, it's about time."[75] Dr. O'Hara traveled by train to a St. Petersburg hotel, while up in Pottsville his family was rooting for him, imagining that he might be playing golf or putting bets on the ponies. He was doing neither, and merely languishing. In early February he was visited by a Pottsville surgical nurse who'd often worked with him, and what she saw alarmed her so that at her urging, Florida friends soon arranged to have Dr. O'Hara returned to Pottsville by way of Philadelphia, with a private Pullman porter in attendance in his stateroom.

On March 12, 1925, John and Joe O'Hara met their father at the Pottsville depot. A quarter century later the first son recollected the scene vividly, in a New York newspaper column written in defense of another small-town doctor, this one charged with a crime:

> About twenty-five years ago a man got off a Pullman car in a small town in Pennsylvania. He was wearing a polo coat and a tweed cap and he was accompanied by a porter. I had a small roadster waiting at the station, and when I saw the man I went to him and kissed him because he was my father.
>
> I took him by the hand and led him to the little car and drove him home. I got him upstairs and helped him undress—he had no luggage on the train—and put him to bed. In a week's time, less one day, he died.
>
> What he died from was overwork.[76]

Dr. O'Hara came off the train fevered and bewildered. He thought he'd been taken into custody by the porter escorting him. He was frightened, but submitted to his sons' urgings that he come home with them.

The roadster was too small to fit them all, and Joe made the crosstown trip on the running board. At 606, nurses put him in a hospital bed on the third floor. He had been a proud, robust, assertive man, puff-chested, Pottsville's own Teddy Roosevelt. Now he was whipped, slack-skinned, and reed-voiced. His son Tom was shaken to hear his father whimper to his mother, "Katharine, I'm going to die."

Tom remembered his mother's response (anxious, and little wonder): "Who will take care of the children?"[77]

"The world will take care of them," he responded, meaning who knows what?

Specialists were sent for, and a kidney man from Philadelphia declared the case hopeless. During his final six days, the Doctor would say other things that meant more or less than they seemed to mean. But oddest of all was a confidence he shared with his Johnny-boy. Perhaps to frighten him out of smoking, perhaps because he believed it was true, he told his son, drawing him near, that John had a spot on his lung. The Doctor's son believed him, of course; the alternatives were so monstrous. Many years of fear—congealing a tendency toward premonition—would pass before John O'Hara knew this curse to have been spurious. And that wasn't the only malediction whispered from the Doctor's deathbed. He also cautioned his wife not to entrust the leadership of the family to John—who, as if to verify this augury, fell ill and took to his own bed soon after his father returned from Florida—though he allowed that the twenty-year-old boy might be reliable in an emergency.

Mary was brought home from boarding school, and the youngest children were sent to kin in New Jersey. Then, on the early morning of March 18, aged fifty-seven, Dr. O'Hara said his last words—"Poor John!"—and died. What an epitaph! How was a son to surmount such an expostulation? "Poor John." What was he to make of that? Pity? Contempt? A censorious father's contrition? A divination privileged by the authority of the deathbed? There is no way to sweeten or temper those words. They make a killing review.

Dr. O'Hara's obituary in the *Pottsville Journal* celebrated his skill and standing: the headline announced him as having been "FAMED AS SURGEON," and the body of the memorial essay declared him to have been "one of the most expert in the country . . . his skull surgery was the marvel of the medical profession. His skill was none the less brilliant in abdominal operations." Beanie Boone was the author, but I wonder if

John contributed to his dad's obit. If so, I wonder too about these absolute and intemperate declarations: "Dr. O'Hara was a man of the most temperate habits. He held the firmest convictions and was a most loyal friend." If sentimentality has been justly defined as a response lushly in excess of a modest provocation, the son's response to his father's death was unrequited love, a potent mix of mortification, regret, and awe. The apt knowledge sometimes weighs on a young man that, were his father unrelated by blood—a chance acquaintance met at school, say, or at a party—the one would not take the other as a friend. This pain could only be sharpened by an apprehension that the rejection might be prompted by disapproval. "Poor John." You can say that again.

The night of his father's death, according to one of O'Hara's less skeptical biographers, the distraught young man ate in a restaurant on Centre Street, "where he overheard a Pottsville doctor comment on Dr. O'Hara's death: 'Well, he wasn't much good any more.' John knocked him down."[78]

Did he really? I doubt it. The story is unattributed, but it much resembles John O'Hara's many other accounts of fists flying in the neighborhood of his father or on account of some perceived insult to his pride, honor, or standing. In O'Hara's many written recollections of his father, two constants animate his esteem: the Doctor was a bravura surgeon, and he was quick with his dukes. In his New York *Daily Mirror* report from the mercy-killing trial of a New Hampshire doctor, O'Hara remembered that the Doctor "broke a man's jaw with one punch because the man, a member of the Ku Klux Klan, called him a 'Mollie Maguire.' " Now there is a complex sequence of circumstance, affront, and outcome: a doctor breaks rather than mends a jaw, a nice inversion of the Hippocratic Oath—Do great harm. The harm is done to someone manifestly deserving of a broken jaw, a Klansman, but what was this unlucky bigot's offense? Denigrating the social and political particulars of a proud gent's Irishness, confusing him with left-wing riffraff.

In a letter to his friend Bob Simonds at Dartmouth, written the day following Dr. O'Hara's death, and in another one a week later, John mentions nothing about having had to knock down a man who insulted his father's surgical skill, but he does mention prominently the mortal warning he got: "He heard me cough and it prompted him to tell me or to reveal to me (I haven't found out which) that I have two spots in the pulmonary apparati. . . . This death thing makes one think. After my father went I began to think—that all this about the immortality of the soul is worth the while of even the most cynical. No one knows better than I what sort of life the governor led. Hard work, a clean life and so little pleasure. No one can tell me that he derived a lot of satisfaction from the knowledge that he was doing good and that alone."[79]

These letters are signed "Doc."

The funeral service at St. Patrick's was, of course, "almost as big as a gangster's or a politician's," as his son bragged, counting the house and its composition with characteristic vainglory and accuracy.[80] The regional papers calculated more than twenty priests in attendance, forty cars in the cortege. Every local physician and surgeon showed up (even the one O'Hara claimed to have punched out that night in the restaurant) and together with some Philadelphia medicine men formed a parade of honorary pallbearers. Finis Farr quotes Tom O'Hara's dim recollection of the scene graveside, where "a small, spare doctor from north of Pottsville burst into uncontrollable tears."

In *Ourselves to Know* (1960), the novel's most decent character is one Dr. Willetts, who has all of Dr. O'Hara's virtues and none of his vices. He is gentle as well as shrewd, self-effacing as well as honorable. He is central to the health of Lyons (the name the author gave to Lykens), and when he dies the mining town and outlying farmers and trappers and loggers give him a "good turnout," a fife and drum corps with muffled drums and funeral beat, a contingent of movers and shakers from the nearby small city of Fort Penn. But all in proportion here:

> The life and death of Dr. Willetts was all over in time for the four o'clock Fort Penn train. The out-of-town people scattered to depots, to the local hotels and saloons and private residences, and by the time the evening mail was being sorted, the doctor and his final ceremony were part of the vanished light of that day, not even much talked about. Death had been sudden and sent forth a shock, but it had been neat in a community where neatness was not always a characteristic of sudden death. He died all in one piece, above ground, and the manner of his death had not endangered others. Where coal is mined, the people of a town can never wholly ignore death-in-quantity, no more than it can be ignored by the people of a fishing village. The colliery and the sea provide their livelihood, but miners and fishermen leave home forever

whenever they go to work. . . . And so the men and their wives and the
older children must always look at the colliery and the sea and at death
and life with the disciplined eyes of all those who are never far from the
ultimate unforeseeable truth. A neat, single death can never have the
same force in a Lyons or a Gloucester as in a town where the place of
livelihood is not itself a hazardous situation. Affection for Dr. Willetts
was genuine and universal, but there was also a contradictory gratitude
to him for being the one who died: for the time being, death was satisfied with one, and not four or forty.[81]

When the Doctor's estate was settled, there would be further cause
for weeping. The high-living patriarch died without a will, and his intes-
tacy—the more unfathomable for the slow progress of his illness and his
capacity to understand the gravity of this situation—only aggravated a
want of prudence in a man making such a show of responsibility, sobriety, and family duty. He had no life insurance, and apart from less than a
thousand dollars in the bank, he left a safe deposit box filled with German marks made valueless by inflation, currency which he stubbornly
speculated was undervalued.* The house at 606 was free and clear, but
no cash had been left to endow its expense. The entire estate—the
Pottsville house and office and the Panther Valley farm, including invest-
ments and assets of every kind—was valued at less than fifty thousand
dollars. A third of that amount went immediately to the state of Pennsylvania, owing to the lack of a will. Money left in trust to the O'Hara children—fifteen hundred apiece—was lost in bank failures during the
Depression, as was Katharine O'Hara's Delaney inheritance, perhaps as
much as sixty thousand dollars.

"He may have been a good surgeon," O'Hara later judged, "but in
money matters he was a fool."[82] Had Mary needed that $2,800 harp the
Doctor had bought as soon as she expressed an affection for the angelic
sound of the instrument? Had the Doctor, shouldering huge past-due

---

*Many years later, reflecting on the mortal injury that a legacy—say he'd got his "hooks on a thou-
sand-grand all at once"—would have done to his writing, spurred as it was by urgency, O'Hara recollected some details of his father's financial acumen. "My old man . . . was many times a
millionaire, but in German marks. He was not overfond of the Germans, but he was sure their
marks were going to come back, and there would be an O'Hara Brothers polo team . . . and the
greatest herd of Jerseys on the North American continent, and Ireland would be free. . . . Well, Ireland is free, because wishing will make it so, and har-de-har-har to you."

accounts for his patients, really needed to bet (and lose) a thousand dollars on the Dempsey-Carpentier prizefight? His son James later recollected a rather cavalier bookkeeping routine: his father would stuff the day's take—cash and checks, uncounted—in a sack and deliver it to the Pennsylvania Bank, without bothering to wait for a receipt (though he did, in a nice O'Hara touch, carry a .32 in case he encountered someone even less unfastidious than he about money). Postmortem, Patrick O'Hara's extravagance quickly lost its patina of charm, eroded by the realities of a large family's needs. Five automobiles seemed now a few too many. The Cressona show farm, growing debts with vegetable fecundity (as much as ten thousand in the red some years), was sold. So too the ponies, to the Stonewall Jackson Riding Academy of New Jersey, a transaction which Tom O'Hara many years later remembered vividly for Finis Farr: "on a cold clear morning in early March, the men came for the ponies and carts. Tom followed the cavalcade to a freight yard on the edge of town, where he saw the men take the wheels off the governess cart, the dog cart, and the little Conestoga wagon, and stack the carts and wheels in one end of a boxcar. Then they lowered a ramp and put web harnesses on the ponies to hold them during the trip. The ponies went up the ramp; the men pushed the door on its grooves across the opening in the side of the car and clamped it shut. And Tom told John that only then did the fact of his father's death at last sink into his mind."[83]

This is a complexly dramatic scene for a biographer to have recovered. Farr abstains from footnotes in his life of O'Hara, but either Tom—a good journalist with a long career on the *New York Herald-Tribune*—wrote it for John (or for Farr), or told it to John (who re-created its filigree for Farr), or else Farr—a screenwriter, spy novelist, and social historian, as well as biographer—dramatized the scene himself, elaborating on the fact that the ponies and wagons were sold to a riding school. The door pushed on its grooves and clamped shut is almost too fitting for memory's resources, but it's the kind of detail—together with the delicately reviewed sequence—that John O'Hara understood how to exploit in fiction.

In fact, the most creative use he made of the emotional aftermath of his father's death is "Fatimas and Kisses" (1966), a first-person narrative in Jim Malloy's voice about a Pennsylvania Dutch convenience-store owner with an unfaithful wife. Lintz has murdered his wife and kids, and "Fatimas and Kisses" is about the ugly progress that led the man to his low state. The convenience store was around the corner from where Malloy grew up, and Lintz's wife (imagine a distant cousin of Tom Buchanan's unlucky mistress, Myrtle Wilson) "was a placid, rather slovenly woman whose hair was never in place. She had an extraordinarily lovely complexion and white little teeth and large breasts."[84] There's something exactly right about that description's cool erotic excitement, and it's freighted with the suggestion of awful trouble.

That trouble comes, but the story ends on an unexpected note, with the Gibbsville police chief walking and talking about the crime with Malloy after sharing a drink with the younger reporter. In a startling change of subject the chief says, out of the blue:

" 'I thought a great deal about your father. What's a young fellow with your education throwing it all away when you could be doing some good in the world?'

" 'What education? I had four years of high school,' I said."

The police chief, surprised by this, says he'd assumed Malloy went away to college.

" 'Away, but not to college.'

" 'Oh, then you're not much better than the rest of us,' he said.

" 'I never said I was, Chief.'

" 'You never said it, but you act it. Your father *was* better than most of us, but he didn't act it.'

" 'No, he didn't have to,' I said."

And with this valedictory the story ends, final words that convey longing, regret, and shame, an everlasting wound. Poor John indeed.

The dream of Yale finally ended with his father's death. Not because there was no money left to pay the modest tuition, but because there wasn't enough to support those bright college years in the style that was to have been the point of the enterprise. O'Hara was careful to insist that he could have entered Yale in the fall of 1925, that he had been admitted (no documentary evidence supports or denies the claim,* though in 1927 he did write—unavailingly—begging Yale to waive their required

---

*In a *New York Times* profile of O'Hara following the stage success of *Pal Joey*, Benjamin Welles reports with improbable melodrama, on the evidence of an interview with his subject, that O'Hara had "passed examinations for Yale and was virtually on the train to New Haven when his father died" (Benjamin Welles, "John O'Hara and His Pal Joey," *New York Times*, 26 January 1941).

board exam, which he had neither passed nor taken) and his mother had
agreed to pay his Yale fees if he got in (despite her insistence that Mary,
in her final year at Eden Hall Convent of the Sacred Heart, forgo college
to help out at home). No, it was simply that he wouldn't countenance
"grubbing out his tuition washing dishes and tending furnaces."[85] As he
told an interviewer, "I couldn't see waiting on tables and worrying over
nickels for four years."

Katharine O'Hara, widowed at forty-five, rose to her crisis with equanimity and good humor. She liked to say in later years that it was commonplace to go broke after the Great Crash, but it had been her family's
distinction to go there during the full flow of the Boom. Then, in 1925,
there were successive family crisis conferences, presided over by Mrs.
O'Hara and her eldest son. Whatever tensions were complicated by their
awareness of their fix, the family tightened, lavishing loyalty and affection on one another. It was from this time that a catchphrase came to be
a familial First Principle: *Cut one O'Hara and eight of us bleed.* There
must have been more emotional serenity at 606 after the Doctor's death
than before it.

Many years later, writing to his *New Yorker* friend William Maxwell,
O'Hara was precise about his mother's good character at this time. Every
night she did the grim arithmetic, without complaining: "She had very
rough going, but she enjoyed it. She baked cakes and sold them for $5,
she gave French lessons and did crocheting, and she was also president
of the Shakespeare Society, active in the D. A. R., gave recitals with the
First Piano Octette of Pottsville, and not too humbly heard herself
described as 'Katharine O'Hara is a remarkable woman.' She loved it."[86]

There's wisdom in this characterization, an understanding of the
mechanisms of another's pride, a pride taken in that pride, a nuanced
and relaxed vision of the human comedy that O'Hara too frequently suppressed in favor of imposing upon his characters desperate shame or
ignoble want.

But this family knew how to have a good time. They played word
games, gossiped, teased one another. Like his father, John had learned
sign language (from a deaf driver of Dr. O'Hara's) and taught it to his siblings. One night in the sitting room, with their mother present, John and
Tom exchanged silent dirty jokes. To their dismay, she was soon busy
with her own fingers, rebuking them. There was good-natured competition between John and his mother, both of whom liked to memorize

poems, tell stories, and laugh. When they played bridge as partners, he would try audacious bidding systems and his mother would sigh, blink, and command, "Just follow the rules, please." Consideration was expressed not only through community and warmth; the older family members knew when to leave one another alone, express respect by silence. This habit of solicitude John O'Hara returned to in his later life: he'd sit hushed for hours watching television with his wife or daughter, the ballgame or comedy's sound switched off; he'd sit alone in his study with his Princeton friends—Dean William Lippincott or, say, Pat Outerbridge—in still quiet, sometimes for hours.

Meantime, after his father's death, John had his job, his friends, his parties at roadhouses and country clubs, his ardor for Margaretta Archbald. There were other women in his life, but she was the One, and she knew it. He'd take her to "rock fights," jazz dances at which the Pottsville rakes pulled out all the stops and the corks from all the bottles. Jimmy and Tommy Dorsey were Schuylkill County boys; the trombonist Tommy, who played with the Scranton Sirens, was born the same year as John, and never forgot the promise of the posters, "The Sirens Are Coming!" The big bands—Cab Calloway's, Kay Keyser's—came to amusement parks out in the country, Lakeside and Lakewood, and to the country club, and wherever they swung in for one-nighters, there was our ace dancer, wowing his partner, humming along to the jazz and knowing all the lyrics.

One singer made a particular impression on him. An Irish tenor, Jack Gallagher, one arm lost to a mine accident, did a version of "Jazz Me Blues" that brought dance audiences to stageside, and got the boys and girls rubbing against one another, "but all the women had their eyes on Gallagher," O'Hara wrote. "When the number ended there would be a mass exit to the bushes."

Hundreds would show up for these dances, across class lines. By prearrangement or chance, O'Hara and his pals would often hook up with girls from the patches (known to the Pottsville bucks as "spivots"), and it appealed to everyone that they weren't apt to run into one another in daylight. While it was not unknown for them to shack up with whores (often along the very thoroughfare later renamed John O'Hara Street), more commonly they'd find quick sex out in the country, where a farm or mill girl might accept an offer of a dollar for a quickie in the backseat. You might hope that a young man with such a hair-trigger sense of resentment, such a furious refusal to be taken for granted, would have had nobler consideration of the "spivots" he put to such blasé use. You'd be dreaming. But later, after three wives and a daughter, after writing from the points of view of memorable women characters, he achieved a binocular vision on his practices with the girls he'd come across way back when: "As we were dirty little snobs, we would have a hard time next week explaining to the spivots why we hadn't danced with them last Thursday," when the young gents had showed up at a dance hall with Margaretta Archbald and her country club friends to listen to Fred Waring's Pennsylvanians. " 'If I'm not good enough for you then, you don't get a dance with me tonight,' the spivots would say." In this 1967 recollection, "When Bands Were Big," O'Hara's keen ear and memory recalled the titles of a couple of Scranton Siren numbers that spoke to the neglecteds' injury and indignation: " 'Aggravatin' Papa, Don't You Try to Two-Time Me,' and 'You Gotta See Mama Every Night or You Don't See Mama At All.' "

You also gotta show up at the *Pottsville Journal* on workdays, or you don't get to show up at all. O'Hara, insubordinate and skipping assignments, was scolded and threatened, to no avail. The managing editor, David Yocum, was short-tempered but long-suffering, due either to his respect for this young reporter's skill as a writer or to the publisher Harry Silliman's sympathy for Mrs. O'Hara. In any case, the miscreant employee—habitually showing up at noon, four hours late, hungover, or not at all—committed serial vocational suicide before his career at the *Journal* finally expired. During the winter of 1926 O'Hara once justified his tardiness to Yocum by explaining that he'd bumped his head during a bobsledding accident and that this had interfered with his sleep patterns; he then was sent to interview a hinterlands weather prophet whose foretelling instrument was a goose bone. When he returned to the newspaper drunk and without a story, explaining that the fabled Gus Luckenbill was unknown in his hometown, that marked the end of the reporter's twenty-dollar-a-week job—or, at least, End Number One. He begged for another chance, and Yocum relented. Two weeks later, his refusal to cover a Lutheran church supper on Margaretta's last night in Pottsville—she was leaving for Montana, to teach school at the Flathead Indian reservation school—occasioned End Number Two, the final finale.

A couple of weeks later he found a job, possibly with Silliman's help, at the *Tamaqua Courier,* fourteen miles northeast of Pottsville. He was bored stiff, but initially dutiful, and soon got a nice raise, from twenty-three to thirty-five per week, which he spent on gas, clothes, and fun. When he had funned away his gas money, he'd commute by trolley, and before long began showing up late, hungover, and . . . so forth. Sacked in mid-March of 1927, he sometimes claimed his separation from the *Tamaqua Courier* was provoked by his Democratic sympathies in collision with the preferences of a Republican newspaper, but was half-hearted in this self-defense. A more ardent champion of his role in the journalistic scheme of things was Walter S. Farquhar, writing more than twenty years after O'Hara's dismissal by (and of) local newspapers: "He was not a thorough reporter, because his artistic soul could not stomach the messenger boy attitude of some of the public, the constant writing of names, names, names and the general humdrum. . . . But he always wrote well and his writings for the Journal were high class. . . . Then he went to the Tamaqua Courier and ran against the same tough proposition. He could not stand it."[87]

In return, the *Courier,* like the *Journal,* could not abide him. Now O'Hara was, if not lost, desperate. Margaretta was beyond his reach in every way, and his will to write had no practical outcome. "Artistic soul"? I don't believe it. O'Hara's appetites in his early twenties were too turbulent and confused to be understood as aesthetically coherent. He wanted to be somebody, but what somebody he might be was outside his field of vision, and why not?

He had been courting "The Conning Tower" since before his father died, and soon after his discharge from the *Courier,* he got a snippet published, if this unpaid item makes the cut as even a snippet: "As our about-to-be-assembled book will be compiled from Tower clippings, it is Mr. John O'Hara's suggestion that it be called 'Files on Parade.' " If you can make it there, you can make it anywhere. . . . Young writers sometimes lean against such slender reeds as a mention in New York, an approvingly lifted eyebrow from an editor or agent, prior to hearing the rest of the story: *Sorry, my list is full.*

Still, O'Hara was in print in New York, and to his mind the rest was mere negotiation. He submitted puns and parodies, imitations and wiseguy observations, which from time to time appeared in "The Conning Tower." Meanwhile he tried to hustle a freelance assignment from *Scribner's* magazine—which passed—about why he planned, at twenty-one, to vote for Al Smith.

At home he tried to pull his weight. But despite the consolations of his mother's affection and his expressions of responsibility toward his siblings—helping them with homework, offering advice—he was too ashamed to linger long in Pottsville. O'Hara's social standing had declined, at least in his own eyes, with his father's death and mismanaged estate. He showed off his resentments by extravagant displays of scruffiness or foppishness, coming unkempt to the country club (acquiring the nickname "dirty-neck," and "dirty-mouth" too) and overdressed to the Log Cabin and Amber Lantern roadhouses.

It was at about this time that a business conversation between O'Hara and a bootlegger inspired two mutually exclusive versions—both retailed by Pottsville's most celebrated fictioneer—of his flirtation with the outlaw life. In the more sentimental variant, a tapped-out and at-his-wit's-end John approaches Marc Antonio Mosolino (aka Tony Moss) to beg for work as an apprentice bootlegger, but the gruff and giant-hearted killer waves him off and says, "You're too good for this. Go out and get yourself a job and stay away from me."[88] In the more circumspect version, Mosolino offers him fifty a week plus a piece of the action to sell to the country club dances, but the young gentleman's probity is affronted and he declines.*

After the Doctor's death, the O'Haras—unable to afford dues—let their affiliation with the Schuylkill Country Club lapse, but John was nonchalant about formalities of membership. He crashed club dances, sulkingly sucked down too much gin in the locker room, cracked wise, blew his top, sneered, nursed a grudge. Already a nasty drinker and a brawler, he was busy practicing exactly what he later preached to his mentor Walter S. Farquhar to make inevitable—by forever proclaiming Fuck you and Up yours—his split from Pottsville, a divorce that might relieve him of his previously quoted disabling bitterness "stored up against all those patronizing cheap bastards in that dry-fucked excrescence on Sharp Mountain."

---

*An elaboration of his rectitude appears in O'Hara's *Collier's* account of Christmas loafing and drinking: "As a physician my father received a book of liquor prescriptions from the government, but as a Dry he promptly returned them. A bootlegger offered me an enormous sum to swipe the 'script book, but I felt that I was too young to die, so I turned him down."

Colonel Archbald continued to offer O'Hara a lift up from his low estate, writing on his behalf to periodicals in New York. Meanwhile—and let's assume without the Colonel's blessing or knowledge—O'Hara appealed to a newspaper in Missoula, Montana, hoping to find work near his beloved Margaretta. He was turned down gently (though many years later, a character in his story "The Girl from California" wisecracks that Missoula "sounds like you ought to use it in cooking"),[89] which was not the tone of his rejection by a newspaper in Allentown, where his pal Bob Simonds was then living.

Now he was almost out of chances. He turned to John McKee, the New Jersey uncle with whom he'd spent weekends when he was at Fordham Prep. As a federal immigration and customs officer, McKee had pull with American steamship companies, and he found O'Hara a job as a tourist-class waiter on the United States Lines' *George Washington,* bound in July for Bremerhaven by way of Cork Harbor, Ireland. Prohibition-era American vessels were dry, and so were tips in steerage. On the plus side, he completed the thirteen-day passage without seasickness, then managed to use his shore leave in Germany to get himself drubbed in a bar fight in Hamburg.

As soon as he returned to the snug and suffocating harbor of Pottsville, O'Hara applied for a purser's job on the *George Washington*'s sister ship *Leviathan,* but his attempt to trade up was rebuffed and he again was offered a place as a waiter, which he refused. That fall and winter of 1927 his career was to dance, and, increasingly, to dismay his mother. The favorite hangout for his gang was a ballroom in Shenandoah, Patrick J. Mahar's Hall. O'Hara liked to wear his coonskin coat to "Patty's," frost or thaw, and he hung it in the bar rather than checking it at the coatroom, perhaps to save a dime, but more probably to show the furry thing off. Finis Farr reports that "the bar patrons were unfavorably impressed, and one night the waiters had to throw out a drunk who swore he was 'going to piss on that God-damn coat of O'Hara's.' "

O'Hara's mother—who had once found John's defiance of the Doctor's excessive temperance marginally amusing, and who had scraped together enough good humor at the breakfast table to tease her son for his theatrical caution when creeping up creaky stairs late at night to escape his father's wrath—was running low on tolerance. She had been sent an anonymous letter, postmarked Shenandoah, narrating her son's scandalous drinking in those precincts. Properly affronted by the anonymity even more than by the narrative, she sent him off to her mother in Lykens for a couple of weeks, where he worked as his grand-mother's chauffeur. Returning from that ignoble visit with a bit more than ten dollars in compensation, he and his henchmen "proceeded to do the town. We did. After getting a good base of Scotch at [a local speakeasy] . . . we went places, all places, till five a.m."[90] While returning home, the young men sang a drunken parody of the mass, in sort-of-Latin, at a street corner on Norwegian Street, near enough for the voices' boozy sacrilege to have carried to 606, where O'Hara "was greeted by the mater," no doubt already dressed to attend her own version of holy mass.

> Where have you been?
> Nowhere.
> What have you been doing?
> Nothing.
> Who was with you?
> Nobody . . .

It was past time to scoot, so O'Hara did. In a flurry of letters to friends,* he contemplated another try at Yale, assisted again by Colonel Archbald (now fondly titled "A'chie"), a classmate and friend of the college's dean, or else a job, mostly in the company of Bob Simonds, from a comprehensive boy's own adventure list: at Yeaman's Hall, an exclusive club near Charleston, South Carolina (where "to live on the island one must belong to the club. Try and get in"), this notion courtesy of the Colonel's brother Albright, "who has made a couple million in gold mines"; or working for United Fruit in Central or South America "as overseer in one of their Latin American plantations, [a job that] consists mainly of ducking malaria, drinking liquor, bossing natives and, if you're so inclined, laying the dusky wenches"; or for Firestone as an overseer of a rubber plantation in Liberia, where the weather "is o-u-t as far as white men are concerned and the family has done a lot of putting-down-feet at the idea of my taking such a job," not the least of Africa's attractions. But in fact O'Hara's scheme to "roam the world" until he hit twenty-five was

*See John O'Hara, *Selected Letters of John O'Hara*, ed. Matthew J. Bruccoli (New York: Random House, 1978), pp. 13–26.

a pipe dream. During the zenith of those boom years, the depressed odyssey he finally made was to Chicago, with his thumb out and his pockets empty. "The thing to do is to go, no matter how," he wrote Simonds. "I simply must get out of Pottsville or I'll buy a gun and use it. . . . I've never been so unhappy, so little enthusiastic about life, and it's all the fault of this place, or of myself." Has the pathetic conjunction *or* ever offered such a collision of possibilities?

Anyone who's ever been older than seventeen and younger than thirty will recognize the ambition to get to a sunny land where all streets are named Easy. O'Hara wrote lists of calculations, spurious pro rata budgets allowing for an apartment, smokes, liquor, carfare, laundry ("sheets, pillowcases, etc."), allocating forty-eight dollars per month for a "nigger cook for dinner & cleaning." In long letters to his wander-lustful friend he debated the pros and cons of shipping out on a cargo vessel, buying a Ford, or hitching, because "bumming it doesn't particularly appeal except as a last resort, in the event everything else fails." Well, everything else did fail, including his erstwhile partner in the proposed adventures on high seas and low roads: Simonds, employed in Allentown, had decided to play the cards he'd been dealt, for which prudence O'Hara rebuked him: "So old man Mammon has got you, eh? In other words, I hear you've been given That Raise and have decided to stick. . . . I must admit I'm a little disappointed in you, young Simonds. After our many arguments in which you upheld the anti-materialistic side I am almost amazed that mere money could lure you into smugness. . . . I thought that any man who deliberately would stick his hand through a pane of glass would be at heart always a non-conformist."[91]

The lone fugitive set out in September. O'Hara's first way station was State College, to watch a football game and sponge off Bob Root, a Penn State pal and fellow Purity League member. From there he hitched to Pittsburgh and cribbed at Carnegie Tech with another hometown and Purity League pal, Ned Dolan. Then, down to five dollars, he tried Columbus, Ohio, where he didn't find a job and the Salvation Army turned him away from its mission because he was too well dressed. Neither did he find success in Chicago. He applied for work as a groom, but the stable proprietor—suspicious of a would-be hostler got up in a Brooks Brothers suit—wanted to know why he needed a job.[92] "To eat," O'Hara replied, evidently just the wrong answer. If the Brooks suit barred him from work and a free flop in Columbus, the want of an overcoat in Chicago let Lake Michigan winds nip him shrewdly in late October. In retrospect he would describe Chicago as the nadir of his life. Many years later he brought his daughter, Wylie, by limousine from the Ambassador East, home of the Pump Room, to the fleabag where he'd roosted way back when, at 600 West Madison Street. But now he put his thumb back out and limped home.

He hid out in Lykens mooching off the Delaneys, doing odd jobs, and saving twenty dollars—judicious John—from jury duty, and driving again for his grandmother, whom he had taken bitterly to calling the "Queen Mother." Meanwhile, sister Mary, who had quietly mastered secretarial skills, announced in the early spring of 1928 that she was moving to New York City to make her way in the world. John O'Hara, two years older, beat her there by a week.

2. UPTOWN AND DOWN

I used to come to New York once a year when I was a small boy. . . .
My special pleasure was the ride on the bus, up Fifth Avenue and
then over to Riverside Drive. The buses always went too fast for
me. . . . On the ride up Fifth Avenue I would see Hispano-Suizas and
Isotta-Fraschinis and Minervas and Daimlers, and Hudsons and Cadillacs and Roamers and Stearns-Knights and Lelands and Cunninghams
and Danieleses and Templars and Marmons with bodies by Brewster
and Schuette and Derham and Fleetwood and Amesbury. On the bri-
dle path on Riverside Drive I would see some fine saddle horses with
beautiful tack and properly turned out riders. From the top of the bus
I would often see footmen in knee breeches opening the front doors
of the Fifth Avenue mansions. . . . I was curious about those car-and-
footmen people, but only moderately envious; I somehow took it for
granted that when I got big I'd have all that too. This was not even a
dream or a hope. I just took it for granted. . . . So my approach to New
York was conditioned very early by a fantastic ignorance of money
matters, so that when I finally did get there, to work and live, and in
spite of the fact that my father had died just about broke—my attitude
was that of defenseless optimism. New York would take care of the
newcomer.[1]

—JOHN O'HARA, UNPUBLISHED DRAFT
INTRODUCTION TO 1960 REPRINT OF *BUTTERFIELD* 8

New York took care of this newcomer, all right, every which way. O'Hara soon had a job; he'd have many in three years, and if he was inexorably fired from one, he was also reliably hired for another, nine of them. Scott Fitzgerald too famously professed that there are no second acts in American lives. What could he have been thinking? O'Hara, during the time of his rising, caught a new act every few months or so.

From his unpromising base at his aunt and uncle's suburban household in East Orange, New Jersey, O'Hara ventured first to the Yale Club's placement office, where Colonel Archbald had arranged to have the would-be newsman's ambitions and bona fides listed, offering as an index of the young writer's achievements his "Conning Tower" credits. The trip into the city, requiring a train ride and a shift to the Hudson Tubes, must have aroused in O'Hara an acute longing to escape the prison of kin, to find his own place in the midst of things. The twenty-one-story Yale Club, at 50 Vanderbilt Avenue, across the street from Grand Central Terminal and near the Biltmore and Roosevelt hotels, was commanding. Built only thirteen years earlier, it gave the imperial sense of having stood forever at the hub of enterprise.

The club's job service forwarded him to *Time*, founded by the Yalies Henry Luce and Briton Hadden. His prospects seemed to the job aspirant promising: he had had a flip letter published a couple of months before in *Time*, and bearing this flimsy credential, together with a note from Vanderbilt Avenue, O'Hara managed to meet with a couple of senior editors and to shake hands with Luce himself ("Well, Mr. O'Hara, after all these years of letter-writing!"), who offered him a couple of books to review on speculation.[2] (The reviews were not accepted.)

The following morning he phoned Franklin Pierce Adams at the *World*, a Pulitzer newspaper edited by Herbert Bayard Swope with more panache than profitability. Encouraged by this conversation to apply for a job at the paper, O'Hara traveled that day to the gold-domed World Building on Park Row. Nothing doing, Swope told the petitioner, "We're loaded." So he showed up without an appointment in Adams's office while that columnist was adding arch and faux-archaic miscellany to the next morning's "Diary of Our Own Samuel Pepys," a Saturday installment of the popular "Conning Tower," a dog's dinner of cultural news, gossip, and quotations. (A characteristic sample: ". . . so to Mistress Dorothy's [P-a-r-k-e-r] and found A. Woolcott there in the finest costume ever I saw off the stage; spats and a cutaway coat, and a silk high hat among the grand articles of his apparel.")[3]

Adams was generously on the lookout for young writers on the way up, and for talented writers stuck at the bottom. He printed—always with full credit—the snippets they mailed him, and in this way did Robert Benchley, E. B. White, George S. Kaufman, and James Thurber first get published in New York. During the past year Adams had used a dozen of O'Hara's observations, parodies, couplets, and whatnot dispatched from Pottsville—not that he was a sweetie or a pushover. Joseph Bryan III, Virginia gentleman—editor, raconteur, and fellow cavalier of the Algonquin's Round Table, not to mention the original husband of (much later) O'Hara's third wife—created a rank order of the most verbally savage wits of this period—"all of them deft with the scalpel and stiletto, and brutal with the bludgeon and blackjack, and each a combination of snapping turtle, cobra, and wolf"—and put FPA right up there in a "Murderer's Row" with Dorothy Parker, Kaufman, and Alexander Woolcott.[4]

Never mind: Adams liked the sound of O'Hara's voice, and this was pay dirt. So influential was "the Boswell of the Round Table"—surely the Algonquin's most ardently plugging press agent—that as grave a personage as Eugene O'Neill inspired himself to contribute "a light-hearted valentine" to "The Conning Tower." All FPA ever offered in payment was an annual award of a gold watch, but in the estimation of an influential magazine editor of the time, "writers would rather have their work in his column than sell it to the *Saturday Evening Post*."[5] (Parker, in the view of Frank Rich, reserved her "most marketable sallies" and calculatedly impromptu ripostes for "The Conning Tower.") He was also the acknowledged boss of a poker game composed of luminaries as various as Harpo Marx and Herbert Bayard Swope, of Harold Ross and Heywood Broun. The Thanatopsis Pleasure and Inside Straight Club became known among gossips for the "merciless vigor" of its card games. (Broun, having lost thirty thousand dollars in a single night, sold his apartment to cover his losses.) But the loose confederation's lasting contribution was its celebration of voices and preoccupations American rather than Continental, and it was FPA's mission to give expression to talkers who followed the backwash of Huck Finn. "The Conning Tower" made room for Grantland Rice and Damon Runyon, for irreverence and experiment. Adams, promoting antipathy to pretense and aiming to elevate "the smart-aleck remark to a kind of civil religion," recognized in O'Hara a distinctly American voice and an unblinking, savage eye for sham and hokum.

In a March letter to his friend Simonds, encouraging "Judge" to come posthaste from the provinces to Gotham, O'Hara re-created the scene in FPA's office after the columnist's boss Swope had sent him packing. FPA had invited him to sit, then "forgot about me in the excitement of editing." Suddenly Adams began to read aloud, and then asked, "How'd you make out?" O'Hara reported "no soap. He said 'Sunnavabitch! Isn't it hell?' " With that Adams phoned the *New York Post* and instructed them to hire his new friend, "Oh, a perfect gentleman," Adams insisted. "Can he *write?* What a question!" After closing that conversation, and immediately before assuring O'Hara he'd also instruct Harold Ross to give the newcomer writing assignments for the *New Yorker,* it occurred to Adams to ask, "Where *is* Pottsville?" O'Hara was impressed: "How about F. P. A., huh? Never saw me before and did more for me than anyone but you would do. With him cheering for me I'll get along. Remember what I told you about 1928 vs. 1927? This time next year I'll *be* somebody."[6]

In the event, the *Post* didn't hire O'Hara, but a better newspaper immediately did. "The Conning Tower" reported days later—under the rubric "Gotham Gleanings"—that "J. O'Hara of Pottsville, Pa has accepted a position on Ogden Reid's newspaper." That would be the *Trib,* the *Herald-Tribune,* the *H-T,* the newspaper—despite its ruling-class editorial Republicanism—of literate features and bravura reporting.

O'Hara was invited to join this admired newspaper by Stanley Walker, so invariably known as the "legendary city editor, Stanley Walker" that "legendary" could serve as his given name. (I exaggerate: he is sometimes titled the "storied city editor.") Walker, who wrote a book titled *City Editor,* needing neither article nor modifier to ratify his standing, was a thirty-year-old, pipe-smoking, bony-faced Texan. When O'Hara came under his gaze, Walker was already fabled in New York for his talent scouting and pinchfist salary negotiations. He offered the young recruit twenty-five dollars per week, which was six bucks more per week than he paid Joseph Alsop a few years later. In the years before Walker's time some of the writers connected with the *Herald* or the *Tribune* had included Karl Marx, Henry James, William Dean Howells, and Bret Harte. During and after his reign the *Herald-Tribune's* payroll included Walter Lippmann, Dorothy Thompson, Virgil Thomson, Grantland

Rice, Walter Kerr, Red Smith, Lucius Beebe, Heywood Broun, Art Buchwald, Wallace Stevens (!), and FPA himself, who returned—with Lippmann—to the paper where he had begun in 1913, after the *World* foundered from an ill-conceived price hike and folded in 1931.

More than twenty years later, O'Hara's old *Pottsville Journal* colleague Walter S. Farquhar, musing about his friend's career as a journalist (and perhaps about his own thwarted ambitions), declared that "People do not realize the difficulty or near impossibility of getting a start. It depends on the caprice of others."[7] Yes, but there was back then more hunch than science in hiring for a newspaper. I imagine that résumés were less checklists than clip files, and no aspiring reporter was going to be advised to get a degree from j-school before applying to jot obits. Many of the upper-echelon editors and reporters at the *Trib* were college graduates—and a good many of these from Yale—but many others were not. (Very few were Jews, and the owners of the paper were known to prefer ads from the better-heeled Fifth Avenue retailers, leaving the Jewish Seventh Avenue garment merchants to enrich the *Times.*) That O'Hara had missed out on Yale wouldn't lift him on or bump him off any competitive New York newspaper. (Alsop's well-connected family got the plump, over-tailored Porcellian fop hired out of Harvard, and Walker described him as a "dreadful result of Republican inbreeding.")[8]

One of the many apocryphal tales of O'Hara's first days at the *Herald-Tribune* has him showing up at the city desk for his first assignment wearing his coonskin coat. In April? I doubt it. O'Hara had many blind spots, but reading a culture's manners and favored costumes was not among them. The city room in New York was not unlike the open newsroom at the *Pottsville Journal,* dressed like a set for *The Front Page* with overbrimming ashtrays on scarred desks, with brown-bagged pint bottles peeking from bottom drawers, with typists wearing battered hats playing "Kitten on the Keys" on the Underwood. It was a stand-and-deliver kind of workplace, nothing cute or collegiate about it.

It is certain that O'Hara was quick off the mark. Very soon after Stanley Walker hired him on the hunch that the aspirant touted by FPA had what Frank MacShane nicely calls an "alertness to trivia,"[9] O'Hara had the good luck to witness the bad luck of a subway accident in Times Square, phoning in details to the paper. For this he was singled out for commendation. Not as lavishly staffed with reporters as the *Times,* which could indulge its taste for team reporting and prose-by-committee, the *Trib*'s editors instead prized resourcefulness and speed of apprehension, tight editing, and prose with a personal signature. Editing was exercised within the bounds dictated by a *Trib* postulate: Write until it gets dull. And the paper enjoyed an owner "rather more benevolent than despotic . . . dignified and somewhat dotty,"[10] indulgent and amiable, a nice situation for a writer.

A *Trib* rewrite man of the heyday—"Inky" Blackman—explained that the distinction between an obituary in the *Times* and in his paper was that in the former a person died, while in the latter he or she had once lived—and another death-notice specialist offered that a fellow with a prolonged Polish name had died of "a contraction of the vowels." Walker remarked that news was "wine, wampum and wrongdoing," but another and much quoted job-description-cum-jeremiad from *City Editor* still adorns many a pressroom wall: "A newsman knows everything. He is aware not only of what goes on in the world today, but his brain is a repository of the wisdom of the ages. He is not only handsome, but he has the physical strength which enables him to perform great feats of energy. He can go for nights without sleep. He dresses well and he talks with charm. Men admire him, women adore him, tycoons and statesmen are willing to share their secrets with him. He hates lies and meanness and sham, but he keeps his temper. He is loyal to his paper, and when he dies a lot of people are sorry, and some of them remember him for several days."[11]

Putting aside both his flourishes and cynicism, the *Herald-Tribune* favored inventive angles teased from the facts by a well-staffed bullpen of rewriters. Whether Walker had decided that O'Hara was too good a writer or too erratic a fact-gatherer to be a reporter, O'Hara was made a day rewrite man shortly after getting a pat on the back for his subway dispatch.

This was bad news for the night owl, obliging him to appear for work during the breakfast hour, and it wasn't long before this proved impossible. At twenty-three O'Hara was unwilling to recast himself as disciplined and responsible. He was a sprinter capable of transcendent bursts of reckless will, but he had no patience, and was cocky and brash. Within weeks of joining the *Herald-Tribune*, after writing Simonds reports on *Trib* letterhead about the celebrities he was drinking among and boasting of his first sale to the *New Yorker*, the self-important correspondent must have provoked from his old pal one of those don't-forget-I-knew-you-when responses, since O'Hara wrote back: "Did I sense faint sarcasm in your being glad to know the great O'Hara? . . . A year from now people will be glad to have loaned me money and proud to have insulted me and, a few, rewarded for calling me friend. . . . I keep prodding myself by a remark the city ed. [Stanley Walker] made the other night; 'In this town the sky's the limit for you.' "[12]

Walker—who got a lot of writing for the *Trib* in exchange for very little in the way of salaries, known by his reporters to "play organ music on their egos"—was laconic but sociable. The principal site of his socializing was the "Artist and Writers (Formerly Club) Restaurant," a speakeasy on West 40th Street more familiarly known by the name of its owner, Jack Bleeck (pronounced Blake). Near the Metropolitan Opera and not ten yards from the *Trib*'s rear door, Bleeck's was the *downstairs* in the city-room sentence, "I'll finish the story soon, I'm going downstairs a few minutes."[13]

As soon as O'Hara was hired, Walker introduced his young "word painter" to the many regulars at Bleeck's who spoke of themselves collectively as "the Formerly Club" and their tavern as "the mission" or "the drugstore." James Thurber, who liked to sketch the bar scene there, was devoted to the match game, a guessing contest played for money or more usually drinks (rye was the house specialty). Contestants, more than two, would each hold matches—from none to three—in their clenched fists, and each would guess the total of all players' matches. He or she who guessed correctly dropped from the game, guaranteed a free drink. The last player remaining bought a round. Bleeck's murals were ten Thurber illustrations of the intricacies and consequences of this contest. A lively tavern, it was said to be more riotous than the *New York Times*'s favored speakeasy, Gough's, or the *Daily News*'s own Costello's. O'Hara soon had a charge account there, and learned how to use it. The saloon's decor ran to a dictionary for consultation, brass spittoons, and a buckler and breastplate set behind the bar. The latter soon suffered an injury, a "dent caused by John O'Hara's fist in one of his anti-armor moods."[14] An adage held that "drink is the curse of the Tribune / And sex the bane of the Times," properly honoring the most determined drinkers in New York. The newspaper's owner, Ogden Reid, remembered by one disinterested witness as a "cheerful tosspot," liked to linger at Bleeck's and spring for rounds for his employees. In this context you might imagine that Walker was unshockable, but his newcomer from Pottsville certainly made an impression, and not the one either might have wished for. Letter after letter from those days finds O'Hara reporting about himself that he was drunk and drinking, on a bender, recovering from a three-day-and-night tear, broke, in debt, up all night braying at the moon or braying at its absence, rising well past midday. Walker's new assignment was meant to save the barfly from himself, but it didn't work, and O'Hara would simply show up after lunch for his morning shift.

After fewer than three months, Walker canned him. O'Hara bore him no grudge, a true wonder, perhaps because he could report that Walker "thinks I'm swell and had tears in his eyes when he fired me."[15] His ex-boss—his tears dried—later told a profiler at the *New York Post.* "He didn't last long. While with us he wrote nothing at all of any distinction."[16] The potential genius's own recollection of the circumstances was even harsher: encouraging Simonds to try for a job at the *Trib,* he remarked that Walker "can't be bluffed," and that he'd been axed by Walker "because I was drunk most of the time and never was punctual." He was unequivocal in an interview with Don A. Schanche preparing for a 1967 *Esquire* profile: "I was a mess. Nobody knew where I was living."[17]

In fact, he was living still in East Orange, or sleeping there—when he didn't miss the last train under the Hudson, which he often did. That he was a mess seems uncontested. His appearance was slovenly. His flannels were uncleaned and unpressed; he slept in his shirts. He was also mastering the art of the awful first impression. Joel Sayre, an established *Trib* reporter five years O'Hara's senior, found a note in his box: "Dear Sayre: Good piece this morning. Congratulations. . . . Since you have expressed your hostility by ignoring me completely, I just want to say that it doesn't bother me in the slightest, NUTS TO YOU, TOO. John H. O'Hara."[18] (Good advice from drinking buddies at Bleeck's encouraged him to drop the middle initial from his byline—not that he ever needed one at the *Herald-Tribune.*) Sayre now took note of his correspondent: "Not even the most grizzled veterans on the staff had ever heard of a cub on day-rewrite carrying a cane, but O'Hara carried one"—a malacca cane, the better to rap against the spittoons at Bleeck's. Moreover, "his ears stuck out, and now and then his deadpan look and cold blue eyes made you think of a young trooper in the Coal & Iron police."[19]

Still, a hindsighted well-wisher wouldn't choose for him more humdrum pleasures, a more orthodox regime. He was learning about urgencies and frailties that would power his fictional characters through their mostly chaotic personal histories. He was witnessing extreme behavior, hearing the grand range of idiom available to such listeners (you bet his "ears stuck out"), particularly to such curators of phrasing as newspaper reporters and editors, themselves from every social class and geographical pocket of America. I wish I'd been around Bleeck's to hear an old waiter's response to a drunk diner's question, "How are your hemorrhoids tonight?" Ernst scratched his head: "Just what's on the menu."

O'Hara didn't mind writing home to brother Tom about the celebs he was running with. The *New Yorker's* Harold Ross ("a queer duck. Funny stiff German hair and a gap between his two front teeth. Like F. P. A. he swears all the time and when I say swear I mean swear"), the *World's* humorist Frank Sullivan, the *Trib's* boxing writer, Donald Skene, the movie critic Richard Watts (who got decked "downstairs" by a writer he'd panned). The drinkers would begin at Bleeck's, move along to Tony's ("another speakeasy where all the celebrities go"), and then to a nightclub, maybe Chez Florence. "Cigarette girls in satin trousers moved from table to table," as Frank MacShane has imagined the flickering, candlelit scene. It was a fluid society, with gamblers and gangsters and showgirls and bond brokers and hustlers and actors and politicians all thrown together, pontificating, laughing, fighting, pairing off, boasting. O'Hara was impressed, not least with himself. He wrote "Dear Judge," asking a question:

> Does it sound horse's-assy to say I've had such a busy life lately? Here is an idea of the people I've met and spoken to either on assignments or socially: F. P. A.*, Frank Sullivan*, Herbert Asbury, W. O. McGeehan°, Dick Watts°, Clare Briggs*, Belle Livingstone*, Walter Winchell*, Charles Brackett, Don Skene, Frank Getty*, Arthur Caesar*, Harold Lloyd* and wife*, father* and daughter; Howard Dietz*, and spouse*, Tommy Guinan*, Senator George, Denis Tilden Lynch*, McKay Morris*, George de Zayas*, Mrs. Harry Houdini*, John Haynes Holmes, Wm. Lloyd Garrison—to name but a gross. Then there are the purely office celebrities and local big and semi-big shots whose names would mean nothing to you. I have marked with a star the names of the people who I think would remember me if they were to see me tomorrow.[20]

Does it sound horse's assy to say . . . ? That's a question for which there's an answer. But I'm worried about Harold Lloyd's daughter: what's *her* problem? And I notice the politicians are, as ever, fickle, funning you at night and forgetting you in the morning. And is it not sobering to reflect how few of these names *we* remember in the morning? For such a smart fellow, it's remarkable that O'Hara was so gee-whizzy a collector, so avid to list and so little at leisure to characterize—or even to sketch— these dropped names.

He went directly from the *Herald-Tribune* to *Time*, probably owing to his companionship at speakeasies with that magazine's Noel Busch and Newton Hockaday. Before Christmas of 1928, typing on *Time* letterhead, O'Hara wrote Simonds a characteristically avuncular letter, urging him again to jump to New York, assuring him with endearing innocence that he'd used his influence with Stanley to put the fix in for a reporting job. "I told him about you. Told him you were a Dartmouthist, age 27 or 28. I told him you had done stories for me while I was an editor of the Pottsville Journal. I told him that your stories were good. I told him that you are steady, reliable, will not cover a story from a speakeasy phone. . . . This is what your next step must be. Write to Stanley. . . . Be brief, but not too brief. Be snappy, but not too snappy. Above all, just merely dash off the fact that you went to Dartmouth."[21]

This Polonial employment counsel lacks only be-yourself-and-if-that-doesn't-work-be-someone-else to stand as a masterpiece of unintended paradox. And it gets worse: O'Hara then offers his dear friend a crash course in the *Trib's* style book ("Notice that instead of saying 14 W. 46th St. it says 14 West Forty-sixth Street. . . . Notice that you don't say secure when you mean obtain. . . . Stanley knows that I wouldn't have a friend who would be dull or nit-witted"). But then, abruptly, he drops the guard of bluster and stands naked before his friend, under the cold light of the New York winter. In the same letter he admits that he scorns his *Time* job "doing these fucking Newscastings" [magazine condensations for radio broadcast] and laboring to compose sentences in cockeyed Timese: ("backwards ran sentences until reeled the mind . . . where it will all end, knows God," as his soon-to-be best friend Wolcott Gibbs would notoriously write in the *New Yorker*), tortured nonce words and "double-barreled adjectives" corrupted from the baroque rhetoric of Carlyle and tricked out with bogus Homeric epithets. O'Hara, to his credit, shunned *Time*style in his pedestrian work as a second-string theater reviewer and religion reporter working on space rates.

He confessed to Simonds that he'd have to "fix up some cock and bull story to the family, telling them why I won't be home for Christmas. The real reason is I'm flat broke." A more distressing shrift followed: "I have just come off a three-weeks' bender, during which I fell down a flight of stairs, was punched in the face, had a mild attack of d.t.'s although maintaining a residence (if such it may be called) at 107 West 43. . . . Things aren't at the best for me just now."[22] He'd fled or been banished from East Orange, and began that winter living in one temporary place after the next, a six-dollar-a-week room in a flophouse or transient hotel room without running water. A friend of the time remembers his quarters as squalid, with dirty clothes littering the floor, food containers here and there, nothing personal in the room, no signatures or marks of pride or memory. During the Depression, looking back at these hard times, O'Hara recollected working as a telephone operator in a fleabag near Bleeck's: "It was full of fairies, a couple of gangsters, and people like Cary Grant, Alan Mowbray, Cesar Romero et al."[23] Even in his nostalgia for the gutter, names will be dropped.

Niven Busch and his younger brother Noel, urbane New Yorkers, made a deep impression on the newcomer. He marked—and for a time aped—their fraternal manner, at ease in the world, amused by foibles, tolerant of eccentricities, sneering at affectation. Niven Busch's first reaction to him, shared in an interview with Finis Farr, displayed the kind of offhand condescension that O'Hara envied and feared, and that so many of his characters used to dismiss and bully the lower orders: O'Hara "looked as though he had cultured his appearance to represent a Yale grad, Class of '27, fast going to seed, the J. Press suit was stained and spotted, shirt slightly frayed, never quite a clean shave, deliberately uncured or early-morning-acquired hangover."[24] Both brothers wrote for *Time* and for the *New Yorker*, profiles and fact pieces. They sometimes used their mother's apartment on East 72nd when she was out of town; they were friendly to O'Hara, and Niven recollected to Finis Farr that his brother, "in a fit of generosity, hearing that O'Hara was without a flop," had a key made for him. Several keys, in fact. The idea was to let him sleep on the living-room couch, but he kept losing the keys. "Finding them gone, he devised different ways of getting in. One way was to pile a crate on top of a garbage can, then leap up and grab the bottom of the fire-escape ladder. . . . Then he would climb up the ladder and bang on a window." An even less ingratiating tactic was to ring the bells of random sleeping tenants, in hope that they might buzz him in. "Noel and I would not." The brothers' benevolence was exhausted after a couple of weeks.

Niven Busch, recollecting O'Hara's career at *Time*, declared that his colleague "had one great piece of luck" at the magazine: "Henry R. Luce detested him." He earned sixty-five dollars per week and for a month made the masthead, but he continued to resist being at the beck and call of the work-whistle, and had imperfectly mastered the technique of leaving a decoy hat and coat on his office rack, to suggest to an importuning editor that he'd just that moment stepped down the hall, when in fact he hadn't yet punched in. *Time*'s managing editor fired him in February, as soon as his only champion at the magazine, the Busches' cousin Briton Hadden, died. At which point, O'Hara appealed to Henry Luce's sense of fair play, with a predictable outcome. Thirty-five years later he recalled Luce giving him "that Protestant look" and pontificating that Luce publications had no place for a rakehell who "lolled in bed after nine o'clock in the morning." (Wolcott Gibbs, confirming Luce's discernment, observed from experience that O'Hara had a "strong distaste for sunlight and preferred to stay in bed until the worst of it was over.")[25]

He hadn't given up on Margaretta Archbald, though she was regularly giving up on him. After leaving the Flathead Reservation she'd moved to New York, renting an apartment with Mary Brooks, a Scranton cousin who was being wooed (and would be wed) by A. Whitney Griswold, twenty-some years later the president of Yale. O'Hara saw much of his first great love. He'd get drunk before he collected her for dinner, and then she'd drink at the speakeasy and pick a quarrel. One night at the St. Regis Roof he fell into such a rage at her that he smashed the crockery. He'd try to provoke her jealousy by making passes at her friends, and she'd judge him to be a fool, and he'd turn surly, and she'd get fed up and date other young men. Then, in despair and feeling sorry for himself, he would bang on her apartment door when the speakeasies closed or his money ran out. She'd beg him to go home; he'd whine and snarl. This went on and on during 1928 and 1929. While it was clear to both that they had no future together, he never lost his root fondness for her, and it seemed they couldn't make a final break. (When, in 1930, O'Hara met and a couple of months later married Helen Ritchie Petit, he took the occasion to dispense love advice to Simonds, who found himself in his own romantic cul-de-sac. O'Hara urged him to avoid "the anguish I had with Miss Arch, and which I undoubtedly caused. If I had had enough sense to break it off early in 1928, or if she had had sense enough to let me alone in 1929, we'd have been spared 1930, the worst year of my life.")[26]

Refusing to give up Miss Arch or to give up on her may have been obstinate, but it was also resolute. Many, many women adored O'Hara. This is a fact, but it is not self-evident. People unfriendly to him—usually men—were quick to remark his coarse face marred by surface irregularities, his ears spread for takeoff, his long jaw, his acne scars, his hammy hands, his bad teeth. Women were attracted, often abidingly attracted. Of his three wives, all remained loyal to him and were unstinting in their affection, including his first wife, who divorced him.* He was a baby in his emotions, easily wounded and perverse when injured, and when he was drunk he could be violent. "He took refusals hard," in the understated judgment of Frank MacShane. But he remained close to his mother, to his sisters, and to many female friends. He was curious about their preoccupations, for one thing, and for another he liked to write about strong women. He took for granted their own sexual drives, and was disinclined to romanticize them.

While still at the *Herald-Tribune,* he had met a young woman equally indifferent to propriety. He had written rejoicingly to Robert Simonds that he was in a "fair way to having the compassionate mistress" of whom he had dreamed aloud. For "compassionate" read pliant, undemanding, and on call. He had met her down in the Village. "On Thursday for the first time—having seen her just three times previously—I slept with her. God! What a body! And what a brain!" And what a rule book: "She announced the restrictions under which she would continue to see me. The principal one is that if I ever *think* of wanting to marry her, I am bound in honor [and here O'Hara draws, within parentheses, a Happy Face, as merry as a kid's snowman] never to see her again. There is to be positively *no* claim on the other by either of us, except that when one of us needs the other he is to call up, whether it's four in the morning or one in the afternoon. Both of us may be unfaithful and have entire freedom. There is to be an absolute Dutch Treat idea as regards the theater, meals, taxis, etc."[27]

---

*Margaretta Archbald was married to Frederick Kroll, the American ambassador to Haiti, when O'Hara's second wife, Belle Wylie O'Hara, died in 1954. Her letter of condolence was extraordinary even in the genre of sympathy notes for its tenderness and hospitality.

A female colleague at *Time* recalled O'Hara as seedy, with "a mean beard," but he was also capable of refined empathy and tenderness. He liked to make women laugh. He was known as an excellent dancer and a good talker. He was also, early in life, a good listener. Many years later, when he'd explain the histories and customs of their own secret societies to Yale seniors, and fail to invite them to slip in a detail edgewise, he was all pitch and no catch. But the young fictionist in the making, whether by vocational design or inquisitiveness, soaked up what he could learn about strangers, speech, manners, and, always, *facts:* names, dates, geographies, metes and bounds, titles, liens, weights and measures, yards gained, speed, dollars made and spent, meum et tuum, dowers, goods, stuff.

A reporter friend from that time, Harry Ferguson, encountered him due to the circumstance that both were dating blondes who shared an apartment on East 34th Street. O'Hara's was Katherine Klinkenberg, a stunning "Viking" who worked with him at *Time.* "When you asked him what he was doing," Ferguson remembered, "he replied: 'I'm a novelist.' John had unlimited contempt for journalism" (though maybe only during that night, since it would pass). After serving bathtub gin from pint milk bottles, the women sent the two of them home, but along the way Ferguson was led up a flight of stairs into a Second Avenue speakeasy, where, after an exchange of good-mornings with the bartender, O'Hara ordered rye on the rocks, "and my friend will pay." Indeed, Ferguson "paid and paid, because O'Hara turned his pockets inside out to demonstrate to me that he had no money." Thereafter Ferguson financed many a bender, but his friend always repaid him, "usually with witty notes accompanying the money." Besides, the financial drain of that "costly night" was worth it, "because for the first time I saw the incredible O'Hara Memory Machine in action."[28]

The newfound sidekicks shared the speakeasy that morning with four other patrons, who were arguing about sports. "One of them kept yelling, 'All right, name the infield, name the infield, name the infield; five bucks says you can't do it.' " The subject was the 1919 Black Sox scandal, when Chicago threw the World Series to the Cincinnati Reds. O'Hara took the bet, or rather took five dollars from Ferguson to take it. "So there was ten dollars on the bar and tension in the air. O'Hara knocked back a shot of rye and spoke: 'First base, Chick Gandil. Second base, Eddie Collins. Shortstop, Swede Risberg. Third base, Buck Weaver.' "

The losers tried to recoup, challenging him to name two outfielders, two pitchers, and the catcher. Another sawbuck pocketed. The losers were now themselves broke and moving sullenly toward the stairs when one called over his shoulder that O'Hara must have been born and raised in Chicago. No, O'Hara said, Pennsylvania, and then for good measure declared himself a Philadelphia Athletics fan "and a cousin fourth removed to Mister Connie Mack, their manager."

Ferguson said, "That's a lie."

O'Hara said, "Truth forever on the scaffold, wrong forever on the throne." And then: "Ten dollars says you don't know who wrote that."*

Ferguson didn't take the bet, but he witnessed many such occasions: O'Hara pitted against theater critics, out-remembering the birth dates of actors famous and obscure; O'Hara out-remembering a newshound as to Pulitzer Prize winners for reporting between 1917 and 1927; O'Hara wondering if anyone would care to recite the full names of Notre Dame's Four Horsemen, which it happened quite a few did, turning his mood black. Well then, how many passes from Gus Dorais to Knute Rockne during Notre Dame's upset of Army? O'Hara knew poems by heart and song lyrics by the yard. At a speakeasy the songwriter Howard Dietz was bowled over by O'Hara's flawless performance—first note to last—of the recorded version of "Washboard Blues," not neglecting orchestral effects. He was a living research library, a prodigy.

You'd think he'd be perfect for *Time,* and it for him, but despite his bias for facts, he was most seduced by psychological conditions, by the undomesticated urges that drove him and his fictional characters. The legend of the *Time* firing, in fact a simple instance of mutual aversion, grew in O'Hara's telling—and his friends' retellings—into a bloodletting crusade of the titans across a battlefield of factchecking.† In this revised version, O'Hara was hired from his bar-stool perch at Bleeck's to serve the magazine as its "super-checker," according to Donald Schanche's

---

*"Yet that scaffold sways the future, and, behind the / dim unknown, Standeth God within the shadow, keeping watch / above his own," James Russell Lowell, "The Present Crisis" (1844), stanza eight of a hymn sung often and athletically at boarding school in evening chapel, stanza five being: "Once to every man and nation comes the moment to decide, / In the strife of Truth with Falsehood, for the good or evil side."

†O'Hara never forgave Luce for being Luce. Not long after the writer John McPhee graduated from Princeton—where he was building a house a short walk through the woods from O'Hara's "Linebrook"—he telephoned on a neighborly matter. McPhee's house, like O'Hara's before it, was being built on a difficult site, from a septic point of view, and McPhee was wrestling with perc tests

admiring portrait in *Esquire.* Luce's neurotic passion for accuracy—at the expense of cogency and surely of truth—was no match for O'Hara's own inspired nit-picking. His "second-guessing [of correct data and diction] so irritated the national affairs editor that he fired him."

Somehow he kept landing on his shaky pins. After *Time* showed him the door, he got hired as a reporter on *Editor & Publisher,* according to his later (and unlikely) report, on Luce's say-so. That employment survived for less time than it took to be listed on the payroll. Desperate, O'Hara bummed with a friend at his Princeton dorm room for a couple of weeks in the spring of 1929, a prophetic visit to that pretty place. Referring to it thirty years later, he was coy about his host, refusing to drop his name but bragging that this friend's family was "really . . . up there in the chips. I don't mean *one* lousy million. I mean Big, Big. I think if I were to mention his last name I think almost everyone here [in a lecture hall at Trenton's Rider College] from the Middle West would recognize it." It was the rich kid's senior year, and he and his guest devoted their energies to lazing around and "violating the Volstead Act, and what with a little luck at golf and bridge—auction bridge, by the way—I ended up with about the same ten bucks I had in my kick when I arrived."[29] In repayment of this hospitality, he offered his host free advice. The Chicago scion had taken it into his head to become a writer, to write a novel. No, no, O'Hara said. Instead of wasting your time as a dilettante, make a bundle and become a patron of the arts. What became of this friendship can only be imagined.

In July of 1929 he was a night rewrite man for the *Daily Mirror,* but

---

and leach field permits; O'Hara, with whom he shared mutual affection, couldn't have been more helpful.

> He was learned in the ways of bedrock and shale, he had mastered the arcana of septic tanks and leach-fields; he was redolent with knowledge. Moreover he had wonderful stories and little dramas about the officials who controlled the fate of my house. He was knowing, and hilarious and, as he talked, he warmed to his work. It was wonderful listening to him. What he knew! Too soon, he was finished telling me about sewage, he asked me where I was working. I said I was at Time. "Oh," he said, and slammed down the phone.

A few years later, O'Hara—invited to submit to a *Time* interview—sent a nasty and sarcastic note to Luce, who replied by rejecting "totally" O'Hara's "derogatory remarks about TIME as being irrelevant, incompetent, etc., etc., etc." In response to the novelist's expressed willingness to be interviewed personally by Luce-and-only-by-Luce, the great man, in "recognition of our long and not unfriendly acquaintance," declared himself to be "rather intrigued by the prospect of presenting myself at your door" (Henry R. Luce, to John O'Hara, John O'Hara Papers, United States Trust Company, New York, April 6, 1962).

that job—which he got with the help of his new friend Jimmy Cannon, who heard about it from a *Mirror* day rewriter, Gordon Kahn, "who subsequently became a Commie and wore a monocle," in O'Hara's recollection—called for his appearance in the office at twilight, interfering with his intake at Racky's, a speakeasy a block distant from the Hearst tabloid. "A job was something that, if you didn't keep it in its place, could get in the way of the really important business of living it up," a pal of the time remembered of his work ethic.[30] O'Hara many years later remembered it this way: "The study of the Martini as prepared at Racky's restaurant, a block from my office, was an enjoyable way to start my day, which was supposed to begin at 6 p.m. Unfortunately for journalism, although happily for my social life, the day side of the *Mirror* would be at Racky's, on their way home, just when I was on my way to work. . . . I hated to leave the *Mirror*. The city editor had a Pierce-Arrow roadster and wore silk shirts, and while I would have chosen a Lincoln phaeton and buttondown broadcloth, the idea was the same. There was money to be made."[31]

O'Hara wasn't making much of that money, but he was spending a good sum. Frank MacShane has justly concluded that "because he cashed his paychecks at bars he tended to spend everything he earned right away and looked upon the resulting impoverishment as an act of God over which he had no control." He earned, when he was working, four or five dollars a day. Yet he patronized the theater, and enjoyed watching Fred and Adele Astaire dance at the Trocadero. A miserable room cost a dollar, a steak dinner a couple of dollars, a pint of whiskey roughly a third of his weekly salary. He ate and drank more modestly at the Type & Print Club, where *Trib* typesetters liked to gather, and where he met John K. Hutchens, son of the Montana newspaper editor who had let him down gently when he had applied for a job in Missoula to be near Marg Archbald. (Hutchens was beginning his long career as the *Herald-Tribune*'s literary critic, and their loyalty to each other endured, and ameliorated some of the pain O'Hara suffered from many unfriendly and influential critics during the next four decades.) The man about town ate and drank more expensively at Tony's on West 52nd, where the owner, Tony Soma—in the memory of Finis Farr—might sing an aria from Verdi or Puccini while standing on his head. He could dine even more lavishly at Jack and Charlie's, across the street at 21 West 52nd. And then there were the nightclubs, the Pre Catalan or the hotel

roofs where Paul Whiteman played, and the Dorseys and Guy Lombardo, or the Onyx Club, where the best white jazz musicians—Miff
Mole and Max Kaminsky, Johnny Mercer and Phil Napoleon—jammed.
O'Hara first met Dorothy Parker, later his loyal pal and most admiring
fan, listening to the Hawaiian house band at an all-night joint called the
Dizzy Club, which served the hardest of hard-core soakers, patrons who
showed near dawn and drank till noon. Finis Farr has invoked the clien-
tele as people "who drank fast, said little and had pistols under their
coats. Others were there only because they did not want to interrupt
their consumption of alcohol, except when unconscious, until they died."
One infamous young customer announced to fellow barflies that he had
just enough money to drink himself to death, which he had, and which
he did. This was the beginning of what the narrator of *Butterfield 8*
terms the "elaborate era" of speakeasies.

From serving furtive drinks of bad liquor disguised as demitasse the
speakeasy had "progressed to whole town houses, with uniformed pages
and cigarette girls, a string orchestra and a four- or five-piece Negro
band for dancing, free hors d'oeuvres, four and five bartenders, silver-
plated keys . . . to regular patrons . . . engraved announcements in pretty
good taste, intricate accounting systems and business machinery—all a
necessary front for the picturesque and deadly business of supplying
liquor at huge financial profit."[32]

O'Hara couldn't afford the costly city, but he didn't stint; he used it
and gave it back to his readers. Let's stipulate that he wasn't a prudent
man. Later, echoing the sermonizing judgment of "deadly business,"
O'Hara—speaking through Jim Malloy in the 1960 novella *Imagine Kissing Pete*—cuts a devious path to account for the ethical lapses of the
postwar generation ("West Point cadets who cheated in examinations,
the basketball players who connived with gamblers"), pinning responsibility on the fruits of Prohibition.* From this cause there were only
deserters, "who were not brave deserters but furtive ones; there was no
honest mutiny but only grumbling and small disobediences. . . . It was
not only a cynical disregard for a law of the land. . . . Prohibition made
liars of a hundred million men and cheats of their children."[33]

*O'Hara beat this drum hard: in a *Collier's* column of December 23, 1955, he reminisced that he
and his Pottsville friends "grew up in an atmosphere of complete contempt for the one law that
affected the rich, the middle class, and the poor" (John O'Hara, "Appointment with O'Hara," *Collier's*, 23 December 1955).

For the love of Mike! Why the long face? It wasn't as though bar-hopping had ended his writing. One might hope, moreover, for a bit less hypocrisy from a lecture he delivered three decades later at Rider College, scolding "no-good bums" who give a black eye to the writer's trade. "The writing occupation is too often used as an excuse for doing nothing and for doing it with a great deal of insolence and arrogance. . . . I don't want the profession I love, the work I love, to attract people who see it as a justification for getting drunk, leading irregular hours, rejecting the conventions."[34]

He seemed to remember everything that happened to him back then. He hoarded with peculiar avidity slights and humiliations, situations in which he'd seemed less than he was, and acted shamefully. From his life at that time came stories and scenes in novels of being snubbed, of exacting revenge, of taking a beating in a speakeasy or from a cop, of waking up with dirty clothes and phlegmy eyes, of disgrace.

There were consolations. In April 1928, soon after he was hired by the *Trib*—and after assailing the *New Yorker* from Pottsville with submissions (rejected) that were brief extrapolations from daily newspaper fluff, on such topics as cigarette smoking, cars, dance steps—he had a story accepted by Harold Ross. The publication on May 5 of "The Alumnae Bulletin" began an association remarkable for its storminess, but even more for the flood of stories and sketches and novellas that surged from O'Hara to that most cosmopolitan of periodicals, two hundred and sixty-five times between "The Alumnae Bulletin" and "How Old, How Young" (1967), his final *New Yorker* piece. The first published sketch is a brief and sour monologue by a woman responding to her Seven Sister college class notes, a slight exercise in up-to-speed diction. He cashed the fifteen-dollar payment check at Bleeck's; as the bartender forked over the money, which would so soon be coming right back at him, he was heard to ask another patron, "The *New Yorker*—what in hell is *that*?" Today—when the magazine's every staffing shift commands headlines—it seems remarkable that anyone should've had to ask. Three years after its founding, on uncertain financial ground, the *New Yorker* was well on its way to becoming a national intellectual and literary phenomenon. By the time "The Alumnae Bulletin" appeared, Harold Ross's staff already included Robert Benchley, Wolcott Gibbs, Dorothy Parker, James Thurber, Katharine Angell, and her second husband, E. B. White—people who became crucial to O'Hara's career and his sense of himself. He came to measure himself by tokens of the esteem in which he was held by Ross and by his colleagues.

As he shinnied up the *New Yorker*'s thorny pole—selling twelve short pieces during 1928—he was slipping fast at the *Daily Mirror*. His high-water mark came in an unbylined feature, "Girl Invades Yale Club Bar, Only for Men," which merely amplifies with a name and a date its head-line. (It's odd that O'Hara believed the event to have been more news-worthy, or amusing, than his own invasion of that bar, but irony was never his greatest strength.) He was fired from the paper for the usual reasons: too often tardy or absent, too flagrantly drunk or hungover. He got hired by Benjamin Sonnenberg's p.r. firm to cover a bridge match but never showed up, and his one-day employment ended when Son-nenberg tracked him to a speakeasy, the Homeless Dogs, where O'Hara had passed out. After the stock market crash, he picked up work as the fabulously generous Heywood Broun's secretary early in 1930. Broun, an idol of O'Hara, liked to eat and drink and talk, and he paid for O'Hara to eat and drink and talk with him. (When Broun died in 1940, O'Hara wrote a letter to the *New Republic* crediting Broun with a paramount influence: "I still have a raccoon coat for the excellent reason that at my age Heywood Broun had one too.")[35] The Great Crash has been described by one witty friend of O'Hara's as the vanishing of huge for-tunes of "notional" money. Finis Farr concludes, with raffish simplifica-tion, that "this money had never in fact existed, but its reported disappearance caused distress." For O'Hara's part, he boasted of his indifference to the calamity: "For what it was worth, I had the advantage of being already broke."[36]

During the late spring and early summer of 1930 he scraped up work as a movie critic and radio columnist (under the name "Franey Delaney," in a tip of the hat to his maternal grandparents) for the *Morning Tele-graph*, a grubby sheet specializing in racing news and professional bul-letins about the entertainment biz. O'Hara, drifting from one dismal little room to another, didn't own a radio, so he covered his beat from bars that did. He wrote especially vividly about jazz, about Louis Arm-strong and Fletcher Henderson, but this newspaper was as distant from the *Trib* as it was possible for a Manhattan newspaper to be, and some index of its standing is offered by the fact that he accepted the job only after failing in his quest to join a newspaper in Trenton ("Trenton Makes, The World Takes"), New Jersey.

Although he worked as a movie publicist, for Warner Brothers and for

RKO, after his inevitable sacking by the *Morning Telegraph*—tardy and drunk—he was repeatedly pulled toward daily journalism. In his own erratic way, by his own timetable and imperatives, he was a pro. In a 1955 interview with John K. Hutchens for the *Herald-Tribune,* he told the truth: "I pride myself . . . on never having missed a deadline. I have failed to show up for work, and separated myself from a job that way. But if a story was due at 10:10, I had it all in by 10:09."[37] Forty-one years after being taken as an unpaid charity case by the *Pottsville Journal's* publisher, looking back in *My Turn,* O'Hara wrote about his lifelong gravitation: "The moment I enter a newspaper office I am at home, not only because the surroundings are as familiar to me as backstage is to an actor, but because, like the actor, I am ready to go on in any part. I could write a headline, take a story over the telephone, cover a fire, or interview a movie queen, and if I had to make up the front page I could do that too, although I might not win the N. W. Ayer Award for it."[38]

Just like him to know—and drop—the exact award he'd have been pissed off not to have received for his makeup skills. For all his comfort in daily newsrooms, newsrooms weren't comfortable with him. But for a long time, he would appropriately identify himself as connected with—and a slave to, at a dime a word—the *New Yorker.*

Harold Ross's young and youthfully irreverent magazine perfectly fit O'Hara's infatuation with material manifestations of standing and aspiration. O'Hara was a whiz at reading mannerisms as well as manners, at recording the revealing tics of idiom that unmasked pretenders and preeners. His early short sketches were caricatures, verbal equivalents of the *New Yorker's* celebrated cartoons. According to Wolcott Gibbs, who personified the arch wit and slant understatement of the magazine, "he is, I think, preoccupied with a great many things that are trivial and not easy to reconcile with a mind that is adult enough in other respects."

Gibbs—in whose honor O'Hara named the seat, Gibbsville, of his serial achievement, that fictional Pottsville upon whose history and sociology he so elaborately improved—became a friend. To be O'Hara's friend necessarily was to endure and forgive a startlingly mercurial disposition. Gibbs wrote ten years after they met that John O'Hara came into his life in 1928 "with some of the accumulating violence of a hurricane." They drank and ate together at such midtown speakeasies as "21" and Matt Winkel's, a period Gibbs remembered fondly as a curious time when "the fact that everybody was part of the same general conspiracy against a silly law broke down many barriers so that it was hard to tell what might happen before any night was over." Among the low-comedy episodes of boozy bewilderment was the occasion when O'Hara complained "in a puzzled way because a lady had taken away his coat and mandolin— God knows what he was doing with a mandolin—and given them to her janitor."[39]

Gibbs, a hard drinker himself, was astute as well as witty. Like O'Hara, he hadn't gone to college, and he understood—if he didn't share—his friend's fetishistic compulsion to "invest those missing years with a warmth and wonder that they could never possibly have had." He knew better than to tease O'Hara about this fixation, but as an established *New Yorker* contributor and editor, he was free with career advice. After acceptance of "The Alumnae Bulletin," O'Hara submitted a sequence of very short pieces, what the magazine called "casuals," in his case patches of idiom in the form of monologues or conversations, locutions "tangled in [their] own draperies," as Gibbs observed many years later in his preface to O'Hara's story collection *Pipe Night*. The necessary trick, if he were to win Harold Ross's favor, was to make these sketches ramify, or at the least connect with whatever was on the boss's unpredictable mind. (It was told to Matthew J. Bruccoli in an interview that Ross had runically groused to O'Hara that "I trust you with nouns, but not with adjectives.")[40] Justly, the *New Yorker*'s editor wished the magazine's fiction to imitate character in action and not merely to record random reels of speech. It wasn't enough that the sketches be accurate, despite Ross's known devotion to facts.

Even if he liked accuracy, Harold Ross still didn't like the man. Perhaps it was to O'Hara's credit that the latter never seemed fully to recognize this antipathy, though it caused him substantial harm. The relationship between a magazine editor and writer is usually out of balance in regard to practical consequence: if a writer decides to submit work elsewhere, the editor may feel resentful or hurt, but the bruise soon heals; but if an editor decides against a writer, especially a writer so singularly suited in his signature wing-shots to a particular outlet, the writer is undone, effectively silenced, and unemployed. O'Hara's submissions, no less than their author, rubbed Ross the wrong way, and it was no small thanks to Katharine Angell and others with influence that he surmounted the high barrier of the boss editor's distaste. Gibbs tossed many a message across O'Hara's wall in an attempt to explain why, and what he needed to do to get them accepted. O'Hara wrote in 1932 to his brother Tom, who had submitted pieces rejected by Gibbs, that he and his *New Yorker* friend had been together at a speakeasy, and "Gibbs was very drunk, and as sometimes happens when he gets like that, he got [in] one of his Brutally Frank moods," allowing on this occasion that "I am the God damn best writer the New Yorker has, but that I am stupid because I don't know what they want; that I am too obscure. . . . 'And that's the trouble with your kid brother. You O'Haras simply refuse to recognize the fact that The New Yorker isn't for clever people. The New Yorker's for people who live on Riverside Drive. But you're stubborn,' etc. etc. Well, he had just returned a piece of mine for that reason. The ending was too subtle."[41]

It's the eternal cry of the disappointed writer: I'm too good for them. But in fact—putting aside the slur on the Upper West Side neighbors of Columbia University—there was wisdom, or at least cunning, in Gibbs's advice. Harold Ross was crafty enough to grant his editors their passions—and O'Hara had an ally in Katharine Angell as well as in Gibbs— but he increasingly chafed at the obliqueness of the short stories. The editor John Mosher, who'd taken "The Alumnae Bulletin" as an over-the-transom submission, got in the habit of accusing him of being "elliptical." As Gibbs recalled in 1938, some of those stories he might've had in mind—"Tennis," a dopey sportsman's locker-room monologue that did without quotation marks, or the self-describing "Overheard in a Telephone Booth"—had been written "for the sole purpose of putting into print some dislocation of the language" while "others were cryptic." James Thurber reported a typical Ross outburst: "I'll never print another O'Hara story I don't understand."[42] (This is the same Harold Ross, let it be noted, who inquired of his factchecking department, "Is Moby Dick the whale or the man?") Gibbs recalled that "it was not unusual for troubled editors to turn up with three contradictory ideas about what Mr. O'Hara was getting at." But Gibbs also recognized that these early experiments were often "startlingly good," the products of "strongly original talent, advancing painstakingly through trial and error."[43] O'Hara's friend and sometime editor was astute to recognize that although it might seem to a reader that the writer was recording the fits and starts and dislocations and solecisms of speech recorded with mindless accuracy, the compositions were in fact artful fabrications, elliptical and truncated artifices calculated to suggest fidelity. Hemingway had done as much, most notably in "Hills Like White Elephants," and Raymond Carver would extend narrative illusion, marvelously subverting the reader's understanding of realistic speech, and of realism itself.

It is notable that the writer who was too "experimental" for the Jazz Age *New Yorker* was later turned on a spit by critics derisive of his expository clunkiness, his interminable explicitness. Maybe, by the time of the long novels, he had learned Gibbs's and Ross's lessons too well. But meantime, after a few years writing for the magazine, he began to refine his art, as Gibbs understood it, and "lost much, though by no means all, of his passion for indirection. One recent story, for instance, ended with its protagonist leaving the room with the bow on his hat on the wrong side of his head, and while it was abundantly clear to Mr. O'Hara that this indicated great spiritual turmoil, it conveyed precisely nothing to many readers, who wrote in, irritably." It is also a fact that whether a hat's bow showed on the wrong side mattered crucially to his characters; right side's wrong, right? It's revealing, but of little consolation, to know that John Cheever suffered the same kinds of chivvying from the *New Yorker* when he submitted "The Swimmer," so abundant in its deliberate improbabilities and dislocations that it had to be published by *Playboy*.

It was often Gibbs's duty to convey to the author that this or that submission had been rejected, most often by Ross, but not infrequently by Katharine Angell or by Gibbs himself. Nevertheless, their friendship survived these stresses, and O'Hara was unflagging in his ambition to associate himself formally with the magazine. He continued through 1929 and 1930 to place his casuals, including a series of fourteen sketches of the proceedings of the Orange County Afternoon Delphian Society; these were exercises in voice, evidently inspired by his mother's women's club proceedings in Pottsville, and rough approximations of the kind of parodic hilarity performed better by Robert Benchley's "Treasurer's Report" and, later, in O'Hara's own "Pal Joey" sequence. The *New Yorker* was thriving, stuffed with so many ads that it was an editorial challenge to drum up enough copy—especially in the back of the book— to fill the spaces between them. Norman Mailer has called this process "feeding the goat," and O'Hara fed the beast reliably, sixty-eight times in the three years following his first publication. The archly patronizing Delphian pieces came to bore him "to madness," in the estimation of Gibbs (Benchley felt similarly imprisoned by "The Treasurer's Report"), and he wrote about their fatuous doings—"turning out Delphians as briskly as a doughnut machine"—only when he needed a payday, which was always.[44]

Another early series lampooned the misdirected enterprises of Hagedorn & Brownmiller Paint and Varnish Co. The risk run, and not always redeemed, with such banal raw material was too faithfully imitating dullness. From the range of his experience of Pottsville, mining, nightlife, sports, jazz, and business he seemed back then ineluctably drawn to what was pinched and mean. His Duffy series in the *New Yorker* played back the voice of the chairman of the Greens Committee of the Idlewood Country Club, confirming what readers must already have expected or experienced of vainglory, smugness, and triviality. Nevertheless, merely by showing up every couple of weeks, the young writer was attracting notice. Jed Harris, an influential theatrical producer, responded to these early exercises in ellipsis and inanity with extravagant praise. Finis Farr quotes him as having declared emphatically that in O'Hara "we might have the greatest natural playwright in America." Matthew J. Bruccoli is steadfast, even ferocious, in his advocacy of his achievement—as might be gathered from his comparison of this early *New Yorker* work with Hemingway's *In Our Time* ("both are attempts to record—action for Hemingway, and speech for O'Hara")—but even so ardent a champion must recognize an incongruity: "The difference is that O'Hara's early sketches have no stylistic distinction."

O'Hara banged away at Ross, trying to sell him book reviews, music reviews, and profiles. (Al Smith was accepted for a fee of a bit more than a hundred dollars; his character sketch of a chorine wasn't, they concluded, for them.) To Katharine Angell he circulated the legend of his bravura memory and acute ear. "What ever happened to the Victrola-record listening department? I am an authority on records. To prove it: my friendship with Howard Dietz dates from the night in Tony's when I hummed and sang the Whiteman orchestration of 'Washboard Blues,' effortlessly."[45] As early as the spring of 1928, about an hour and a half after landing his first job in New York, he had been hounding Ross: "I am at the Herald Tribune, but positively not of it." The aspirant—a mere twenty-three, but "for years now . . . laboring" to get a spot on "your magazine"—then thought to add, "Please don't let my unenviable reputation as a frivolous person affect your judgment of my qualifications." Nothing came of that beseeching letter other than a "part-time racket,"

probably arranged by Ross, editing a newsletter for the Crescent Athletic Club in Brooklyn, but he kept trying. "I don't want much
money. . . . And like every little boy who comes up from Princeton some
time in senior year, I'm just full of ideas. If the matter should come up,
I'm on the wagon (the matter inevitably comes up when I ask for a
job)."[46]

He wasn't on the wagon for longer than a day or two, and neither was
he up from Princeton, unless freeloading in a dorm room reckons as
affiliation, though he was certainly full of ideas—a twin profile of the
musical comedy stars Betty Compton and Bobbe Arnst, a "Talk of the
Town" piece on male waiters at Schrafft's, a series on Speakeasy Knights
(the column's rubric was itself a tip of the hat to Niven Busch's fort-
nightly New Yorker sketches, "Speakeasy Nights"). He proposed to write
"The Wayward Press" column in Heywood Broun's absence, to compose
profiles of the Yale-graduated father of the Princeton polo captain; of
Harvard football's Waldo Peirce, son of a lumber tycoon; of Yale's Cole
Porter; and of Harlem's Fletcher Henderson.

O'Hara was a snob, forever judging the best this and the oldest that,
the wealthiest, the biggest. His early attitude toward race and color
ranged from the casually vicious to the complex. He was both a bully and
an underdog, and his offhand slurs about Jews and blacks ("dinges") and
east Europeans ("Schwackies," a Pottsville aspersion) were as commonplace as his angry, early 1931 letter to Ross was extraordinary. The occasion was a New Yorker piece titled "Court Games," about a squash
player—with whom O'Hara was unacquainted—named Harry Wolf:
"For all I know he may be the most obnoxious Jew that ever trounced a
Gentile favorite. But I object to the New Yorker's panning him the way it
has. When a man gets to be as good in his line as Wolf apparently has,
you simply haven't any right . . . to be so cavalierish merely because he
also happens to be a wet smack. If he is."[47]

How quickly he changes the subject from anti-Semitism to anti-
assholery, in transparent consistency with his credo that excellence is its
own excuse. Still, it's gallant for a supplicant to reproach, from a position
of powerlessness, a bigot.

O'Hara's temperamental and circumstantial fragility at this time cannot be exaggerated. He was a hostage to his compulsions, his ill temper,
his preposterous and heroic pride. He was a prisoner of poverty, which
during 1930 grew alarming. Among O'Hara's Selected Letters is only one

from 1930, to Katharine Angell White, who had married E. B. White at the end of the previous year. She had rebuked O'Hara twice for scrounging from the *New Yorker* advances of twenty-five dollars against unwritten work, a habit she scolded as "pernicious," adding with frosty disdain, in that first-person plural voice so many shabby hat-in-hand writers were learning to recognize as the rusty squeak of a gate swinging shut, that "we don't really know whether it is better for you to have us do it, or not, but we could not have you evicted I suppose."[48] His response was compliant, almost whipped down: "I am afraid I've been, latterly, more of a liability than an asset to The New Yorker. . . . Right now I am in a State about various things, not the least of which is My Work."[49] His lot was not improving, and just now he was measuring his value while doubting his future. He and Margaretta Archbald were colliding like bumper cars, with about as much sense of purpose or destination. He relied on his sister Mary for companionship and for reminders of better days. She worked at the *Daily News,* which might explain why he never blotted his copybook at that newspaper, and she'd stand him lunch at Schrafft's when she sensed he needed nourishment. He'd recollect later in writing that he once went three days without eating. In the timeworn way of such things, she'd venture to advise him to improve his habits, which of course would prompt her older brother to ask, "Do I have to pay for lunch by listening to a lecture?" One night at a party he was introduced to the wife of Mary's boss. "Are you *John* O'Hara," she asked, and he assumed she knew his name from the *New Yorker,* and was flattered. Not so, as he wrote Simonds. " 'You're not at all like I expected you to be. Mary was at our house for dinner . . . and I gathered that you always needed a shave and a haircut. Why, you're really very nice-looking.' " So he got drunk, phoned his sister, and dressed her down, "but you can't intimidate Mary. The hell with her."[50] (Kathleen O'Hara Fuldner, the youngest of the siblings, assured me of her elder sister, "Oh, Mary! She could *do* indignation.")

He was reduced to sleeping on couches, and even to mooching again off his East Orange aunt and uncle. His hangovers were a chronic illness now, and he was picking more fights than he won. The sketches he submitted to the *New Yorker* during this period attested to his despair and isolation, his Darwinian anxiety that maybe he wasn't among the fittest after all. He was chagrined to have been unable to give more—in coin or esteem—to his siblings and mother, and Margaretta Archbald had accepted a proposal of marriage from a rival. When even the lowly *Telegraph* showed O'Hara the door, he signed off with a dog-Latin misquotation of Suetonius's "Ave Caesar" valediction in his final column—"Te morituri salutamus." Then, shortly before Christmas, he limped home to Pottsville.

Here was a bitter pill. He described himself to Kyle Crichton, an editor at *Scribner's Magazine,* as playing "Artist in the Family": brooding, writing, drinking, borrowing. Not a good time, and maybe he even thought about killing himself. His brother Tom seemed to believe as much when he remembered for Finis Farr that cold, dark time at 606 Mahantongo, with John slumped deep in a big, green chair: "He seemed to hunch down as if he wanted, more than anything, a feeling of shelter. I couldn't do anything to help except by trying to make him aware of my love and admiration." In his younger brother's judgment, "I doubt that he ever felt any worse," except when family died, "in the rest of his life."[51] There are depressions and there are depressions. There was also the Depression. O'Hara's enervation might have been chemical, but it was surely circumstantial. He knew he had frittered away great chances in New York, much as he had with his earlier dissipations at school and in Pottsville. He must have felt cornered.

Fiction writers are in the business of cornering their characters. Their work lives by the principle of obstacle and resistance, its heat issuing from friction. The most memorable characters are driven by thwarted hot-rod engines of will. Plot offers illusory routes forward, ways out, a sequence of turns to choose, errors to enact. And the cruelest twist on the hard fate set in ambush is, as codified by Aristotle, that constitution is fate. Or, as O'Hara at forty remarked not at all casually of F. Scott Fitzgerald, "an artist is his own fault." So it is natural that any serious writer would think systematically about suicide—what Camus called, perhaps too glibly, the only serious philosophical question.* As sober a sage as William James believed that suicide consecrates a character, and what does fiction propose if not the consecration of character? O'Hara knew in his bones the ache of self-defeat, the tinny taste of hangover, the

---

*"There is but one truly serious philosophical problem and that is suicide. Judging whether life is or is not worth living amounts to answering the fundamental question of philosophy. All the rest— whether or not the world has three dimensions, whether the mind has nine or twelve categories— comes afterwards. These are games; one must first answer" (Camus, "Absurdity and Suicide," *The Myth of Sisyphus,* translated by Justin O'Brian [New York: Vintage, 1961], p. 3).

abrasions on a scratched face you feel waking on a badly upholstered couch. Given the shame of not having clean clothes, what difference would a shower make? These are specific griefs, and writing can invoke them. Again and again—most exquisitely in *Appointment in Samarra,* more perfunctorily in too many later fictions—O'Hara turned to suicide as a way out of a tale, or a fix, or a personal history. A way, too, to translate impotent rage into nourishing concentration.

During that brief, miserable stay in Pottsville on the cusp of 1931, writing and grieving for the chances gone out of his life, John O'Hara mastered a narrative equivalent of a serial suicide note that a reader might receive and say, Yes, that was a star-set course, the only available escape route. For students of life's selective cruelties, he was consistently emphatic in his defense of suicide as a rational *quod erat demonstrandum.* As depressed as he was by Ernest Hemingway's solution to his own depression, he never pretended not to understand it. Two years after Hemingway shot himself in 1961, O'Hara wrote a short story, the writer at his bleak, hunch-honoring best, at that clean-to-the-bone top of his form he had conceived by the time he left Pottsville in 1931, that mastery to which he sometimes managed to return even when he himself was no longer at bay. Here it is, "How Can I Tell You?"

HOW CAN I TELL YOU?*

A T-Bird and two Galaxies was very good for one day, especially as the T-Bird did not involve a trade-in. The woman who bought it, Mrs. Preston, had come in and asked for Mark McGranville and shown him a magazine ad. "Do you have one of these in stock, in red?" she said.

"Not on the floor, Mrs. Preston," he said. "But I can have one for you inside of two hours."

"You can? Brand-new?"

"Brand-new," he said.

"Red, like this?"

"The exact same color, the same body job, white walls, radio and heater. I could have it in front of your house inside of two hours. And if you were thinking of getting rid of your ranch wagon, I can allow you— well, let's see what the book says."

*The Hat on the Bed (New York: Random House, 1963), pp. 116–122.

"Did I say I wanted to trade in my ranch wagon? I love it. I wouldn't think of getting rid of it. I want the Thunderbird for Buddy. He just passed all his exams and he's coming home for the weekend."

"Well, you know exactly what he wants, Mrs. Preston. Because he's been in here a couple times, looking at T-Birds. He's a very lucky boy."

"He's a good boy, Mark. Not a lucky boy."

"Yes, he's one of the best," said Mark McGranville.

"And you say you can have a car just like this in two hours? Where do you have to go for it?"

"Oh, all I have to do is pick up the phone, call the factory distributor, and tell him what I want."

"But how do you know he has what *I* want?"

"Because we dealers get a list of what was shipped to the factory distributor. I guarantee you I have just what you want. I'll bring it to your door this afternoon, personally, and be glad to take care of the registration, insurance, all the details. Would you want us to finance it for you?"

"I would not. You bring the car around and I'll give you a cheque for the whole thing, license and everything. I don't suppose you could have his initials put on today?"

"If you let me have the car overnight I can have his initials put on and bring it back to you before noon tomorrow. R. W. P.?"

"R. W. P. That's right. In yellow. Yellow would be better on red."

"About three quarters of an inch high? Or smaller? Maybe a half an inch. A half an inch in yellow shows up well. If he wants bigger initials later, that's easy to fix."

"I'll leave that to you, Mark. And you'll take care of everything? He gets home tomorrow afternoon."

"He couldn't have a nicer surprise. It is a surprise, isn't it?"

"It certainly is. It's a surprise to *me*. I wasn't going to buy him a car till he graduates. But he's been so good, and why not let him have the fun out of it?"

"You're right, Mrs. Preston."

"How's Jean? And the children?"

"They're fine, thank you. Very fine."

"You get credit for this sale, don't you?"

"You bet I do," he said. "Appreciate your asking for me."

"Well, you've always been a good boy, too, Mark. I'm sure your mother's very pleased with you."

"Thank you."

"Your mother's a fine woman, Mark. Any time she's thinking of going back to work again, I hope she lets me know first."

"She would, that's for sure. But I guess she likes keeping house for my sister. They have that little ranch-type out at Putnam Park, the two of them. Mary has her job at the Trust Company, and my mother has enough to keep her occupied."

"Very nice for both of them. Well, I mustn't keep you any longer. You have some telephoning to do."

"Thank you very much, Mrs. Preston," he said. He accompanied her to her ranch wagon, held the door open for her, and waited in the parking lot until she turned the corner.

The other transactions of the day were more typical, not sales that were dropped in his lap by a Mrs. Preston. But all three sales should have made him feel better than he felt on the way home, and he did not know why he should find himself wanting a drink and, what's more, heading for Ernie's to get it.

He locked his car and entered the taproom, hung his hat and coat on a clothestree, and took a seat in a booth. Ernie came to wait on him.

"Well, hi, stranger," said Ernie.

"Hello, Ernie," said Mark McGranville. "Quiet."

"Well, a little early. Never much action before six. The lunch trade till ha' past two, then maybe a few strays during the afternoon. How's it with you?"

"Not bad. Pretty good."

"Ed and Paul were in last night, them and their wives for dinner. Paul made a pretty good load. What's her name, his wife?"

"Charlotte."

"She snuck over and asked me to cut his drinks, but I couldn't do that. I said to her, what'd she want to do? Get me in trouble? You know Paul, he caught me watering his drinks and he'd have it all over town in no time. He's no bargain anyway, Paul."

"No, he's a noisy son of a bitch when he makes the load."

"But he's a friend of yours, though, isn't he?"

"I guess so," said Mark. "Let me have a bourbon and soda, will you, Ernie?"

"Why sure. Is there anything the matter, Mark?"

"No. Why?"

"I don't know. You want any particular bourbon?"

"I wouldn't be able to tell the difference. You know that."

"*Okay, okay,*" said Ernie. He pantomimed getting a kick in the behind and went to the bar to get Mark's drink. He returned with a small round tray on which were a highball glass, a shot glass with the bourbon, a small bottle of club soda. "There you are. That's Old Gutburner, the bar bourbon."

"Old what?"

"Gutburner. Old Gutburner. That's what Paul calls the bar bourbon. It ain't all that bad. You want some music?"

"Christ, no."

"You just want to sit here and nobody bother you. Okay," said Ernie. He walked away, spinning the inverted tray on his forefinger, and Mark had a couple of sips of his drink. He waited for some pleasant effect, and when none came, he finished the drink in a gulp. "Ernie? Bring me another shot, will you?"

"Right," said Ernie. He served a second shot glass of the bourbon. "You got enough soda there? Yeah, you got enough soda."

"I don't want any soda. I'm drinking this straight."

"Yeah, bourbon ought to be drunk straight. Bourbon has a flavor that if you ask me, you oughtn't to dilute it. That is, if you happen to like the taste of bourbon in the first place. Personally, I don't. I'll take a drink of bourbon, like if I'm at a football game to see the New York Giants. Or you take if I'm out in the woods, looking for deer, I usely take a pint of rye with me, or sometimes bourbon. It'll ward off the cold and the taste lasts longer. But for all-day drinking, I stick to scatch. You don't get tired of the taste of scatch. Your rye and your bourbon, they're too sweet if you're gonna drink all day. You know a funny thing about scatch, it's getting to be the most popular drink in France and Japan. That was in an article I read, this magazine I get. You know, in this business we get these magazines. I guess you have them in the car business. Trade publications, they're known as."

"Even the undertakers."

"Huh?"

"The undertakers have trade publications."

"They do, ah? Well, wuddia know. I guess every business has them."

"Every business is the same, when you come right down to it," said Mark McGranville.

"Well that's a new one on me. We're all in it for the money, but what's the same about selling cars and pushing Old Gutburner?"

"What you just said," said Mark McGranville. "We're all in it for the money. You. Me. Undertakers."

"You're talking like an I-don't-know-what," said Ernie.

"I know I am. What do I owe you?"

"Be—nothing," said Ernie.

"On the house?"

"Come in again when you'll get some enjoyment out of it. I don't want to take your money under these conditions."

"You, Ernie?"

"Yeah, me. You got sumpn eatin' you, boy, whatever it is."

"I know I have," said Mark McGranville. "Maybe it's the weather. I don't know."

"Well, my booze won't do it any good, Mark. I get days like this myself, once in a great while. The women get them all the time, but that's different. Take in a show tonight. You know this English fellow, with the big gap in his teeth. Terry?"

"Terry-Thomas."

"He's at the Carteret. He's always good for a laugh. You're not a booze man, Mark. Some are, but not you. You were taking it like medicine, for God's sake. Castor oil or something."

"Yeah. Well, thanks, Ernie. See you," said Mark McGranville.

He could not understand why he went through dinner and the entire evening without telling Jean about the T-Bird and the two Galaxies in one day. He knew that it was because he did not want to give her any good news; that much he understood. She would respond to the good news as she always did, enthusiastically and proudly, and he was in no mood to share her enthusiasm or accept the compliment of her pride in him. All that he understood, but he could not understand why he preferred to remain in this mood. She would cheer him up, and he did not want to be cheered up. He was perfunctory when the kids kissed him goodnight, and after the eleven o'clock news on the TV he rose, snapped the power dial, and went to the bedroom. He was in bed when Jean kissed him goodnight and turned out the light.

"Mark?" she said, from her bed.

"What?"

"Is there something the matter?"

"Nope."

"Goodnight," she said.

"Goodnight," said Mark McGranville.

Five, ten dark minutes passed.

"If you don't want to tell me," she said.

"How the hell can I tell you when I don't know myself?" he said.

"Oh," she said. "Shall I come over?"

"I just as soon you wouldn't," he said. "I don't know what it is."

"If I come over, you'll sleep better," she said.

"Jean, please. It isn't that. Christ, I sold two Galaxies and a T-Bird today—"

"You *did?*"

"That ought to make me feel good, but I don't know what's the matter with me. I had a couple drinks at Ernie's, but nothing."

"I knew you had something to drink. It didn't show, but I could smell it."

"Oh, I'm not hiding anything."

"You hid it about the Galaxies and the T-Bird."

"I know I did. I'd have told you in the morning."

"All right. Goodnight."

"Goodnight," he said.

He thought his mind was busy, busy, busy, and that he had been unable to get to sleep, but at five minutes past two he looked at the radium hands of the alarm clock and realized that he must have slept for at least an hour, that some of the activity of his mind was actually dreams. They were not frightening dreams or lascivious ones; they were not much of anything but mental activity that had taken place while he thought he was awake but must have been asleep. Jean was asleep, breathing regularly. She made two musical notes in deep sleep, the first two notes of "Yes Sir That's My Baby"; the *yes* note as she exhaled, the *sir* as she drew breath. And yet he could tell, in spite of the dark, that she would be slightly frowning, dreaming or thinking, one or the other or both. He had so often watched her asleep, physically asleep, and making the musical notes of her regular breathing, but the slight frown revealing that her mind was at work, that her intelligence was functioning in ways that would always be kept secret from him, possibly even from herself. It was not that her sleeping face was a mask; far from it. The mask was her wakeful face, telling only her responses to things that

114   THE ART OF BURNING BRIDGES

happened and were said, the obvious responses to pleasant and unpleasant things in life. But in the frowning placidity of sleep her mind was naked. It did not matter that he could not read her thoughts; they were there, far more so than when she was awake.

He got out of bed and went to the warm living room and turned on one bulb in a table lamp. He lit a cigarette and took the first drag, but he let it go out. He was thirty years old, a good father, a good husband, and so well thought of that Mrs. Preston would make sure that he got credit for a sale. His sister had a good job, and his mother was taken care of. On the sales blackboard at the garage his name was always first or second, in two years had not been down to third. Nevertheless he went to the hall closet and got out his 20-gauge and broke it and inserted a shell.

He returned to his chair and re-lit the cigarette that had gone out, and this time he smoked rapidly. The shotgun rested with the butt on the floor, the barrel lying against his thigh, and he held the barrel loosely with the fingers of his left hand as he smoked. The cigarette was now down to an inch in length, and he crushed it carefully.

Her voice came softly. "Mark," she said.

He looked at the carpet. "What?" he said.

"Don't. Please?"

"I won't," he said.

The situation of "How Can I Tell You?" is simple: For reasons less clear to Mark than to the reader, the day's events sadden the salesman, husband, and father, and he stops on the way home for a couple of drinks of bourbon. Afterward, in response to his wife's simple, eloquent plea—"Don't. Please?"—the sixth personal question he has been asked in the story, the previous five having generated five lies, he says, "I won't."

It's difficult to imagine how so short a story can give more. Here are the assured cadences of particular speech that O'Hara had painstakingly developed in his apprentice sketches for the *New Yorker*. But here, too, is the choreography of the novelist he was on the point of becoming in the early 1930s: three characters bear down on Mark McGranville, the only one of the four dignified with full identity, both Christian and family names. The outcome of this pressure is developed with a speed that in his earliest fiction failed for haste and in his prolix novels was lost to languor. The matter-of-fact third-person announcement that McGranville's sales history was "very good for one day" is immediately unbalanced by the peculiarities of at least one of these transactions.

Like Bartleby's boss waving a bouquet of papers to be copied by the scrivener without troubling to engage his employee's eye, Mrs. Preston imperiously and without prelude to the son of her former servant points to a magazine ad and demands to know, "Do you have one of these in stock, in red?" When the salesman assures her that he can get one, his dignified solicitations are met with belligerent interrogations, she jabbing and him dodging. The salesman does his work well—his rope-a-dope bags him a sale—but the combat is not without cost. Mrs. Preston exercises her power brutally. Her power derives from money—to which Mark McGranville might reasonably aspire—but more fundamentally from social superiority, against whose givens he can't hazard to beat his fist. This despair might have been sufficient to corner a character in a lesser O'Hara story, but "How Can I Tell You?" goes further: "He's a very lucky boy," the salesman observes, almost wistfully. Then he's pulled up short: "He's a good boy, Mark. Not a lucky boy." And when McGranville agrees, Mrs. Preston is indifferent to his "Yes, he's one of best," returning at once to her peremptory interrogations, climaxing with the urgent and resonant question at the core of this story titled with a question: "But how do you know he has what *I* want?"

Finally, Mrs. Preston, who has met no resistance to her capricious wants, is mollified. The deal is cemented with the salesman's deferential, "You're right, Mrs. Preston." Now she donates some small talk, asking cursorily after his wife and children. "They're fine, thank you. Very fine," he lies. She remarks that the fellow who has just so faithfully served her fancy has "always been a good boy, too," but it can't be lost on the reader that nobody is presenting Mark McGranville with a red T-bird, that luck just may have something to do with outcome. Finally, Mrs. Preston's notice is drawn to the salesman's mother, her former housekeeper. This is conveyed with appropriate and masterful delicacy, taking care not to lean too hard on the mistress-domestic configuration. It is a restrained and scrupulous virtue that McGranville is not revealed to brood about this indignity; O'Hara trusts the reader to allow the transaction between buyer and seller to ramify, not as an illustrated meditation on Class and Power but rather an illumination of one character subject to life's accumulated blows, a man cornered.

McGranville can scarcely explain to himself why he feels so uneasy, or why he tries Ernie's taproom for consolation. This is not his custom, though there is some suggestion in the story that it might once have been. As deliberately as Nick Adams would prepare a campsite, the salesman locks his car, hangs "his hat and coat on the clothestree." Ernie's "Well, hi, stranger," stuttering with commas, bristles with resentment. *Stranger* reverberates, leaving Ernie's customer—now in a caricatured inversion of the role of Mrs. Preston—accused and alienated. "How's it with you?" Ernie pretends to care to know. "Not bad. Pretty good," McGranville again lies. Then Ernie casually defames the customers of last night, and the customer of today heedlessly colludes in the slander of Charlotte and Paul (himself a gossip in this mean, small town). "But [he's] a friend of yours, though, isn't he?" Ernie disingenuously wonders, stabbing with emphatic redundance, *but* and *though*. "I guess so," Mark McGranville lies. "Is there anything the matter?" Ernie again pretends to care to know. "No," McGranville continues to lie. "Why?"

This *Why?* is shrewd and grievous. It has the subversively bank-shot indirection of O'Hara's signature dialogue-as-combat that cleared the way for a dialectic revolution in dramatic action brought to its recent apex by Harold Pinter and David Mamet. A speaker can't ask a Pinter character what's the time of day without getting in response the equivalent of that *why*, a self-inquisition that asks as well: why should I prefer one bourbon over another, why doesn't bourbon click in, why would I want to listen to music?

Ernie, in the story's longest speech, and second-longest paragraph, delivers a monologue of such relentless banality that it is a mark of McGranville's dislocation that he actually listens—through a choking fog of anxiety—to its untransitioned sequences, and responds, "Even the undertakers," to which Ernie sensibly comes back, "Huh?"

The salesman then embarks on a meandering diatribe against capitalism, the system, ambition, human nature. Ernie's alarmed: "You're talking like an I-don't-know-what." This isn't a town where you lightly call a customer a Commie, but Mark McGranville knows what the barkeep means to say. With one stunning achievement of irreducible clarity, he says, "I know I am," and then asks—is there any crueler way to wonder?—"What do I owe you?" And my God, Ernie, elliptically yet with an answering clarity, says "Be—nothing."

This is writing, this is feeling, of a high order. Everything that O'Hara would need to know for the composition of this story he had learned by the time he turned tail from his cheerless home in Pottsville, where his mother fretted how to put an extra meal on the table for her eldest son, and tried to divert him with amusing vignettes of the very proceedings of her women's groups that had fed his *New Yorker* Delphian sketches, which now so wearied him. O'Hara was already a virtuoso of the music of exhaustion. Mark McGranville, like John O'Hara that Christmas season, "did not want to be cheered up." "Is there something the matter?" Jean asks. "Nope," he lies. The acts that confirm his resolute despair—snapping off the power dial on the TV, lying silent in their shared bedroom while "five, ten dark minutes passed" (an excruciating duration in so short a story)—these dead-end choices, hammered shut by a series of "Goodnight"s, close his case.

The deliberation he brings to his surroundings as his story winds down is a final oppression. The odd sentence "He thought his mind was busy, busy, busy" has access to the conscious state of the near-suicide that the living can only stab at imagining. To hear the musical notes of a wife's deep sleep—"Yes Sir That's My Baby"—that's pure O'Hara, a reaching down to observe some essential detail, the *telling* detail. And the cigarette lit and—like whiskey, music, the TV's power, good news of good business—immediately snuffed: what more can be said? One more thing, after marking time by the cigarette re-lit and smoked to mark an end to time: "I won't."

These final words go, I think, beyond *non serviam*.

What happened to O'Hara in Pottsville during those dark months in 1930 of soul-scouring can't be specified, but it's reasonable to guess that he sounded a kind of abyss. Writers—or anyone who has suffered the flu—will recognize that odd state he must have entered, a numb reverie not unlike the fevered sweats Keats endured from consumption, and an extraordinary out-of-himselfness (gussied up in Keats's case as selfless "poetical character . . . not itself, everything and nothing," having "no Identity," continually "filling some other Body")* physiologically congruent with the creative state. Keats complained that "I am in that temper that if I were under water I would scarcely kick to come to the top." But the reason his state then is available is that he composed it, considered an order of words that would reveal it, and by this process kicked right on up to the top. Although O'Hara sank into an overstuffed chair moping and despairing—from his younger brother's vantage—he was also fever-

*To Richard Woodhouse, October 27, 1818.

ishly trying to place work at *Scribner's Magazine,* sending proposals and reams of pages to Kyle Crichton. Charles Scribner—book publisher of Fitzgerald, Wolfe, and Hemingway—had one of the three magazines that, with the *New Yorker* and *Vanity Fair,* might be suited to O'Hara's preoccupations and gifts. When he submitted to *Scribner's* stories that had been declined by the other two, he was candid about their histories, even telling Crichton why they had been refused—too oblique, too limited in range, too dirty.

Crichton said no, and no, and no, but he also explicitly framed for the writer his inherent weaknesses and potential strengths. In one rejection letter from those dispiriting weeks, responding that a particular story was "a bit slight for our use" (and don't you love "a bit" in such a charge?), he allowed that what O'Hara did best was "modern conversation," and urged him to combine that virtue with "a little deeper content" (ditto "a little" in such an exhortation?).[52] Well, a little deeper was where O'Hara was digging. If it hadn't quite yet shown in his work, he was meditating on those personal and family and social histories that were within a year or two to ripen into his breakthrough story and breakthrough novel, "The Doctor's Son" and *Appointment in Samarra.*

Meantime, he was crazy lonely. His eldest brother, Joe, was bunking with the long-suffering McKees in East Orange during the week and driving home on weekends to comfort his mother in her failure to do the same for her sad boy. Later, for interviewers, Joe would compete with Tom in his account of the extravagance of John's melancholy, noting that it got so bad that he'd passed the hours memorizing *A Farewell to Arms* beginning to end. An unlikely story, I think, but it is surely true that O'Hara was sedulously studying the structure of extended narrative from Hemingway's example. Almost thirty years later, in one of the few craft lectures he consented to deliver, he remembered having been so struck by Hemingway's paragraphing—blocks of type—"that I remembered it photographically."[53] Though Hemingway's music, what William S. Gass has called in reference to Stein "the geography" of the sentences, did not seep into his customary straight-ahead expository beat, what is certain is that O'Hara courageously, in the face of hard news from New York, continued to instruct himself how best to write.

At the end of the Washington's Birthday holiday in 1931, Joe drove John to East Orange, and six days later, on February 28, after a cycle of flamboyant New York parties culminating in a scene hatched at a speakeasy, John married Helen Ritchie Petit at the city hall. He and "Pet" had met, at a New York Equity Ball, no more than a couple of months before they married. Slight, with a delicately boned face and deep blue eyes and gold hair to her waist, she was twenty-two, an aspiring actress, a graduate of Wellesley who had studied at the Sorbonne and had an M.A. from Columbia. Several interviewers got dissimilar versions of her character from different friends. If one declared that her Wellesley classmate was "fastidious," another noted that her clothes often seemed to need cleaning. She was said to have had an "Alice-in-Wonderland" air, or else to have been "jumpy." She was bright and witty, and was accused of indulging in enigmatic conversations that were onerous to follow (maybe only to friends who were not bright and witty). There was general agreement that she gave off an "iridescent air," and O'Hara is quoted by Finis Farr as remarking that "she had a shine all around her."

Miss Petit was off to a quick start in the theater, playing the ingenue opposite Eddie Albert's lead in *Room Service,* a successful Broadway farce. She enjoyed speakeasy culture and spirits, and evidently believed it to have been the soul of wit when her suitor rode off on a horse belonging to a (dis)mounted policeman watering at the trough of Tony's, where the wedding plans were raucously laid, including a solemn promise by Jimmy Walker to perform the ceremony. Walker was not known as the "late mayor of New York" for nothing, and when Hizzoner's tardiness gave way to absence, a city clerk was press-ganged into officiating. O'Hara's mother—together with Mr. and Mrs. America, from Border to Border and Coast to Coast and all the Ships at Sea—first learned of the "welding" from Walter Winchell's evening radio broadcast, to which she listened faithfully, as her firstborn and recent boarder well knew. Taking into account O'Hara's enduring affection for his mother, it is difficult to imagine what provoked such a slight or such cowardice. That the impulsive bride and groom were married at city hall and not in a church? That Helen Petit was Episcopalian? Mrs. O'Hara understood that her son, drifting far from her faith, was long gone over the horizon, and she had written letters to his former Niagara schoolmate—the soon-to-be-ordained Father Beatty—anguishing about the apostate libertine's scandalous New York life. (In fact, the day after the civil ceremony, from remorse, the newlyweds proposed to Beatty that he bless their marriage, but he piously declined, inasmuch as the couple had been "living in sin.")[54] Still, O'Hara's failure to phone or cable his mother seems aberrant. Did he nurse some resentment from his weeks under her roof as an almsman? Or, more likely, did he know that his mother would be dismayed that he had undertaken, with so few prospects, so great a responsibility?

Surely the bride's mother, similarly kept out of the loop, was aghast and then some. So hostile had she been to her only child's friendship with the detested ne'er-had-done- and probably-ne'er-would-do-well that she refused to convey courtship telephone messages from him to her. So hostile was she that Miss Petit's collision with her mother's stonewall resistance, in the timeworn way of such things, bounced the promising young girl back into O'Hara's arms. On form, it is not difficult to sympathize with Ma Petit's misgivings. But it is also generally acknowledged by everyone consulted in this matter that the woman was a battle-ax. Previous accounts have judged her a "dragon," an "appalling woman," "monstrous," "odious," the "world's champion bad mother-in-law." Pet Petit's father had walked out on her, and nobody at the time or later seemed puzzled by his outing. The shrew was said to have been "incurably unhappy," given to hand-wringing and heaving sobs. It was told by a college friend of her daughter (known as "Petey" to her friends and "Stubby" to her mother, before O'Hara re-nicknamed her "Pet") that Mrs. Petit had characteristically made good on a threat to scream her lungs out in the middle of the Budapest Corso in response to her daughter's reluctance to accompany her to an American restaurant there.

Until her marriage, Miss Petit lived with her mother in the Flatbush quarter of Brooklyn—540 Ocean Avenue—under the generous protection of her bachelor uncle David ("Dee") M. Mahood, a prosperous inventor with profitable engineering patents and a fondness for his niece. His ameliorating influence had inspired Mrs. Petit to announce the wedding in the *Brooklyn Eagle* (which had the groom a graduate of Fordham University), and secured the bride an allowance—nominally funded by her mother—of a hundred dollars a month. By means of this money and a loan co-signed by Joe O'Hara, the couple set up housekeeping at 41 West 52nd, an apartment recommended by his sister Mary and all too convenient to Tony's and "21." It was a renter's market for apartments after the Crash, and no trick to find a nice place for fifty a month, with a loose lease and the possibility of having the first month's rent forgiven. Even so, having subtracted rent from the dowry, O'Hara understood that he needed a job.

He got one as a New York press agent for Warner Brothers, writing movie ads and flacking for stars needful of interviews in the many papers from which he'd been fired. Matthew J. Bruccoli has tracked down his hokum for James Cagney's *Public Enemy,* a gem of fluff and nonsense that ran in the *New York Times* seven weeks after the wedding:

> There exists today a world within our world that we dare not ignore. And monarch of this unlicenced kingdom is "The Public Enemy."
>
> He is here! We know he is here! . . . But what is he? Why is he? Who is he?
>
> Thursday morning you will meet him face to face. Thursday morning you will witness a new milestone of cinema accomplishment—a slice of today's life—quivering!—real!—unadorned!—astounding![55]

Astounding is right! O'Hara hadn't plumbed bottom in Pottsville, after all. Not to solemnize the asinine, but how many times could a writer of his gifts compose humbug such as this and rise to write again?

An abrupt reversal of fortune came in the form of a thousand-dollar gift from Uncle Dee, earmarked for a honeymoon. The couple considered Paris, and then—thinking practically and productively—they settled on a trip to Bermuda, to the end of giving the new husband a serene and healthful situation for his work. (Wolcott Gibbs had taken his wedding trip to Bermuda, and this encouraged O'Hara's interest in the island.) By the end of June they found themselves at Paget East, in "Greenway," a two-bedroomed yellow cottage near Elbow Beach. The rent was fifty dollars per month, and they immediately settled into a routine of reading, and he into steady, ground-gaining writing. They walked, rode bikes, relaxed, kept regular hours, and—in the miraculous manner of work's potent cures—forgot to drink themselves silly.

In a letter to Bob Simonds, mailed a couple of weeks after they arrived, O'Hara described the routine: "We just don't drink. No resolutions or anything of the kind. It just doesn't seem to occur to us. We bought a bottle of gin when we got here, and we still have it, two weeks and one day later. Pet reads, and I have done a lot of writing. We eat and smoke, and at night we sometimes knock off a bottle of ale and a bottle of porter, and that's just about our life. I bike to Hamilton (about twelve minutes going, fifteen coming back on account of a hillock) once or twice a day to mail letters and buy the papers and magazines and cigarettes. I haven't even got a sunburn. . . . So far I have resisted the impulse to buy a pith helmet, but I do wear linens or flannels all the time."[56]

At the time, Simonds was enduring his own frustrations of career and doubts about his future with a steady girlfriend. The O'Haras invited the couple to visit Bermuda; the two friends, who had plotted before the marriage to travel together and make together a two-member frat house in New York, now found themselves domesticated. Perhaps this unsettling change rather than shallow envy spurred Simonds many years later to abet Beverly Gary's bloody hatchet job in the *New York Post*'s serial catchpenny defamation of O'Hara. She revealed that when his best friend met Simonds's boat at the Bermuda dock he was a "sporting fashion-plate," an overnight Bermudian "wearing Bermuda shorts, a pith helmet and riding a bicycle."[57]

This petty matter—hardly petty to its victim at the time—is a casebook instance of biography's limits. In a dispute freighted with malice— the warring versions of a particular Paris dinner as narrated by Gertrude Stein in her *Autobiography of Alice B. Toklas* and by Ernest Hemingway in his *Moveable Feast*—memory's rearview mirror is clouded by the smog of righteousness and repudiation. Gertrude Stein recalls that Hemingway and his first wife invited her and her companion to a simple meal at their romantically simple flat above the romantically redolent saw mill. It was a fine dinner, until Hemingway ruined it by insisting that Stein read his latest short story, right there, right then. In *his* version, he and his wife had invited Miss Stein and her companion to a simple meal, etcetera, a fine occasion until, against all that he understood to be decorous, she insisted on reading his latest work, right there, right then. Who's lying? Probably neither. I suspect that—accompanied by unserious offers and unfelt murmurs of modesty—Gertrude Stein did actually, there and then, read pages by Ernest Hemingway. But whose idea, or fault, this was . . . who knows?

Did O'Hara wear a pith helmet in Bermuda when he met Simonds's boat? I don't know, but would guess that he didn't; and I also imagine that if he did, it was by way of a joke. Did Simonds mean to injure his old friend when he passed this slur to Beverly Gary, *if* he blabbed it to her? I think maybe, a little. I think, too, he may have mistaken, thirty-eight years after the event, a phrase in a letter—"So far I have resisted the impulse to buy a pith helmet"—for a confession of ungoverned and ill-calibrated display that corresponded with his least fond memories of the writer. It matters, because the mosaic of O'Hara's reputation has been fabricated from such farcical snapshots: Cowpoke O'Hara in chaps and ten-gallon hat, Colonel Blimp O'Hara in walking shorts and a pith helmet.

In fact, Simonds and his Coaldale fiancée, Catherine Melley, had a convivial visit with the O'Haras. The four danced to "Star Dust" at a dinner party on the roof of the Hamilton Hotel, inspiring Simonds to recollect many years later for Finis Farr that "the sky was so clear it seemed one could reach out and pick a star." Then, by coincidence, singing their way home in a horse-drawn carriage, the four bumped into a female friend from Miss Melley's hometown. What was really going on in O'Hara's Bermuda—as he well understood—was the assembly of O'Hara's own native haunt, his Region, which he began layering into one fictional representation after another. In addition to working on "The Doctor's Son," he had been stimulated by Scribner's announcement of a short-novel prize of five thousand dollars to undertake a novel set in a society and geography much like Pottsville's. Kyle Crichton—whose annual salary was thirty-six hundred—encouraged O'Hara to apply, and between late June and mid-August he worked frantically to finish a draft of his first book, *The Hofman Estate*, the sole copy of which he mailed to New York on August 18.

Crichton was a fellow Pennsylvanian, raised in the soft coal region, a miner's son educated formally at Lehigh and politically by laboring in the state's bituminous pits and at Bethlehem Steel. Using the pen name Robert Forsythe, he wrote acerbic profiles of American celebrities for the *Daily Worker* and the *New Masses*. The two had first met face to face at Scribner's editorial waiting room, before the trip to Bermuda. Crichton later remembered an old wooden bench with a high back: "This was the mourner's bench on which I, as the second editor, met the yearning geniuses with their manuscripts. . . . We struck up an immediate friendship on the basis of the fact that he knew almost as many recent graduates of Lehigh as I did."[58]

O'Hara had every reason to assume Crichton's friendliness toward his work, and he corresponded with the editor as though he were an accomplice in the competition rather than a judge. *Scribner's Magazine* had just paid seventy-five dollars for his story "Alone" (which condemns the *New Yorker* as a magazine its protagonist has always "vaguely resented"). His trust in Crichton's advocacy might have prompted his bumptious candor in a cover letter sent with *The Hofman Estate:* "Here is the short novel by that amazing young genius, O'Hara, who will be hurled into the literary spotlight by winning the Scribner's contest. . . . The piece, you will find, moves fast. . . . The pace is mine and the piece has been written so fast (it's really journalistic) that there hasn't been much time for Influences."[59] He added that it needed retyping, that he was mailing the original and had made no copy, and that he'd welcome a decision "as soon as possible," together with "any moneys accruing to the author at this point."

The greenest tenderfoot among today's aspiring writers would know better than to mail such a brash appeal to an acquiring editor. The craft of the cover letter was long ago thoroughly mastered: never explain or apologize; be brief, be blunt, be gone; keep a copy and send an S.A.S.E; don't beg, whine, or carry on. Such taciturnity must be taught because it runs counter to every instinct of a writer who has just put "The End" (or "—30—") to the final page of a first draft. Whatever chemicals are released in the brain during prolonged concentration and invention, they cloud common sense, and if chemicals didn't distort reason no one would make it halfway through the composition of a book, let alone finish it. It's such an improbable notion at heart, to imagine that the world wishes to shut up and listen to one's account of the Hofman estate— whatever that might be—or of a solo fishing trip in Michigan, or of growing up in a prairie town. To make up stories and then expect to be paid to have them spread to the four corners, why this is rash and unguarded, a formula for making a jackass of oneself. So hooray for O'Hara that he didn't know better how to manage his career, or didn't care to know, or fooled himself into having faith that the world hungered to know what he hungered to tell.

Crichton—responding indeed "as soon as possible"—rejected *The Hofman Estate* ten days after it was mailed. His bluntest criticism was of erotic passages, on the grounds that they were erotic, just as he and Maxwell Perkins would object later to O'Hara's unsentimental portrayals of priests and nuns in his short fiction. Such editorial delicacy, in the context of Perkins's resistance to Hemingway's rougher diction, casts a shadow of doubt over Crichton's sunny 1960 remembrances of *Scrib-*

ner's editorial fearlessness: "Being an editor at *Scribner's* was pure joy. There were no sacred cows to worry about, there were no prejudices or taboos or angles. Nobody was concerned about the teen-age public, or the woman's audience, or the churches."[60] In 1933, refusing *Appointment in Samarra,* Crichton spoke for Perkins when he objected to passages too blatantly carnal, and to others offensive to Catholics: "The theme again—the terrible theme. They [*Scribner's* upper echelons] just won't look at anything like this, and there is no use in my passing it on. You'll have to push yourself around and give out an aura of sweetness and light some way or you'll have a hard time with us."[61]

O'Hara took the news well, almost too well. He now began a habit of redoubling his effort when he lost sight of the goal, and his loyalty to *The Hofman Estate* was contingent upon its being agreeable to publishers. He had always met rejection with renewed submission—in the resonant term—and the first paragraph of his response to Crichton's crushing rebuff (not only for the prize but for publication as a runner-up) was stouthearted. "I'm still a bit groggy," the spurned and sapped writer wrote, "having just received The Hofman Estate and your note, which, I must say, broke it as gently as possible, and thanks for so doing. Anyhow, here are some pieces."[62]

It does not require exquisite insight to imagine how it must have felt—how it feels—to have such an offering returned to sender. The very speed of the gesture, thumbs-down, must have stung. Writers never forget that particular pain, a stab of shame that something tended and tendered has been repulsed. It is a short hop from the fact of denial to a vivid sense of the denier's repulsion. (More than once, more than a dozen times, I have heard writers confess variations on a common visualized theme, that of an agent or editor—eyes averted and nose pinched shut with one hand—returning with the other extended arm a box of pages, holding the pathetic thing like a turd at the end of a very long set of tongs.) By the accumulation of not-for-mes an imaginative inventor might become "a master of the fancied slight." The flat-broke and rejected author's steadiness in the face of so large a failure, the persistence of "some pieces" sent into the cold wind of Crichton's dismissal, these acts steeled him to be a pro, for better and worse.

The for-better facet was stamina, tenacity in the performance of his labor. Unbroken stream doesn't begin to describe the widgets that coursed down this writer's production line. But factory recalls weren't in

the picture, and that was the for-worse aspect. If a piece of work wasn't
accepted, the rejecting editor's hostility toward that submission was no
match for its author's. According to Pet and John both, he flushed the
only copy of *The Hofman Estate* down a storm drain after it didn't make
the cut at *Scribner's.* This is no more true than the myths Faulkner per-
petuated about his habit of writing in the furnace room at Ole Miss (in
1933 O'Hara wrote a letter of apology to Crichton, whom he had
wrongly accused of losing the typescript, which in fact was squirreled
away in a file marked "Second Thoughts"), but the fib signaled his dis-
loyalty to work that didn't give an immediate return on its investment.
The Hofman Estate represented too substantial a promise of acceptance
for O'Hara not to submit it elsewhere, which he did. But Crichton, in a
letter mailed a few days after the return of the typescript, was prescient
in his warning against sloppy impatience, urging him "passionately to
rework" rather than immediately to resubmit the book, to Ogden Nash
at Farrar & Rhinehart, who had expressed interest in seeing it. "I think it
would be a mistake for you to waste the thing and also harm your reputation by giving it publication without first working on it more. . . . For
God's sake don't rush into print and get the reputation as a light
weight."[63]

This would become a recurring tension at the *New Yorker,* O'Hara's
refusal to revise in any but the superficial manner. Other prolific writers
have shown contempt for a return to the drawing board, for reshaping,
even for sanding and polishing. Anthony Burgess comes to mind; he had
a theory that the integrity of the creative process was fundamentally
diminished by tuning up, or by the coldblooded rearrangement of the
parts in what he took to be an organic whole. Some writers—few to my
knowledge—can only make successive drafts worse, piling on detail
willy-nilly and slopping ever thicker and more garish coats of paint on
the delicate surface of a simple fabrication. Others, recognizing their
congenital vice, swear off the practice of revision, trusting absolutely the
hot promises of the Muse, that treacherous bitch. Thomas Mann's attentive power was said to be such that he composed and stored his work in
his mind, and much later revised it there, and then—to make it available
to those who didn't live in his head—transcribed the revised version into
what was only nominally a first draft. O'Hara made something of the
same claim for his own cohesive power of composition. He testified
more than once, perhaps too defensively, that deadline pressure when

he was a reporter and rewrite man had taught him to get the story—or novel—just so on the first go, and that he wouldn't tolerate editing because his work didn't need any. In common with many of his principles, this hardened into sometimes blockheaded obstinacy. Certainly his stubbornness made an impression on out-of-town newcomers to literary New York. Jerome Weidman, twenty in 1933, remembered for Matthew J. Bruccoli his encounter with O'Hara in the lobby of the *New Yorker,* after Weidman had had a stormy editorial meeting with Harold Ross. O'Hara stood the younger man to a cup of coffee, and offered what Weidman characterized as the "only lesson I ever had in how to write a short story." Listen sharp: "Once you have finished a story, there's only one way to improve it: tell the editor to go to hell."[64]

Nonsense. Such bully-boy posturing must have done great damage to O'Hara's work. It can be destructive, of course, to accept on faith editorial direction whose aim is to smooth, sweeten, regularize, remove difficulty, sap surprise. But even then, such editorial counsel is only damaging to the degree that the writer enacts it. A refusal to listen to an editor's response is no wiser than a refusal to listen to yourself build a vagrant story idea into a story. The issue of line-editing, the attempt by literalists—especially at the *New Yorker*—to correct on behalf of standard usage some of O'Hara's inspired dialogue solecisms,* became a red herring, an insupportable rationale for artistic sloth. Even admiring editors, Crichton and Katharine White especially, rightly begged him to slow down, to consider, to review. No way. The older he grew, the more stubborn. His friend and fan David Brown, a movie producer, likened O'Hara's chosen method—"he wrote for the printer"—to shooting live television, trying to edit in the camera. O'Hara had no such gun to his head, but speed-typing on pulpy paper, keeping no carbon copy, as though being a daily reporter on deadline, suited him—as long as he wasn't being paid to do it for a magazine or newspaper.

Crichton, responding to his plea from Bermuda for quick money during the brief period when *The Hofman Estate* was under consideration, also

---

*O'Hara's characters' speech enacts exactly Ambrose Bierce's definition of grammar as "a system of pitfalls thoughtfully prepared for the feet of the self-made man, along the path by which he advances to distinction" (Ambrose Bierce, *The Devil's Dictionary* [New York: Oxford University Press, 1993], p. 44).

urged him to come back to New York, "where you b'long." He counseled him not to let "a little thing like money worry you. Borrow it from the in-laws."[65] The O'Haras arrived in New York in mid-September and, having given up their apartment, moved in with uncle and mother-in-law. It was a horror, a Punch 'n' Judy show of recrimination, I-told-you-sos, fore-head-smiting, maledictions both sotto voce and shouted. Mrs. Petit had been steered to believe that O'Hara had taken a leave of absence, rather than quit, his Warner Brothers job. Shortly after a late-October retreat from Brooklyn to 19 West 55th, another fifty-per-month apartment, O'Hara wrote to Simonds to explain his failure to promptly answer his friend's premarital grumblings:

> I was then in the throes of something which, I daresay, was a bit more immediately troublesome than your own problem in Coaldale. I was having mother-in-law trouble, which can be all that the comic supple-ments reveal. . . . The result was simply hell. . . . On at least one occa-sion I got so drunk that I passed the evening in a speakeasy and did not return home to Brooklyn. . . . Mrs. O'Hara and I have done a good deal of drinking since Bermuda, you will not be interested to know. We have a nice enough apartment; very likely will look very lupine when the rent comes due, which is Dec. 1, thus leaving me flat on my ass for Christ-mas, which is as it should be. It will be something not to have to be sorry about not giving Christmas presents this year. I've been sorry so many years that it almost spoiled my holidays.[66]

The move to West 55th had been made possible by the *New Yorker,* which gave him a drawing account of seventy-five per week to produce "Talk of the Town" pieces. Like so many unions between this writer and that institution, it would soon end badly, with bitterness on his side and a good share of blame on the magazine's. Six months earlier, shortly before the newlyweds went to Bermuda, Harold Ross had advanced a small sum to the flat-broke bridegroom. When O'Hara thanked him, Ross responded with disarming humility that the management had lent him the money: "I didn't. There is quite a distinction there as I am trying to get rid of the paternal and financial aspects of this job."[67] The managing editor at that time, James M. Cain, surely not a name that leaps to mind when one considers bureaucratic propriety, had established a policy that all advances had to be cleared through him. When he learned of the

O'Hara pittance, Cain complained to Ross, who rescinded the advance, bitterly blaming the blameless writer for his own embarrassment. Cain told Matthew J. Bruccoli that this caused him to feel such guilt that he quit, and lit out for Hollywood.

This was not a happy marriage. According to Bernard Bergman, who edited "Talk of the Town," Ross "took a dislike to O'Hara from the day he was hired and rejected every O'Hara piece I turned in."[68] (Ross's animus was not exclusively against O'Hara, but also against his journalism, as the editor preferred him to stick to fiction. In 1978, Bergman told the *Pottsville Republican* that "O'Hara didn't realize that if someone hired you for a job, you were supposed to show up nearly every day, and usually sober." But Bergman's versions to others took a more bewildered line, recalling that O'Hara had been "a hard worker" with "a lot of talent," who had produced commendable work during his time on the staff, most notably an "especially charming" account of a slow air voyage over Manhattan in the Goodyear dirigible *Columbia*. No matter; Ross "didn't want O'Hara around. . . . Why I never knew."[69] Bergman's boss commanded O'Hara's boss to fire him, complaining that he was "into us for three hundred dollars. Fire him before we're in him for more."[70] Though Bergman found the once-again-canned reporter a job as a movie flack at RKO, O'Hara never forgave him. Years later, running into his former employee in a bar, Bergman tried to shake hands. He got the iceman's stare, and "Bergman, you fired me, you sonofabitch. Now look at me and look at you."[71]

The other marriage wasn't any happier, though there were pacific interludes. Kyle Crichton remembered Pet Petit fondly as "nice and pretty," a young married woman "whose parents [sic] used to send over their dinner by cab in a specially-made aluminum warming contraption." (Despite the stormy fiasco that fall in Brooklyn, the O'Haras nevertheless ate dinner there with Mrs. Petit at least once a month, and went with her to listen to the New York Philharmonic.) The young couple would host modest parties, playing charades and serving bathtub gin, and then—Crichton remembered—they might wander over to a pool hall on Sixth Avenue, "wholesome and innocent, and I think we had a good time."[72] A friend of Pet O'Hara told Finis Farr that often John was chipper, "amusing, amused, in tune with the world."

But more often he quarreled bitterly with Pet, jealous, to an acute degree, of imaginary rivals, or of his wife's imaginary flirtations with actual friends. Let her speak to any man at Tony's or Bleeck's and O'Hara would accuse her publicly and in full cry of laying plans to sleep with that man. She complained to her friends that life with him was becoming "unendurable." Finis Farr, with the advantage of personal observation, reasons that O'Hara was tormented by his "vivid imagination, for in those days he had cast everyone he knew in a melodrama . . . and he had a theory that he needed to study people under stress. If there wasn't any stress, he appeared . . . to be trying to create some." He mocked his wife's theatrical yearnings. When Pet later opened in the "damn" revue, *New Faces of 1934,* O'Hara wrote Simonds that he hated the very thought of it. "I think all actors are terrible people. As Benchley once said, Scratch an actor and get an actor."[73] O'Hara's *New Yorker* profile of a chorine begins with a spiteful, glancing ricochet off a theatrical type, the "sloe-eyed lady in the Living Picture number, who is a Phi Beta Kappa from the University of Wisconsin, and is taking an extension course, on Dante, at Columbia."[74] Pet wearied of his increasing preoccupation with the Region, and her boredom ignited his temper. When he was drinking, which was most nights, his grievances and antipathies smoldered dangerously. No episodes in O'Hara's personal history are as ugly as his explosive indulgences of ferocity against men, women, and—on that one ghastly occasion at "21"— midgets. In this notorious incident, O'Hara insulted—or decided he had been insulted by—a gruff Lilliputian, and threw a punch. The bantam's buddy, returning from the men's room, joined the fray, and between them the peewees won on points, giving the heavyweight a unanimous- decision whipping.

Let's call getting beaten up in bars a lifestyle choice; hammering women and knocking them down at parties and in bookstores is something else altogether, and it was something O'Hara did in his drinking days. In self-vindication he later explained, helpfully, that "although I may often have felt like belting a woman, I have never actually taken a poke at one except in anger."* Stories circulated that he had shoved Pet, pushed her out of a moving taxicab, slapped her. These scenes are difficult to picture. Of course everyone knows by now that no awful act is inconceivable in privacy, and that an ashamed, drunk, and truculent hus-

---

*Peter S. Prescott, quoted without citation in the January 12, 1981, *Newsweek* review of Frank MacShane's *The Life of John O'Hara.*

band was brutal to his wife is within the range of experience. But it is difficult to picture these scenes being acted out in public places. Any writer—and for sure any drinking writer—is familiar with the outrageous. Bar fights, fuck-yous, drinks thrown in a perceived jerk's face: it happens, but in my experience seldom, and I don't think of myself as cloistered. There is no tolerance these days for wild pain-in-the-ass drunkenness among even the baddest boys and girls. Furniture breakers and shouters get the gate as soon as they stumble across a line not that distant from civility.

Now is now and then was then. James Thurber's second wife summarized O'Hara as "a cruel and neglectful son of a bitch," and on drunken fury and viciousness has to count as a connoisseur. Her own husband was repellent. Gentle E. B. White was his closest friend, and White "spent a lot of evenings with him but I didn't enjoy them. Jim had it in for women and he was obnoxious about it. He would lash out at the nearest woman, and one night the nearest woman was my wife, Katharine. I wanted to hit him, but I couldn't hit a one-eyed man."[75] Wolcott Gibbs, another friend, swore that Thurber was "the nicest guy in the world" until five in the afternoon. After his third drink, he'd begin to brood, and squint his half-good eye, and mutter imprecations, and soon enough he was maligning the speakeasy patrons with filthy language and hurling glassware. In a notorious incident at Tony's, Thurber pitched a glass of whiskey at Lillian Hellman, an event she described in "Julia." Dashiell Hammett, also drunk, shoved him against a wall, so Thurber pitched another whiskey (so quickly refilled?) at him, hitting a waiter, cousin to Tony, who called the police, "an extreme action for a speakeasy proprietor," as Burton Bernstein appropriately observes, adding in a footnote the kind of ad hominem aside that threatens to make the writing of biography pleasurable: "There is something about Lillian Hellman that makes men, and some women, want to throw whiskey at her. Thurber simply and inexcusably did what everybody else thought better of doing." (I'll bet a glass of "scatch" that someone—maybe Bernstein's better angel—made him add "and inexcusably.")

Back then, otherwise smart men and women subjected themselves to the torments of keeping company with morose, bellicose, incomprehensible, drooling drunks, and these otherwise astute men and women came back for more, and even invited such sots as Thurber and O'Hara to parties that began more than three drinks into the cocktail hour. Either their memories of pain were truncated by their own snuffed synapses or their tolerance of it was heightened by the numbing consequences of gin. But Thurber and O'Hara were almost never ostracized by their friends for their loutish conduct. It's as though "speakeasy" signified not quiet speech—the whispered "Pal Joey sent me"—but easy democracy, the license to say and do any damned thing that seemed promising at the moment. And I was taught that "speakeasy" was a corruption of "spake-ayezee, boyo," coined in an unlicensed Pittsburgh grog shop as an admonition to keep it down, put a sock in it. Anyone who has sat on a barstool and listened to a drunk share his flossiffyalife, anyone who has labored to seem innarested in a drunk's rhetorical question, Y'know-the-matter-with-you?-well-I'll-tell-you-the-trouble-with-you-is . . . what's-wrong-with-you-is you're a silly-looking-cocksucker, will wonder how a night at Bleeck's or Tony's could conceivably resemble what is sometimes termed "fun." It isn't only that everyone got away with murder back then, it's that everyone also seemed willing to be murdered.

Thurber, in a letter to Malcolm Cowley composed from self-interest, created a complex taxonomy of alcoholism which O'Hara would surely have underwritten: "I do not believe that Fitzgerald was a worse drinker than most of us, but this is always mystical ground. Hemingway called Scott a rummy, O'Hara says that Eustace Tilley has no right to talk about Hemingway's drinking—obviously a crack at Gibbs . . . as if O'Hara could not have held his own with Scott or anybody else, except Benchley and Sinclair Lewis. . . . I also give my own definitions of rummy, souse, drunk, sot, and the others. The drunk, for instance, is the stranger who annoys your party on the sidewalk as you are leaving 21; the rummy has several suits, but always wears the brown one; and the sot doesn't know where he is, or who you are, and doesn't care."[76] These are distinctions without a difference to the wife who gets shoved from a moving taxicab. In light of the graphic accounts of Thurber's viciousness, it's sobering to be taught that he was a sweetheart set beside O'Hara, "the one everybody fought with."[77]

Back then falling down drunk was a cause of mirth, and a bad story told well on oneself was a reputation-enhancer. Cartoons amused by featuring top-hatted barflies with Xs for eyes and grog blossoms for noses. Blackouts were especially droll. Jiggs got bopped on the bean with a skillet by Maggie, and to shock the proprieties was an honored hobby among the gang O'Hara ran with. His jocose letters to Simonds from this time have buried within them alarming—given the reality of his actions—warnings. From Bermuda, in reference to his short-lived ambition to live there year-round, he discussed overcoming his bride's objections to such a plan: "Sweetheart this is so heavenly that we must spend most of our time here, and if you don't like it I'll knock your God damn block off, sweetheart."[78] Writing to his brother Tom about some writing he'd sent, he encouraged him by reporting that "my wife read your pieces and her conclusion was that you today have a better mind than I have. I bopped her on the snout and let it go at that."[79] A few months after Simonds married Catherine Melley, O'Hara proposed that he and Pet visit them in Allentown, where "I could show you how to administer a punch in the jaw without inflicting an embarrassing bruise on your wife's chin. . . ." I guess this is why it's a good idea to burn letters before they get into the hands of biographers armed with ellipses; after my dots there are his words, the balance of the sentence reading ". . . and my Mrs. could show your Mrs. how to place crackers in a husband's bed with maximum effectiveness."[80]

The problem for a biographer with no direct experience of the young John O'Hara is the necessity of leaving unexplained the major mystery of his personality; namely, why so many men and women found it pleasing to be in his company. An ambitious and resentful writer who seems superficially to have been a monster of solipsism was clearly something more various. He didn't reproduce the cadences and underlying reality of spoken idiom without listening to voices other than his own; he couldn't have so accurately drawn pictures of his times without staring out, at the integrities as well as the incongruities of his companions, as well as selfward. Without these nuances of motive and act, certified by the fact of his friends' loyalty as well as by the specifics of work, it would be easy to write him off as a coarse bully and a social climber, a mean drunk and a brutal husband. And indeed, hanging judges among critics have for years dismissed him along with his work in just such terms. Here is Peter Prescott's 1981 summary of O'Hara's personal history in New York: "There he drank late in the speak-easies, slept later still, became thoroughly acquainted with chorus girls and gonorrhea, and, as an apprentice journalist, managed to get fired from the best newspapers and magazines."[81] (It was Prescott's stern father, Orville, whose *New York Times* reviews stirred O'Hara to publish his books on Thanksgiving Day. In those times, publication dates were honored, and Orville

Prescott—one of the cohort O'Hara referred to collectively as "little old ladies of both genders"—was on the Monday-Wednesday-Friday shift.) However hard his friends, and sister Mary, should have come down on him for his bad-acting—and he was so notoriously umbrageous that friends who wished to be friends kept their sermons to themselves—he was harder on himself.

By the autumn of 1932 O'Hara was on the skids again. During the year he sold eleven stories to the *New Yorker* and one to *Scribner's*. He earned at least five thousand that year, including his up-till-then record payment of $175 from the *New Yorker* for his profile of a chorus girl, "Of Thee I Sing, Baby." This was much money then, and added to Pet's allowance it should have been enough. Reason not the need. The theater cut deep, dinner after the theater, nightclubs after dinner, taxis home. They were tapped out. His phone had been disconnected, and not for the first or last time that year. Broke as he was, as a benefit of his work at RKO some press agent might slip him an expensive hat or tickets to the Beaux-Arts Ball. Around publishing and writing such paradoxical lagniappes abound, the publication-day lunch, say—with fine wines and rare cheeses and eau de vie—that costs in excess of a book's advance against royalties, not to mention its earnings.

O'Hara was readying himself for a move. In December he reported in a tender letter congratulating Simonds on his marriage that "today was my last under the happy sign of RKO, or the sign of the viscera. [O'Hara had begun this letter in October and kept adding to it till year's end.] They fired me, pardner; they ousted me, and only because I missed, on the average, a day a week from hangover trouble. . . . I always was the last in the office." How did he manage to show up at all? All this time he kept plugging away at *New Yorker* submissions, and was trying unavailingly to dream up a piece of long fiction to enter—with fifteen hundred other applicants—in the *Scribner's* contest. His preferred cycle was the night shift; he liked to begin writing after midnight, and to sleep till the lunch hour. RKO kept a different clock. He had to beg for a twenty-dollar-a-month reduction in rent, since he'd received a hundred percent cut in pay, but when he caught that landlordly break, Mrs. Petit cut her daughter's allowance by twenty-five.

And then Pet, at her mother's insistence and against O'Hara's wishes, had an abortion. He felt bitter shame. He never expressed anger at his wife for her decision; that he reserved for petty torts and imagined wrongs. But he felt pain that his failures, his unreliability, had inspired in his wife such a conviction of hopelessness, and now he indulged even more in prolonged benders, what he called "overnight vacations; getting so cockeyed drunk that twenty hours elapse before I recover." In a heart-breaking throwaway sentence to his best old friend, with whom he'd shared his longings and hubris: "I wish I could take a vacation from myself."

This letter is unusual for its compressed emotional music, and gives the impression of coming direct from the heart, an impression that can be achieved only with passionate composure. A mature, moving, and troubled run of prose, it tells in part of driving with Joe to take their brother Tom to his first year at Brown, and forecasts that Tom will do fine there and after college as well.

> A change of scene is what I need more than anything else. Even so short a trip as the one to Providence made me realize that New York is licking me. I couldn't help thinking that the other day in a street car. A few years ago—say seven or eight—I could go to a town like Philadelphia, stay at a hotel, and get a swell kick out of listening to the city noises. I could get a kick out of uniformed delivery boys, and electric motor trucks, and elevated trains and orchestras unobtrusively playing at luncheon in the hotel dining-room; mounted police and shops that sell $20 shoes. Maybe I could recapture that swell feeling in another city. Chicago still seems to me more of a city than New York, because I know New York so well. God, to think that I recognize the faces of scores of cops and doormen between 42nd and 59th! Waiters in speakeasies and the Algonquin and Sardi's and B-G sandwich shops know me by name better than the same craftsmen [in Pottsville]—and in essence I don't like it. Perhaps that's the reason I liked Chicago. It was so completely foreign and strange, and I was so completely an outsider. And yet it isn't that I am really an *insider* here. I have few enough friends, and a lot of people who speak to me really hate my guts. The spurious attentions, if you can call them that, of waiters and the like are entirely the result of 15% tips.[82]

This is O'Hara at his unprotected best, without the armor of derision, or even of irony, let alone spleen. It is also a remarkable instance of a kind of third-person nostalgia, as though some precedent writer had enjoyed sufficient narrative omniscience to recover the immediate noises and rumbles and music of the city now lost to the letter's first-person composer. Let me try to articulate this: as a reader I am stirred by O'Hara's powerlessness to be stirred by New York precisely because the artist forming these impressions has an acute ear and eye for the very things he believes himself to have mislaid. Now, fired by RKO, he declares he has been left with no excuse to fail to do "some decent work." He mentions a couple of plays—one of them what might have been a treatment for *The Big Chill*, had that movie been set in Pottsville in 1922 and the Christmas of 1932—and "the item known as Novel, which I do want to get over and done with."

The novel, of course, would be *Appointment in Samarra*, and O'Hara had been accumulating its vivid details from the first time he registered a distinction between a Shetland pony and a polo pony, between a Harris tweed and a Donegal, between a Packard and a Cadillac, between a roadhouse and a country club, between a doctor and a coal miner. He had been preparing for this performance since he was at dancing class, maybe before. Now was the moment. He had been fretting to Simonds that his memory for particulars of the Region was waning. He was losing his mining vocabulary, and even his geographical understanding of where one patch stood in relation to another. Toward the end of refreshing his sense of place he had spent a weekend with the Simondses in Allentown, and now planned to visit near Pottsville, keeping clear of home, maybe holing up in Tamaqua, or Schuylkill Haven.

Trouble outran him. In his distress and regret he was increasingly churlish. When an old Pottsville friend visited the couple, a drunken O'Hara dressed him down as a social climber and refused to shake his hand when he left. When the friend phoned the next day to invite O'Hara to dinner to make amends, Pet went in his stead. And then she went further—home to Mommy. Life like that was too exhausting, even for the young. O'Hara understood his inadequacy better than anyone, and in all his correspondence there is not a phrase that could be construed as bitter toward Pet, or cruel, or self-excusing, unless you'd want to count the modifiers in a June letter to F. Scott Fitzgerald, reporting that "my pretty little wife is rolling out to Reno next week, and the girl I loved from the time I was 17 got married in Haiti last month, to a Byronic lad whom she'd known about two months. And she was the shadow on the wall that broke up my marriage. Oh, my."[83]

TOP LEFT: *Dr. Patrick Henry O'Hara*
ABOVE: *Katharine Delaney O'Hara*
LEFT: *Remaining O'Haras at 606
Mahantongo Street following the
death of the Doctor, 1925. (From left,
standing) Thomas, Martin, John,
Joseph; (sitting) Eugene, Mrs. O'Hara,
Mary, James; (on floor) Kathleen.*

ABOVE LEFT: *With Pet, Bermuda, 1931*
ABOVE RIGHT: *Belle Wylie O'Hara*
RIGHT: *O'Hara and Belle, swinging on
the moon, lit by stars, Bachelor's Ball,
Los Angeles, 1940*

RIGHT: *O'Hara, Wylie, and beach wagon, Quogue, late 1940s*

BELOW: *Belle, Wylie, and John, the dunes at Quogue*

BELOW RIGHT: *O'Hara at Quogue*

O'Hara, wearing OSS disguise, 1943

ABOVE LEFT: *O'Hara, seated between Walter Winchell (left) and John McCain, Stork Club, on O'Hara's thirty-first birthday, January 31, 1936*
RIGHT: *With F. Scott Fitzgerald, Los Angeles*
BELOW: *With Ernest Hemingway and Sherman Billingsley, owner of the Stork Club*

RIGHT: *With John Steinbeck, Quogue*
BELOW: *With JFK and W. H. Auden,*
National Book Awards, 1956
BOTTOM: *Katharine "Sister" Barnes*
O'Hara

ABOVE: *O'Hara in monogrammed MG-TC, Princeton*
BELOW: *Between Albert Erskine and Bennett Cerf, fellow admirers (perhaps) of O'Hara's Rolls-Royce Silver Cloud III, parked in the courtyard of Random House offices on Madison Avenue*

LEFT: *With Thomas O'Hara, New York, 1960*
BELOW: *With Wylie at "21,"
1965*

O'Hara wrote this on the letterhead of the William Penn Hotel, in Pittsburgh, where he'd been living since May. He had applied for a job as managing editor of the Pittsburgh *Bulletin-Index*, a *New Yorker* knock-off among the many that had sprouted in such get-up-and-go American cities as Los Angeles, Cleveland, and Chicago. He was by now convinced that New York would, in the aftermath of his breakup with Pet, not only lick him but kill him. He'd lurched into a comical but potentially termi-nal dispute at a gangster party in Greenwich Village, when a female guest accused him of stealing her jewels. As if that collision weren't chancy enough, the reporter in him liked to grill mobsters about the peculiarities of their business, and some of them began to wonder why, aloud. But the gravest threat to O'Hara was from himself. Matthew J. Bruccoli relates an incident when a morose O'Hara bumped into Mil-dred Gilman, a friend, in front of a movie theater: " 'Mildred, you will be the last person to see me alive.' Since he seemed reasonably sober, she took him seriously and persuaded him to go into the theater with her. They sat in the back row, and he talked about his depression over his failed marriage."

Still careening, he stumbled that spring into a want ad in a trade pub-lication inviting applications for the *Bulletin-Index* post, hence Pitts-burgh. O'Hara wrote the owners, J. Paul and Henry Scheetz, a detailed proposal that was frank about the shortcomings of the issue he had been sent for study. The brothers Scheetz had made it clear that they were interested in making money, but were undecided whether the best means to this end was to kiss or kick the asses of Pittsburgh's industrial and commercial aristocracy. O'Hara came down on the side of *Timely* sassiness, sobered by careful factchecking. (He used the occasion to scold the publication's current editors for allowing into its pages a mon-strous solecism that seemed to suggest that the nuptials of Miss Pennel to Lt. Boyd—an infantry officer—had been concluded with a recessional beneath an arch of sabers, when every damned fool should know that "the saber is a cavalry weapon.")[84]

The Scheetzes were evidently kinsmen in masochism, because the surly supplicant got the nod and began work in May. He negotiated a fifty-dollar weekly expense allowance at the William Penn, where he set up housekeeping on the twelfth floor, sharing a room with his typewriter and golf clubs, weapons with which he meant to bring the Iron City to its knees. Pittsburgh was ground down by the Depression, but an outsider wouldn't have known as much from the spring and summer seasons' polo matches, coming-out parties, fancy-dress balls, and foxhunt. From his office a few blocks from the hotel, in the Investment Building, O'Hara commanded a staff of two, paid seven and eight dollars per week, about the price of the Brooks Brothers neckties with which he wowed the boys. At least one of these, Frank Zachary, later remembered O'Hara as a considerate boss, and impressively fast on the keyboard whacking out stories for the so-called *B-I*, or for the *New Yorker* and for *Vanity Fair*, which finally accepted a story, "Hotel Kid," while O'Hara was in Pittsburgh. Zachary told Finis Farr that it seemed to him O'Hara "could finish one of these before going out for lunch."

As managing editor, by inference rather than by masthead title, O'Hara put the magazine to bed in the predawn of Tuesday mornings, and celebrated the achievement, *Time*style, by an assault on the local speakeasy, standing drinks for his lads. But he began his stay in a temperate phase, realizing at twenty-eight that he was running out of fresh chances. He intemperately and shamelessly stole diction and syntax from Henry Luce: "A leonine person in appearance, temper and will, was Henry Clay Frick, bearded Pittsburgh steel & coke master, Carnegie friend & foe; but a very gentle lion when he thought of children."[85] This was about as bad as it got; as good as it got were his savvy portraits of the city's rough underside, "Plush and Velvet" (about Plush Alley, the vice zone) and "Joe: Straight Man" (about the Democratic patronage boss).

Then he began to slip. Pet visited him several times before lighting out for Reno, and he confessed to Kyle Crichton that "I now fully recognize that I love my wife," and indeed he hoped to remarry her after the divorce, if—as she insisted—he made enough of himself to free them from Mrs. Petit's financial dominance. This bizarre plan was made weirder still by O'Hara's continuing preoccupation with Margaretta Archbald. After a spell on the water wagon he began drinking again, and hard by early July. He was overrunning his due bill at the William Penn, putting in very late nights at the hotel's Urban Room, where he was infatuated with a chanteuse named Dolores Reade (later Mrs. Bob Hope), who inspired a *B-I* piece titled "Torch Singer."

Late on the eve of Independence Day, he cracked. His submissions to *Scribner's* were being rejected with mortifying regularity, and he was tugging his forelock hard in his cover letters, taking on faith the justice of

Kyle Crichton's condescension. With a recently submitted story about a sportswriter, he had invited Crichton to "do as you like. That is, make any changes you deem essential to a sale." In return, the editor felt free to condemn his story as at once insipid and "too damned emotional. I have tried it on everyone else in the office and there is no shouting—no flag-waving . . . the story as a story isn't no good. . . . We should like to have a story of yours here if ever you should dig down deeper into that shallow Irish nature of yours." How in the world could O'Hara keep coming back for more of this? Wiseass or not, such a flip insult must have been excruciating to endure, and even more bitter was to realize how actively he had collaborated in his abasement. (In 1960, Crichton wrote O'Hara begging for a review of his memoir, *Total Recoil*, adding that he didn't like the title but that "Doubleday think it's cute and will sell some books." He assured O'Hara that "you're in the book," along with Pope Pius XII, Hemingway, Faulkner, and Sinclair Lewis. Like all writers of such letters, Crichton—as he toots his own horn—scuffs the rug with his toe, admits to "a lot of crust on my part," but explains that Joyce and Proust "went to all lengths to plug their books," and "I've never had much critical attention and I'd really like a little this time."[86] O'Hara responded generously, without noting the ironies, but tried to save Crichton from himself: "If your book is good, you are not going to feel any better about it if you do personal plugging of it. And if your plugging is not successful, you are going to feel ashamed." He added, ". . . and if I don't like what you've said about me I will kick you right in the balls.")[87]

And there was more. He was brooding about Marg Archbald's wedding to that "Byronic lad," the son of the Episcopal bishop of Haiti, and the forlorn and friendless liberty of the holiday at the William Penn inspired a binge that sent him out on the sill of his twelfth-floor window. When he crawled back inside, he resolved to save himself and, not for the last time, gave up drinking. He reported this event because he wished to have someone know, and believe, that hurt had pushed him to the edge, and that he'd paused there, looking down or looking in. It is easy to assume cynically that such a moment's gravity is in inverse proportion to its publicity. But whatever happened in his frenzied imagination just before and while he was perched above that unforgiving city—whether or not he was actually so perched—he never forgot the availability of a final option, jumping, pulling the trigger, turning the key in the ignition.

It would be pretty to report that coming off alcohol had lifted O'Hara's spirits, as temperance had in Bermuda. In fact, perhaps the most self-scourging letter he ever wrote was provoked in early August by another rejection letter from Crichton, this one patting the submissive would-be *Scribner*ling for coming close—no cigar—with an effort not without a hint of merit, chin up. O'Hara's response was immediate: "I think a lot of what you said is a lot of crap, for the reason that I know so much better than anyone else that I have an inferior talent. The reason I think I have an inferior talent is that when I write I can't sustain an emotion. It isn't that I don't feel things, but when I begin to write out of hate, I find myself being diverted into tolerance; and when I write about love, or from love, I get critical and nasty. . . . I'm not important, and I never will be. The next best thing is to be facile and clever."[88]

Let it be noted that he was deep into the fiction that became "The Doctor's Son." Meantime, thanks be, the market for facility and cleverness was drying up in Pittsburgh, the Scheetz brothers growing impatient. The bar bill at the William Penn was the least of it. O'Hara had made a small scandal with a recently married local woman, according to Matthew J. Bruccoli, and his employers were weary of his undisguised scorn, and of his habit of writing on the *B-I* time clock submissions for fancy New York publications. For his part, he didn't like that they'd taken to opening personal mail addressed to him at the magazine, and sometime in early August there was an office dustup. Bruccoli reports that the incident grew in legend to a fistfight, that O'Hara was said to have "knocked one of the owners across a desk, but it probably involved only pushing or shoving." At any rate, he quit without notice and had his things shipped to New York. Pet was with her mother in Nevada, where she divorced him on grounds of extreme mental cruelty. Within days he had settled into a tiny eight-dollar-per-week room at the Pickwick Arms Club Residence, 230 East 51st, no bath and within easy earshot of the squeal and rumbling thunder of the Third Avenue El. Now he was ready to ready himself for *Appointment in Samarra*.

The novel that began life as *The Hofman Estate*—first book in a prospective trilogy of which an extended "Doctor's Son" was to be another installment—now bore the working title *The Infernal Grove*, from a line of an untitled Blake poem. (O'Hara's ear had an unfortunate inclination toward the most melodramatic tropes of great poets; cf. *A Rage to Live* from an otherwise acidulous poem by Pope.) This title in fact was a hand-me-down from Dorothy Parker, who had provisionally attached it to a story collection published as *After Such Pleasures,* from Donne's "Farewell to Love" (when only the best will do). In some self-reported versions, O'Hara began writing the novel in September 1933, and in others not until December. "There was no desk—only a chair, a bureau, and the bed," he told Robert Van Gelder in an interview for the *New York Times Book Review* in 1940. "I used the bed as a desk—put my typewriter on it—and each night I'd work until my back began to hurt."[89] The portable typewriter was new; he made no carbon copy. Perhaps his aching back wasn't always a reliable signal, since he noted in an author's foreword to the Modern Library edition of *Appointment in Samarra* that "the places where I have ex-ed out lines in the original manuscript were a result of trying to force the writing when I was tired."

He wasn't drinking, or by the evidence of a letter to his brother Tom was drinking very little; it was a peculiarity of the times and perhaps until very recently, that to confess to having sworn off was to reveal the abasement of having been a slave to alcohol. But the evidence is strong that in fact he was drinking black coffee at Tony's, where he went clubbing before he worked from midnight to dawn, or on a bad night for a few hours. He laid off Thursdays and Sundays. He later remembered that period—despite his poverty—with fondness, testifying that he was "a reasonably happy man." It is difficult to overstate the retrospective euphoria that coherent work, however painful or shaming the story being told, can confer on a writer.

He was also seeing much of Pet, with whom he'd rendezvoused—unknown to his bygone mother-in-law—as soon as she returned to New York from Reno. She would come over from her uncle's place in Brooklyn and they'd go to afternoon movies together, and he'd sneak her back to his cubicle at the Pickwick Arms. The clandestine quality of these encounters did nothing to diminish their glamour, and he was again falling in love with her, or falling in love with love.

Habits died hard with O'Hara, and the habit of the *New Yorker* seemed unbreakable. Having turned down an offer from the Broadway producers of *Tobacco Road* to be that play's press agent, he wangled an assignment as the *New Yorker's* football correspondent. In October he wrote to his brother Tom, who had decided not to return to Brown, in Pottsville; he told of the divorce, and reported that he had "got good and drunk, I mean good and drunk," back on Independence Day, and "then went on the wagon," confining himself to "a cocktail and a glass of wine at dinner." He was down to one hundred seventy-four pounds—two hundred plus was his customary weight—and was worried, skinny as he was, about the onset of winter, with his topcoat in storage at Macy's, the warehousing fees unpaid. "I am leading what is called a life, but there isn't anything to it. . . . I have a feeling that all this is time-out preparatory to something awful happening to me, but I almost don't care. My little pieces in The New Yorker, unimportant though they are, are the only things that make the difference between my being dead and alive. I don't mean that the money keeps me alive. I mean that I do nothing else, and except for them I might as well be dead."[90] What was preparing to happen to him, of course, was his remarkable first novel, but he can be forgiven for not putting an accurate name to his apprehension. Writers are notoriously unable to judge the richness or poverty of work in progress. But a couple of weeks before he wrote his brother, O'Hara had submitted to *Scribner's Magazine* "The Doctor's Son," which he rightly judged to be "a beautiful story," and it had been turned down.

However bleak the history he conveyed to Tom O'Hara in that letter home, there is no trace of self-pity, but rather a steely resignation to tastes indifferent to his graces. "So I *accept* this mantle of mediocrity, from whatever source it came, without even bothering about whether it fits." In later years, this indifference to the judgments of his critical tormentors became unduly mannered, an unthinking (and often unfelt) *Fuck you*. But in 1933, what's at work is good work driving out bad luck; he is simply too busy being a good writer to take the time to consider his wrongs and faults.

Besides, room-without-bath or no, he was having fun. The *New Yorker* sent him to cover games at Harvard Stadium, at Princeton's Palmer Stadium, and—Valhalla!—at the Yale Bowl. In the snows of yesteryear, these Big Three teams enjoyed a national following. He rubbed tweeded shoulders with "the courtly Georgian Grantland Rice," as Finis Farr recalled him, and with "the old Princetonian Lawrence Perry," who reported only on amateurs in his column "For the Game's Sake." He was a colleague of "George Trevor, who wrote his weekday copy in the library at the Yale Club and sent it downtown by messenger to the *Evening Sun*. O'Hara also met Damon Runyon, the star of the Hearst papers, who wore a belted polo coat and a velour hat the size of a coal scuttle."[91]

And when he wasn't lionizing some heroic Bulldog's run into the center of the line against bloodied Tiger defenders, he was spending his
time in New York in the company of Gibbs, Benchley, and Dorothy
Parker. Parker was his best friend by now, and her influence was decisive
on his determination to go forward with his novel. It hadn't damaged her
standing that she'd told him that he'd never be happy because he was a
genius, and that if Hemingway had read "Alone" he'd want to cut his
throat from envy. It also hadn't hurt that she evidently said many of these
same things behind O'Hara's back, violating the custom of her judgments. Writing about her sixteen years later, Norman Mailer caught the
essential Dorothy Parker. She "looked like a bird at the mercy of every
beast with teeth, a flurry of feathers up in a tree. . . . She also had a manner that was gentle, full of praise, and treacherous as a scorpion. . . . Still,
Norman wanted Dottie Parker's real affection. He wanted the lovely
things she said to him on one side of the door to be repeated on the
other."[92] To stay on the safe side, Mailer made it his practice to be the
last to leave a room with Parker in it.

(It wasn't even safe to have her approval. I found in the 1934 O'Hara
files of the *New Yorker* archive at the New York Public Library a press
clipping that somebody at the magazine decided belonged in their former colleague's folder. It was a Walter Winchell item, titled "The
Squelch Swelegant," lampooning "a brandy-foolish author of a recent
bestseller" who had been "doing a table-thumping 'I am' solo in Tony's.
'Dorothy Parker,' he thundered, 'called me a genius.' 'Oh well,' depre-
cated I, 'you know every funny thing that's said here is credited to
Dorothy.' ")

There is every reason to believe that her goodwill toward O'Hara was
unconditional. She much later told the *New York Post*'s debunker, Beverly Gary, that John was a "talent that blazed, but he hadn't yet steadied
himself as a writer" before the composition of *Appointment in Samarra,*
which she tirelessly promoted. He was "broke and depressed and
needed to be nagged."[93] When he reported that Ross had turned back a
piece, leaving him strapped, without a word she got up and wrote a
check so he could spend a weekend in the country with Pet. (In the
event, he used the money to liberate his winter wardrobe from hock at
Macy's.) According to her biographer Marion Meade, Parker "ordered
him never to mention the matter again, because she was so deeply in
debt that fifty dollars made no difference." There seems to have been no

physical attraction between them, and he was no match for her verbal fencing speed and wit, a word attached like a title of nobility to her name, Her Wittiness, Dorothy Parker.

In addition to a tendency toward dark moods, which Parker termed "Scotch mists," they shared admiration for F. Scott Fitzgerald, who by 1933 needed all the admiration he could get. Wolcott Gibbs wrote that *This Side of Paradise* was "a sort of textbook" for O'Hara, "to be reread at intervals."[94] (This was not a novel that encouraged rereading, even by its author.) The most touching of his fan letters to Fitzgerald followed the death of Ring Lardner, a great influence on Parker's despairing, deadpan stories, and for whom Fitzgerald had written a memorial in the *New Republic*. O'Hara detailed how he had heard of this essay at Tony's, from Thurber, who was praising it. He and Parker had gone to an all-night newsstand to buy it, and the news-seller, explaining that the issue had already been taken off the stand and bundled to be returned, added in an unlikely aside, "You want it for the article on Lardner I guess." An issue was extracted from the bundle and removed to a beanery—the Baltimore Dairy Lunch—and read "over and over" by O'Hara, and then by Parker, "and she wept tears." O'Hara admitted to Fitzgerald that all he could think to say was, "Isn't it swell?" This made Parker bristle, and say, "The Gettysburg Address was good too."[95]

Literary friendships are probably no worse than friendships between politicians, or between matadors, or between tenor saxophonists. But neither are they any less troubled and tense. It isn't just the obvious—though cynical outsiders would like to believe it. Envy and rivalry are such obvious challenges to goodwill that they mostly derail friendships that never were. The late Stanley Elkin, blessed with a breathtaking vocal range and inventive brilliance, had a comically exacerbated envy of other writers' worldly good fortune, of bigger advances, bigger sales, sweeter movie deals. But in the crucial matter, his response to their work, he was dying to be bowled over. He'd read any seriously wrought sentence not his own and clap his hands. He wasn't a pushover, but he wanted other work to be good. And at this point in his life, O'Hara, too, wanted other work to be good. He especially wanted Fitzgerald to know how much he respected him, perhaps because his hero's star was in eclipse and O'Hara knew how to root for an underdog.

This may explain his tolerance of Fitzgerald's bad behavior. Not long after getting that fan letter, he had come to New York from Maryland to drink with the gang at Tony's and to meet pliable young women. At the end of a night of drinking coffee and watching Parker and Pet and Fitzgerald drink what they drank, O'Hara found himself in a taxi with his two friends and his ex-wife. "Very late," as O'Hara remembered the scene thirty years later in a letter to William Maxwell, "on the way to [Pet's] apartment, Scott was making heavy passes at [her], and she was not fighting him off." At this time Pet lived in a swank Park Avenue building, and Fitzgerald, propped up by the doorman, followed her into the foyer, pawing at her. "Meanwhile Dottie had said to me, 'He's awful, why didn't you punch him?' I said [Pet] seemed to like it and we were divorced."[96] Now it is also true that O'Hara didn't want to leave the taxi, as he was afraid that the doorman would report his presence to Mrs. Petit. But given his aggravated jealousy, it might be expected that such a drama would have called out O'Hara's blackest rage. Maybe coffee canceled it, or maybe his knowledge of Fitzgerald's brittle vulnerability in the final days of submitting *Tender Is the Night* (whose galleys O'Hara had proofread) spoke to his insecurities about his own novel. Thirty years later there is no tinge even of disdain in his speculation to Maxwell that Fitzgerald probably had listed Pet "among his conquests."

This was the beginning of 1934, twenty-five or thirty thousand words into his novel, the football season spent as an income pump, and O'Hara's billfold was cleaned out. He wrote Tom that he had begun to get "little notes, then bigger notes from the proprietors of [the Pickwick Arms], reminding me that the most important rule of the place was Payable in Advance."[97] He anguished about eating, let alone paying his room rent. He tried to wheedle money out of Ross, reviewing his productivity (more than a hundred "casuals" printed!) and tooting his own muted horn—the "good pieces have been recognized . . . and the bad pieces have been forgotten by my enemies." He suggested it might be appropriate to give him a bonus of a dollar per casual, but even in need his attention also turned to less pragmatic emblems of Ross's esteem: "And so I think it would be nice if you were to have a medal struck."[98] Suppress the temptation to smile; he wasn't kidding. He was kidding himself—which is easy to forgive—for trying to believe that their "association has been uniformly pleasant for me, and I hope satisfactory to you." Lots of luck there at the *New Yorker.* Now O'Hara took a more direct approach. He sent special-delivery letters to Harcourt, Brace, to Viking, and to William Morrow, offering to show them what he had written, in return for their agreement to read it and decide overnight whether to advance him living expenses while he finished the book. Having mailed the letters, he spent all day in nickel-and-dime movies near Times Square. All three publishers replied by telephone that same afternoon—that really *was* special delivery!—and O'Hara chose Harcourt's Cap Pearce, because he had phoned first; the next day, during a visit to his publisher, Alfred Harcourt asked a single question, "Young man, do you know where you're going?" O'Hara assured him that he did. The advance was fifty per week for eight weeks, a sweet deal for Harcourt, a lifesaver for the young man. If indeed he hadn't begun this submission draft till December, he had written more than a thousand words per day, a fine run even for him. Writing to Tom in early February, he described his regime: "What I'm doing now is stalling. I work in jags. I work like the devil for days at a time, and then suddenly I dry up or get stale, or get physically too tired to go on."

The book was due April 1, an absurdly tight schedule but well suited to O'Hara's pell-mell preference. There's always in the writing of a novel the difficulty of ongoing revision, of amending on page two hundred of a manuscript a detail that creates a trickle-back adjustment to myriad tributary passages upstream. This is such a fundamental feature of longer work that novelists come to learn quickly that memory of the details of the text is a friend easily betrayed by inattention. Familiar now with computers, novelists speak of loading their work into memory each morning, as though it were as simple as punching a few keys. How this is done, in fact, is either by uninterrupted concentration, carrying the novel forward regardless of football articles, gigs at writers' conferences, or days abed recovering from hangovers. Without evading these interruptions, before pushing forward the novelist must fall into the dream of the narrative voice, and maybe once in a lifetime a novelist manages to remain unjolted from that odd trance. And this is how it happens—as it did to Faulkner with *As I Lay Dying*, for instance—that a finely joined novel may be fashioned in a matter of weeks by a writer normally requiring years for the same achievement. Owing to poverty, or fruitful compulsion, or good artistic instinct, O'Hara drove through *Appointment in Samarra* in an ecstatic reverie.

In March, even the solitude of the Pickwick Arms wasn't solitude enough, so he shipped out with his typewriter on the cruise ship *Kungsholm*, bound for Barbados and the eastern Caribbean. He was, this hot new property of a venerable New York publisher, the chief contributor to the *Kungsholm Cruise News,* Editor: John O'Hara. Well, nobody ever promised that writing was a predictable vocation. The job aboard, he claimed, required twenty minutes of his day, and the chatty newsletter shows it. Why—having his weekly advance from Harcourt, Brace—did he sidetrack himself? Well, for one thing the *Kungsholm* was scheduled to dock in Haiti, where he might be able to visit Margaretta Archbald Kroll. He tried, but she was off-island, sailing on her own cruise, so instead O'Hara got to meet her father-in-law, the Bishop, a "pompous horse's ass."

Never mind, even on the *Kungsholm* and a victim of his own baneful influence, he couldn't be stopped. Back on dry land in New York, he surrendered the novel April 9, one week late. With five bucks and change to his name, he wrote Tom that day to confess that he was afraid he'd "muffed the story." This is not an unusual response—postcoital tristesse, postpartum blues—for the surrender of a book to an editor. What was unusual was O'Hara's persistent underestimation of *Appointment in Samarra,* a book from which he might have taken more pleasurable pride and better instruction about the peculiarities of his narrative strength. Just now, he received from Fitzgerald an inscribed copy of *Tender Is the Night,* and in expressing his awe of that novel's ambition, O'Hara felt the need to diminish that of his own, falsely confessing that "the best parts of my novel are facile pupils of The Beautiful and the Damned and The Great Gatsby. I was bushed, as Dottie says, and the fact that I need money terribly was enough to make me say the hell with my book until you talked to me and seemed to accept me. So then I went ahead and finished my second-rate novel in peace. My message to the world is Fuck it."[99] Clearly he had enjoyed crucial encouragement from Fitzgerald, but *The Beautiful and the Damned* ran out of oxygen before it reached base camp beneath *Appointment in Samarra,* and why couldn't O'Hara judge accurately what he had made? Perhaps because the unobstructed directness and primary colors of his sentences lack the music and prettiness of Fitzgerald's least efforts, and because he now understood that accuracy of recollection and description was to be his literary destiny.

Perhaps he also felt too acutely like an apprentice among his admired friends. The novel's new title was another hand-me-down from Dorothy Parker. One afternoon at tea in her apartment, after reading and admiring O'Hara's pages, she pointed him toward a possible epigraph, in W. Somerset Maugham's play God-awfully entitled *Sheppy*. The passage tells of the encounter in the Baghdad marketplace between a merchant's servant and the female Death. The servant, jostled by Death and startled by a shock of recognition on her face, flees, riding his master's horse north to the putative safety of Samarra. What a coincidence! Death had been surprised to see that very servant in Baghdad, "for I had an appointment with him tonight in Samarra."

O'Hara, studying the passage, said, "There's my title."

Dorothy Parker, according to him, said "Oh, I don't think so, Mr. O'Hara."[100]

Alfred Harcourt—suggesting, with an unpersuasive quorum of Harcourt, Brace, editors, that he call his first novel *Swell Guy*—abhorred the title. So did Sinclair Lewis, who called it "atrocious philosophy, and—since it is both meaningless and difficult to remember—shockingly bad box office."[101] Apart from the difficulty of remembering whether Samarra has two *m*s or two *r*s, I think it's a fine title, tantalizing and appropriately deterministic, which is, I suspect, what Lewis found so "atrocious." "I bulled it through," O'Hara later boasted in an author's preface to the Modern Library edition of the novel. It was thereafter a mark of his nerve, if not of his judgment, that he looked only to himself for literary counsel, just as his successful auction of the novel to three publishers caused him to overvalue his cunning as a literary agent.

Appointment in Samarra comes out the gate with speed and authority. The omniscient narrator is wholeheartedly invested in each consciousness he inhabits, and he begins in the mind of an auxiliary character, Luther Fliegler, in the dark of Christmas morning, "lying in his bed, not thinking of anything, but just aware of sounds, conscious of his own breathing, and sensitive to his own heartbeats." His awareness—avid and alert—has the standing not only of thought but of action. The point of view is handed off easily to his wife, Irma, and after less than a page in the dramatic propinquity of present tense, the narrative attains sufficient velocity to shift into past, the comfortable overdrive of historical reverie, and for the balance of its journey smoothly rolls unobstructed toward its final catastrophe, Julian English wrecked by Julian English.

Perhaps it's too cute to invoke automotive conceits in rendering the tale of a Gibbsville Cadillac dealer who, during the onset of the Depression, kills himself by idling his Cadillac in his own tight-shut garage. But in fact cars—the novelty of them, the various personalities they expressed during the first third of the twentieth century, the social and physical freedom they promised, the very sound of them—in convoy comprise a *primum mobile* of this novel and most everything O'Hara would later care to write. The novel's scenes are difficult to forget. The countenance and costume of Harry Reilly—in whose face Julian English throws the fateful drink, at the Lantenengo Country Club—I remembered better than the fact that he is introduced telling a dirty story. I recalled after many years that "his white tie was daintily soiled from his habit of touching it between gestures of the story." I remembered without effort Julian, in the last minutes of his life, holding a flower vase very recently full of booze, pounding his feet to the time of a jazz record, drunkenly breaking his favorite where it lay discarded on the floor then picking up its pieces, losing his balance, and sitting on another, "crushing it unmusically." Most literary experiences that readers can recall with clarity are visual. It is rare that a patch of prose conveys dramatically the tactile sense, which is why Melville is so justly celebrated for that shock of recognition when the narrator of "Bartleby" touches the wasted scrivener, employee, and scourge. O'Hara's "crushing it unmusically" is an audacious sensation to invoke, a ruinous sound, and he quickens the first chapter of his first novel with another sequence of sounds destined to be grooved into the memories of its readers.

As Irma lies in bed beside the thump of her husband's heart, she hears another noise: "cack, thock, cack, thock, cack, thock." Such ostentatious onomatopoeia is usually sentenced to the parodic hell of rhetorical self-pleasuring. But O'Hara pushes way into the sensual immediacy, as natural as heartbeat, of listening: Irma is hearing "a car with a loose cross-chain banging against the fender, coming slowly up or down Lantenengo Street, she could not make out which." This is a bravura succession of frequencies and receptions, of discords and interpretations. It is pleasing to imagine O'Hara in his bed at 606 Mahantongo Street the snowy and frozen Christmas of his humiliating flight from New York, lying listening, trying to unriddle the source of that memorable slap, coming or going? "Then it came a little faster and the sound changed to cack, cack, cack-cack-cack-cack. It passed her house and she could tell it was an open car, because she heard the flapping of the side curtains. It probably was a company car, a Dodge. Probably an accident at one of the mines and one of the bosses was being called out in the middle of the night, the night before Christmas, to take charge of the accident. Awful."[102] Irma's progression from high-fidelity recording to narrative invention is an inspired enactment of O'Hara's creative process. From ferocious attention, aggressive scrutiny and audition, comes suggestion, inference, an instinct to link discrete pieces in a chain of circumstance.

Such, too, is the general knitting and unraveling of character in *Appointment in Samarra.* Julian English is at thirty a wellborn and well-married son of a prominent Gibbsville doctor, the kind of doctor whose unmerited sense of superiority beset and enraged Dr. Patrick O'Hara. (Dr. English, the son of a bank embezzler and suicide, and a surgeon inferior in his skills to Dr. Malloy, has no other grounds for his sense of social invulnerability than a long line of Gibbsville men named English coming before him, which in Gibbsville is grounds aplenty.) Julian was a Deke at Lafayette, a welcome relief from the relentless Big Three credentials of O'Hara's later major characters in novels.

His father wouldn't send him to Yale out of spite and exaggerated, pinchfist rectitude because Julian as a child had been caught stealing. Chip off the old block; like grandfather like grandson. Once a thief, and so on. Never mind that Julian never stole again. If O'Hara's characters believe in anything more passionately than they believe in hierarchy, it is destiny as character. His wife, Caroline, is ashamed of Julian's drunkenness and extravagance. Alternately a charmer and a boor, with the boor ascendant, Julian has run up a personal debt to Harry Reilly, he of the anxious fingers soiling his white tie in the country club locker room. Reilly is a social climber, Catholic in a scarcely fictionalized Pottsville whose social Olympus is dominated by Protestants. Reilly has small, shrewd eyes, "a big, jovial white face, gray hair and a big mouth with thin lips." This is a face upon which to launch a highball. His "clothes were good, but he had been born in a tiny coal-mining village, or 'patch,' as these villages are called." He tells his story in a brogue, whistling "faintly when he spoke," a ludicrous music made necessary "by the fact that his bridgework, done before the Reillys came into the big money, did not fit too well."[103]

When the novel was published, the scandal in Pottsville was provoked not by the town's citizens owning individual keys to open a roman à clef of character (Harry Reilly is invented from bits and pieces of many,

including the author himself, as is Julian English), but by a single com-
munally owned master skeleton key: O'Hara's pitiless fictional autopsy of
his hometown, which "all those cheap patronizing bastards" he would
soon describe to his mentor Walter Farquhar somehow thought "that
dry-fucked excrescence on Sharp Mountain" was theirs, not his.

Appointment in Samarra is lovingly filigreed, warmblooded in its
engagement on behalf of even the least of its characters' interests. But it
is also a group portrait of narrow self-interest, of greed, alcoholism, and
intolerance. Because the narrative vantage is third-person omniscient, it
is difficult sometimes to be confident who—the author, or the character
his eyes are resting upon—expresses some of the novel's baser bigotries.
During Irma Fliegler's attention to the tire chains slapping past her
house, she turns her aspiring middle-class attention to her neighbor
across Lantenengo Street, Mrs. Bromberg, whose religion has supposedly deflated the street's property values, even though the Brombergs
had paid more than half again the asking price of the house to buy it; this
illogic is manifestly Irma's and not O'Hara's. Similarly, it is her ignorant
fear that "pretty soon there would be a whole colony of Jews in the
neighborhood, and all the Fliegler children and all the other nice children in the neighborhood would grow up with Jewish accents." Her husband sells Cadillacs for Julian English, and she's hoping to be invited to
join the country club next year.

It is Julian's—and not O'Hara's—shame that driving mindlessly and
bareheaded he reflects that "he did not like to see men driving hatless in
closed cars; it was too much like the Jews in New York who ride in their
town cars with the dome lights lit." For that matter, the bootlegger Al
Grecco doesn't approve of English earlier in the novel, wearing "his hat
on the back of his head." It is Julian's thought—and also a Gibbsville, and
no doubt a Pottsville, fact—that a country club girl could marry the
"worst heel," brutal, stupid, and ill-dressed, "so long as he was not a Jew."
But when the observation is repeated—"Not that any Gibbsville girl of
the country club–Lantenengo Street set ever married a Jew"—there is
an inescapable atmosphere of narrative complicity in the emphasis,
together with a mean threat in the following sentence: "She wouldn't
have dared."[104] On the following page, Caroline's education at Bryn
Mawr is invoked as a pretext to indulge a far-fetched distinction between
her and her friend Constance, "the plain girl who goes to Smith and
competes with the smart Jewesses for Phi Beta Kappa." And Robert

Cohen, that Princeton Jew who so disfigures *The Sun Also Rises,* isn't a patch for nastiness on a "handsome young Harvard Jew, who turned out to be something fancy" in Caroline's sexual education, which included a perverse Paris sex circus and the Harvard Jew's (it's difficult to know which adjective lavishes the greater contempt) creepy voyeurism watching Caroline watch, all of which she describes in creepy detail to a girlfriend.

Not that Jews have a monopoly on these characters' prejudices. Poles come in for casual abuse, and Catholics, and Italians, and hunkies and schwackies and roundheaders and broleys. And these coarse animosities, pea-brained and dully predictable, are set against the complicated and tender anxieties of a small city whose purpose has been outlived, whose time came and is now ebbing. *Appointment in Samarra* is about serial death: in the season of the Depression it is about depression; in the figurative marketplace of Baghdad it is about the failure of commerce. Like Fitzgerald, who had such an exacerbated sensitivity to time slipping away, O'Hara was always good at snow. And nowhere better than in this first novel, on the cold night of a club dance shortly after Julian threw that drink in Harry Reilly's face, the ice cubes giving the blowhard a black eye. He's brought his wife to the club, "arm in arm he and Caroline, their arctics flopping," and soon he'll be drunk and fighting in the locker room with his friends, but now he's alone on the verandah, looking across the snow-covered golf course, a place designed to honor boundaries of every kind. "But now in the night there was no way of telling, if you did not know, where club property ended and real farmland began."

In Fitzgerald's "Winter Dreams," which begins so memorably at a Minnesota summer resort, time passes with dizzying and terrifying speed, like a series of time-lapse photos of the seven ages run seriatim, lickety-split from infancy to mere oblivion. Dexter Green is bewitched as soon as the story begins by the seasons running past, fall "crisp and gray, and the long Minnesota winter shut down like the white lid of a box," while "Dexter's skis moved over the snow that hid the fairways of the golf course."[105] In that story, plans are planned, ambitions thwarted, chances lost to careless choices. The implacable enemy of Dexter Green's longing is time. A regard for chronology's antagonisms is not a strange characteristic for an artist. John Cheever's "Swimmer" manages to represent a character's terminal upset by subtle suggestions of cosmic dislocations, a winter star in what was an instant ago a summer sky, seasons escaping unnoticed. But Fitzgerald was a class apart in his attunement to loss measured by season giving way to season. When he wrote "Winter Dreams" he was twenty-six, and already acutely alert to decay. He was like a dog that answers a whistle at a pitch too high for us to hear. A promising up-and-comer with a good business in New York, Dexter—no older than his author—learns casually that Judy Jones, the first love of his life, a legendary beauty, is now a married mother of twenty-seven with "nice eyes," a woman other women respect. That's it. The story's climax. And Dexter weeps, the tears streaming down his face: "The dream was gone. Something had been taken from him. He pushes his palms into his eyes, forcing himself to see her and him as they were, the waters lapping on Sherry Island and the moonlit veranda, and gingham on the golf-links and the dry sun and the gold color of her neck's soft down. . . . Why, these things were no longer in the world! They had existed and they existed no longer."[106]

Fitzgerald's "Babylon Revisited"—his other grand dramatic meditation on temporal undoings and dissolutions—appeared like *Appointment in Samarra* in the wake of the Great Crash. Think of them as hangover parables. Charlie Wales has been a drunk, and one wild night in Paris he did the kind of rash, irreversible thing that Julian English did at the country club; but as a result of locking his wife outside in the snow she has died. He has quit drinking—excepting a whiskey a day to attest to self-control—so as to earn respect and claim custody of his daughter, Honoria, who is nine. Fitzgerald's story is controlled by every kind of time signal—tenses, modifiers, synonyms for "then" and "ago" and "any more," memory tags, fading light—available to the language. And its unexpressed but screwy premise is simple: he wants Honoria back before it's too late. Yet it soon will be, since at nine she will soon be too old to cherish. He wants to protect her, to "jump back a whole generation [putting him at twenty-five] and trust in character again as the eternally valuable element. Everything else wore out."[107]

Appointment in Samarra is the biography of a man wearing out. It is to O'Hara's credit as a novelist of manners that to have Julian English neglect to wear a hat while he drives his Cadillac is as scandalous in his society as appearing without a wig at the court of the Sun King. As long as the customs and decorums which O'Hara understood and dramatized were vital to his socially mobile readers—that is, from the late 1920s until 1960 or so—he was unsurpassed in his ability to chart the advance and decline of characters by their diction (whether self-consciously formal or casually solecistic) and by outward shows of style, the absence of Julian's hat or the wardrobe of Caroline Walker English's mother: "You would look at Mrs. Waldo Wallace Walker, dressed in a brown sweater with a narrow leather belt, and a tweed skirt from Mann and Dilks, and Scotch grain shoes with fringed tongues, and a three-cornered hat. You would know her for all the things she was: a woman who served on Republican committees because her late husband had been a Republican. . . . She would be a good bridge player and a woman who knew the first two lines of many songs, who read her way in and out of every new book without being singed, pinched, bumped or tickled by any line or chapter."[108] But what singes the reader of *Appointment in Samarra* is the awful spectacle of Julian English running out of character, thus out of life. The act of humiliating Harry Reilly occurs off the page, and is reported by an aghast onlooker to a couple of unnamed fellows in the stag line near the dance floor. This is a shrewd narrative maneuver, leaving the reader to imagine—over and over—the noise and sight of such an outrage. It makes the reader complicit in gossip about this life-changing episode, and free to exaggerate or extrapolate consequences from it. Julian's hungover memory of what he did last night with that drink to that face returns to him "as though in a terrible, vibrating sound; like standing too near a bell and having it suddenly struck without warning."

What sounds that bell is waking to find himself alone in his bed. Writers as far apart in time as Dorothy Parker and Fran Lebowitz have remarked on O'Hara's extraordinary power to enter heart, soul, and organs his female characters. Late in life he perverted this power into a kinky claustrophobia: whether out of inspiration or aspiration, he finished the race breathing hard to imagine the erotic lives of lesbians. But at the height of his powers, his interest in exploring female characters was fearless and persuasive. Fitzgerald's most memorable women— Daisy Buchanan, say, or Nicole Diver—were facets of Zelda, made memorable by a rhetorical virtuosity masking opacity of motive; and Hemingway's Brett Ashley was one of the guys, and his Katherine Barkley was victimized by her ovaries, and the woman in "Hills Like White Elephants" was an unseen manipulator of a laser weapon of responsive speech. But John O'Hara's engagement with female characters was and is radical for its insistence on their particular properties. Take Caroline English, even as imperfectly understood by her husband: "Upstairs was a girl who was a person. That he loved her seemed unimportant compared to what she was. He only loved her. . . . Other people saw her and talked to her when she was herself, her great, important self. It was wrong, this idea that you know someone better because you have shared a bed and a bathroom with her. He knew, and not another human being knew, that she cried 'I' or 'high' in moments of great ecstasy. . . . But that did not mean that he knew her. Far from it."[109] It's a genius touch, " 'I' or 'high.' " Julian's uncustomary humility here is a tip of the hat to his uncustomarily modest creator, an acknowledgment that some riddles are destined to remain impenetrable, even as it is the fiction writer's privilege to aim to infiltrate them. Not for O'Hara the dismissive shrug—women, they drive you crazy, bless 'em—although in his essays he was capable of being boneheadedly reductive. For all his rightheaded if bleak understanding of the limits put on any husband's imaginative and social intimacy with his wife, or vice versa, Julian still wonders aloud why women seem to go to restaurant bathrooms together, and when Caroline grows irritated with being mauled and felt up in the front seat of their car, Julian wonders aloud if she's "got the curse," which notion and locution provoke her to fury. Nevertheless, he weighs Caroline's moods, talks to her, tries to imagine what she feels. And all of this he does despite his suspicion "that a man who is good with women, as good as he had been, is not wholly trusted and liked by men."

During the three days of the book's action, he is serially distrusted and disliked by men. Harry Reilly won't accept his apology. Julian gets into a drunken brawl with a war hero and other friends at the country club. Even bootleggers condescend to him, and one of their molls toys with him. But what really hurts, after all, is his loss of Caroline, and the even deeper loss—prophetic and irreversible—signaled by the tense shift in his sentence expressing suspicion, "is good with women" to "as good as he had been."

The novel is not without defects. The sex scenes, admirably uncowed and direct, in which the dignified but unseemly Caroline refers to her black lace negligée as a "whoring gown," are undecided whether to be as cold as plumbing manuals or as coquettish as vaudeville kick lines. (Show me a writer other than Nabokov who can write persuasively about eros and I'll feel worse about O'Hara's failure to raise a reader's sensual temperature.) His celebrated dialogue sometimes works so strenuously to be idiomatic that it descends to exercise, like a busy piano piece played too fast. And the third time the narrator uses a broken cross-link on tire chains to create an atmosphere of deterioration, a reader might feel impatient.

But the big things are in place. To be sure, serious critics have accused O'Hara of killing off Julian English without first winning in the court of probability a death sentence for the disgraced, indebted, about-to-go-belly-up car dealer whose parents don't bother to disguise their disdain for him and whose wife has left him. There are two prolonged and daring passages—in the minds of Caroline and much later Julian—that brilliantly dramatize their mutual humiliation. The first of these interior monologues catches her alone with ruminations about Julian, and more specifically about his faithlessness:

> He did. What's the use of trying to fool myself? I know he did. . . . He did. I know he did. And what for? For a dirty little thrill. . . . Ah, Julian, you stupid, hateful, mean, low, contemptible little son of a bitch that I hate! You do this to me, and *know* that you do this to me! *Know* it! Did it on purpose! Why? . . . But you get a few drinks in you you want to be irresistible, but you're not. I hope you found that out. But you didn't. And you never will. I love you? Yes, I love you. Like saying I have cancer. . . . You a big charmer, you. You irresistible great big boy, turning on the charm like the water in the tub; turning on the charm like the water in the tub; turning on the charm, turning on the charr-arm, turning on the charm like the water in the tub. I hope you die.[110]

And so he must, soon enough. And not least because he has indeed "found out" that he is not irresistible. In fact, resistance is all he can count on as the hours retreat from Christmas morning. He quarrels with the cook, Mrs. Grady, about how long to boil his eggs. "He was annoyed with her contemptuous manner. . . . There it was again: servants, cops, waiters in restaurants, ushers in theaters—he could hate them more than persons who threatened him with real harm. He hated himself for his outbursts against them." His dominion is constricting. Anyone who's made it to middle age will recognize the authentic desperation in Julian's dawning awareness that the bright young kids at the country club— "nineteen, twenty-one, eighteen, twenty"—don't want him at their house parties and football games. He's about to hit thirty, " 'and if I dance with their girls they do not cut in right away, the way they would on someone their own age. They think I am old.' "

Late in the novel, shortly before he shuts himself off, he makes a pass at a society reporter for the local paper, a woman he considers so far beneath him that he's not sure—drunk and lonely as he is—that he'll welcome her in his bed. It's not his choice to make; she's not interested, having a boyfriend, a married man with kids and a buck-an-hour job. Worst of all, she lets Julian down gently—" 'you're married to a swell girl. I don't know her at all, but I know she's swell' "—and her mercy is decisively cruel. Julian was "thinking of the time after time he was going to hear those words. 'You're married to a swell girl.' " He thinks of all the mouths that will issue such sentiments about his estranged wife. "Telephone operators, department store clerks, secretaries, wives of friends, girls in the school crowd, nurses—all the pretty girls in Gibbsville, trying to make him believe they all loved Caroline. In that moment the break with Caroline ceased to look like the beginning of a vacation."[111]

Given such a vivid account of deterioration, it's difficult to understand why critics as shrewd as John Updike and Edmund Wilson can—despite their sympathy for this novel—charge O'Hara with failing to dramatize the inevitability of Julian's suicide. Wilson—in what edges toward a buck-up-boy sentiment—wrote in 1940 that Julian "is apparently the victim of a bad heredity worked upon by demoralizing influences; yet the emotions that drive him to suicide are never really explained."[112] Allowing that suicide is a mystery prudently approached on one's knees, and allowing that O'Hara in his later work came to use suicide's convenient finality as a way to escape a plot that had failed to hold his interest, Wilson's is a bum rap. It's one thing to have a character in his 1966 story "Natica Jackson" boast in advance of his imminent self-gunning, "I'm thirty-seven. Life has had its chances to be attractive to me, and I say it's failed dismally."[113] Flip, frosty, false. But the preparation for Julian's end makes his death seem like a mercy. This is his final meditation on shame:

> Thirty years old. "She's only twenty, and he's thirty. She's only eighteen, and he's thirty and been married once, you know. You wouldn't call him young. He's at least thirty. No, let's not have him. . . . Wish Julian English would act his age. He's always cutting in. His own crowd won't have him. I should think he'd resign from the club. Listen, if you

don't tell him you want him to stop dancing with you, then I will. No thanks, Julian, I'd rather walk. No thanks, Mr. English, I haven't much farther to go. Listen, English, I want you to get this straight. . . . Julian, I wish you wouldn't call me so much. My father gets furious. You better leave me out at the corner, becuss if my old man. Listen, you leave my sister alone. Oh, hello, sweetie, you want to wait for Ann she's busy now be down in a little while."[114]

O'Hara enables him to hang on like grim death to such lucidity even in the face of his decline into soporific speechlessness. "I am . . . drunk. Drunk. Dronk. Drongk. . . . No ice I get drunk kicker," he says aloud to his lonely self, about finished now. On the next page he climbs in the Caddie's front seat and turns the key. "It started with a merry, powerful hum, ready to go. 'There, the bastards.' " And that's it.

For Julian. A lesser novelist, especially a green one, would have exited on his dying fall: "He had not the strength to help himself, and at ten minutes past eleven no one could have helped him, no one in the world." *Appointment in Samarra* in effect returns death to the marketplace, to give an accounting. "Our story never ends," this story begins to end. "You pull the pin out of a hand grenade, and in a few seconds it explodes and men in a small area get killed and wounded." That's the beginning. Following the explosion come stories of fatherless children, widows. Or "a man out of the danger area sees the carnage . . . and he shoots himself in the foot," perhaps from a wish to join the club, or sneak home on a cheap pass. "Another man had been standing there just two minutes before the thing went off, and thereafter he believes in God or in a rabbit's foot."[115]

Now the pebble tossed in the pond will lap ripples at Gibbsville forever. Caroline holds Dr. English accountable. Dr. English directs his pain and rage at the Deputy Coroner, Dr. Moskowitz, who has publicly declared Julian's act a suicide. "Let the little kike quack Moskowitz have his revenge, which Dr. English knew Moskowitz was doing." Why? Something about a dinner for the County Medical Society, arranged by Dr. English at the Gibbsville Country Club, from which Moskowitz had been excluded, owing to club policy and the host's bias. It is not clear whether O'Hara is reconfirming a narrowness we had already registered in Dr. English, or dramatizing the bitter fruits of social injury, or making the larger claim that Julian was doomed by the poisoned Gibbsville air he breathed, as noxious an atmosphere as his sealed garage.

Caroline, oddly, misses most the "collegiate sound" of Julian's metal v's striking the sidewalk. You wouldn't imagine that heel inserts, their tapping on concrete, would be peculiar to walkers with university training, but it's what O'Hara believes her to miss, and he makes me believe this. Caroline also believes that Julian "was like someone who had died in the war." This I cannot not believe.

And it was on this point that unfriendly criticism of *Appointment in Samarra* turned, on the question of consequence, the question asked so reasonably yet irrelevantly of all novels of manners: Who cares? O'Hara would suffer throughout his creative life from the unanswerable charge that his characters cared about the wrong things, and that he therefore cared about the wrong people. When he says on Julian's behalf that "it was no more difficult to face a fist or to enter the front-line trenches than it was going to meet [his parents], especially his father," he makes a claim untrue in a general sense and perfectly true in the particular case of this book. The movements that cause a character in fiction to fall in love are without limit: sight, smell, a hoarse voice, a strand of hair falling across the mouth, an abstract notion of beauty or goodness. Kindness may work as effectively as cruelty, though unrequited love is the more common literary maneuver, honoring resistance, the novel's friend. Why then is it meant to be discreditable for characters in fiction to be inspired to rage or lofty ambition by the obstacles raised by an unfriendly society? Hunger, war-terror, the ache of malady: these no doubt take physical precedence over the ache of disgrace or longing, but it is not necessary for a young man to be apprenticed to a blacking factory to feel the pain of alienation. Torment is not merely literal, or why write about it except clinically and remedially? Why not honor the reality that a rejection works wonders against the spirit, as does a snub, or a distracted look over your shoulder by someone you have hoped to interest.

Of course, following the Great Crash, and in the first frost of the Great Depression, and with Europe unraveling like a cheap suit, our country's most serious cultural critics had put on their long faces and were impatient with the complaints of fictional characters dressed by Brooks Brothers or Peck & Peck, characters whose bellies were full and dwellings sited lakeside, adjacent to the fairway, or overlooking Central Park; to be sent packing by the upper middle class to the lower middle didn't seem then a decline fit for empathy or even curiosity. Let's say that to write a novel of manners was considered politically, thus aesthetically, incorrect. To be serious was to be engaged with the historical rather than transitory consequences of capitalism, and social Darwinism was too busy in its cruel communal labors to be reproached for clubhouse postings and exclusions. America's official readers were suspicious of the novel of manners even before Henry James's time, and during Edith Wharton's, and F. Scott Fitzgerald's, and J. P. Marquand's. They are suspicious of it now, assuming that "manners" refer to social climbing and that climbing is a fit action only for mountaineers, that slights are life-changing only if suffered by those of a minority religion or with off-white skin pigmentation. Novelists of manners—faced with this humanly comprehensible hostility to the pain of palefaced, educated, fully employed, or trust-funded characters—must be resigned to critical indifference. Oddly enough, this critical unfriendliness has often been the handmaiden of popular success: Wharton, Fitzgerald (while the Jazz Age was still on), O'Hara, Marquand, Auchincloss.

O'Hara understood American critics' ("professional pipe-smokers," he called them) reflexive hostility. "It is a dangerous thing to bother about the rich," he wrote in an introduction to *The Portable F. Scott Fitzgerald*. "A writer who does it in this country—at least during and since the times when barbers and bootblacks were piling up fabulous fortunes of from five to forty thousand dollars—will find himself regarded a toy." (The ridicule of teensy sums—"five to forty thousand dollars"—was not designed to ingratiate.)[116] Even at their most catholic, serious American critics find it difficult to take seriously coded behavior, systems of civility and discrimination, "the rich" and their damned manners and mannerisms. Charles Child Walcutt, writing one of the first extended appreciations of O'Hara's fiction, concluded in 1969 that he was a grand and gifted writer of short stories and a mediocre novelist. "The weakness of O'Hara's novels is related to the excellence of his short stories: America lacks the manners to sustain what Aristotle called a 'significant action of some magnitude.' "[117] It isn't, of course, that "America lacks the manners," but that our manners are so fluid. For a reader to feel deeply a character's resistance to the oppression of an arbitrary system, it is necessary for the reader to believe a system in place and to comprehend its quiddities. The devil is in the quiddities: a short story may extrapolate—as "How Can I Tell You?" surely does—from a sequence of comprehensible acts of battery on a character, in this case the cul-de-sac of serial belittlings; there is neither need nor leisure in so few pages to invoke or create the Great Chain of Being that is a system of manners. In *Appointment in Samarra,* O'Hara relied on his readers to understand at once the consequences of Julian English's recklessness at a moment in American history particularly intolerant of gratuitous gestures. He threw his drink in the face of a man who had money just when he was going to need some himself, because it was understood that the drivers of Gibbsville were going to do without Cadillacs. Much later, discussing a possible film adaptation of his first novel, O'Hara insisted that it be set during the Depression, and in particular in 1930. He reminded the producer David Brown that "in 1930 there was not yet an FDR to revive hope. . . . In [Westbrook] Pegler's great phrase, the Era of Wonderful Nonsense was at an end, but the only hope people had was that the Era was not over; the hope was not for a bright future; the hope was for the resumption of the immediate past."[118]

Julian English's situation within a small city's depressed situation is coherent. To kill himself by Cadillac is congruous. Walcutt is on to something in his suggestion that such tragic inevitability is missing from O'Hara's episodic later novels—*A Rage to Live,* say, or *From the Terrace.* In these discursive wanderings, he sets himself the task of inventing not only the social obstacles that his characters batter against, but also the foundation, furnishings, and filigree of a society zigzagging across great fields of time; these family sagas depend for narrative coherence on the constants of money and privilege.

As many readers have noticed, O'Hara did not—in his novels, at least—take a position on "the rich." He was neither a bomb-thrower nor the moneybags' running dog. He meant to describe rather than to deride, decry, or cry up. He surely believed, with Fitzgerald, that the rich are different from you and me (or "from you and I," in one of the favored extended-pinky solecisms O'Hara bestowed upon the children of the rich). Clive James has tellingly written in the *New Yorker* that for bright children who, like George Orwell and O'Hara after his father's death, grow up in the "impoverished upper class," poverty is "a potent incubator" of lively perception as to how hierarchy works. "Either they acquire an acute hunger to climb back up the system—often taking the backstairs route through the arts . . . or they go the other way, seeking an exit from the whole fandango and wishing it to damnation." O'Hara climbed, but on the way up he licked no heels. Norman Podhoretz concludes that "despite his meticulous care in describing the way they live and think, he draws no conclusions from class. Which is to say that he is not a snob." This is too generous: of course he was a snob, always within a self-described meritocracy, on and off as a connoisseur of bloodlines, a close reader of that stud book the *Social Register.* But Podhoretz explores an abundant vein in his next conclusion: "The rich appear to him most representative of the human condition, because their lives are frankly, clearly, and fully implicated in the life of society."[119]

This incendiary theme—that the rich are not merely different but also more interesting—is developed by Matthew J. Bruccoli, who argues O'Hara "focuses on middle and upper-class people because their lives are more complicated."[120] This charge's axiom is confounded by its corollary on the same page of *The O'Hara Concern*—"Environment is heredity"—which proposes the opposite of a "complicated" life: a life that is hostage to convention and expectation, defined by limits. By contrast, it is the lower-middle-class Flieglers whose wakeful anxieties and class ambitions open *Appointment in Samarra.* O'Hara described his novel in his letter to David Brown as determined by a moment in social and economic history as surely as *Wuthering Heights* was determined by its time.

Even as he undervalued the virtues of *Appointment in Samarra,* O'Hara thought of himself as playing in the same league with the best of his contemporaries. *Fine*—as in "it was a fine night"—has been "a romantic word" in Julian's vocabulary ever since he read *A Farewell to Arms;* an offstage character's only distinction was that he had known Scott Fitzgerald at Princeton, "and that made him in Caroline's eyes an ambassador from an interesting country." Fitzgerald returned the favor of O'Hara's unstinting admiration with a blurb, and Hemingway wrote in *Esquire* that he was "a man who knows exactly what he is writing about and has written it marvelously well." Thus began a sequence of logrolling that climaxed with O'Hara's notorious review on the front page of the *Times Book Review* of *Across the River and into the Trees,* in which he judged Hemingway "the outstanding author since the death of Shakespeare."[121] For this panegyric he would be made to pay, not least by its beneficiary. Perhaps Papa was sore about a *New Masses* review of *Appointment in Samarra,* which claimed that "O'Hara reports like Sinclair Lewis and has more guts than Hemingway."

For whatever reason, Lewis himself—whom O'Hara had so admired—lit into *Appointment in Samarra* in the *Saturday Review,* the magazine's second hostile response. The first, by its editor Henry Seidel Canby, was headlined "Mr. O'Hara and the Vulgar School," a slightly less brutal attack than the one by Lewis, who had twice commended the novel in pre-publication squibs (a not-unheard-of paradox suggesting that he loved his fan's book until he read it). His condemnation was comprehensive, beginning with the title, which he wrote might as well be *Assignation in Abyssinia,* and priggishly summarizing its sensuality as "nothing but infantilism—the erotic visions of a hobbledehoy behind the barn."[122] O'Hara later tried to badger Lewis at "21," standing beside him at a urinal, but his quarry fled and he was obliged to content himself with a nasty little sketch in *Butterfield 8* of a writer almost as sad a drunkard as Lewis getting shown the wrought-iron gate by the fed-up management of that celebrated hangout. To O'Hara's credit, however much he came to despise the man, he continued to admire and emphatically praise Lewis's work.

Appointment in Samarra, dedicated to FPA, works the author's mentor into the action by way of a plug for his column in the *World* and for Adams's wisdom overall. Adams naturally—the way of the *World*—returned the favor, with interest, in a "Diary of Our Own Samuel Pepys" entry: "So home, and read all the afternoon John O'Hara's *Appointment in Samarra* . . . with some of the best talk, especially between husband and wife, that ever I read, and I got a great glow when I saw that the book had been dedicated to me." Six days later, another hooray: "Boy, I yell for *Appointment in Samarra* / A dandy novel by John O'Hara."[123]

O'Hara also felt some need to honor the *New Yorker* explicitly. At a crucial moment in Julian's decline, after Harry Reilly refuses to forgive him, coming home to break the news to Caroline, he discovers her reading the *New Yorker,* and there follows a detailed description of the precise issue, "not the newest one," but rather one with a Ralph Barton cover drawing, and it seems important to describe both the drawing and its caption. This favor was not returned. The magazine published three reviews of their contributor's fiction, all pans: in the first dismissive review of their admirer's most ambitious work (another to come from Clifton Fadiman, topped by Brendan Gill's devastating response to *A Rage to Live*), the magazine printed Fadiman's charge that the novel was all surface, smooth enough at that superficial level, but without ideas or effect.

That review ran as the football season of 1934 began, and O'Hara—

whose novel would soon be in its third printing—had re-upped as foot-ball correspondent of the *New Yorker.* This led to the ugliest dustup yet. Don Wharton, one of Harold Ross's editorial delegates, was put in charge of the football columns, and by the first week in October had challenged an expense report of $47.25—"this ridiculous expense account," as Wharton termed it—that included a subscription to the *Yale Daily News.* Two days later O'Hara wrote Ross, resigning from his foot-ball job,* also "severing my connection with the New Yorker as a con-tributor of casuals. . . . I am quitting as a contributor. . . . That's all. You keep Mr. Wharton." Ross responded that he had got the note and was "passing it along to our headaches department. . . . I wish you hadn't got your shirt off so quickly and so completely." Enter Gibbs, to mediate, observing that O'Hara had "simply lived in some style" on the *New Yorker's* arm. But he also reported that the fracas was escalating: now O'Hara demanded payment of three hundred dollars for the pieces unused after he quit. His cold fury, Gibbs ventured, was "the result of being a novelist, I'm afraid."

That tore it. With an up-yours, and a first book being trumpeted as brilliant, O'Hara left for Hollywood, where it was debasing to enumer-ate—he elaborated to Gibbs, who conveyed the intelligence to Ross—sums as pissant as three hundred dollars.

---

*He was replaced by Rogers E. M. Whitaker, O'Hara-like and then some in his passion for railroads and the facts of their comings and goings. He claimed and was believed to have journeyed 2,748,636.81 miles by trains, worldwide. When Whitaker died his lawyer remarked, "You could call him up in the middle of the night and ask him how to get to Tulsa or Medicine Hat by train and he'd give you all the times and connections" (Herbert Mitgang, "Obituary," *New York Times,* 12 May 1981, D-23).

3. TWENTIETH CENTURY LIMITED

I went out there for a thousand a week, and I worked Monday, and I got fired Wednesday. The guy that hired me was out of town Tuesday.

—NELSON ALGREN, *WRITERS AT WORK*

They ruin your stories. They massacre your ideas. They prostitute your art. They trample on your pride. And what do you get for it? A fortune.

—A VENERABLE HOLLYWOOD REFRAIN

I'm going to work for Paramount. They read galley proofs of my novel, and they said they couldn't buy it, but they want me, so they got me. . . . A week from today or tomorrow I'll be in greener pastures, pastures made green by exactly the fertilizer that I have to offer.

—JOHN O'HARA TO THOMAS O'HARA, JUNE 4, 1934

Appointment in Samarra was passed over by movie studios as too explicitly erotic, too raw, too bleak. Twenty-five years later, O'Hara showed 'em: he instructed H. N. Swanson, his Hollywood agent, to set a deal-busting million-dollar floor on the movie rights to the novel: "It's like putting the Koh-i-noor diamond in Tiffany's window," he boasted to

Swanson. "They won't pay the price, but it brings them into the store."[1] Later, in 1960, thinking better of luring certain window-shoppers into the store, he explained to the producer David Brown that the unheard-of price "keeps out the grocery clerks."[2] A superior television movie, faithful to the spirit of the novel and starring a young Robert Montgomery as Julian English, was directed by Herbert Bayard Swope Jr. for *Robert Montgomery Presents* in the spring of 1953, following the novel's reissue by the Modern Library. In 1959, O'Hara evidently counted among those gawking grocery clerks Paul Newman, who offered half a million cash outright, and the other half of the asking price on the come from profits; but O'Hara held firm—a cool million up front, my way or the highway—and the Hustler had to content himself with starring in *From the Terrace,* one of O'Hara's baggier monsters translated into a meanderingly episodic melodrama.

Despite declining to buy rights to his first novel in 1934, Paramount recognized O'Hara's gift, and aspiring to make use of it offered him a ten-week contract as a writer of what was termed—by grocery clerk bookkeeping—"additional dialogue," at two hundred and fifty a week, with an option to renew for another ten weeks. It's one of the more affecting credulities of moviemakers that they continue—in a triumph of hope over experience—to confuse the art of dialogue on the page with the art of dialogue on the screen. In a story or novel, voice must enact the most explicit of actions; a prose character's speech and language of meditation is that character's performance, the principal display of motive, sense, and judgment. On the screen, a character's words serve best to punctuate acts, or lie at cross-purposes to those acts. The screen-plays of America's best literary writers make a dreary filmography: Fitzgerald bombed, as did Dorothy Parker; Faulkner *was* bombed during most of his serial visitations, though he managed to come up with a nice credit on *To Have and Have Not.*

In the human comedy, Hollywood is top banana, whether the subject is boastful ignorance, mad vanity, vulgar gimme, automotive or architectural novelty, eccentricity of wardrobe, or unfelt sentiment. When I was a greenhorn novelist, beckoned from New York to that palmy colony by first-class air tickets for a first chance to be professionally lied to, a more experienced writer friend took me to an instructional lunch, as if to a briefing at the Explorers Club. My friend assured me that if I refrained from scribbling sums on the backs of hotel envelopes in the expectation that I'd soon be able to afford an imported roadster, and if I understood that any woman asking in a friendly way whether I hailed from out of town was a hooker, and if I NEVER returned ANY phone call from ANYONE in the movie business more than once, I'd limp home with my skin and some of my self-respect. He sagely explained that it was best not to debate whether it were a pardonable sin to sell one's soul, at least until someone offered to buy it (with a cashier's check), and that should I be so lucky as to sell mine, for God's sake get a hefty chunk on the front end. I got no hefty chunk but I enjoyed a limo trip from LAX to the Beverly Hills Hotel and heard swell reviews of my book by people who hadn't read it. What a visitor makes of such circumstances pretty much sets in stone whether he'll read the pretty blandishments of Hollywood as the talent-thieving seductions of the whore of Babylon or as the razz-ma-tazz of a pretty cheerleader. Here John O'Hara had his head on straight. For one thing he was cocky, which sold a whole lot better out west than hangdog. He arrived late to work his first day on the job, and Matthew J. Bruccoli reports that he explained in extenuation, "You should have seen her." For another thing, he desired a car, and Hollywood had an abundant inventory and was a capital place for a writer to carry away money enough to buy a fine ride. A feature writer for the *Los Angeles Times* recently remarked that "for almost a century, writers have been coming to Southern California for the same reason that Willie Sutton robbed banks."[3] The more sardonic writers didn't announce themselves to be bank robbers, but thought of themselves as hookers. From the prominence of Stockholm, after bagging his Nobel, Faulkner explained to an interviewer who'd asked how he bore his two-year sentence at Warner Brothers: "I just kept telling myself, 'They're gonna pay me Saturday, they're gonna pay me Saturday.' "*

The money *was* there, and O'Hara had a reasonable shot at it. He was still on the wagon, and luck seemed to be breaking his way. He wrote his brother that this was a trip he welcomed; he was "excited . . . about the prospect of being able to buy a Ford phaeton of my own, and a new suit, and some razor blades."[4] Having duly bought a Ford roadster, he moved into an apartment in the Ravenswood, on North Rossmore, across the

*Quoted by Patricia Ward Biederman, "Literary Legends," *Los Angeles Times,* 24 February 1995, Valley Life, 8.

street from the Wilshire Country Club and four easy blocks from Paramount and its studio lot, a crazy quilt of stage sets backed up against a cemetery whose dead were guarded by towering palm trees in whose crowns nested a colony of huge and—according to Finis Farr—"intelligent" rats. His first day on the job he persuaded his impressed bosses—by identifying a saddle as a Whippy—that he was a virtuoso of horses and horsemanship, and for this was put to work on a cavalry movie for Cary Grant and Carole Lombard.

Work was not O'Hara's paramount priority. Fun was. He ganged up with Robert Benchley and Dorothy Parker, who wore celluloid lapel pins marked *New York 2500 Miles* and initialed around the edges *W.T.F.A.Y.D.O.H.A.C.:* What The Fuck Are You Doing Out Here Athletic Club. What they were doing was eating lunch at the Brown Derby—that monument, shaped like a hat, to a Cobb salad—and at the Vendome, where he found himself in the same room, if not at the same table, with such as Marlene Dietrich and Dolores Del Rio. It was a high-octane dream. The cupidity and ignorance were on such flamboyant display that it seems natural that Nathanael West's end-of-empire *Day of the Locust* would be set within a short walk of O'Hara's apartment and office, but it wasn't compulsory for a sensitive soul to be broken by glut, rapacity, and vainglory. It must have been a hoot to hang around Musso & Frank's, or the Melrose Grotto, where movie people and eastern writers told awful stories about other movie people and other eastern writers. The stories just kept coming: the outlandish promises, corruptions of beauty, name-droppings, plentiful follies. It was possible to loiter, to observe, to listen for the punch line, to get a tan and play tennis and play the role, as Finis Farr suggests, of "the talented man who sees through it all. He sees through the false tinsel, as [West's brother-in-law] S. J. Perelman said, to the real tinsel underneath."[5]

More than thirty years later, writing about Hollywood for *Holiday*, O'Hara recollected that first visit unironically in reference to his seduction by as gaudy an icon of extravagant display as any newly arrived starlet could have conjured: a white Rolls-Royce phaeton, vintage '25, with a price tag of fifteen hundred at a Sunset Boulevard garage. He'd stop to look at it day after day, feel the haul of temptation, and, unaccountably, resist it. But to own a Rolls became a fixation, an emblem of arrival frankly aggressive. (It never entered O'Hara's mind to buy a Bentley, even after those cars and Rolls-Royces became twins except for their grilles.)* For now, despite what he remembered in *Holiday* as his "horror of going into debt,"[6] he traded his recently bought used roadster as down payment on a new sand-colored V-8 Ford phaeton, which he paid off at fifty per week.

He was feeling flush. Paramount, pleased with his script-doctoring, renewed its option to employ him for another ten weeks. Advance sales of *Appointment in Samarra* were a promising five thousand, and in mid-August he was given a Beverly Hills publication-day party by Herbert Asbury to which actors and producers and directors came, together with S. J. Perelman. Asbury had been a rewrite man with O'Hara at the *Herald-Tribune,* and contributed to the *New Yorker;* he had recently published *The Gangs of New York,* a vivid account of nineteenth-century lowlifes and their hangouts, and this mixture of history and legend had paid off prettily. After dinner Asbury's butler was sent to buy fifty copies of the *Los Angeles Examiner,* whose reviewer brought the welcome news that *Appointment in Samarra* is "too good to be true," a peculiar compliment for any novel, good or bad.

O'Hara was getting around, making the nightclub scene, pitching woo, and learning to put topspin on his forehand. On the surface, where it likes to stay, Hollywood is a jolly place, all garden, payday, and fiesta. The newcomer had already mastered the odd economies of windfall, learning that eastern money—royalties and magazine payments—was "hard money. Real money" that he deposited in a New York bank, and

---

*"Do not buy a Bentley," O'Hara instructed the readers of *Holiday.* "The Bentley, costing $400 less for the same car without the Rolls-Royce radiator, is a form of inverse snobbism that I, for one cannot afford. . . . The Rolls-Royce radiator guarantees instantaneous recognition of your rolling stock wherever you go. . . . The Bentley is all right for Jock Whitney and Bob Lovett, but Johnny O'Hara from Pottsville, Pennsylvania, needs the full treatment" (John O'Hara, "On Cars and Snobbism," *Holiday* [August 1966]: 52, 53).

Similarly Dexter Green's post-Princeton stylistic choices in Fitzgerald's "Winter Dreams" seem bound by iron imperatives:

> When the time had come for him to wear good clothes, he had known who were the best tailors in America, and the best tailors in America had made him the suit he wore this evening. He had acquired that particular reserve peculiar to his university, that set it off from other universities. He recognized the value to him of such a mannerism and he had adopted it; he knew that to be careless in dress and manner required more confidence than to be careful. But carelessness was for his children. His mother's name had been Krimplich. She was a Bohemian of the peasant class and she had talked broken English to the end of her days. Her son must keep to the set patterns.
>
> [F. Scott Fitzgerald, "Winter Dreams," in *Babylon Revisited and Other Stories* (New York: Scribner's, 1960), p. 123.]

around which designed a budget. Hollywood money was "pretend money in a pretend-world,"[7] but he knew better than to knock its uses.

Even so, good fortune had its limitations. "I am no happier than ever," he wrote his brother Tom in August of 1934. "I am going nuts with a headache." He went to doctors, and ordered x-rays, worried about Bright's disease or the aftereffect of a concussion got tobogganing many years earlier in Pottsville. (Bright's, the constellation of kidney ailments that killed his father, was the fancy name he gave to what in fact were serial doses of the clap. So conspicuously handsome was his Ford phaeton that O'Hara emerged from the office of a doctor celebrated for the speed and efficacy of his venereal cures to find an unwelcome note from S. J. Perelman on his windshield: "Don't worry, it's no worse than the common cold.")[8] He was brooding too about sour reviews of *Appointment in Samarra,* at that date fewer and less interesting than the raves. He also wrote to Tom, with more hurt than his rhetorical manner suggested, that he suspected the publication of his novel "will have the curtains drawn at 606, but why should it? I certainly have been repudiated there as thoroughly as possible, and what I do there is on my own head." It would be nice to believe so, but the good people of Pottsville, perversely straining to fit their feet into fictional characters' shoes, complained to Mrs. O'Hara about her awful boy by telephone and up and down Mahantongo Street and at the country club and bridge table. An editorial in a Danville, Pennsylvania, newspaper deplored the local scandal-monger's novel, remarking its "cruelly clever caricature" of Caroline Walker English's mother, helpfully identifying that made-up battle-ax as the mother of a young Pottsville woman O'Hara had unsuccessfully courted. The editorial ruefully noted that when the author was home with his own mother "last Christmas" he "didn't get asked out so very much during his stay." And as for Katharine O'Hara, the scolding paper bedewed its schadenfreude with the crocodile tears of an anonymous Pottsville lady's commiseration: " 'And now he's brought all this disgrace on her after her life of hardship,' sighed our fair informant."[9]

His mother's disapproval, or disgrace, stung, even though by then his skin should have thickened. In my experience, seconded by O'Hara's history, no writer's skin ever sufficiently toughens. Eternally writers long to be outlaws, but all-loved and all-forgiven. The open-eyed and rhetorically gutsy critic of his home town and its "patronizing cheap bastards"[10] was now the wronged, crybaby victim of Pottsville's misreading of his roman à clef that wasn't. O'Hara was still explaining almost three decades later that while Gibbsville was Pottsville and—okay—Lantenengo Street was Mahantongo, and ditto their respective clubs, he hadn't in fact killed himself by carbon monoxide poisoning. "The Region," here as in his later Gibbsville fiction, was compounded of memory and invention, of faithfully recorded geography and history washed by the artificial light of imagined circumstance and created character.

That a writer might consider this a natural confabulation should go—you might hope—without saying. But it needs saying, because writers as well as readers are in such radical disagreement regarding what is fictional "truth," what is fictional "fact," what is "documentary," what is "creation," what is "art." (Even as friendly a reader as O'Hara's biographer Frank MacShane grumbled that he found it "curious" that in *Appointment in Samarra* the novelist had been "so uninventive.")[11] Readers, notably those whose neighbor's lock has been picked by the clef of the roman, ask another question, in truth a tort: What is "fair play"? Having written a novel titled *Providence,* for its interest in chance and (ill) fortune, but set in that actual Rhode Island city, I have felt the lash of parochial resentment. To neaten my fictional topography I rerouted a couple of rivers, which was no more than the city grandfathers themselves had done. I helped myself to a few of the city's great family names and invented others, used Rhode Island's history in the slave trade, invoked one of its rhythm-and-blues bands, and narrated certain felonies committed by its mayor, charges lifted from its major newspaper's vivid crime pages. I exploited the city's street names and its best-known hotel. And boy-oh-boy did I irritate some of its citizens. A lifer at the state penitentiary, previously a busy and efficient hit man, managed to convey by phone that he'd never forgive me for giving Rhode Island "a black eye."

I think now I understand, sort of. It's a question of scale. No reader would expect the Plaza Hotel to sue Fitzgerald for setting the climax of *The Great Gatsby* in a hot, close-aired suite in that New York hotel. It's as though big cities are just asking for it, much like the abstract World (as in "the world" of fiction or of the imagination). They and their landmarks belong to everybody, to readers at large, citizens of "the world." But Providence is different: it had set itself aside to be left alone, meant to write its place names in a privately published atlas and leave its characters themselves unlisted. At a tenth the size of Providence, Pottsville was twenty times as outraged to have been published. O'Hara, naturally, in defiance of reason, believed for the rest of his life that "the dry-fuck excrescence" should have been grateful.

Instead the burghers were furious to be held up for infamy and derision. O'Hara's brother Martin remembered that as soon as *Appointment in Samarra* was published, John "was a bum in Pottsville. It was pornography." This recollection was harvested by the *Pottsville Republican* in 1978, on the occasion of a Pottsville John O'Hara conference, and Martin, his brother Eugene, and some O'Hara cousins were eager to catch the small wave of publicity before it petered out. Like most family legends of fellow townspeople's censure and ostracism, a concealed motive was ascribed: "the people who protested most loudly about the book," Martin assured the reporter, "were probably those who owed money to Dr. O'Hara." The local librarian, Miss Peterson, wouldn't stock the book, declaring herself "shocked. I didn't like the things O'Hara wrote, nor the way he wrote them. He brought a foreign vocabulary to our people, one they were not used to." (In fact, she went so far as to return a complimentary first edition of *A Rage to Live* to Random House: "Too trashy for our shelves.")[12]

Ex-neighbors' and dancing classmates' resentment lit in him a simmering brood. A year after the publication of *Appointment in Samarra* its author complained to his friend John McClain in a *New York Sun* interview that Pottsville residents who were near strangers approached him on visits home "with fire in their eyes, calling me names for holding them up to the ridicule of all their friends and threatening to sue me for defamation of character." As late as 1962, in a defensive letter to Gerald Murphy, regarding the notion that Murphy had been the inspiration for Dick Diver in *Tender Is the Night*, O'Hara was still answering questions no competent reader would think to ask: Was the likeness of Julian English a haphazard snapshot or a composed portrait? But, for his creator, this distinction reached beyond art into honor. That O'Hara was writing an unsolicited letter to a fellow famous for being a scrupulous gentleman—and for having been poorly used by his ill-mannered, frequent guest F. Scott Fitzgerald—itself tells a tale. O'Hara, like most nervy writers, used people. In fact, in a revealing phrase, following his petulant observation that Fitzgerald had been shocked by the salacious in *Butterfield 8*, O'Hara charges his late friend with having had "a fastidiousness that . . . should be no part of an author's equipment." (He did not scruple to varnish his own distastes, goodness knows; in a letter he wrote Hemingway while working on *Butterfield 8*, he declared of Maxwell Perkins and of Murphy's wife, Sara, "they don't like me, and I don't like them, in spades.")[13] What one may choose to think about the ethics of appropriation, and whether—in the notorious calculus of William Faulkner—any number of sweet old ladies might without tears be put to the blade to make possible one "Ode on a Grecian Urn," the old ladies have their own point of view. Whatever decency a writer salvages from his personal history, moral punctilio, bushido, or common consideration is incidental to a writer's essential selfishness. Claim as we might to be Robin Hoodish houseguests, helping ourselves to the manners and idioms and tics of friends and neighbors and kin in order to animate imaginary characters, the towels and silver are still missing at the end of the weekend. It would be best, I think, to concede as much; and then to decide, without resorting to self-justification, if one has the stomach for serial exploitation.

O'Hara insisted that Julian English was in fact based on some poor Joe (whom he named to Gerald Murphy) "who was definitely not country-club, but had charm and a certain kind of native intelligence, and who, when the chips were down, shot himself. I took his life, his psychological pattern, and covered him up with Brooks shirts and a Cadillac dealership and so on, and the reason the story rings so true is that it is God's truth, out of life."[14]

Whoa! "I took his life" is, in the novel's context, a hell of a claim. And where to begin with the fallacies of logic strewn through this boastful summary: if a Brooks shirt and country club membership were, as he claimed to Murphy (himself the scion of Mark Cross!), merely "superficial characteristics" or peripheral accessories, then what has furnished the "psychological pattern" of Julian English? He dies of hubris, having believed himself to be beyond the reach of consequence, armored as he has been by his breeding, tailoring, and club membership. If details are extraneous, then why would O'Hara choose to indulge the promiscuous overspecification that depressed his critical reputation during his creative life and beyond? In his novel *The Big Laugh*, published the year of that letter to Murphy, he writes about a Hubert Ward, a talentless and nasty actor who prospers by playing a "shitheel"—which his peers judge him to be—without winking at the camera, if only because he doesn't know himself well enough to wink. Ward drifts from the New York stage to Hollywood, where he succeeds tolerably in an art film, sets up housekeeping in an apartment-hotel on North Rossmore, buys a Lincoln convertible, and sends "English coach-at-the-inn" Christmas cards to those studio personages more powerful and celebrated than himself.[15] They in turn invite him to dinner parties, tennis, and beach luncheons. They lavish on Hubert Ward the same gold cuff links and gold cigarette lighters and gold pencils they lavish on everyone else, but they won't give him high billing on movie credits. There is, of course, a pecking order. Here are its "characteristics," and if they are "superficial" in the sense of being on the surface, they are not superficial to *The Big Laugh,* a fiction like all others in that it communicates interior turmoil by means of surface representation:

> He moved right into Hollywood Society, a curious combination of the powerful, the able, the glamorous, and, among the males, the wearers of the Brooks Brothers shirt. The actor or writer who continued to get his shirts by mail from Brooks after beginning to make movie money was somehow considered to be well connected socially back East, and in some cases was. But Hubert Ward's connections with Eastern Society were remote. . . . Hollywood Society, however, took him up without any investigation of their own claims for him. They appeared to like what he was not: he was not unemployed, he was not from Los Angeles, he was not a Latin or a Jew (the older Jews in Hollywood Society rebuffed younger Jews, even their own children) . . . he was not actorish.[16]

Despite the third-person voice, the perspective here—revealed by "appeared"—is Hubert Ward's. Whatever the absolute value of an amply cut, long-tailed blue oxford-cloth button-down, to Ward and, evidently, the society he wished to manipulate, such a shirt was as profoundly "superficial" as skeleton and skin, hair and eyes, the architecture of nose.

Despite, or because of, his friendship with Gilbert Roland and his wife, Constance Bennett, with Humphrey Bogart, Lauren Bacall, Tallulah Bankhead, James Cagney, Peter Lorre, and Cedric Hardwicke, O'Hara retained the contempt for actors that had poisoned his marriage with Pet Petit. When he enumerated not being "actorish" among the awful Hubert Ward's supposed virtues, he wrote from the heart. And in "Drawing Room B," a 1947 story as sneering as it is furious, O'Hara catches a falling star, Leda Pentleigh, whose manifestly fabricated name is no longer on everyone's lips.* Said drawing room is located on the Broadway Limited, a train assumed inferior to the Twentieth Century Limited, just as its point of departure—Penn Station—is seen as less desirable than Grand Central, which is closer to the Waldorf, where Pentleigh no longer is installed by her studio. Nor has she been conveyed to Pennsylvania Station by the Rolls or Packard that once carried her valued person. Crossing the terminal to her train, her eyes cast down to avoid celebrity-seekers who seem not to be seeking her, "pounding her Delman heels on the Penn Station floor, she recalled a remark she was almost sure she had originated, something about the autograph hounds not bothering her; it was when they didn't bother you that they bothered you. Of course it was Will Rogers or John Boles or Bill Powell or somebody who had first uttered the thought. . . . Well, whoever had said it first could have it."[17]

Seated in a corner of her drawing room, "on the wrong side of the car" so as to watch people on the platform, she leaves the door open to contemplate entraining passengers. She opens a "high-class" book and "watched the public (no longer so completely hers) going by. They all had that beaten look of people trying to find their space; bent over—surely not from the weight of their jewelry boxes."[18] Leda and the swine. O'Hara wrote ten-pound novels that couldn't convey, in their sum, as acute a distress as that faded glory cornered on an inferior train at rest in an inferior railroad station choosing to study her beaten-down fellow travelers "trying to find their space." Pitiless precision and a flawless ear for the cadences of disappointment, revealed through a series of "superficial" manifestations, create the story's peculiar genius. It is invigorating to read such an account of displeasure. The energy O'Hara spends on Leda Pentleigh is respectful; he weighs with her jeweler's delicacy the weight of those jewelry boxes.

She is approached in her drawing room by Kenyon Littlejohn, an amiable character actor who hopes that she might've seen him on the Broadway stage, might remember him. She hasn't, or doesn't, or won't. Never mind, he would like to ask her advice about securing a Hollywood agent, since he's going west for a screen test, "the older-brother part in 'Strange Virgin,' " and thinks he might like to stay. Leda Pentleigh interrupts him:

*This story was adapted for the off-Broadway stage in 1999, a production entitled *Train Stories* that also included "Travelogue" by Ring Lardner and Mary McCarthy's "Man in the Brooks Brothers Shirt," citing the eponymous and most notable characteristic of the man with whom her heroine, Peggy, has a drunken one-night stand in fact in a drawing room much like Leda Pentleigh's.

"New York actors come out for just one picture, or, at least, that's what they say. Of course, they have to protect themselves in case they're floperoos in Hollywood. Then they can always say they never planned to stay out there, and come back to New York and pan pictures till the next offer comes along, if it ever does. . . . 'That place,' they say. 'They put caps on your teeth and some fat Czechoslovakian that can't speak English tries to tell you how to act in a horse opera,' forgetting that the fat Czechoslovakian knows more about acting in his little finger than half the hamboes in New York. Nothing *personal*, of course, Mr. Little."[19]

Shortly into his second option period, O'Hara boarded the Twentieth Century Limited bound east to Grand Central. He'd be back, sooner than he believed. But he never did learn to write memorable film dialogue. His friend David Brown told me that he believed his dialogue—whether for film or fiction—"didn't play well for actors," and he wasn't saying anything he hadn't said to his friend's face. "His dialogue parsed. Was too pregnant. Not broken off. Like real speech. Wouldn't act." Had O'Hara been serious about writing for the screen, he might have found a method for that medium as effective as the indirection and compression and surprising collisions of his story dialogue; and in a way, Harold Pinter, David Mamet, and Neil LaBute are in the line of succession from O'Hara's most combative fictional set pieces.

But he had no need of another medium. He returned to New York to work on a new novel, *Butterfield 8,* and to await publication in 1935 of *The Doctor's Son and Other Stories.** O'Hara's first novel had been a success, going through three printings by October, when Harcourt, Brace, printed a full-page ad in the *Herald-Tribune* with twenty-six endorsements from A (Dorothy Parker's "A fine and serious American novel . . .") to Z ("Zest is the outstanding pleasure I derived," by Louis Untermeyer). Though his first address back in New York was once more the Pickwick Arms, he wouldn't stay long in that low-rent roost. He was restless with ambition, never more oddly expressed than by his reexploration that fall of Yale's admission procedures. Matthew J. Bruccoli reports that O'Hara expressed a desire of going to his dream-college

*He recollected his abrupt return east three decades later in "Hello Hollywood Good-Bye," as having been provoked by reading "week-late New York papers about the Ivy League football prospects, and the plays that would soon be opening on Broadway."

pre-med, with a view to becoming a psychiatrist or—even more risi-
bly—a ship's doctor. It's safe to assume he got the thin thanks-but-no-
thanks envelope, ameliorated somewhat by a mailing at about that time
from *Who's Who,* with a form to be filled out. (In a silly boast, O'Hara
had predicted to his father, who couldn't have cared less about such
things, that he'd be a listee before he hit thirty, and he was only a year
late.)

More important, the publication of *The Doctor's Son and Other Stories,* six months after *Appointment in Samarra,* confirmed his gift and
range. The title novella had not been previously published, and the other
thirty-six stories had made less of an impression appearing in magazines
than when taken together. Of the thirty-seven, two others, both written
during 1934, are first-rate: "It Must Have Been Spring," that self-
revealing memory (previously discussed) of a young horseman walking
through the withering fire of his father's appraisal; and "Over the River
and Through the Woods," a close third-person account of a Mr. Winfield's Thanksgiving journey from New York to the Berkshires, accompanied by his granddaughter and her two school friends to visit the house
he was obliged by declining fortune to sell to his son-in-law. This story is
remarkable for its inhabitation, by a writer still in his twenties, of a man
of sixty-five. Most young writers make a hash of this visionary undertaking, driven by either offhand pity or sentimentality to caricature what is
unimaginable to the young: a state of conservative expectation. Winfield's feebleness is never exaggerated, but he chills easily and has a
turbo-alertness to discomfort; he stumbles on ice, and doesn't get up
quickly, though he is never as imperiled as his young companions
assume. He is a courtly gentleman subjected by age and personal history—there is a suggestion that he was a drinker—to small humiliations.
His bedroom shares a bathroom with that occupied by one of his granddaughter's school friends, and when he knocks on her bedroom door to
offer her a cup of hot chocolate, since his hearing is imperfect, he mis-
takes her "wait a minute" for an invitation to enter. He opens the door to
find the girl undressed:

> Mr. Winfield instantly knew that this was the end of any worthwhile life
> he had left. There was cold murder in the girl's eyes, and loathing and
> contempt and the promise of the thought his name forever would
> evoke. She spoke to him: "Get out of here, you dirty old man."

He returned to his room and his chair. Slowly he took a cigarette out
of his case, and did not light it. He did everything slowly. There was all
the time in the world, too much of it, for him. He knew it would be
hours before he would begin to hate himself. For a while he would just
sit there and plan his own terror.[20]

The gulf between O'Hara's best stories and his least sketches is conspicuous in this collection. His failures here are seldom of music or situation, of observed detail or persuasive characterization. He writes about
hookers and about a counter girl in a fur-district lunchroom run by a
Chinese man caught in a tong war. (In "Ella and the Chinee" his narrator
manages to slander a whole world of the oppressed: "Micks" and "Wops"
and "Kikes," not to mention "old geezers.") He eavesdrops on the Afternoon Delphians, on partners whose attempts to name a coffee shop
result in "Coffee Pot." He overhears a deb's monologue about cutting
another girl dead at a dinner in New Haven before the Boat Races. He
oversees a petty crook and pool-hall hustler getting his hands smashed
for reaching in the wrong pocket. These are finger exercises, hasty sil-
houettes sketched on the fly, done and sold for a dime a word. By contrast his stories, and of course his first novel, prosper in direct proportion
to their consequence. Julian English famously throws his drink, in a
moment's surrender to boredom and distaste, in the face of a man to
whom he owes twenty thousand dollars. Mr. Winfield thinks to make
kind use of an extra cup of cocoa the maid has brought him. Both are the
agents of their undoing, and both act, in the Aristotelean sense, in har-
mony with their flaws. In Mr. Winfield's case, he wants the girl in the
next room to notice him and hold him in esteem, but what happens next,
in the space of a door-opening, is just about everything: the final door has
slammed shut behind him, and the fields before him will be swept by
enfilades discharged by the hostile society on the other side of his guest-
room door. No reader can offer to him the least consolation, can say, *Oh,
don't worry. They all know you aren't a dirty old man. It was a simple
misunderstanding, and will blow over.* At least Adam, cast from Eden,
made his solitary way hand in hand with Eve. Mr. Winfield is alone,
another of Julian English's lost tribe.

On the dust jacket of the Harcourt, Brace, edition of *The Doctor's Son*
appear two likenesses of O'Hara: a flattering sketch on the front, wavy-

haired and strong-chinned and soft-eyed; in the photo on the back flap, his face is lean and alert. After the obligatory biographical swagger—Mr. O'Hara "has jerked sodas, worked on two railroads and in a steel mill, on an ocean liner and a farm . . . he bummed east and west; was a day laborer"—he caused to be reported that "he was married once, is six feet one inch tall and weighs 184 pounds." (So he added an inch; doesn't everyone?) Putting aside the sass and bogus intemperance of the curriculum vitae—a template of its kind—it's clear that the author was in fighting trim, on the wagon, and that Pet was on his mind.

The stories were reviewed in the *New York Times Book Review* by Edith H. Walton, who for the most part is pleased ("shrewd, savage, merciless and apparently fertile in ideas") and manages in a short space to skim the prominent surfaces. She concludes, justly, that the lesser sketches are "thin, trivial, synthetic." She rightly invokes Ring Lardner as having influenced the idiomatic lowlife exercises and Hemingway's "Killers" as having inspired the brutal "Sportsmanship" of the broken hands. But there are two throwaway lines in Walton's review that were to become a mantra of O'Hara criticism, and both are wrongheaded.

The most damaging charge—imbedded in the review's final sentence—is that O'Hara "has no viewpoint to offer, that he records instead of judges." But how, in a work of fiction, can there be "no viewpoint"? Without p.o.v. there is no story (not even a flawed story), and point of view is always a *position,* in all senses of that word. It is a vantage, of course, the "location" from which the world is regarded and interpreted. But it is also, in the case of *Appointment in Samarra* and "Over the River and Through the Woods," an attitude about the dominant culture's point of view. This fiction reveals a society unflinching in its swift judgments, unblinking in its predations.

Walton's other charge is even more absurd. Applauding the "widening of range" in *The Doctor's Son* from *Appointment in Samarra,* whose milieu she flatly dismisses as "wastrels of the country club crowd," Walton gives birth to a canard that still quacks after O'Hara's reputation. The fallacy of his exclusive focus on the wellborn and rich began with one reviewer ignoring Luther and Irma Fliegler, ignoring bootleggers and molls, ignoring the bounty of characters and the fundamental lineaments of a novel published only six months earlier.

Some fictional properties are questions of opinion; others are matters of fact. In fact, O'Hara's social range was always expansive. In geography,

however, he inclined toward the binary—Gibbsville and its satellites
Harrisburg or Scranton, or New York and its own (Hollywood, generally)—whether writing about nabobs or about what he memorably called
"small-time smallies."[21]

Considering John Updike and William Maxwell, the critic Brooke
Allen wonders "what is there about American small-town life that so
many writers have found nurturing? What is there in these seemingly
dull and convention-ridden backwaters that obsesses certain writers and
provides them with apparently unlimited fictional material? Thurber's
Columbus and Anderson's Camden [Winesburg], Ohio; Maxwell's Lincoln, Illinois; Updike's Shillington, Pennsylvania." Allen postulates that
the draw of these "small, unexciting" communities is that "fixed social
structures and limited casts of characters are ideal for framing narratives. To know several generations of a family, however superficially, is to
be given the narrative satisfaction of seeing how a story turns out."[22] In
this deceptively plain-minded description of narrative impulse and
selection feeding a curious reader's appetite, Allen has gone to the heart
of both O'Hara's technical imperative—to fabricate a coherent narrative
design—and his destructive misapprehension—that he could again and
again chronicle successive generations of a family, or even several families, within the compass of single narratives, those monsters of extended
genealogy like *A Rage to Live* and *From the Terrace*.

In his long story "Ninety Minutes Away," O'Hara writes about a seedy
police reporter, Harvey Hunt, working his beat in a hinterland of Gibbsville (South Taqua, the burg is named, and it's probably okay to read that
as Tamaqua). Harvey weighs lighter on the social scale than Jim Malloy
or O'Hara himself, though like those fellow reporters he's a naysayer. A
local police sergeant explains, "If you're *for* something, he'll be against
it."[23] And Harvey, too, feels the pinch of a small town—where, knowing
so much, he can learn too little—and on an impulse moves to the Big
City, which on his cramped map means Philadelphia. He finds a job as a
night rewrite man and is flabbergasted not just by the noise of a metrop-
olis, but by the prodigal, outrageous luxury of stories, stories enough to
waste. "You simply could not have two million persons living together
without creating the frictions that result in news items. To a man who
had worked in the small towns of eastern Pennsylvania the city was inex-
haustibly rich with unwritten columns of wonderful, exciting stuff . . .
and in the excitement of his first year in a big city he felt the need to live

forever. . . . He had never seen so many rich people, so many poor people, so many people, and he wanted to know all about them."[24]

O'Hara's second novel, imagined even before *The Doctor's Son* was ready for the printer, would be *Butterfield 8*. If, like Harvey in Philly, O'Hara was stirred by "so many people" to want to know "all about them," how was he to impose narrative control in New York on such an appetite, such abiding curiosity? Not easily, was the immediate answer. Even more immediate than the problem of fictional abundance—all those characters, all their stories—was the problem of work itself, of discipline undone by distraction. Like most writers who have enjoyed a flash of attention, O'Hara took advantage of his small celebrity to extend his social reach, to get out and about. Now, this sort of horsing around isn't necessarily the venal sin that artistic piety so often condemns. There should be a mindless break between books, a holiday from preoccupation, an opportunity to encounter what serendipity instead of purpose might provide. Later, and most likely too soon, O'Hara would lay away the coonskin coat and flask, and direct the Prince Hal in him to renounce its Falstaff. He would finish one book and begin another as though they were widgets coming off the Acme production line, and as he grew older too much of what he understood was about beginning and finishing books, and too little was about the lived experience that books use and serve.

For now, he was experiencing life fully. After rooming briefly with Quentin Reynolds, a Brown University friend of S. J. Perelman and Nathanael West, he moved into a bachelor brownstone on East 55th, near Lexington, with John McClain, a sandy-haired and blithe football star at Brown, one of that team's "Iron Men." He was the ship news reporter of the *Evening Sun,* a sweet deal in the mid-1930s, when the great Cunarders and French Line passenger steamers brought cargos of the glamorous home from London and Paris. McClain, columnist of "On the Sun Deck," conveyed to the mouth of New York harbor by pilot boat, would board the ships before they docked, memorializing the banalities of celebs and practicing his genius at friendship. Finis Farr writes that McClain, from Marion, Ohio, had "special interest for O'Hara because from his first day in New York [he] behaved like an accepted insider, and in a short time that was what he was." O'Hara had met him at Tony's speakeasy through Dorothy Parker, who was infatuated with him. McClain was himself infatuated with money and prominence; enjoying a reputation as an able swordsman, what the French delicately know as *beau sabreur,* he resolved all too publicly to fuck his way up whichever social or pecuniary ladder was handiest. He worked out daily at a gym, and his fitness was expressed by a physique that was—in the judgment of Joseph P. Bryan III, a pal of O'Hara and Benchley and McClain[25]—"the male equivalent of a Rubens nude: a big, blond, handsome hunk of roast beef and cold cream." Soon this body went to his head, in the inevitably witty complaint of Dorothy Parker, of whose remorseless ardor he tired. He became a fixture as the extra man, and as Bryan tells it:

> At fashionable estates from Old Westbury to Bernardsville, guest books began to carry this entry, in John's clear, beautiful handwriting:
>
> > From east to west,
> > The nation's guest.
> > —John McClain
>
> Dottie said of an extremely rich Long Island hostess at whose house he had become almost a weekend fixture, "He'll be back as soon as he has licked all the gilt off her ass."[26]

And that was how one of his best friends wrote about him. In a few years McClain took his buff good looks to Hollywood, where he prospered as a friend to Robert Benchley and David Niven. But in New York he and O'Hara shared the ground floor of the place on East 55th, two rooms apiece. The writer was unreserved in his deference to McClain's social grace, what Ivy-Clubbed Princetonian Bryan summarized as "clean fingernails and a smooth tongue." The roommates' pleasures were unimpeded, and money was in good supply. For their valet, bartender, and chauffeur they hired a brooding former ship's steward called Burton—it sounds like a stage name—whom McClain had discovered. He drove the boulevardiers around New York in O'Hara's Ford, enduring the sophomoric ignominy of its vanity plate—the first of many secured from friendly politicos. "D-69"* evidently provoked in the phaeton's owner excessive mirth, and it was his routine to tell confused acquaintances that he continually found strange women sitting in it. (He liked to park it across 55th, in front of a notorious whorehouse.) But after six months of service, Burton quit, complaining that "there was too much action around the premises."[27]

---

*That would be *D* for *Doc.*

With McClain as an unwholesome model, O'Hara became a flagrant kisser-and-teller. He'd always liked to shock, but during this stint his manners with women coarsened. McClain, with his artless charm, slipped his serial conquests by as boyish mischief. Easygoing was his manner to a marked degree: Farr wrote of O'Hara's roommate that "McClain's charm lay in the broad tolerance of his views, and . . . his willingness to overlook shortcomings in others was so well known that the height of horror was expressed when some disgraceful affair took place and it was said that 'even McClain was shocked.' "

Eventually he was shocked by his roommate, when he returned home from the *Sun* with a young woman to pick up O'Hara for a lunch date. Having forgotten the engagement, O'Hara greeted the couple wearing his underpants, instructed them to wait while he concluded an ongoing chore, and, without closing the door to his bedroom, wrapped up a performance—theatrically strident—of lovemaking. He had partners aplenty, and each was destined to learn from O'Hara the names and preferences of the others. Such narratives, even more than the knowledge of his promiscuity and his frequent contagions of the clap, tempered the devotion of the women he pursued during the McClain period. Yet contrary to Edith Walton's charge, in these pursuits he was democratic: he went after debutantes and semi-pros from the kick lines.

A frequent target of his attention was Ruth Sato, a Japanese showgirl he had met at Billy Rose's Casino de Paree, a dinner club at which Benny Goodman's orchestra provided the dance music. Her working hours suited his: at night, while she showed off what nightclub revue patrons pay to see, he wrote; in the early morning they'd go to the Stork Club, or she'd come to East 55th for cookies and hot chocolate (as he was still on the wagon that winter of 1935). He read dialogue to her from the early pages of *Butterfield 8,* and in the name of research for the novel's first chapter, set in a Park Avenue apartment, he took her to one that was offered for sale; they feigned marriage, and an interest in buying. O'Hara was comfortable enough with Sato to mock her origins, to take liberties of a kind that today would get a suitor carried off in leg irons. He found it amusing to make lame jokes about the opium trade—Japanese or Chinee, what's the diff?—and Matthew J. Bruccoli reports that O'Hara was extravagantly amused to learn that "Hara" in Japanese means large valley, as in yodeling in the breast-rimmed ravine. He nicknamed her "Sato San," with what passed for affection, and "Peril," as in Yellow Peril. "It's a good thing you are the only Jap I know," he wrote to her from North Carolina in February, during a road trip to Key West. "Think of the confusion. Ah, but confusion was Chinese!"[28]

Meantime, he was seeing Pet. From Hollywood he had written his brother Tom that while "Marg was the one for me; Pet I love actively and deeply." He also offered his naked chest to the sword of confession: after reassuring his closest brother of his fundamental decency, he allowed as how he was "fundamentally decent," too, but on the other hand "I was— am—a weak character." He advised Tom to settle down, to get himself "a good girl and stick with her."[29] He then meditated about the nature of the "congenital tendency" of O'Haras "to dominate your wife or your girl" and offered an unsolicited exhortation—"Never forget that your girl or your wife is every damn bit as much a person as you are"—which he then elaborated: "She regards you as another person, just as you regard her as another person. She thinks the world revolves around her just as you do around yourself, just as anyone does. She has a vote in life as well as in politics, she eats and sleeps and suffers and thinks (regardless of how badly you and I may think she thinks) like you and me. She was born, she lives, she's got to die; and for you the attempt to dominate her, to pinch her personality, is some kind of sin."

Putting aside the bully-boy parenthetical, this passage has the atmosphere of felt homily. It may even explain in part his lack of gallantry toward women at this time, his disregard of the convention of reticence— otherwise peculiar in a man bent on being known as a gentleman—in his erotic affairs. He thought of women as fellow seducers, or accomplices in seduction. He surely thought of them as powerfully endowed with points of view, capable of commanding narratives as well as relationships.

Another of these relationships was with Zita Johann, a stage and movie actress memorable—or not—for *Grand Canary* and *Voice from the Grave*. Walter Winchell told his readers that O'Hara and Johann "are having an appointment in Samarra,"* and in fact he discussed marriage with her even as he was discussing remarriage with Pet. But Johann didn't love him, and didn't even much like him. For one thing, she was put off by his touchiness. Introducing him to a friend, she forgot his name and called him Irving Thalberg. He was hurt; and who wouldn't

*My god how flattered, bored, and finally haunted O'Hara must've been by unimaginative variations on that title in interviews, profiles, reviews, his own columns ("Appointment with O'Hara"), and parodies ("Appointment with the Dentist").

have been? But he was so easily hurt. Frank MacShane tells of O'Hara feeling stung to see the songwriter Howard Dietz leave a nightclub with an acquaintance, and announcing to all nearby: "I've slept with that woman!"

There was this recurrent progression in O'Hara's associations at that time: he'd become increasingly childish in his demands, and draw down to zero balance the patience of friends. It had happened in Pottsville, then in New York, in Pottsville again, in New York, in Hollywood, and now back in New York. Pet would drop by his 55th Street apartment in the company of a little dog, and they'd sometimes even dream aloud of returning to each other. Then he'd become jealous of some man, or of Pet's yappy pet, or he'd spill his guts about someone he'd taken into this very bed. In February, Pet told O'Hara that it was over for her, and she meant it.

It's difficult to know how deeply, if indeed at all, this affected him. Soon after the terminal breakup he left New York for the trip south, during which he wrote with such self-pleasuring jocularity to Ruth Sato. He drove to Key West with the notion of writing a profile of Ernest Hemingway for the *New Yorker*, which had advanced him money for the piece. He hid his purpose from Hemingway, who didn't even know O'Hara was bearing down on him, who might in fact have been in Africa, or Cuba, or even New York. In fact he was in Key West, but O'Hara decided not to bother him when he learned that Hemingway was entertaining some swells, so the *New Yorker* was obliged to reconcile itself to Lillian Ross's famous anatomy (and autopsy and interment) of the celebrated writer, perhaps the most influential and style-setting profile the magazine ever published.

From Key West he made his way to Miami, where he settled in at the Hotel Cortez to work on *Butterfield 8* and pitch woo to a showgirl appearing in *Earl Carroll's Vanities*. He later wrote Hemingway: "It took me a week to find out that she was Lesbian. They have to wear suits and smoke cigars before I recognize them."[30]

He was jittery, and this time—unlike his experience of restlessness while he was trying to get a grip on *Appointment in Samarra*—he knew what to do about it. He had explained to friends that he could best plunge into the imaginative life of small-time Gibbsville from the vantage of a city like New York; now, to see with fresh eyes the rudiments and textures of New York's nightlife and the demimonde of Gloria Wandrous—*Butterfield 8*'s heroine—he needed to decamp to a small town. After visiting F. Scott Fitzgerald in Baltimore,* he returned briefly to the East 55th apartment, packed, and headed north to Cape Cod, to the Oceanside Inn in East Sandwich. There he dug in for several months of the kind of committed attention to his work that he hadn't managed since his honeymoon trip to Bermuda. In East Sandwich he was undistracted. As a weekly draw against a total advance of one thousand dollars, O'Hara received fifty per week from Charles A. ("Cap") Pearce, his editor at Harcourt, Brace, and this was sufficient. As he wrote to Pearce fifteen thousand words into the novel: "My room has two windows facing the sea, and a third looking out on the long beach. I am less than 50 yards from the surf. The food is good and plain, and I am the only guest. I pay $25 a week. There is no sex, no nothin'. I work in the afternoon and in the evening, and quit at one a.m. It is now after that."[31]

By the time he next wrote, perhaps a week or two later, he was growing a beard and had twenty-five thousand words. (The words came out of the typewriter "*zip-zip!* just like that," O'Hara wrote eleven years later, in his introduction to *Here's O'Hara*, a collection of stories and three short novels.)[32] From this shutdown off-season seaside isolation, New York must have taken on precisely the unforgiving grandeur, the noise and bustle and impatient expectation, that O'Hara sought for his novel. Just as Hemingway had best reentered the Big Two-Hearted River from Montparnasse, and Edith Wharton's New York and Newport gave up their quiddities from Italy and France, or James mapped Washington Square in Sussex, the mind's eye was naked, focusing from memory and coloring by invention and without reference to those research tomes that O'Hara later so excessively relied on for narrative credibility. The world of Gloria Wandrous became his *only* world, and in his solitude he populated it and occupied her.

Her name in the newspapers had been Starr Faithfull, and her interpreter adhered with rough fidelity to her lurid story. In June of 1931 a drugged and battered body, dressed in silk and three days in the water, washed ashore on Long Island's Long Beach. She was twenty-five. There

---

*Many years later O'Hara told his stepson C. D. B. Bryan that Fitzgerald had taken Zelda from the sanatorium for the afternoon. While O'Hara drove, with Zelda between them on the front seat, Fitzgerald—fastidious when he was, not when he was not—began petting his wife. "See, I can still get her hot." Bryan writes, "I never felt the same about [him] afterward."

is a patina of allusive irony in O'Hara's title, inasmuch as Faithfull may have been (as Gloria Wandrous suggestively was) a call girl. Though she lived in Greenwich Village (on St. Luke's Place at an address the tabloids enjoyed reporting was "a few doors down" from Mayor Jimmy Walker), she was a fixture with the fast crowd from that Upper East Side neighborhood—Park Avenue between 70th and 80th—whose telephone exchange had recently been changed to BU(tterfield) 8, one of those Manhattan exchanges, like RH(inelander) 4 and EL(dorado) 5, ubiquitous in the *Social Register.*

The drowned girl was pretty enough to have had her personal history made notorious not only on the front pages of the tabloids (emphasis on nails painted bright red, clad "only" in silk, fashionably bobbed hair bobbing seaweedy in the surf) but also in a *New Yorker* article. Faithfull had lived a gothic horror of bad luck and bad judgment. While suicide notes were produced to account for her death, these were properly regarded with some suspicion, since a good many older men had reason to feel relief that this adorable and difficult young woman was no longer present to be difficult. It's likely that O'Hara also learned about her from John McClain, because Faithfull was a fixture aboard transatlantic ships, what the tabs termed "a good-time girl" who had made a specialty of bon-voyage parties. The theory was that she didn't make the final gangplank call for the *Franconia*'s all ashore that's going ashore, and so she got to shore from beyond Lady Liberty, the hard way, following a jump or a shove.

In 1994 Gloria Vanderbilt's novel, *The Memory Book of Starr Faithfull,* an imaginary diary, emphasized her precocious eroticism and enthusiasm for ether—"creamy dreamy," in the Vanderbilt lexicon. This account seems consistent with what is known of the facts, that in puberty (or possibly before), her cousin Andrew J. Peters, the mayor of Boston at that time and thirty years her elder, used ether—and, even worse, the words of Havelock Ellis—to put the girl in a semi-swoon so that he could more conveniently abuse her at his leisure. O'Hara's *Butterfield 8* dramatizes the final days of Gloria Wandrous's life, but accounts for her promiscuity, flakiness, and alcoholism by an exposition of flashed-back facts in which the heroine has been molested at eleven first by her uncle's friend Major Boam; soon after, following a train ride, she is improbably seduced by Joab Ellery Reddington, a portly school principal and major creep out of Victorian melodrama, equipped with both ether and a Phi Beta Kappa key chain hung over his vested belly (but somehow denied waxed moustaches). "Within a month he had her sniffing ether and loving it. It, and everything that went on in that room."[33]

Soon enough, every aspect of her character turns contrary and perverse. She won't allow a physical relationship with her best friend Eddie, whom she loves, precisely because she loves him and he loves her. Gloria's self-disgust is relentless, and owing to that shame she will not cease punishing herself. O'Hara was thrusting here at a fictional fashion of the day, subconscious motivation, psychologically determined characterization. But his lunge was halfhearted. He was more beguiled, of course, by social determinism, and would have felt more comfortable with Marx than with Freud. But he also seemed to retain those Manichean habits of belief trained in him by nuns and priests: reflecting on Gloria, the dreadful Reddington says to himself, "God damn that girl! I am a good man. I am a bad man, a wicked man, but she is worse. She is really bad. She is bad, she is badness. She is Evil. She not only is *evil,* but she *is* Evil."[34] The train of thought is so corrupt a denial of responsibility as to approach parody, but O'Hara is at ease with the dualistic lexicon.

There was another, coarser incentive for him to seek a ready explanation of Gloria's neurotic and self-destructive behavior in his novel. He was in a hurry, and counted on plot—what Hollywood calls "backstory"—to solve character. This expository temptation forever dogged him, and the less he listened to editorial advice, the lower his reluctance to pluck all-too-fitting causes for effects rather than develop dramatic outcomes—at their best surprising—from enacted provocations.

He finished *Butterfield 8* at the George V in Paris. In one of those touchingly self-memorializing plaques to which writers long have been susceptible once they reach the final full stop after the final sentence of a final page, he noted: "Exactly 2 o'clock p.m., August 5, 1935/Paris France."[35] Perhaps remembering his plan to finish *Appointment in Samarra* aboard the *Kungsholm,* he had taken the manuscript of his new novel to Genoa aboard the *Conte di Savoia* on borrowed money, and from Genoa to Florence, and from Florence to Paris. There was never any danger that O'Hara would become an expatriate, or even much of a tourist. As he wrote Cap Pearce, "I have only seen Paris from the taxi window, from the station to the hotel."[36] He didn't leave the hotel—not even his room!—until he finished the book, having his meals sent up and writing until he fell asleep.

He assured Pearce in the letter that he'd made time during the crossing to win the ship's rifle-shooting contest "with a score of 57 out of a possible 60. Only one passenger ever has made a 60; that was last year when the weather must have been a good deal smoother. . . . I got a cup as a trophy." He provided Pearce with the firearm's make and model, but on the merits of the novel he would ship off to him the following day he was less forthcoming: "I don't know how it is. Sometimes I think it's good, sometimes I think it stinks." This prophetically anticipated the critical range of its reception.

Butterfield 8 has continued either to excite or numb readers who have good reason to respect one another's judgment. In this the novel is a critical touchstone, with the delighted hooraying its scope and the dismayed deploring its sprawl. Among contemporary writers Louis Begley is a booster, admiring the moral seriousness of O'Hara's treatment of the collision between Gloria and Weston Liggett (Yale, Skull and Bones, first-eight oarsman), with whom she falls in love. That he is twice her age and a social-climbing ass—who has roughed up Gloria during a first-night stand at his Park Avenue apartment just before the novel opens—strikes friends of the novel as organic to its virtues, a putatively unsentimental group portrait of café society and its commingling of Piping Rock golfers and speakeasy hoods. In this reckoning *Butterfield* 8 flows from *The Great Gatsby* toward *Bonfire of the Vanities.* Here is Begley applauding the 1994 Modern Library reissue: "It is high time to bring back *Butterfield* 8. We need the astringent of O'Hara's idiom and the moral sense that makes him able to show the somber American colors and intimate ugliness of vice: paunchy old men whose hands suddenly go wild over bodies of little girls; gin-sodden remittance men and stockbrokers in Brooks Brothers suits; Park Avenue doctors scraping out pregnancies; the terror of past-due club bills and checks written on depleted accounts."[37]

The story begins arrestingly. Gloria wakes early on a May Sunday in a stranger's bed. Half-drunk and already hungover, she finds herself in a man's undone pajama bottoms. She holds the drawstring open, and laughs: "I wonder where he is."[38] At any rate, he isn't at home on Park Avenue. As to who he is, she soon pieces together his c.v. from framed and "enlarged" photos: men and women and girls standing beside saddle horses. ("There was one snapshot of a girl in a tandem cart, a hackney hitched to it, but if you looked carefully you could see that there was a tiestrap, probably held by a groom who was not in the picture.") On Gloria's behalf, O'Hara looks very carefully: prize ribbons, several viewpoints of a family yacht, and—almost too inevitably—"one picture of an eight-oared shell, manned; and one picture of an oarsman holding a sweep." This picture she inspects closely, the three-button crew shirt with the inescapable crotched letter over its heart. But she also notices that "his trunks were bunched in the very center by his jock strap and what was in it."* Poking around the empty apartment, whose dining room "made her think of meats with thick gravy on them," Gloria discovers a woman's closet in which is hung a mink coat; she discovers, too, that her evening dress has been torn, "ripped in half down the front as far as the waist," and that Weston Liggett has left her a note and three twenty-dollar bills. "This is for the evening gown," to which her judicious response is, "The son of a bitch." She leaves with the sixty dollars, a Liggett daughter's black felt hat, and Mrs. Liggett's mink.

Had *Butterfield 8* sustained the furious social comedy of these lacerating introductory pages—the collision between Gloria's ferocious vengeance and Liggett's smug peacock vanity—the novel would be all that Louis Begley claims for it. In the event, *Butterfield 8* is almost conquered by its disjunctions—of story, sentiment, and moral precept. At the source of this fractious confusion is its author's divided attitude toward two of its principals: Gloria and Jim Malloy.

Malloy, O'Hara's stand-in, would reappear again and again in stories and novels and novellas set in Pennsylvania and New York, but it isn't clear how he got invited to *Butterfield 8*'s party. His rant about all Irishmen being the same "Mick," noted in an earlier chapter, gives us an understanding of O'Hara, but is irrelevant to Weston Liggett or to Gloria Wandrous, both of whom happen to share a city, but not their lives, with this newspaper reporter whose narrative purpose is obscure. In this novel Malloy and a Gibbsville woman drinking in a speakeasy notice across the room Caroline English of *Appointment in Samarra*, and many tales later he is the narrator and central to the action of *Imagine Kissing Pete*, a 1960 Gibbsville novella with cross-references to the night Julian English threw a drink in Harry Reilly's face. A character in *Imagine Kissing Pete* refers to Reilly as a "cheap Irish Mick," to which Malloy, who

---

*When a bona fide ex-oarsman—a press agent, of all people!—revealed to O'Hara that rowers didn't wear jockstraps, that smart aleck made a lifelong enemy.

has no fondness for Reilly but has evolved from his *Butterfield 8* certitudes ("We're Micks, we're non-assimilable, we Micks"), responds, "call
him something else."[39]

If Malloy is a stowaway, Gloria is a multiple personality. O'Hara can't
decide whether she's an embittered victim of cynical abuse, a bad seed, a
personification of the lawlessness of speakeasy culture, a romantic heroine, or just a good little gal who wants in her heart of hearts to settle
down with an upstanding guy and raise decent kids. She hates Liggett
(with good reason) and also loves him (for no evident reason at all). Her
cruelty is perverse and arbitrary on one page, her generosity boundless
on another.

In *The Confidence-Man,* Melville's narrator inquires rhetorically,
"Where does any novelist pick up any character? For the most part, in
town, to be sure. Every great town is a kind of man-show, where the novelist goes for his stock, just as the agriculturalist goes to the cattle-show
for his."[40] During O'Hara's visit to the man-show he seems to have been
undone by his confusion of plenty with magnificence. This is a common
miscalculation of second novels, those frequently overweening exercises
that are set up by their ambitious authors for bruising falls: if they liked
Appointment, wait till they get a load of *Butterfield!* If Pottsville had
ideal scale for O'Hara's first novel, with its social variety and small population, its constricted economic and geographical scope, New York was
fundamentally inchoate, a collection of discrete societies which O'Hara
could only cause to overlap by the exercise of arbitrary plot devices and
such institutions as the newspaper (allowing license to brush up against
Eddie Brunner, who loved Gloria) and the speakeasy, where people
unknown to one another gathered together. Malloy never meets Gloria,
and fifty-plus characters wander hurriedly and distractedly through the
novel's pages, like strangers passing on Fifth Avenue.

There are passages in *Butterfield 8* which face and audaciously exploit
the daunting hodgepodge of New York's concurrent stories. At the
novel's midpoint its fifth chapter begins:

> On Monday afternoon an unidentified man jumped in front of a New
> Lots express in the Fourteenth Street subway station. . . . Robert
> McDermott, a student at Fordham University, was complimented for
> his talk on the Blessed Virgin at the morning exercises in her honor. A
> woman named Plotkin, living in the Brownsville section of Brooklyn,

decided to leave her husband for good and all. William K. Fenster-macher, the East 149th Street repairman, went all the way to Tremont Avenue to fix a radio for a Mrs. Jones, but there was no Jones at the given address, so he had to go all the way back to the shop, wasting over an hour and a half. Babe Ruth hit a home run into the bleachers near the right field foul line.[41]

The sequence of field notes continues for another page—"John Lee, a colored boy, pulled the wings out of a fly in Public School 108"—and concludes with Gloria Wandrous "worrying over what she should do about Mrs. Liggett's mink coat" and with Eddie Brunner playing a Rudy Vallee recording. The experiment is attentive to cadence and detail. "The" East 149th Street repairman is nicely contrasted to "a" Mrs. Jones, with the articles equipping a reader with telephoto or wide-angle lenses. The effect, artfully random, is akin to reading a great city's newspaper. Notwithstanding the formal achievement of John Dos Passos's *Manhattan Transfer,* such news-clipped and news-reeled roll calls, absent mosaic calculation, are generally antithetical to the composition of a novel with a cohesive social and moral purpose.

Butterfield 8 reaches for coherence—or perhaps transcendence—by way of notional abstractions applied to two historic circumstances: the Depression and Prohibition. Jim Malloy's rumination on the latter, from *Imagine Kissing Pete,* has been quoted on previous pages: a stupid law imposed by zealots translated honorable citizens into cheats and cynics, "making liars of a hundred million men and cheats of their children."[42] Wised-up skepticism hard-boils *Butterfield 8's* prose and characters. As Jim Malloy recollects in *Imagine Kissing Pete,* "we knew so much, and since what we knew seemed to be all there was to know, we were shock-proof."[43] And, still in an aphoristic mood, he concludes—updating Gertrude Stein's French auto mechanic—that "we were the losing, not the lost, generation."[44] As in losing money, that is. This was the conjunctive role the Crash and Depression played,* and the experience of economic collapse surely confounded cosmopolitan savoir faire, the confidence that "we knew . . . all there was to know." Because less than a page after boasting of "shockproof" comprehension, Malloy declares that "we had grown up and away from our earlier esteem of God and

*Not for nothing was Fitzgerald's searching account of his depression titled "The Crack-Up."

country and valor, and had matured at a moment when riches were vanishing for reasons that we could not understand."[45]

In Gibbsville, the consequences of crashed stock prices and sluggish spending are immediately evident in unpaid grocery bills and club resignations, unbought Cadillacs, downward mobility, and shocking social realignments. Jim Malloy, in *Imagine Kissing Pete,* describes his hard times as a free lance in New York, the many jobs he's lost, and tells his boyhood friends that he's living on the edge and might have to limp home. They in turn let him know that in Gibbsville it's even worse, having to move to "parts of town that were out of the way for their old friends. There is no town so small that that cannot happen, and Gibbsville, a third-class city, was large enough to have all the grades of poverty and wealth and the many half grades in between, in which $10 a month in the husband's income could make a difference in the kind and location of the house in which he lived."[46]

In the New York of *Butterfield 8,* the sums were greater, the shocks less immediately evident, narrative synergy less reliable. O'Hara is very smart about how the Depression registered on the generation of Weston Liggett.

> These men began taking stock of what life had given them or they had taken. Usually men of this kind began counting with, "I have a wife and two children . . ." and go on from there to their "investments," cash, job, houses, cars, boats, horses, clothes, furniture, trust fund, pair of binoculars, club bonds, and so on. They were—these men—able to see right away that the tangible assets in the Spring of 1931 were worth on the whole about a quarter of what they had cost originally, and in some cases less than that. And in some cases, nothing. By the time the depression had reached that point such men accepted as fact the fact that nothing you could buy or sell was worth what it once had been worth. . . . Then a few men, a few million, asked themselves whether the things they had bought ever had been worth what had been paid for them. Ah! That was worth thinking about.[47]

As a run of prose, this passage has brisk immediacy, and its stern assessment of the value of value predicts the journalism of Tom Wolfe. Still, it is of a taxonomy not far removed from "the very rich . . . are different from you and me." Fitzgerald transcends his generalization of

"The Rich Boy" by specifying and dramatizing the singularities of Anson Hunter: "solid rock" yet "sybarite," sentimental yet scornful of "unstable women," a man trusted and admired by old people and young alike. O'Hara's Weston Liggett never surmounts his classification: "men of this kind," "these men," "such men." Narrowed for an instant to "a few men," plenty enough characters to drive a novel, the increase to "a few million" is epidemic, a sum better suited to economics or sociology than to visionary portraiture.

Butterfield 8 was published in October and sold out its first printing of fifteen thousand in two days, but the second printing of ten thousand moved slowly. The quick sell-through of a first printing is a notorious sucker-trap for writers inclined to trust the myth of eternal progress. What such early book sales often indicate is simply, and happily, that the author now has a core audience; O'Hara's, developed by his stories and first novel, amounted to some fifteen thousand people, impatiently awaiting any book he wrote. Matthew J. Bruccoli reports that O'Hara's royalties for 1935 came to $8,502.53, a fair sum for an observer of the "losing" generation.

Many reviewers were scandalized by the book's dirtiness. English editors, who had taken warmly to *Appointment in Samarra,* shied till 1951 from *Butterfield 8.* In the *New Republic,* a couple of months after the novel's publication, Malcolm Cowley—reviewing the reviewers whom O'Hara had dubbed "little old ladies of both sexes"—spoke for the prigs in describing the novel's characters: "The people John O'Hara describes are as limited in sensibility as so many shellfish. . . . They are confined to four interests in life: getting money, getting drunk, going to bed and going to the bathroom." Warming to his work, Cowley added that "they have boorish manners and the morals of a pink-nosed Chester boar."[48] Harcourt, Brace, had excised the word "fuck" and references to pleasure-giving body parts. Twenty-two years later, in a lecture at the Library of Congress, O'Hara remembered and quoted from O. O. McIntyre's review: "Some of the literati say John O'Hara's *Butterfield 8* is swell. I say it's swill."[49]

But what must have stung—indeed it is every novelist's pride-sapping dread—was to be told in public that the would-be daring *Butterfield 8* was tedious. And imagine the hurt to be told in print by his old friend, employer, and benefactor Heywood Broun that his novel was dull! Broun confessed that he wouldn't have read past the middle, where he was "bogged down, had he not been on a train journey," had "it been possible to find a fourth for bridge—or even a third, for that matter."* For a writer who rightly prided himself on the delicacy of his ear, it must have been especially galling to read of Broun's "uneasy sense that all the speeches were delivered by the same person. The lady of not very difficult virtue spoke exactly like the newspaper reporter, and for the life of me I could not distinguish the idiom of the illustrator from California and that of the business man who rowed on the crew at Yale." And then he piled on, accusing the novel's "people" of being "not only dull but unrecognizable. Quite frequently their actions are as puzzling to me as their words. Even the major premise of Gloria's many affairs found me dubious. It seemed to me that the lady did protest her lack of virtue far too much. So much of her time was spent in talking about sinning that I wondered how she ever managed to catch up with her homework."[50] To stand accused of having written a dirty book was no shame, but of having left out the good parts? What fresh hell was this? as Dorothy Parker liked to ask.

Butterfield 8 was not without its admirers, then as now. John Chamberlain, on publication day in the *New York Times,* read it as a "highly moral tale." The *Saturday Review,* so mulish in its aversion to *Appointment in Samarra,* defended the new novel against charges that it was raw journalism, declared it to be satire, and about the characters assured readers that their creator "knows exactly how they behave in all the typical circumstances of their lives."[51]

It is in the treatment of Gloria Wandrous that O'Hara wanders, at times seemingly bewildered. Crucially, he leaves ambiguous how she died. She might have thrown herself into the water forward of the ship's side-wheels, to be sucked into the housing together with "floating timber and dead dogs and orange peel" and crushed. "It was half an hour before they got what was left of Gloria out from between the blade and the housing, and nobody wanted to do it then. . . . There was no place in her body where there was a length of bone unbroken more than five inches. One A[ble] B[oatman] fainted when he saw what he was going to have to

---

*O'Hara's finely tuned perception of justice sometimes overrode his finely tuned sensitivity to grievance. When Broun died late in 1939, O'Hara wrote the *New Republic* that "He made a lot of people seem right by letting it be known that they were his friends. He honored me, by God, by letting me sit with him, work for him, drink to him." O'Hara, *Letters,* p. 157.

do." There's something prurient about the tabloid verve of that description, O'Hara approaching scopophilia in his close-up view of Gloria's mangled corpse. Weston Liggett has a different version of events. She died running from him after he'd tried to take her to bed aboard the Boston-bound steamship. As readers had been warned pages earlier, the hand railing around the top deck "was too low; it was dangerous." Liggett knows that's what killed Gloria: owing to "the motion of the ship she ran smack into the rail, which is extremely low." In other words, *Butterfield 8* has not advanced Gloria's story beyond the casual journalistic speculation—inferring rival and mutually exclusive possibilities from the single fact of a dead body—that inspired the novel. It's difficult to imagine O'Hara as one of those laissez-faire novelists who—when asked which was it, suicide or accident?—shrugs and says, Suit yourself, one reading's as good as another.* Malcolm Cowley took particular offense at what he took to be resolution-by-accident. This judgment must be read in the context of his conviction that "Gloria is an appealing character and a real one," whose "acts ring true" until the final act. "Mr. O'Hara denies her [the right to die tragically] and makes her die by accident because *The City of Essex* had a low guardrail. It is this slovenly handled death scene that changes the story from drama to melodrama, from Hemingway at his best to Hemingway mixed with Hearst."[52] Cowley had reason to feel strongly about death by separation at sea from the sanctuary of a vessel: in 1932 his wife, Peggy, was homeward bound with Hart Crane from Mexico via Cuba when the poet jumped overboard and was swallowed up.

*Judging by a letter Starr Faithfull wrote four days before her body washed ashore, suicide was a probability. In this letter—to a man for whom she felt unrequited love—she begins, "It's all up with me now. This is something I am GOING to put through. . . . If one wants to get away with murder one has to jolly well keep one's wits about one. It's the same with suicide. I intend to watch out and accomplish my end this time. No ether, allonal or window jumping. I don't want to be maimed. I want oblivion. . . . Nothing makes any difference now. I love to eat and can have one delicious meal with no worry over gaining."

And on the subject of murder, a local district attorney described the event as "death by drowning, brought about by someone interested in closing her lips." This, together with her letter, is quoted by Lisa Grunwald and Stephen J. Adler in *America 1900–1999: Letters of the Century* (New York: The Dial Press, 1999), p. 205. The editors cite the source of this suicide note as *Postmortem: The Correspondence of Murder* (1972), whose author, Jonathan Goodman, published in 1996 *The Passing of Starr Faithfull*, which argues that the young woman was murdered by gangsters prying into rumors of her love affair with a friend of Franklin D. Roosevelt, either that ethereal Boston mayor or the more earthy New York mayor.

Not every reviewer regarded Gloria as worthy of a tragic death, or as worth a reader's interest, let alone sympathy. One of the cruelest notices was Clifton Fadiman's, titled by its *New Yorker* editors "Disappointment in O'Hara." Fadiman's pan wasn't a patch on Brendan Gill's nuclear *New Yorker* strike against *A Rage to Live* fourteen years later, but till that hostility was expressed with relish, this would do: the critic declared himself to have "not the slightest interest" in these "small" characters, whose conversations, lusts, and yearnings were "small," and their author hadn't redeemed the risk of being dull about the dull. Most bitter was Fadiman's prophecy about the future of a young and serious writer who had tried hard to trust the goodwill of the magazine he had hoped would nurture him: "the path" he'd cut for himself in *Appointment in Samarra* "is bound to end in a blind alley."[53]

Once again, O'Hara decided that he had best go west, that he was "sick of New York and New York was sick of me."[54] If Cowley had been too cruel in his summary dismissal of *Butterfield 8*'s dénouement, he might have been too kind in his enthusiasm for Gloria's clarity as a character. Following her opening scene, lucidly and corrosively vengeful, in Liggett's apartment, Gloria becomes arbitrary, opaque in her motives, virtually unknowable. It is irresponsible to account for a writer's failure with a fictional heroine by invoking his recent history of failed love relationships, but this was as perplexing a period as O'Hara was ever to experience in his associations with women. There were so many pursued, and of such various temperaments and circumstances, that it's necessary to keep a playlist to make sense of the chronology.

Following Ruth Sato and Zita Johann came Dorothy Van Hest, another showgirl announced in a Walter Winchell column as O'Hara's bride-at-hand. Then, during the busiest days of his composition of *Butterfield 8*, at a house party in the Berkshires he met Barbara Kibler, a nineteen-year-old Wellesley sophomore from Ohio. He broke his routine at the Cape to court her in Boston that spring of 1935, and by publication date wrote Fitzgerald that he was in love. "She is 5'3", dark, beautiful figure and looks younger than she is. She is from Columbus, and her family are nouveau riche and Protestant. You would like her. . . . Barbara and I are most likely going to get wed the minute I sign a Hollywood contract."[55]

During the previous year, thanks in part to the interest excited by *Appointment in Samarra* and *The Doctor's Son*, O'Hara had begun hob-

nobbing with people too good for Weston Liggett. Among these were
John Durant, from an esteemed Connecticut family with deep and
spreading roots at Yale, who had made a fortune on the stock market and
lost it in the Crash, incurring huge debts that he famously repaid, a dollar on the dollar, down to the last penny. Though he routinely beat
O'Hara at tennis, Durant told Finis Farr, "he kept challenging me. I cannot recall an opponent that I ever faced with such confidence. . . . All I
had to do was simply to get the ball back to him and he would eventually
make the error. He was a cinch." Another new friend was Robert M.
Lovett, a New York banker (Averell Harriman's partner) and later secretary of defense, and his wife, Adele, a short-term close friend to Dorothy
Parker and—for the long haul—to O'Hara. (Frank MacShane explains
that when O'Hara inevitably quarreled with her, she reminded him that
he had "incurred" her friendship, and that he was stuck with it.) In her
biography of Dorothy Parker, Marion Meade reveals how the radical
wiseacre's self-proclaimed socialism coexisted with the companionship
of Wall Street millionaires and pretty remittance boys. She kept company with Herbert Bayard Swope, and with Jock Whitney and his sister
Joan Whitney Payson and with Pierpont Morgan and, especially, with
Adele Lovett. For their part, the Piping Rock nobility found the Weston
Liggetts of the world tedious and predictable, and they liked having wits
like Benchley and Parker at their dinner parties. As Meade explains,
"these friendships had undeniable advantages because the rich could be
generous suppliers of cottages on their estates for little or no rent, memberships in racquet and tennis clubs, and gifts of money and stocks."[56]
Moreover, as in Parker's sometimes treacherous case, professional epi-
grammatists were skilled fifth columnists, and as Truman Capote later
showed in the social suicide of his "Côte Basque," sport was to be had
with America's aspirant aristocracy. "There was a wonderful tawdriness
to be found in their drawing rooms," Meade writes. "Their stupidities
were of course ideal targets for all manner of wisecracks and gossip."[57]
This is a bit too easy; closer to the reality was Parker's later self-derision,
her conclusion that the opposite of slumming was an expression of what
Meade characterizes as the "natural social-climbing instincts of indigent
writers."[58]

    Well, that's a bit too hard. Whatever O'Hara's vices—and social climb-
ing was among them—he was never faithless, and never a hypocritical
user. That he so wholeheartedly took the wellborn wealthy to his heart—

that he mistook their security for grace, their good manners for warm-heartedness, their diffidence for honor, their good tailoring for beauty, their faux-Gothic college dormitories for Oxford's Christ Church or Cambridge's King's—might well cast doubt on his judgment, but it doesn't reflect ill on his fidelity. Whereas Parker dedicated a book to Adele Lovett, and dropped her, O'Hara presented the valued typescript of *Appointment in Samarra* to Robert Lovett, who had begun their friendship at Tony's by proclaiming the book was a masterpiece. At the end of October 1935, Adele gave a party for O'Hara's friends to meet Barbara Kibler. Among the guests at their apartment on the East River at 83rd Street were Deems Taylor, Robert Benchley, Hoagy Carmichael, George and Ira Gershwin, Tallulah Bankhead, Burgess Meredith, John McClain, Pauline and Ernest Hemingway. It was to invite Fitzgerald to this party that O'Hara had written him about Miss Kibler. Years later, in *True at First Light,* Hemingway remembered O'Hara that night "fat as a boa constrictor that had swallowed an entire shipment of a magazine called *Collier's* and surly as a mule . . . plodding along dead without recognizing it," the love-struck young guest of honor in a "white-edged evening tie he had worn at his coming-out party in New York." Hemingway also remembered Adele Lovett's "nervousness at presenting [O'Hara] and her gallant hope that he would not disintegrate."[59] This skepticism was not unfounded: When O'Hara's sister Mary asked that night if he loved Kibler, O'Hara responded, "What business is it of yours?"

In December of 1935, having tried fruitlessly to talk the commissioner and editor of Clifton Fadiman's review of *Butterfield 8* into making a place in the *New Yorker* for "Footloose" pieces detailing his westering drive cross-country with his brother Eugene and John McClain, O'Hara set out for Columbus, Ohio, to woo Barbara Kibler's family. He didn't succeed. The Kiblers, despite O'Hara's protestations to Fitzgerald of Barbara's Protestantism, were Jewish, and they objected to their daughter's suitor partly on the grounds of religious incompatibility. "I have no money, and her family is against me," O'Hara had written Fitzgerald even before meeting her parents. In Columbus their opposition hardened; they were anxious about the age difference between their daughter and O'Hara, offended by the public response to *Butterfield 8,* and won over neither by John nor his brother. When Barbara Kibler returned to Wellesley from her Christmas vacation in Ohio, the engagement was broken off.

To friends, O'Hara obliquely hinted at and even directly threatened suicide, and from Hollywood, in April of 1936, he wrote Fitzgerald in response to his extraordinary essays—later published as part of *The Crack-Up*, then appearing in *Esquire:* "I was in love with a girl, as I wrote you; she gave me the air, and on the rebound I got a dose of clap. I apparently suffer more in the head than in the cock, and much more than most men."[60] Well, has any lovesick sufferer ever failed to calculate his wretchedness as extraordinary? In fact, O'Hara's misery following this breakup did seem inconsolable. He had been in Hollywood since February, mooching off Dorothy Parker and her husband, Alan Campbell. The couple earned as much as twenty-five hundred a week (multiply that by six or seven for today's dollars, and don't subtract income tax) writing a courtroom picture for Paramount and Claudette Colbert, and they did all in their power to spend it on a household at 914 North Roxbury Drive, just north of Sunset Boulevard and near the Beverly Hills Hotel, which it resembled in scale. Of his hosts and their circumstances O'Hara offered Fitzgerald an ungracious report: "They have a large white house, Southern style, and live in luxury, including a brand-new Picasso, a Packard convertible phaeton, a couple of Negroes, and dinner at the best Beverly Hills homes. Dottie occasionally voices a great discontent, but I think her aversion to movie-writing is as much lazy as intellectual. She likes the life."[61]

In this same letter O'Hara also gives a cross-grained account of Donald Ogden Stewart, a well-liked humorist and screenwriter, close and loyal friend to Parker and Robert Benchley, among many others, including Fitzgerald. Perhaps his most notable achievement was to have served as the prototype for Hemingway's Bill Gorton in *The Sun Also Rises*, as affectionate and flattering a portrait as a model could wish for. (Of course Hemingway turned on his old friend, for the crime of having reproached Hemingway for mocking another old friend, Dorothy Parker.) Like O'Hara, Stewart was beguiled by great wealth, but comme il faut in mid-1930s Hollywood, he was also a would-be revolutionary. O'Hara declared that Stewart, "full of shit, has converted himself to radical thought, and goes to all the parties for the Scottsboro boys." Educated at Exeter and Yale, Stewart was earning five thousand a week as a screenwriter, and was as popular a dinner guest as Hollywood had. He wrote the screenplay of *The Philadelphia Story* (Philip Barry was another chum), and then—during the war and after—

became a tediously committed Stalinist, and was blacklisted in 1951. Stewart's wife divorced him to marry Tolstoy's grandson, Count Ilya Andreyevich, and Stewart married Lincoln Steffens's widow. What particularly abraded O'Hara was Stewart's patient and humorless explanation of why he made a superior radical, "because, he pointed out, he'd *had* Skull & Bones, he'd *had* the Whitney plantation, he'd *had* big Hollywood money."

O'Hara had a little New York money, seventy-five a week from Harcourt, Brace, and he used it to rent a cramped apartment on Ohio Avenue, in Westwood south of Wilshire but within an easy drive of Beverly Hills. Suffering a fit of self-improvement, he planned to study French and American history at neighboring UCLA—a spasm that almost immediately passed. He now owned two Fords, and felt secure enough to refuse screenplay work for less than a thousand dollars a week. (The average wage of a screenwriter at that time was forty per week, and the average term of service was two weeks in a year, and that was for the lucky ducks not writing on spec.)[62] In his letter to Fitzgerald he fretted incoherently about his relationships with the "lovely dishes" in California: he would meet a "dame," and "want to be friends with her in a tentative way—for future." But their instinct—for what?—and his "subconscious and my conscience"—say what?—kept him from closing the deal, "from throwing in the old Sunday punch." Reading these sentiments, it is little wonder that he hadn't been able to decide what to make of Gloria Wandrous.

Moreover, his dumbfounded solitude was shot through with self-doubt. "I am lonely," he wrote Fitzgerald. "I have no social grace, either. I lack the Princeton touch. People do not invite me out much, and the only way I can climb is down." So he was climbing down fast. When he'd worked in Los Angeles the previous year, and when he was on the wagon, he had led a sociable life. He'd gone to the Cocoanut Grove to dance and the Brentwood Club to play golf and Stanley Rose's bookstore on Hollywood Boulevard to browse the shelves and connect with other East Coast writers. There he met Rose's store manager, Meta Rosenberg, who became his friend and a lunch date next door at the Musso & Frank Grill, where it's still good times to eat unfashionable food and be treated rudely by waiters who have been past retirement age since the place began business on Hollywood Boulevard in 1919.

Now, during this self-exile in California, he was changed, drinking again, often drunk, frequently loutish, sometimes cruel and even brutal. His coarseness was in the spirit of the time and place. In his notebooks of this period, Edmund Wilson referred to a conversation between O'Hara and the Jewish wife of a well-raised Main Line friend of Wilson's: "John O'Hara had said to Felice one day: 'You know, Felice, I ought to have laid you that day I had the chance.' 'When was that?' 'That afternoon at the country club,' etc. 'Oh, that was the day!—I had a dose of clap.' [Wilson's friend's] father . . . would rather have died than talk like this before ladies—in fact, this roughneck vein hadn't been invented yet.* They had evidently been associating a good deal with the Jewish comic writers out there."[63]

For his biography published in 1980, Frank MacShane interviewed several people who knew O'Hara then in California, and the stories they told were not pretty. Not long after receiving Barbara Kibler's pink slip, and soon after catching the clap, O'Hara pursued a schoolmate and friend of Meta Rosenberg, Betty Anderson, who also worked at the bookstore. MacShane seems to lump her among the "two or three carloads of girls" conveyed to Union Station by the Super Chief every Friday afternoon, pretty hinterlanders aspiring to make their fame as actresses who would instead, "like the characters in Nathanael West's *Day of the Locust,* [live] marginal lives as models, salesgirls, secretaries and call girls." But as MacShane later details, Anderson wasn't a quick trick, and she explained to O'Hara the night of their first date—a quiet party at Dorothy Parker's—that she had a boyfriend. Having declared himself the "shyest writer there is," he offered to give her "a chance to see" whether she might not prefer him to her boyfriend. She went out with him, he made an aggressive pass; she rebuffed it, he became enraged. She left his car—whether by choice or at his insistence—and had to hitchhike home from the San Fernando Valley. Following that misadventure, he would come to the bookstore and make nasty remarks

---

*It may be useful for perspective to note that Wilson, in the same passage, describing the manners and political scruples of that delicate father's Paoli neighbors, recollects a conversation in which a Main-Liner was "denouncing" Hitler and was admonished, " 'I think you're going too far: you're talking about him as if he were Roosevelt!' "

And to put the Main-Liner in perspective, perhaps O'Hara was not exaggerating when he recalled that when he "first arrived in Hollywood there were Jews who regarded Franklin D. Roosevelt as more dangerous than Adolf Hitler" (O'Hara, "Hello Hollywood Good-Bye," pp. 54, 55, 125–29).

to her, or he'd drive up at closing time and try to get her to join him in his car, and when she wouldn't he'd crawl alongside in low gear and alternatively wheedle and insult her, jamming traffic along Hollywood Boulevard. At length, after making her life a nightmare, O'Hara came to Stanley Rose's to announce to her, "You'll be glad to hear that I'm going back to New York," and when she answered "Good riddance," he hit her, knocking her down in the bookstore aisle "with such force that she banged her head against the wall of the shop."[64]

He had hit women before. He'd been briefly banned from "21" for having clouted a date who'd come late for lunch. Now, in Hollywood, he seemed out of control. He was drinking at the Clover Club, a gambling casino, with a writer friend, when the friend introduced him to a young woman, an admirer of his work, who was visiting from Minnesota. After snarling that he was surprised that anyone in St. Paul knew how to read a book (would that include his pal Fitzgerald, born there?), he asked, "Why don't you go and fuck yourself?" His companion that night, Alan Rivkin, designated him an "uncouth son-of-a-bitch,"[65] and he conceded as much himself, just as he had confessed to Cap Pearce at that time that "I regret to report . . . I have been living at the bottom of a bottle."*[66]

O'Hara even managed to enrage the sweetest-disposed and best-mannered of his friends. Robert Benchley flew into Los Angeles just as O'Hara divorced—again, and not for the last time—the *New Yorker,* which had rejected his recent submissions. O'Hara's letter to Wolcott Gibbs was sore and sulky, instructing him to instruct Ross not to bother answering his recent letter (which Ross evidently had had no plan to do anyway) and instructing the magazine's administrators, "Please don't use my name in any advertising,"[67] a show of petulance that will kindle a frisson of recognition in any writer feeling—as we will—aggrieved by neglect. Perhaps Benchley's own rock-solid standing at the *New Yorker* was irksome, but whatever the motive, O'Hara tried his best to undo a persistent friendship he had reason to treasure.

Benchley, when he came to Hollywood, shared a bungalow with John

*This would not have shocked, or perhaps even dismayed, the prickly Cap Pearce, who was—a colleague has written—a "bender" drunk, who would disappear for a week or more into "oblivion," before drying out in a New York hotel room, from which he'd presently emerge to manage the business affairs of his firm (Stan Hart, *Fumblefinger: A Life Out of Line* [New York: Abeel & Leet, 1999], p. 246).

McClain at the Garden of Allah (formerly the mansion of the silent star Alla Nazimova), by this time a louche but outrageously comfortable hotel on Sunset Boulevard. Benchley divided his time between the East Coast (which Dorothy Parker had begun despairingly to refer to as "The Coast") during New York's theater season, and Hollywood, where he was in eternal demand as a performer in the short movies that brought his fortune and his fame. He made forty-eight such shorts, beginning with the 1928 film version of his fabled "Treasurer's Report," the first continuous sound movie ever produced. Shirley Temple begged Benchley for his autograph, and in 1935 *How to Sleep* won an Oscar for best short film. Faced with the bitter irony of a celebrity he neither courted nor enjoyed, what could Benchley do but show himself and his friends a good time? And the Garden of Allah was a fun factory. There was a swimming pool, of course (roughly shaped to resemble Nazimova's beloved Black Sea, and just a bit smaller), and starlets sunning near mimosas and bougainvillea and palm fronds. (Birds, too, which Benchley loathed for their irrational cheerfulness and hangover-exacerbating breakfast-hour racket.) And it was here that Benchley and McClain opened their bungalow bar come the cocktail hour to what McClain termed "the drop-in trade": among many others could be expected Dorothy Parker, Humphrey Bogart, the bogus prince Mike Romanoff, and John Steinbeck, a new friend to O'Hara. Writing ten years later, McClain claimed that the "chatter and laughter" could be heard at a block's distance from their merry salon.

It has always been a crime against good sense to fail to chatter and to laugh in Hollywood. Long after she turned self-deludingly sorrowful about her richly rewarded sellout to Paramount and MGM, Dorothy Parker could still find something worthy of her wit and observation under the dazzling natural light at a Beverly Hills scene. She described in a *Paris Review* interview having noticed near the Garden of Allah "a Cadillac about a block long, and out of the side window was a wonderfully slinky mink, and an arm, and at the end of the arm a hand in a white suede glove wrinkled at the wrist, and in the hand was a bagel with a bite out of it."[68]

Despite such entertainments, O'Hara kept his lower lip pouted, his grog-blossomed face long. F. Scott Fitzgerald's friend Sheila Graham, who titled her memoir *The Garden of Allah*, recalls him at these gatherings, leaning against a bungalow wall, glass in hand, "listening intently to the conversation but not joining in. . . . He always seemed ill at ease. He never smiled. He never laughed."[69]

As Robert's son Nathaniel Benchley told Frank MacShane in 1978, one night O'Hara pushed away from the wall against which he'd leaned brooding and began wrestling roughly with a woman who had no wish to wrestle. Robert Benchley, to whom the title "gentleman" was attached as though it were a portion of his name, tried to stop these churlish antics: "He went up to O'Hara who had a hammerlock on some woman, and said, 'All right, John, isn't that about enough?' to which O'Hara replied, 'Yeah, and that goes for you, too,' and swung at my father, knocking the cigar out of his mouth." Awful enough, of course, but then Benchley turned the moment to laughter—and O'Hara to a laughingstock—by declaring that "he would get a new cigar if it was the last thing he did." The following morning, as sure as hangover, Benchley's phone rang with a remorseful O'Hara on the other end, saying he just wanted to say he was sorry. "For what, John?" Benchley asked. For what I did last night, he explained. Oh, *that*, said Benchley, "please don't apologize to *me*. You're a shit and everybody knows you're a shit, and people ask you out in spite of it. It's nothing to apologize about." O'Hara asked his friend if he meant what he'd just said. "Of course I mean it, John. You were born a shit just as some people were born with blue eyes, but that's no reason to go around apologizing for it."[70]

A variation of this phrasing was told me by Nathaniel Benchley's widow, Marjorie: "You will always be a shit, but you are our shit." Small and cold comfort in that first-person possessive; to have been dressed down by so courteous and generous a friend might have prompted an irascible soak to dry up his act, but fat chance. Worse aftermaths than O'Hara's chastening followed those sodden jamborees. His friend Charles Butterworth, an actor, was killed when he flipped his sports car driving home from the Garden of Allah bungalow. O'Hara himself was in a car wreck with the actress Madeline Carroll, the director Lewis Milestone at the wheel. And Benchley—only forty-seven years old, and having managed to get all the way to thirty-one without drinking at all—was now killing himself slowly—"Who's in a hurry?" he wondered—with alcohol and unearned self-contempt. Now O'Hara, *he* was in a hurry.

Love rescued him. It sounds corny, but this was an age when corny contested with hard-boiled, and both styles—comic romance and film noir—had their heads in the clouds of exaggerated emotional recoil. O'Hara, lost to self-pity and resentment, was found by a young woman as unlike him in temperament as could be imagined. Theirs was a good love story, and it began with Belle Wylie's head-over-heels crush on *Appointment in Samarra,* which she had read soon after it was published: "I'd like to meet the man who wrote that book," she had told her sister Lucilla. (One variation, a hoary staple worldwide of family legends, has Belle declaring her wish to *marry* him, but I don't believe it.) She was twenty-three, with two sisters and two brothers, the daughter of Robert Hawthorne Wylie, a New York physician (and Yale graduate), and an affectionate, witty, and well-read mother, by this time a widow.

The first meeting of Belle Wylie and John O'Hara has been reported variously: it was at the West Side Tennis Club, near his Ohio Avenue apartment, on a transcontinental train, at the railroad station in Chicago, or at the Pump Room between trains.* In fact, as O'Hara's inscription to her on *Pipe Night* affirms, Belle Wylie first noticed him when he was paged at the Newark airport; they happened to share a plane to Los Angeles, and he tried to pick her up during a fueling stop in Wichita. She politely demurred: she was shy, and punctilious. Belle Wylie's heart, though, "went thump-thump-thump," in the resonant words of her childhood friend Kate Bramwell.† O'Hara was struck immediately by her grace. Willowy, dark-haired, with what Frank MacShane has described as "a slightly Asian look to her eyes,"[71] she was invariably characterized as gentle, and just as invariably her friends hedged that delicacy with modifiers: iron-willed, determined, unflinching. It was in that resolute spirit that she prevailed upon her older sister to invite O'Hara to a dinner party Lucilla was giving in Los Angeles with her husband, Henry Codman Potter, a Broadway and Hollywood director and the son and grandson of Episcopal bishops (and Yale graduates). At Belle's request, O'Hara was seated next to her. Politicians dazzle citizens with the hocus-pocus of recollecting the name—and spouse's name, and dog's

---

*Mary Leigh ("Lili") Pell, now Mrs. Robert Whitmer, who was a companion to the O'Haras' daughter Wylie in Quogue and Princeton, understood the meeting to have been during a "leg-stretch" in Chicago. Belle saw a man debark from a train, "wearing a trenchcoat, a mysterious, powerful presence." O'Hara, asked by Lili Pell after Belle's death to confirm this account, "opened his closet door. 'Here is that coat. I was married in it.' "

†Second wife of Henry Gardiner, who had previously been married to Belle's sister Winifred.

name—of campaign contributors, and O'Hara flabbergasted with a related party trick. He knew and would recite the maiden names of newly met married women at dinner parties, and sometimes their childhood nicknames, and he informed Belle Mulford Wylie that she'd studied in New York at Brearley and gone away to school at St. Timothy's, and that she designed her own clothes. The uncharitable could regard this as the fruit of a climber's systematic study of the *Social Register,* but Miss Wylie—and many another shrewd woman—interpreted the novelist's notice as attentive curiosity (or perhaps curious attentiveness), and she was flattered. They left that dinner together before the final course had been served, and went nightclubbing and to a gambling ship anchored off Long Beach, and they talked until sunrise. Considerate and deliberate, Belle was also "fast," according to her friend Kate Bramwell, who believed the love-struck couple drove that morning to Tijuana to elope but, moved by prudence or sobriety, turned back at the border. From that morning forward, O'Hara never considered not longing to marry her.

In fact, he loved her so unresistingly that he found in himself the solicitude not to rush her, and to consider whether what he wanted was good for her. Biographers try not to be suckers for panegyrics to the dearly departed. (We're not as skeptical of malice.) Most of what has been written about Belle Wylie was subsequent to her death, in 1954, of consequences of a congenital heart defect, and if anyone has said a cruel word about her—or expressed the least reservation about her warmth, kindness, intelligence, and loyalty—I don't know of it. A surprising number of the people I interviewed who knew John O'Hara had difficulty recollecting exactly why they liked being his friend, and what it was like being in his company. But people who knew Belle Wylie knew why she was remarkable. The reasons were not always the same—brave, "original and gay," stylish (a friend remembered vividly the evening dress, half black and half white, she'd designed), adventuresome, "independent-minded"—but the memories were specific, and they were expressed emphatically. "She did what she wanted," Kate Bramwell was happy to declare.

Her family only augmented her allure. Socially prominent in New York and in Quogue, Long Island, they were not snobs. Mrs. Wylie had been a nurse, and she enjoyed—like her late husband—a tolerance for human weakness and folly, together with inquisitiveness about what

made the intricacies of human clockwork tick. Understanding the rami-
fications of her daughter's cardiac affliction—Belle Wylie was born a
blue baby—she encouraged the fragile young woman's interest in tennis,
and even yielded to her determination to get a pilot's license, which
Belle then did.

If she could be a pilot, her beau could be an actor. Unable to find writing assignments at the high price he set, his newfound friend Clifford
Odets and the director Lewis Milestone (he of the car wreck) offered
him fifty dollars a day for three days of work* on *The General Died at
Dawn,* Paramount's movie shot from Odets's screenplay about fashionably costumed gunrunners and a sinister Chinese warlord. O'Hara plays
opposite Gary Cooper, whose moody adventurer (named O'Hara!) is a
cynical/idealistic Friend of the Oppressed Chinese People. In a slouch-
brimmed hat and white trenchcoat, he makes a pretty conspicuous
undercover agent. Odets's campy tough-guy script—"Pal, my nose
bleeds for you," he snarls, when he's not snarling the nickname "Sweetheart" to all nonoppressed people, or showing off his pet monkey Sam,
who manages by force of cuteness never to get eaten, even by the warlord's henchmen—unintentionally reveals him to be preposterously
slow-witted, and the story goes that Cooper kept tripping over his lines
when (the actual) O'Hara said, as he was scripted to say, "Hello,
O'Hara." In a letter to Bruccoli, Milestone remembered Odets telling
budding actor O'Hara that he was to play "a corrupt newspaperman who
could be bought for a bag of salt," and recalled having to reshoot that
scene, because Cooper would complain, "But *he's* O'Hara." Our O'Hara
did his thing in the dining car of a train to which Cooper's O'Hara has
been lured by a hard-boiled and squishy-hearted femme fatale, played
by a gorgeously lit and unhappy Madeline Carroll: "Maybe someday
there'll be a law to abolish the blues," she moans in B-flat, without much
conviction. The real O'Hara looked good by contrast, tastefully dressed,
mumbling his lines—"Waiter?" is one of the longest—and shuffling cor-
ruptly. This picture was not worth a thousand of his words.

During the spring and summer of 1936 he was uncharacteristically

---

*In Hollywood, accounts—narrative and fiscal—are elastic. In 1954, writing in *Collier's,* O'Hara
inflated his take to four hundred dollars. In fact, he and John Steinbeck—at their first meeting—had
laughed about how to describe a "Hollywood Millionaire": there was your "fifty-thousand dollar millionaire," who was worth a great deal more than twice as much as your "twenty-five thousand dollar
millionaire."

drawn to two dramatic adaptations. O'Hara generally reserved his creative enthusiasm for fiction, but the Hollywood novel he was trying to write for Harcourt, Brace—provisionally titled *So Far, So Good* (published in 1938 as *Hope of Heaven*)—was moving slowly. It was conceived as a response to Fitzgerald's notion that in *Appointment in Samarra* and *Butterfield 8* he had limited his repertoire to blues chords, striking his notes only percussively. Fitzgerald suggested a "bucolic idyll," and—an even trashier proposal—insisted that O'Hara must learn to embrace both the bucolic and the idyllic. In Hollywood? If ever there was a less suitable notion, it was Fitzgerald's own ambition to write a chivalric romance set in the Middle Ages. So, unsure for once of his art, O'Hara caught a dose of Development Deal Syndrome, and angled to adapt *The Great Gatsby*, Clark Gable to play the hero, and Miriam Hopkins to play Daisy. Fitzgerald feigned enthusiasm, though he was aware that his friend's preoccupation with the leisure class was encouraging reviewers to link his own achievement and O'Hara's ambitions; in his scrapbook he referred to "THE CROSS OF JOHN O'HARA."[72]

At the same time that he was eager to show the world moving pictures of Gatsby's shirts and the green light at the end of an East Egg dock, O'Hara was negotiating to adapt for the stage *In Dubious Battle*, John Steinbeck's proletarian novel propagandizing labor unions. The two met at Steinbeck's cottage in Pacific Grove, south of Monterey and Cannery Row, to discuss the project, and Steinbeck—who didn't invite collaboration any more than O'Hara did—appreciated his directness. For O'Hara's part, this marked the beginning of his lifelong affection for the man who won "his" Nobel Prize. They cooked themselves Mexican food, and many years later O'Hara recalled that afternoon, and Steinbeck's English saddle hanging on the wall beside his high school diploma.

In Dubious Battle was a far more dubious project for O'Hara than *The Great Gatsby*, which was hazardously appropriate. He had been friendly with many left-leaners in Hollywood, and during those Depression days of Hitler's rise it would've been surprising if he hadn't. Two of his closest friends in this period were Clifford Odets, whose *Waiting for Lefty* had been produced the year before by the Group Theater, and Budd Schulberg. O'Hara recollected fondly how it was among the three of them in an essay for *Holiday* in 1967, by which time he was as mossbacked in his political and social views as any Main Line Republican. The three spent hundreds of hours talking about the ways of the world, about experience and work—both as manual labor and as a calling—about generational conflict and generic resentment, about politics and about manners. "[Schulberg and I] were men of passion, of violence; intemperate in matters that had nothing to do with alcohol. . . . We would *inform* each other, without ever once changing the other's mind about anything. About *anything.*"[73]

The tenderness with which O'Hara treated those thirty-year-old memories was an index of how centrally they influenced his understanding of decency and honor. In "Hello Hollywood Good-Bye," a *Holiday* essay written a year later, he was still hanging around the subject of Odets, Schulberg, and Steinbeck: "It was no more my nature to write a proletarian novel than it was for John Steinbeck to write a novel about Hobe Sound, or Fitzgerald to write a documentary about Pacific Grove. Because I was involved with the New Deal I attempted a dramatization of *In Dubious Battle,* but I abandoned the project when I found that in those moments of truth when a writer must believe what he says, a thing is not finally true because another has said it is true."[74] O'Hara elaborated: he gave money to good causes, listened to Dorothy Parker's harangues or pretended to, he had worked with his hands "and been miserably poor." But he resisted depicting all wearers of Brooks Brothers shirts as fascists and all laborers dressed in overalls as "crusaders for freedom, decency and truth. My memory of fascists in overalls and genuine liberals in button-down shirts was always getting in the way." Such memories—and let's assume that in 1936 his "memory" of fascists in overalls was fairly scant—also impeded his escape from the fate of Fitzgerald, whose *Tender Is the Night* had been repudiated as tiresome rich-kid fluff, much to O'Hara's alarm, as he reported in "Hello Hollywood Good-Bye": "I continually wondered about the parallel between [Fitzgerald's] early career and mine that had just begun: a big success with *This Side of Paradise,* followed by unjustified chastisement for *The Beautiful and Damned.* . . . I had read proof on *Tender Is the Night* . . . and I was shocked and probably frightened by what the critics and the public had done to it and to him. People from whom he had the right to expect respectful treatment were condescending or worse, and I was convinced that I had nothing better to look forward to."

The choice was not, of course, between honesty and propaganda; it was between conviction and attitude, between writing what one truly felt in the moment, as Hemingway had it, rather than what one thought one ought to feel. O'Hara sometimes made too little of much (as in his thinner stories) or too much of little (as in his thicker, later novels), but he didn't fake and he despised cant: for worse, but mostly for better, he would continue to write about personal rather than political and economic cataclysms. If this meant he was to be consigned by conventional-wisdom critics to the particular hell—triviality—where novelists of manners are indicted for all their stylish dining, dancing, weekending, playing, and climbing, he'd live with that.

Budd Schulberg wrote his most celebrated novel, *What Makes Sammy Run?*, about that kill-or-die experiment in pure exploitation, the Hollywood studio system, in which his father "B.P." was a bona fide mogul, production chief at Paramount. Schulberg was asked by the local cell if O'Hara might be coaxed to join the Communist Party. Frank Mac-Shane writes that he was certain O'Hara wouldn't join, owing more to his temperament than to his politics, which were then to the left of Roosevelt's.[75] O'Hara, the anti-whatever-you've-got, a fellow traveler, a collaborator, a Popular Frontiersman? Not likely. Schulberg, nine years his junior, was a grown-up writer, and ideological right-think didn't bar him from writing about the underworld of boxing (*The Harder They Fall*) as well as about shepherding Fitzgerald through a drunken weekend at the high and chilly reaches of Dartmouth Winter Carnival (*The Disenchanted*), and later, in his screenplay for Elia Kazan's *On the Waterfront*, about the travails of longshoremen (and, by not-so-subtle inference, the virtue of having informed on commies to the House Un-American Activities Committee during the blacklist). Schulberg himself broke with the party in 1939, after its leaders insisted that *What Makes Sammy Run?* be vetted for its concordance with Marxist dicta.

O'Hara was nothing if not an equal-opportunity sidekick in those days. Eventually, in his Princeton squirehood, he would have a restricted notion of the kinds of people who offered him comfort and security, and one of his best friendships of this sort dates from Los Angeles. Alfred M. "Al" Wright Jr. met O'Hara while he was at home in Pasadena on vacation from Yale. His father was a successful lawyer who lived in Pasadena, a town unfriendly to "dirty celluloid" and movie parvenus. The younger Wright, who married Joan Fontaine and became an editor at *Time*, shared his memories with Finis Farr in 1971, and admitted that what always brought O'Hara to mind were the photos hanging in the Yale Club in New York of "the 1895 crew or the 1907 golf team. . . . That was the world he really loved—and lived in, or tried to. I don't think John gave a damn about anything that happened after World War II. His era was that eighty-five years from the first shot at Sumter to the scene on the deck of the *Missouri*."[76]

They first met in the Trocadero nightclub in Hollywood, where O'Hara was sitting with a college classmate of Wright's, Chad Ballard, a fellow with deep pockets (his father owned a circus) and a wooden leg. The trio went on a three-day bender, driving around town in O'Hara's phaeton, being chauffeured by a Filipino who "looked out after him," as Wright told it. When the hilarity ended, O'Hara "poured me on the [Super] Chief to return to New Haven," and thereafter, once he'd returned to New York, the older man would visit Wright at Yale to drink himself "into insensibility" at the Fence Club bar.

O'Hara was welcomed at tennis clubs and dinner dances by the Wrights and their friends in Pasadena, where the huge houses were red-tile-roofed Spanish, but the manners eastern. When Al Wright thought back on his old world, he was precise in saying that Pasadena's bygone Midwick Country Club had "the best polo in America . . . outside Meadowbrook" (on Long Island), and that O'Hara "loved to go to the polo. He was not in the least interested in the Hollywood polo at Riviera and Uplifters . . . and made fun of it." At Midwick he managed not to knock cigars out of the mouth of Mr. Wright, or to put a hammerlock on Mrs. Wright. Many years later, in *The Big Laugh* (1962), O'Hara made fun of his protagonist, the calculatedly non-actorish actor Hubert Ward, social-climbing, having himself photographed "chatting between chukkers at Midwick Country Club" with Louis Rowan, "young Pasadena polo star" (and a friend of O'Hara's), and with "Mr. and Mrs. Alfred Wright, of Pasadena."[77]

A fundament of Hubert Ward's spurious respectability is his marriage to a Lake Forest widow, whom Ward meets at a party given by her sister, and with whom he leaves that party to spend a romantic evening. Nina Ward has manners, family, nerve, and an estate. It would be simple-minded to confuse Hubert Ward with John O'Hara, or Nina Ward with Belle Wylie, but in *The Big Laugh* O'Hara clearly toys with material from his courtship and Belle Wylie's position, subverting the actual outcome to create a love perverted by miscalculation and mutual suspicion. Nina Ward's money gives her the kind of freedom O'Hara always liked to bestow on his stronger female characters, and he himself was soon to be protected by Belle's property, what Finis Farr delicately terms "a modest competence." When she returned east, O'Hara warned her that he'd follow, and having drunk himself into despair, having found himself unable to make progress on his Hollywood novel, he made good on his word.

He was in New York by early 1937, falling deeper and deeper in love. Belle returned his affection but was not to be railroaded. She had reservations about O'Hara, of course: he spent so lavishly on clothes and cars and nightclubs that he couldn't afford to marry; he was eight years older and divorced; he had been a notorious skirt-chaser; he had a volcanic temper and a growing roster of enemies. Her mother—together with Lucilla and her straight-arrow husband and Belle's other sister, Winifred, or "Winnie"—shared these reservations. From his base at a Chelsea apartment on 24th Street west of Eighth Avenue, paying his rent with *New Yorker* stories and meager Hollywood savings, O'Hara was living his life at night. (Several friends I asked about his taste in apartments described them as unmemorable except for their darkness: the shades were down, a wall outside hard by the window, or—as in the case of his Ohio Avenue apartment in Westwood—the windows too high to afford a view.) He was drinking a bottle and more a day, and as Al Wright reported to Finis Farr, O'Hara, got up in a trenchcoat and felt fedora, "had a regular circuit around town, and he was as methodical about it as a night watchman," his stops including Bleeck's, "21," and the Stork Club. Frequently he'd quarrel, and one night he chased a guest from "21" along 52nd Street, with a view to beating him in consequence of some fancied or authentic slight, then gave up the chase when he decided that a policeman—whose ambition was to assassinate him—was lying in wait down the block, his pistol drawn.

To keep company with a drinking O'Hara was always a high-maintenance operation, but if bluster and tears had been the whole story, Belle Wylie wouldn't have stayed the course. Gentle teasing was also their experience, and they loved to dance. Nevertheless, in the spring of 1937 Belle went to France to visit her sister Winnie and to stare at her hole cards before she played her hand. O'Hara begged her by cable to come home and marry him, and she came home.

He rented a house that summer on Dune Road in Quogue, to be near Belle and her family. That drowsy summer resort was a self-conscious counterculture to the fast life in New York; it was reserved, pretty, and serene. The Wylies' house at Quogue Street and Shinnecock Avenue—a mansion referred to, in the preferred way, as a cottage—was near the lit-tle village with its golf club, inn, and maple- and elm-edged streets with shingled and picket-fenced shops and an interesting old grocery store whose treasures were squirreled away in dark aisles and corners that must have reminded O'Hara of his grandfather's store. Eighty miles from Manhattan, set on the east end of Long Island's Atlantic shore near Southampton and Westhampton, Quogue has a determined indifference to dazzle.* It suited the Wylies as well as the Wylies suited the place, and O'Hara had to train himself quickly in family virtues. Remembering his first summer there, he confessed sheepishly that during his initial visit to the Beach Club he'd stupefied the bartender, not to mention the Wylies, when he requested a Scotch sour.

The beach is stunning where O'Hara's rental house—an honest-to-Betsy cottage—was set at the far end of Dune Road, with sea-grassy dunes providing a lee from the fresh afternoon southwesters. He played tennis at the Field Club, and quickly forged a close bond with Belle's mother, with whom he liked to trade literary opinions, joke, and play bridge. She liked him well enough to give O'Hara the security to confide in her his anxieties about his drinking. With two sons in addition to three daughters, Mrs. Wylie was not likely to be surprised by much, but her tolerance and friendship didn't extend to enthusiasm for a match between Belle and her suitor; it is not certain that O'Hara knew as much, because the Wylies were not people to cause needless pain, and it is probable that Mrs. Wylie understood her daughter's self-reliance well enough to realize that it would be fruitless to forbid her anything. For her part, Belle worried that to cast her lot with O'Hara would mean los-ing those many old friends who—she well understood—would not abide his tantrums or his thin-skinned self-regard.

She saw both sides of her future husband that summer and fall. He had finished his Hollywood novel, *Hope of Heaven,* hiding out in a Philadelphia hotel room to sweat it through. He honored his contracts, and for him—even in those chaotic years—his notion of honorable pro-fessionalism often trumped his self-indulgence. But back in New York,

---

*In a 1949 letter to John Steinbeck—who settled summers in Sag Harbor, twenty-four miles to the east-northeast—he declared, "Here. Here is my Pacific Grove. I love Quogue. Quogue is unique in that it is the only real family place-cum-Social Register on the Eastern Seaboard" (O'Hara, *Letters,* p. 225).

with the book finished, he had leisure to dance and drink and prevail on Belle to marry him. He would typically phone her late in the evening, after sleeping in, and they'd make their rounds. Frank MacShane tells of a New Year's Eve when Adele Lovett was home alone and got a phone call from O'Hara inviting himself and Belle, whom Mrs. Lovett had not met, for drinks. They had champagne, and O'Hara passed out, Belle betraying no dismay, merely chatting serenely with her hostess till O'Hara stirred awake. This was the pattern of their relationship, and the expression of her steadfast self-confidence. She fiercely protected him from disrespect, from any who might wish him ill, even from teasing. A few weeks before Christmas of 1937, she and O'Hara eloped to Elkton, a Maryland town informal about its marriage requirements. The bridegroom was so tapped out that he had to borrow nine hundred dollars from his brother Tom to pay for the trip and the ceremony.

O'Hara had seen little of his family in Pottsville since that ugly Christmas of 1930, shortly before he married Helen Petit. A year earlier, on his way from California to New York in pursuit of Belle Wylie, he had stopped at 606 Mahantongo Street to see his mother and sixteen-year-old sister Kathleen. His brothers Eugene and Martin also lived in Pottsville, Joseph in New Jersey, and Tom in Philadelphia, where he wrote for the *Evening Ledger*. The situation at home was grim. A neighbor from the good old days at the farm stopped by with a free chicken and some eggs, and O'Hara—trying to reach Belle—discovered that the phone had been disconnected. He made arrangements to pay utility bills, and to send money now and then to help out his mother and siblings, but the inevitable result of his determination to leave Pottsville behind in favor of New York, Hollywood, and his very own Gibbsville was estrangement. The dynamic is as familiar as family: the successful eldest brother blows into town in a pretty new car, dispenses concern and stern homilies, together with a trim sheaf of small bills, together with a reminder that this lucre didn't grow on trees. The siblings are rescued, if perhaps a touch less grateful than their redeemer might have hoped. Smiles are thin. It seems that there's pressing business in New York that makes it necessary to leave Pottsville sooner than expected. Everyone is sorry to hear it, having so enjoyed gathering again in the old homestead. But come up to New York, soon . . . when I'm settled. And a Merry Christmas to all.

O'Hara's relationship with his eldest sister Mary was more personal, more openly combative, for one thing. And he would grow close to his witty and irreverent youngest sibling, Kathleen. His kinship with Tom was unaffected and mutually heartfelt. As early as Tom's junior year in parochial school, O'Hara had micromanaged Tom's future, assuming he would want to go to Yale, to try out there for the *Daily News* in preparation for a job on the *Herald-Tribune,* and by the way, on the byline "sign your name simply Thomas O'Hara when you write pieces. No middle initial."[78] He advised his younger brother Polonially at times, but Tom invited the direction: his father was dead, and John's unembarrassed devotion was forceful. "Don't let anything get in your way," he exhorted. "I wish I'd had sense enough to take advantage of the chance you're giving yourself." John O'Hara would tap into that vital and benign gusto that comes of rooting for another again when his daughter Wylie was growing up; this was a virtue worthy of his outsized ambition.

Mr. and Mrs. O'Hara returned to New York the night of the unceremonious civil ceremony and made a few phone calls. One was to Winnie, who was delegated to tell their mother, who either "shrieked," "wailed," "howled," "screeched," or "screamed," depending on who's remembering. This was evidently a cry of surprise rather than pain, or at worst a final convulsion of disapproval, since from then on O'Hara was welcomed without restriction into the Wylie family. Surely Belle never looked back: she was one who might hesitate at the edge of the high board, considering whether she really wished to dive, but when she went she *went,* and when she came up from the depths she swam, and if someone was in the water with her floundering, she towed him to safety. He made her laugh, adored her, and—when he was sober—behaved as if he did. Kate Bramwell tells of having been at a small family dinner at which O'Hara accused the Wylies in general of not being as fancy as they liked to imagine, and tormented one of Belle's brothers for being foolish. "Belle said, 'That's terrible to say, John,' and O'Hara got up from the table, came to her, kissed her head and said, 'I'm so sorry, sweetie.' That was John, always surprising you."

Many surprises—if anything done under the rule of whiskey can be accurately described as surprising—were ugly. Finis Farr quotes an unidentified witness to a scene from the marriage: "I could have brained John in the Stork Club one night when he spoke sharply to Belle, who took it without flinching, then he began to needle her and kept it up, really bullying her and lousing up a nice dinner, until at last she burst into tears. It was a shameful performance and I never forgave him for it. . . . I left murmuring to myself, 'He may be a successful and talented writer but he is at heart a cheap bastard.' "[79] (Protect drunkards against witnesses who leave murmuring to themselves complete sentences, which years later they remember for biographers.)

Belle, however, was aboard for the long haul. No matter her husband's provocations, she seemed to take it as her mission to make his life better. She learned the ruses and maneuvers that many living with an alcoholic come to master: she watered the bottles, or made drinks with alcohol floating on top, unmixed, so that they'd seem stronger than they were. She asked some people—Al Wright was one—to forgo drinking with her husband. Above all, she stood up for him always, and no friend seems ever to have reported to any journalist or biographer any instance of her having complained about her situation or having suggested that her patience was finite.

Not that she martyred herself to his cause. Egregious episodes such as his bullying that night at the Stork Club are so hateful as to threaten to dominate any judgment of their early marriage, just as accounts of his fisticuffs with women and midgets might abruptly curtail any curiosity about his "character." But please, some balance: it was not a nightmare to be married to John O'Hara. For many it might have been an ordeal, but for Belle Wylie he was, taken all together, the love of her life. Once married, her friends agree, she wouldn't have had him any other way, except perhaps better satisfied with himself.

As with Pet, the honeymoon with Belle was palmy. The Lovetts had lent the couple their house in Hobe Sound, a retreat for old money (by American time) that was to nearby Palm Beach what Quogue was to ostentatious Southampton. Of course the house was beautifully furnished, and O'Hara in his thank-you note to Adele Lovett just barely resisted the urge to make sport of that understated perfection. Upon arrival he and Belle did not know how to take it, but after "seven or eight seconds" the house had grown on them. "At first I went around admiring things. The *Chinese* prints, and the *Chinese* statuettes, and the *Chinese* bowls and other things you picked up in *China* last year—I liked them."[80] They rested, read, played tennis at the Jupiter Island Club. (Ten years later—writing to Harold Ross, of all people—O'Hara confessed that his "usefulness to the Hobe Sound set" had ended during

"our wedding trip. After that, I was not asked to rejoin the club.")[81]
Needing Henry Luce's address to thank him for a wedding gift, O'Hara
remarked in another letter to Adele Lovett, less facetiously than he perhaps knew, "I'm just *lost* without my Social Register!"[82] Beginning at this
time, that black stud book with its orange lettering would be one of his
primary reference tools. Together with club membership directories and
Who's Who it charted the changing fortunes of those people who had
title to a large portion of his attention. In acronyms cryptic to an outsider, the *Social Register* of New York or Boston or Philadelphia listed
the academies attended, clubs joined, maiden names, yachts owned, and
"dilatory domiciles" (vacation addresses) of those people who, in
Pottsville, would have been mine owners. O'Hara's daughter Wylie
remembers having cleaned house at the beach cottage in Quogue, thinking to please her father with her industry and consideration. Among
other accumulations of what she took to be junk she threw out bygone
and redundant membership lists of the Quogue Field Club and the
Beach Club. O'Hara was furious, and explained that those primary documents—who'd been added, who dropped, who divorced—were his
life's blood, sky-charts of sidereal motions in the social firmament.

He understood that his own star, through no agency of his own, had
risen. Many years later, writing to his brother Tom, he put it bluntly: just
as the Major had "married up" into the Franey family, climbing from
"violent and spectacular" into the "gentle Irish," just as his father Patrick
had "married up" into the Delaney tribe, he himself had enacted this
"instinct for natural selection" by marrying Belle Wylie, and then, in
1955, after Belle died, Katharine "Sister" Barnes.

At this time Barnes was married to Joseph Bryan III. O'Hara's letters
to Bryan are among his most unbuttoned, and open a window (as the
generality of his businesslike and self-conscious correspondence too
often does not) on what it would have been like to hang out with the
man. Teasing self-deprecation marked the style of their correspondence.
Bryan, born and raised in Richmond, Virginia, was handsome and quick,
a man reliant on and overcompensated for his charm. Through him,
O'Hara hoped to establish a relationship with the *Saturday Evening
Post,* thereby improving on his mendicant status at the *New Yorker.*
From Quogue that summer of 1937 he had written Wolcott Gibbs—and
the following spring Ik Shulman, another *New Yorker* editor—begging
for greater respect and a raise to twenty cents per word "for good old
faithful O'Hara."[83] Failing to achieve either the raise or the respect, he

then tried Bryan—unavailingly—for "some of that Post gold."[84] It was characteristic of Bryan's supple tact that he managed to decline the invitation without causing irritation.

Oh yes, there was always Hollywood. But the Hollywood novel, *Hope of Heaven,* was a letdown, both for his ambition and his reputation. That town has probably done more harm to good writers by way of fictional excesses into which they have blundered all by their lonesomes than by the fabled soul-stealing powers of the studios' gilt. Nathanael West's *Day of the Locust* is the gold standard of Hollywood novels, and Fitzgerald's *The Last Tycoon* surely has its adherents, but these are the only two novels written by the eastern sightseers of O'Hara's time that can make a claim for narrative achievement as glittery as the subject. (Schulberg's *What Makes Sammy Run?* is the work of a native son, effortlessly authentic in its flamboyance of action and setting, too at home in Sammy Glick's extravagant society to bother exclaiming at its awfulness.) The material is seductive, of course; to discover in Allah's lush garden a Gothic gingerbread house of yummy treats—the elegantly extended gloved hand Dorothy Parker noticed holding a gnawed bagel—can cloud a wanderer's judgment and make a writer lazy. O'Hara had hoped to escape the blatant traps: skull visible beneath the skin, broad farce, Fatty Arbuckle's idea of a good time. He didn't concentrate on desperate starlets mistaking the objective and subjective case, or quote a cigar-munching Sam Goldwyn knockoff proclaiming of a film "Too caustic? To hell with the cost. If it's a good picture, we'll make it," or complaining of writers that they forever "bite the hand that lays the golden egg," or boasting that he had read "part of [a book] all the way through." Instead he put his money on Jim Malloy, an almost-thousand-dollar-a-week screenwriter, transplanted from Gibbsville to Hollywood by way of New York.

He had aspired to write an allegory, and with an eye to shaping it as a novella had studied Mann's *Disorder and Early Sorrow* and *Death in Venice.* This length was perfectly suited to O'Hara's gifts (*Imagine Kissing Pete* and "The Doctor's Son" profit from both their unities of action and their extended duration), but allegory was not. As explicitly hostile to conceits and to veiling as he was to whispered inference, O'Hara made his expository points bluntly and repetitively, and in all but his briefest stories was eager to tell plainly as well as show unambiguously. *Hope of Heaven* divides its attention between Malloy and the young woman he pursues, Peggy Henderson, like Betty Anderson a pretty employee of a local bookstore and sympathetic to left-wing causes. Like O'Hara's, Malloy's chase proves fruitless, but for rather more noble reasons. Here the problem is Malloy's refusal to swallow the cant and right-think diction of the object of his affection. The tone between them is hard-boiled, and O'Hara may have left some autobiographical scat on the trail in the following exchange, wherein Malloy asks Peggy "Do you love me?"

" 'No.'

" 'Well, then, why don't you marry me?'

" 'I don't like you.' "

No problem. He asks her again to marry him, and whines, "We're friends, aren't we?"

" 'Yes, and that's all. Just because I *sleep* with you?' "[85]

There are plot complications. The creepy son of a Lutheran pastor from Malloy's Region is forging stolen traveler's checks as he is "on the lam" (the diction is fatally perishable: money is "kale . . . wampum . . . spinach . . . mazuma . . . cabbage"), from New York, a long and tortured tale. Malloy, who never knew Reverend Schumacher's son back home, asks reasonably enough at a lunch meeting: "Why did you tell me all this?" The reader some time back began asking the same question, and the answer's not helpful: "I should of been a rich guy instead of a minister's son without any dough." He wants, that is, to be an actor. Meantime, Peggy Henderson's mysterious father just happens to be a detective (or "dick") who happens to be on the hunt for some guy "on the lam" from a petty crime involving traveler's checks . . . and so on, unto an accidental killing meant to leave everyone with a good reason to feel sad. Malloy visits New York on a trip that lasts half a paragraph, and seems to serve no purpose other than the display of some inside dope about Tony's, "21," and the Stork Club. It's a dog's dinner, *Hope of Heaven,* with its title mystifyingly inspired by Alexander Pope's *Essay on Man* and its allegorical underpinnings effectively obscured from my view. Its characters are introduced by essayistic biographical profiles, so the novella is lacking dramatic revelation as well as clear purpose. O'Hara's vision was clouded by Fitzgerald's exhortation to compose an idyll, by his own peculiar ambition to compose an allegory, and by his uncharacteristically abstract desire—expressed to his editor while the novel was under way—to represent altruism and "regeneration."

He worked hard on this book, bulled it through despite the distractions of courtship and marriage and studio work and nightclubbing and hangovers. It is no disgrace to write a failed novel, and no prophecy of future failure, since there are so many ways for a writer to get off track along any single leg of the journey. O'Hara confused courage with stamina, understood bravery to be a function of enduring pain rather than abandoning its cause. Valor was important to him: he was bravely candid in his clinical self-estimation of his courage, noting that he'd stood up to beatings in some fistfights and had been willing as a boy to jump in front of a runaway horse, but reporting also that he'd backed down from fights and too often swallowed his pride. He didn't dare back down from *So Far, So Good,* even after it became a hopeless *Hope of Heaven.* The novel is dutiful, a self-imposed assignment completed, and there is evidence throughout its pages that its author's heart was not in it. Perversely, it is often those very fictional undertakings about which a writer is least enthusiastic that summon the most exertion. With *Hope of Heaven,* typing away at it in Westwood or New York or Philadelphia or Quogue or at a hotel beside the Hudson in West Point (where he felt he would be immune to any temptations, nocturnal or otherwise), O'Hara honored the notion of preparing a perfect—by his lights—typescript. He typed on cheap rag paper, and if he made a change or committed an error, he retyped the sheet, thus making it impossible to know the extent of his revisions on a given piece of work.

The real danger of this book was only collaterally to his career and critical reputation. After *The Doctor's Son* and *Appointment in Samarra* he had enough credit in the bank to bounce back from a critical pounding, and despite his thin-skinned disposition he was fundamentally sturdy in his response to reviewers' abuse. No, the harm of this failure was to stunt his appetite to undertake another sustained work of imagination without looking over his shoulder at all those judges so quick to remind him of some spurious "promise" he has failed to keep and might have lost the art to fulfill. O'Hara didn't write another novel until *A Rage to Live,* published eleven years later. Meantime, he wasn't idle. A story collection—*Files on Parade*—came in 1939, followed a year later by *Pal Joey,* those linked stories that made his fortune, the following year. Whatever his confusions and doubts about his third novel, O'Hara remained loyal to *Hope of Heaven:* in a 1941 column in *Newsweek* he judged it to be not only the work on which he had worked hardest and longest, but also his "best written," and many years later he inscribed a copy to Wylie with the judgment, "This is my best."[86]

On the strength of O'Hara's previous success, Harcourt, Brace, sold thirteen thousand copies within two months of publication, and soon the author was chivvying his publisher to commit to a new story collection, which they refused to do unless the novel sold thirty thousand copies. Here was a collision of interests. Publishers don't like to print books they can't sell, and beyond the obvious reasons they also don't like to be the instruments by which a book is ignored. Failure is no fun; it's profitless and, even worse, it invites the irritation and contumely of the writer. But of course O'Hara was right to want the publication of his stories written since *The Doctor's Son:* there were many good ones. So perhaps spurred by one outcome controlling another—no story publication without a rewarding sale of the novel—he was almost obliged to study the advertising budget, and to pester Samuel Sloan and Cap Pearce to up the ante. Editors will react with familiar repugnance to the breezy sarcasm in a letter O'Hara wrote six months or so after publication, ham-handedly ironic about the single ad extolling *Hope of Heaven:* "But don't infer that I am complaining. I think it is sound business psychology to make the reading public think a book is hard to get."[87] This is an old, old story. A certain respectable number of readers—thirteen thousand, say—buy a book because they want to read whatever that writer writes. Then the reviews arrive, and maybe they're so-so, maybe they're even bad, and these were very bad. The book stopped selling, and stopped finally for the reason many books stop selling: because it was not very good. I feel like a fifth columnist here, but the sad fact was and is that nobody but a student or a reviewer reads a book because he has to, and advertising cannot necessarily persuade any reader to buy it. Reading a book is a discretionary enterprise, and that so many people chose to spend their hours reading O'Hara after *Hope of Heaven* is more interesting than the fact so few read that one.

Heywood Broun again was disappointed, and Clifton Fadiman scolded the author for writing "ads for Brooks Brothers" and offered headmasterly advice: "you go ahead and be a novelist." (This review incited a sneering response from O'Hara, that if Fadiman wore a Brooks suit he would be recognized at once as an incognito spy.) Alfred Kazin deplored *Hope of Heaven* as a "woefully empty book." Sterling North, writing in the *Chicago Daily News,* a review that could provoke a legal action in these sensitive days, labeled O'Hara one of the "bright young drunks of American literature," and showed in the sententious tag one of the ways in which then was not like now: "The mere fact Mr. O'Hara writes like a drunk, thinks like a drunk, brags about wenching like a drunk is of no particular consequence. If anything, it is in his favor."[88] In case you missed it, that was meant I think to be a compliment. According to North, "bright tipplers" offer "good drunken conversation" and are properly uninhibited regarding sex and violence, proving that O'Hara was either "a very good Irishman or he has the most vivid imagination of any young man who ever earned royalties on his indiscretions."

They were rough in the old days, but it's also worth remarking that to a drinker back then being called a drunk was merely descriptive. The criticism (or boast) that *Hope of Heaven* was sex-soaked was more complicated, morally and aesthetically. North's unstructured stream-of-unconsciousness, for all its own slurred imprecations, is lucid about this, that Jimmy Malloy and the "clear-eyed amorous girl to whom he makes scarcely interrupted love" know how to have a good time. Reading the novel today, one has to wonder: the he-ing and she-ing seems as lubricious as Prozac:

"I turned over and we lightly kissed each other and felt our passion slowly coming on again. 'Ah, this is nice. This is what we're here for, isn't it?'

" 'Mm-hmm. Want me to stay all night?'

" 'Sure. It's a long time since we've done that.'

" 'Am I good for you, Jim?'

" 'Yes, you're good for me. Am I good for you?'

" 'Yes. Yes,' she said. 'Yes. Yes.' "[89]

Putting aside that Molly Bloom was a superior yes-woman, such passages can't raise anybody's temperature today. Now now is now and then was then, and the mere fact that these two were in bed together, and talking about what they had done, would do, and were doing—this was a big deal. Interviewing people of O'Hara's generation for this book, I was struck how often they would mention how dangerous it had felt to read him on sex, and many of them recalled exactly where they were and with whom when they first read about Caroline English's lusts or Gloria Wandrous's fingers running across her own skin. These bygone readers couldn't quote a memorable sentence from O'Hara's fiction, but they by God recalled heating up when they read the Good Parts.

Waiting for the reviews to run their course and the ads not to run, O'Hara settled with Belle into the Wylie house in Quogue. Gradually these time-outs from the harum-scarum of Hollywood and especially New York—Bermuda had been the first, then Cape Cod and Hobe Sound—came to dominate O'Hara's choices. Belle had an influence here: she knew how to protect her husband from his worst temptations. But recess—not confined to a modest atmosphere—had been O'Hara's tropism since those long-ago visits to his maternal grandparents' modestly serene house in Lykens, and those retreats with his parents to their modest farm. Keeping company with the wealthy was also for O'Hara an elegant keep from the grubby exertions of striving, and country clubs (grand as well as bucolic) were barbicans, refuges on the right side of the moat, illusory sanctuaries from all that might ail a set-upon and deserving fellow. At Quogue he worked in the late Dr. Wylie's study, which Frank MacShane has described with all its "memorabilia, fishing tackle, shotguns, copies of Galsworthy and Yale year books." After O'Hara moved to Princeton and built his own refuge, Linebrook, such a collection of caste-referenced totems would be the furnishings of his office. He rose early, ate a big breakfast, read the newspapers, worked, went to bed early.

When he and Belle went to the city, they stayed either at her mother's apartment at 1115 Fifth Avenue or at the Algonquin. O'Hara continued to have business with the *New Yorker*, submitting stories and complaining about his treatment by editors and paymasters. He wrote Ross: "I want more money [repeated ten times]. . . . You might at least give me a gold watch and chain, suitably engraved. I want appreciation. I'm only human."[90] It was an accumulation of such complaints that prompted one of Ross's more charmingly exasperated outbursts: "What I'm running here is a goddam bughouse. Not a man in the place without a screw loose. Look at ——, who thinks his balls are swelling, and ——, who thinks his ass-hole is closing. Jesus Christ, aren't there enough real troubles in the world without brooding about crap like that?"[91] But in fact, Ross had the inspired notion to take O'Hara's message literally, ignoring its just plea for better pay for his work. In 1948 he bought from a Third Avenue pawnshop a cheap pocket watch, gold-plated and "fat," in Katharine A. White's memory, "studded with turquoises." Ross had it inscribed with after-dinner-testimonial flummery, and indentured O'Hara once again as his—no, the *New Yorker*'s—loyal serf.[92]

This bad marriage hurt—Ross's excessive scorn butting against O'Hara's tetchy self-regard and quantification of his standing—but the longer O'Hara wrote for the magazine the better for literature. When *Files on Parade* was published in 1939—five years after *The Doctor's Son*—it collected thirty-five stories, some of O'Hara's most affecting and daring work. Edmund Wilson was particularly enthusiastic about "Price's Always Open" (1935), a study of a townie from a summer resort striving to rise socially. Owing a debt to Fitzgerald's "Winter Dreams" does not diminish the story's power. Price's is a gussied-up diner and its owner has one leg, "having left the other somewhere in a dressing station back of Château-Thierry."[93] His place is the place to eat when there's no other place to eat. "Not that anyone ever wondered about it, but it might have been interesting to find out just when he slept." This unnoticed but priv-ileged observer has earned the right to judge his customers, and he has opinions, especially about the late crowd that drops by after the yacht club dances shut down. He likes the summer kids well enough, "and they always said *Mister* Price. . . . But they were summer people and the winters were long." So a year-rounder is his favorite, Jackie Girard, the son of a local carpenter, a Holy Cross boy with a summer job as clerk at the local hotel and not a member of the yacht club but often invited to its dances owing to his usefulness as a piano player. With the bravura social calculation that characterizes Dexter Green's unstable position in "Win-ter Dreams," O'Hara's narrator explains that Jackie is not invited to the small dinner parties that precede the dances, nor to satellite parties that spin off from them. The story ends with a scene of stunning brutality involving Price's blackjack laid vigorously against the head of a nasty and violent summer kid, a comeuppance for a cruel snob who has sucker punched Jackie. In a delicate touch, O'Hara engages the night counter-man in a general rout of the summer kids: "In his hand was a baseball bat, all nicked where it had been used for tamping down ice around milk cans."[94] Like Dexter Green refusing to caddy at the country club for the young and bratty rich girl with whom he will fall in love, or the checkout clerk in Updike's "A & P" who responds to the manager's act of cruelty by quitting his job, Price has effectively put himself out of business.

The conjunction of O'Hara's direct observation—the nicked bat, the ice held over from winter realities to accommodate summer pleasures—shows the story writer at his most alert. Wilson singled out "Price's Always Open" as a rare and excellent instance of democracy striking back: "The cruel side of social snobbery is really Mr. O'Hara's main theme."[95] If the violent striking back here has been indisputably commensurate with its provocation, this is not invariably the case in O'Hara's work. As Louis Auchincloss has written in *Reflections of a Jacobite:* "In the strange, angry world that he describes, the characters behave with a uniform violence, speak with a uniform crudeness. . . . The most casual meeting between a major and minor character will result in an ugly flare-up or a sexual connection, or both. It is impossible for an O'Hara hero to order a meal in a restaurant or to take a taxi ride without having a brusque interchange with the waiter or driver."[96] Auchincloss is addressing the novels rather than the stories, and he has somewhat over-sharpened his point, but motiveless truculence is often a feature of O'Hara's unsuccessful characterizations. Resentment is animating, but only when the acuity of the hurt—as opposed to a reader's personal judgment of the stakes—can be felt through the writer's sentences. "Surely," Auchincloss writes, "there is a difference between the feelings of the man who has not been asked to dinner and those of the man who has been thrown down the front stairs." O'Hara, who wrote both crudely and subtly about both, might not agree. Hurt—unlike the narrative that attempts to convey it—is not subject to an exegesis, but it is reasonable to argue that injury suffered from an abuse of power has a better chance of exciting pity and terror than the delayed petulance of an individual scorned.

Consequential abuse of power is dramatized in another story from *Files on Parade*, "Do You Like It Here?" (1939). A student has been at an unnamed boarding school fewer than six weeks, having entered in midyear. Roberts is an outsider, a child of divorce whose parents' travels have given him many different educational opportunities. In his brief time at this school he has managed to be hated by, and learned in return to hate, the only other student the story characterizes. He is summoned to the housemaster's office and accused of having stolen a watch, though there is no evidence suggesting that he is a likely suspect; and the third-person narrator, with access to Roberts's consciousness, declares that the boy testifies "truthfully" that he believes he has never seen the watch in question. The four-page story does not settle the facts, and O'Hara seemed deliberately misleading in reporting them himself, writing to an editor at the *New Yorker,* where the story first appeared, that it was about a boy who stole a watch. Steven Goldleaf's recent book, *John O'Hara: A Study of the Short Fiction*, admirably summarizes the almost farcical bafflement of critics wrestling with "Do You Like It Here?"[97] Their perplexity has been exacerbated by the account in Frank Mac-

Shane's biography that O'Hara himself, as a young man, was accused of filching a watch from the locker room of the Schuylkill Country Club, a crime of which he was almost certainly innocent. (And, as reported in an earlier chapter, Kathleen O'Hara Fuldner has said that O'Hara's father "knocked John down" for stealing five dollars in fact stolen by another boy named John.) A similar irresolution had beset the death of Gloria Wandrous; it was such coyness, or haste, on O'Hara's part that led Harold Ross to his exasperated proclamation to James Thurber that he'd no longer print any O'Hara story he didn't understand.[98]

At any rate, readers have suspected that Roberts did steal it, that he didn't, that it was never stolen at all, and that, if it was stolen, the house-master dunnit. Certainly this housemaster, a graduate of the school where he has taught for more than a decade, the brother of two gradu-ates, the son of a graduate, the classmate of fathers of his students—tor-tures Roberts. Van Ness does this by asking, as though from a summit of indifference, mocking questions about the boy's family, social instability, loneliness. He is pulling the wings off a fly, as he is licensed to do by the arbitrary entitlement of the boarding school hierarchy, a caricature of the caste system devolved into despotic abuse all the more grotesque for its plummy idiom of high-mindedness. Anyone who has ever been called to any master's office at a boarding school will recognize as authentic the helplessness of the boy at the mercy of Van Ness's interrogation. He begins by remarking, "Strange. Strange. Six weeks and I really don't know a thing about you. Not much, at any rate." This, of course, sets the table for what follows, a grilling so relentless in its self-pleasuring malice that the story comes at the reader like a battery of punches that never ceases:

> "Roberts, tell me a little about yourself."
>
> Roberts wonders what Van Ness means.
>
> "How do I mean? Well—about your life, before you decided to honor us with your presence. Where you came from, what you did, why you went to so many schools, so on."
>
> "Well, I don't know."
>
> "Oh, now. Now Roberts. Don't let your natural modesty overcome the autobiographical urge. Shut the door."
>
> [With the door shut, the master's malevolence heats to an erotic degree]:
>
> "Good," said Van Ness. "Now, proceed with this—uh—dossier. Give

me the—huh—huh—*lowdown* on Roberts, Humphrey, Second Form, McAllister Memorial Hall, et cetera."

Roberts, Humphrey, sat down and felt the knot of his tie.

[He tries, stumbles through chaotic personal history, asks] "Is that the kind of stuff you want, Mister?"

"Proceed, proceed. I'll tell you when I want you to—uh—halt."[99]

The rest is painful to read, a nutty, perverse, and credible overload of spite. When Van Ness finishes he sits back, "almost breathless." The effect is so crushing that it leaves O'Hara's story broken, like Roberts, at the end. All that the boy, alone in his room, has breath enough of his own to say—all that O'Hara can say on his behalf—is, "over and over, first violently, then weakly, he said it, 'The bastard, the dirty bastard.' " It's not enough. O'Hara trusted sometimes lazily his conviction that no story ever really ends, that its outcome can be imagined beyond the final sentence. This is what Grace Paley termed "the open destiny of life," an author's bountiful impulse toward her characters' vital faculty for surprise. But that destiny shuts at a story's edge, and what O'Hara has not set in motion will not yield anything after his final word is spoken. A character's reprisal against a bully is available only within the story's language, and O'Hara is made speechless by the quotidian sadism of his housemaster.

To imagine the consequence of a snub, one might better read "Olive" (1935), named for the hotel switchboard operator who listens in on guests' conversations. Here the power lines are tangled: Olive is the servant, and the hotel's guests are free to give her orders. The Colonel, lonely and polite, is a generous tipper, but Olive resents what she takes to be his lack of esteem for her. Miss Bishop, shy and also lonely, begins a friendship with the Colonel, and Olive subverts their affection by innuendo and a treacherous failure to deliver messages between them. Here the subservient character has the story's point of view, and what has Olive's attention controls the fate of her supposed betters. "Olive," notably un-Chekhovian in its sour malice, is interesting to read with Raymond Carver's story "Errand," which is gradually revealed to be about a great European hotel's bellhop, one of those conventionally invisible presences. Carver's story—drawing on facts of Chekhov's dying days told in Henri Troyat's biography—is a comment on biographies' pecking order, their ignorance of, indifference toward, or generalized references to nameless little people (a bellboy, a chambermaid), as though in the tale of a personage these extras exist merely to dress, rather than animate, a scene. "Errand" reclaims for the bellboy his primacy in the hotel-room drama of characters attending a dying personage's death. In that hotel room are Chekhov's wife and doctor, and they send for champagne, which the bellboy brings. In Carver's story, after all, this is *his* hotel, and what he's thinking about is *his* tip, and how that tip might be diminished by the guests' taking notice of a popped cork littering the carpet. The chief distinction between O'Hara's and Carver's preoccupations in "Olive" and "Errand" is that Carver uses his story to redress an imbalance of seemingly settled authorial attention, and O'Hara uses his to settle, with gratuitous cruelty, an aggrieved character's petty score.

In April of 1938, upon the proximate spur of having seen a romantic movie that made Europe seem grand, the O'Haras sailed tourist class aboard the French Line's *Paris*. He talked themselves into the venture by claiming that he'd get more work done in Europe than at home; she prophesied that they'd live cheaper than in the (albeit free) house in Quogue. He promised that the trip would recharge the old batteries; she reasoned that her mother and sister were in London, and she missed them. It was a bad year, of course, to tour Europe or, worse, to live there. Never mind: Paris would be safe from Hitler, and if it weren't, there was always London, where Faber and Faber was about to publish *Hope of Heaven*.

Belle might have wished she had stayed home when, upon sailing, she discovered that a passenger in first class was the earlier Mrs. John O'Hara. Pet entertained the couple, and O'Hara drank too much, and wife and ex-wife were civil, even friendly, but Belle balked at Pet's proposal to tour with them. O'Hara gave Samuel Sloan an account of the crossing from the Hotel Scribe in Paris, where the weather was so foul that spring that he joked that the "ski trains [were] coming down from St. Moritz to take advantage of the wonderful skiing."[100] That letter has a paragraph worth quoting at length for its uncommon drollery. In his correspondence O'Hara could press hard on irony and sarcasm, but his letters (except to Joseph Bryan III and, later, to his daughter) were written not to please but to instruct, generally in the parlance of his wishes or grievances. This, by contrast, is sheer fun: "The trip across was made without incident. Rats in the hold caused an outbreak of bubonic plague, which was quickly stamped out. A time bomb exploded in the fo'c'sle head, but the loss of life was slight. . . . A lady on B Deck was seasick all the way, and the commandant was buried at sea, with traditional honors. Belle had twins, back to back. . . . But nothing really happened except a Miss Fenstermacher, of Davenport, Iowa, won the ping-pong tournament with a furious, slashing forehand. . . . Mike Romanoff was unable to make the trip."

O'Hara went to a lunch party out at Senlis, at novelist Louis Bromfield's house; he was irritated, met "some of the prize pricks of three continents. Only two prize cunts: third prize," he told Sloan in a later letter.[101] Listening to Parisians speak French instead of English and the cold spring soon got on his nerves, so at the end of the month he decided to cross to London and give the English a chance to annoy him, which they did. He might have preferred that they speak French, because he didn't enjoy what they said to him. The O'Haras stayed first with Belle's family at a small hotel near Bond Street, but presently a Faber and Faber editor found them a flat in Chelsea, near the Thames and right off Cheyne Walk, that favorite street of comfortable American expatriates.

The Thurbers were in London for the year, and it galled O'Hara (even if perhaps it had the effect of granting his letters a lighter touch) that his friend's charm on the page and a London gallery show of his drawings had won him so many foreign admirers. O'Hara's jealousy was premature but prophetic; over the following decade Thurber would win a remarkable following in England for his fantastical observations in essays, fiction, and drawings, and such fans as W. H. Auden and T. S. Eliot (Faber and Faber's very own) found virtues in his work that were exactly those virtues O'Hara found in his own. For a *Time* cover story in 1951, Eliot applauded Thurber's "serious" humor, "serious and even somber. Unlike so much humor, it is not merely a criticism of manners— that is, of the superficial aspects of a society at a given moment—but something more profound. . . . They will be a document of the age they belong to."* Two years later Thurber was given an honorary Litt. D. by Yale, where he, too, wished he had studied, if that's the best verb to describe what he and O'Hara hankered to have done in New Haven.

O'Hara arranged for guest memberships at second-tier London clubs,

---

*Quoted without citation by Charles Holmes, *The Clocks of Columbus: The Literary Career of James Thurber* (New York: Atheneum, 1978), p. 289.

and Frank MacShane tells that Alec Waugh invited him and Thurber to a self-consciously bookish dining society self-styled Ye Sette of Odde Volumes. Perhaps the view from outside the windows of such precious gatherings is distorting; it might've looked like fun, the white tie and tails, badges, such nicknames for members as "Brother Idler" and "His Oddship." There were arch and tedious speeches, and O'Hara became bored, then drunk; when the boorish Yank lit a cigarette before the king had been toasted, he was reproached by a waiter, and—fight or flight—elected to keep his fists in his lap. Still, Waugh came back for seconds and gave a dinner party on their behalf, to which he invited Pet. In a letter to Adele Lovett, quoted by MacShane, O'Hara catalogues the guests, including a "Lord who seems to have committed a murder, a fairy with a beautiful wife, an Asquith with teeth that she copied from Mrs. Roosevelt." In a letter to Charles Pearce and Samuel Sloan, addressed "Dear Cheps," O'Hara remembered that also in attendance was the curator of reptiles at the London Zoo, and "a Lesbian who loved Butterfield 8 and didn't know anything else I'd written."[102] (What babies writers can be about this kind of thing! Fighting words for some newly met to an author with two or more books in print: "I love your book!")

Stylistically an Anglophile, with his lifelong enthusiasm for bespoke clothes and Peal and Lobb and Leathersmith and MG and Rolls-Royce and English saddles, O'Hara resented the English and they didn't care for him. The Irish in him, despite himself, might have prevented him from sucking up to the gentry, and notwithstanding his intolerance for inferior presentation—Wylie remembered him cutting cold an adolescent date because the boy's *father* neglected to shine his loafers—he sometimes showed up at dinner parties in London not only without black tie, but without any tie, and without a shave. He liked to make cracks about Wallis Simpson, author of Edward VIII's scandal. He resented the right-wing, even fascist, politics he encountered at some of these very parties, and bolted a London restaurant when some of its young, university-educated patrons burst, without irony, into the "Horst Wessel Lied."[103]

When he and Belle wondered why they weren't having a better time, O'Hara made friends with T. S. Eliot's sometime flatmate, John Hayward, an acerbic and learned doctor's son. This was an unlikely fellowship, of the kind that should remind biographers to mind the essential mysteries, whether chemical or capricious, of human associations. Hayward, a bibliophile with a caustic curiosity about erotic compulsion and folly, was wheelchair-bound. He prized speed of verbal response (never O'Hara's strength) and range of scholarly erudition (never O'Hara's interest). Evidently Hayward delighted in O'Hara's fluency in Broadway double-talk, and his appreciation of that facility might have been a nice push for Pal Joey's coming soliloquies.

The O'Haras had meant to spend a year in Europe, but after three months they sailed home in August aboard the *Champlain.* "Suddenly," Belle wrote Adele Lovett, "John couldn't face another Englishman without wanting to kill him."[104] He'd done little work in France and England, and resigned himself to the reality that *Hope of Heaven* was hopeless as a money-pump, and he knew it was past time to dig in again and write something that mattered to him, because this was his only hope of writing something that mattered to anyone else. Swallowing his pride, he once again threw in his lot with the *New Yorker.* Katharine White, in a 1971 sketch of O'Hara for her archive in the Bryn Mawr College library, noted that she had edited nearly all of his short stories until her retirement in 1962. Perhaps, but beginning early in 1938 O'Hara's principal contact at the *New Yorker* was William Maxwell, who began working with O'Hara when the junior editor was filling in for Mrs. White. O'Hara trusted, respected, and liked Maxwell, and this goodwill was returned with interest. Katharine White was so accustomed to her rectitude and gravitas—to being, as she quoted someone else as saying, "the literary conscience" of the *New Yorker*—that she found it difficult to regard O'Hara from any point of view other than her own, and her vantage was always from on high, looking down. Even her 1971 sketch reveals an essential disdain, in her apology for writing four whole pages about her experience over three decades in which she read hundreds of his stories; this, she notes, is all out of proportion with her opinion of O'Hara's "value" as measured against some other *New Yorker* writers.

She remembers him condescendingly as an importuning young cub, "difficult" and "drinking badly" and "making his way in the big city by his talent, plus arrogance and bravado." Then, tempering disapproval with justice, Mrs. White notes that he quickly developed into one of "our" most brilliant short-story writers, and I assume "our" refers possessively to a magazine rather than to the perhaps grander universe of American literature.

Mrs. White recalls that she and Ross "coddled" O'Hara, a memory unsupported by the record. He instead was dismissed, mocked, scolded, and almost always patronized. When she had written him in 1932, master to apprentice, that "it does seem the greatest of pities that you can't spend a little more time on your manuscripts for The New Yorker,"[105] she was only saying what was so,* and no doubt it needed saying, and no doubt his work would have profited greatly from deliberate consideration, had he possessed the patience for revision. But subverting this reproach is a touch of self-interest—"your story in—was it Scribner's—which . . . seemed to me a much more finished work"—that could only emphasize O'Hara's precarious standing. And then the letter ends with a plea, from the low road, to help the fiction editor feed the goat: "Do please think about this and write a lot for us." Mrs. White would lay herself on the line with a long-faced report: that not only had a story been rejected but that "the final sorrowful news" was more fundamental: "I think you could have something very striking here if only you felt it deeply and cared enough about it to write it that way. It now seems as if the writer didn't care, had no emotion about the whole thing."[106] This is brave candor, and it is clearly designed to inspire a rethinking of O'Hara's enterprise and working methods, indeed his calling. But he either wouldn't listen or couldn't hear: he sent back a day later—revised, by his lights—the story she had returned. In her subsequent rejection, she hoped he would "take another whack at it" later. "I sound so violent because I am so disappointed, and I don't mean to be rude for you know I really do think you are a first-rate writer and only suffer from haste or something."

It is the combustible combination of dismay expressed with regretful and self-justifying delicacy that inflames rejected writers beyond any pain rejection itself can cause. To be told no—nope, not for us—is disappointing and can bring a flush to the cheeks. But when rejection comes bundled with hand-wringing, how-can-I-tell-you and what-can-I-say-to-make-you-understand and have-you-any-idea-how-unpleasant-this-is-for-me, well—the correspondence is soiling. Mrs. White never forgave O'Hara for writing stories she didn't like. She didn't like it when

---

*In 1941 O'Hara boasted to Lucius Beebe, interviewing him for the *Herald-Tribune*, that "my short stories for the New Yorker never have taken me more than two hours to write" (Lucius Beebe, "Stage Asides," *New York Herald-Tribune*, 12 January 1941).

he wrote the word "latrine," when he wrote another "dirty phrase," and she didn't like it when Ross decided to raise O'Hara's word rate from 6.3 cents to a dime (nine cents, Mrs. White advised, was plenty). And later she justified what O'Hara took to be a short payment (yes, he counted) by explaining "we don't pay by the word, but by the inch." Well, by inches their string was running out. As "a matter of publishing policy," she rejected an essay that she admitted to O'Hara everybody at the magazine "thinks is great," because it was experimental. Behind his back she wrote her colleagues that she'd "stake [her] reputation . . . that O'Hara will not go down as a first-rate writer unless he reforms on both dirt and clarity." But still, the goat needed feeding: "We wish you could send us some more stories. Can't you bring yourself to write some?"[107]

William Maxwell and O'Hara learned quickly how to work together. A taciturn prose stylist, born and raised to celebrate the quiddities of Lincoln, Illinois, Maxwell understood the precarious hold that a writer keeps on dignity and self-assurance. He had matters of life and death in proportion, having experienced in his near and extended family calamities: kin burned by kerosene, a grandfather dying in slow agony from a rat bite, a brother losing an arm in a horse-drawn carriage accident. His mother had died in the influenza epidemic of 1918–19 that O'Hara had invoked with such emotional precision in "The Doctor's Son," and they shared a clear understanding of injuries that are not merely self-referential, but have terminal outcomes. Maybe Maxwell sensed how vulnerable one feels when submitting work, and took a long view of the distinction between short-term failure and long-term success, but for whatever reason, he knew how to say "no" to O'Hara without rubbing disdain into the superficial wound of rejection; he understood, that is, and conveyed to O'Hara, that he was rejecting a piece of work and not its maker.

While O'Hara was in London he tried, as Maxwell knew, to influence Faber and Faber to publish Maxwell's first novel, *Bright Center of Heaven*. Two weeks later Maxwell returned, without hand-wringing, O'Hara's "Big and Dumb," saying plainly that "we are all against this, and each one for a different reason, which I hesitate to convey to you, lest we sound collectively foolish." It is difficult to articulate how exactly the tone of Maxwell's rejection contrasts so favorably with White's, but it has to do with modesty and restraint, and an absence of dolor or vexation. "Me," he continues, "I think it would be better in the long run if you just sat down and wrote us another story." Well, wasn't that what Mrs. White asked? But for her the asking was always within the context of the *New Yorker*'s wishes and desires. Shortly after that rejection, O'Hara wrote Maxwell, "all right is what you're doing, and thank you is what I say." Craftsmanlike square dealing made all the difference to O'Hara, who understood that Maxwell's comfort with him was based on felt respect. Alone among *New Yorker* editors—from that cohort of Ross, Gill, Fadiman, Gibbs, Thurber, Mrs. White—Maxwell had from then on with O'Hara a rational, helpful, and friendly working relationship. There, that wasn't so difficult, was it? That didn't hurt, did it? Almost twenty years later, during "Remarks on the Novel" at the Library of Congress, O'Hara rounded—gently, for him—on his critics, promising that "I am going to go right on writing in spite of their stern refusal to grant permission." But he knew how pugnacious this sounded, and also said, "I don't *want* to be known as a sorehead. But if I am one, it may be because I have been clouted on the skull so many times."[108]

Soon after returning from Europe, the O'Haras were in Los Angeles, staying briefly in Brentwood Heights with Lucilla and Henry Potter, Belle's sister and brother-in-law, while they settled on a Westwood apartment to rent at 471½ Landfair, a block from the UCLA campus. Even now it wasn't *all* peaches and cream with the *New Yorker:* he was soon complaining to Maxwell that his copies of the magazine were arriving "exactly a week later" than anyone else's, and "what the hell's the matter with the Circulation dep't?"[109] He had come to Los Angeles looking to stuff his billfold, but despite encouragements from RKO and Twentieth Century–Fox, the projects he worked on were stillborn. He could make a decent living as a script doctor, doing emergency cosmetic surgery, but he needed to hit the mother lode to support the lavish style in which he was learning to live. That's where his pal, Joey, came in.

In 1948 O'Hara gave an interview to the gossip columnist Earl Wilson about the origins of the series of letters from a nightclub MC, collectively titled *Pal Joey*, most of which were published in the *New Yorker* beginning in 1938. The account was Wilsonized, fattened with hyperbole and then sliced like baloney into mini-graphs that could be fully comprehended as a reading passenger rocked to and fro hanging from a subway strap. The topic was Writing While Drunk, and according to O'Hara he was very drunk indeed at the dawn of *Pal Joey*. This was when he and Belle were just back from England and living at Mrs. Wylie's apartment on Fifth Avenue. He had decided to hole up alone in

Philadelphia to write something—anything, really. The night before departing, he and Belle had been on the town, and he'd had a snootful. The hangover next morning was a killer, and heading downtown on Fifth to the station, O'Hara, realizing he wasn't going to make it, told the cabbie to drop him off at the Pierre. After a couple of drinks, he felt better, decided he needed a nap, and checked in. " 'Then,' said O'Hara, looking down at the table, shaking his head, 'began a real beauty. Just getting stiff and passing out. I started Thursday. By Saturday morning I'd drunk myself sober."[110] The switchboard operator—kinder than Olive—told him what time it was, and which seven o'clock she meant (the breakfast seven), and that it was a day or two later than he thought it was. " 'At that point remorse set in. I asked, *What kind of god damn heel am I? I must be worse 'n anybody in the world.'* " So he pondered this, allowing that there must be somebody worse than him, but who? " 'Al Capone, maybe.' " Then it hit him, the hit hit him: a nightclub master of ceremonies, he'd be worse than John O'Hara. Here the myth clears its throat, and the snare drum rolls: "O'Hara took a cigarette from his handsome gold case. . . . 'I went to work and wrote a piece about a night club heel in the form of a letter. I finished the piece [in a couple of hours]. The New Yorker bought the story the same day, ordered a dozen more, and then came the play. . . . That was the only good thing I ever got out of booze.' "

After the submission of that first piece, Ross took O'Hara to lunch at "21" and told him, "sober," as O'Hara later remembered it, that if he wrote him ten more Pal Joeys "I could say the hell with Hollywood."[111] It's not difficult to understand his enthusiasm. To read a few lines of Joey's solecisms and inventive misspellings—to hear him boast and lie in first person, to hear his mind angling for advantage—is to recognize a perfect seeding of O'Hara's gifts in shallow but richly manured soil. Joey is a Broadway blowhard, widely if not deeply in debt, reflexively cynical. The lowlife vernacular is right up to the bygone minute—every chorine is a "mouse," and every time Joey gets a "load on" he "tumbles" for one of them. The brief pieces are letters to his on-and-off friend Ted, and once O'Hara heard them in his imagination, he could write them by the yard.* They owe debts to Ring Lardner, whom O'Hara rightly respected,

*This patch comes from "A Bit of a Shock," about a babe Joey bumps into while he's preparing a burlesque nightclub act in Chicago: "Well we are rehearsing and I am doing a patter with the kids in

and certainly to Damon Runyon, on whom he looked down. Like Robert Benchley, crushed by the deathless popularity of his "Treasurer's Report," O'Hara feared from the beginning that he'd become the hostage of a series that he soon came to consider a stunt.

By May of 1939, when Ross rejected a couple of letters from Joey to Ted, O'Hara bristled with irritation in a letter to Maxwell, and threatened to put the series to sleep.† While drawn to Joey's eclectic voice, Ross was also apt to reject an O'Hara piece whose idiom challenged him. He was, as always, vigilant about letting double meanings slip past his censoring eye, and from his first submissions to the *New Yorker* O'Hara was required to fight to exercise his acuity for malapropisms, neologisms, and inspired barbarisms. ("Wuddia hippum the mob" was his variation on *What do you hear from our friends?*) Ross recognized that his strength was the singularity of his usages, yet he labored with dumb resolve to regularize them. The tension inspired one of O'Hara's most articulate defenses of his style, in a 1939 letter to Maxwell: "I wish to hell there would be an end to this quibbling about my use of the vernacular. Even if people don't get it at first, they will. I was the first person ever to do a piece about double-talk. . . . It is a point of artistry with me. I like being first in those things, but you-all make me nervous. . . . I have been unable to use the verb to make in the sense of recognizing and/or identifying. Detectives are always saying 'I made him the minute I sore him,' meaning 'I recognized him . . .' But Ross would think the detective was a fairy."[112]

the line where they come up to me one by one and ask me what I want for Xmas and it is all the double entender. But it is the way I play it that is funny. I do not know exactly who to compare myself with but for illustration Maurice Chevalier. I am having trouble with one of the mice because she is mugging even in rehearsal and as far as I could make out is doing her impression of Kate Hepburn and any minute will go into her impression of L. Barrymore."

†At about this time O'Hara wrote a bitter letter to Ross about the editor's close friend Dave Chasen, of the eponymous restaurant on Beverly Boulevard that was soon to become famous. Ross had invested in the restaurant, which became at once a hangout for Robert Benchley and Dorothy Parker, the Marx brothers, James Cagney, and W. C. Fields, among many others. O'Hara had either overpaid a thirteen-dollar lunch tab, or had been overbilled, the exact nature of the crime lost in the heat of his rhetoric. The gist, though, was that Ross's dear chum was a crook. The editor responded with greater patience than his author deserved: "If any gypping goes on, it must be the waiters. . . . I think you should have written Dave about it, or told him. . . . But don't come to me with any more restaurant problems, for the love of God" (Harold Ross, "Letters from the Editor," in *Letters from the Editor: The New Yorker's Harold Ross,* ed. Thomas Kunkel [New York: Random House, 2000], pp. 139, 140).

By late 1939, O'Hara reported to Maxwell that Ross was "getting bored with Joey too." That "too" included, of course, his creator, although O'Hara admitted that it had pumped forth the easiest money he could get without "actually inheriting it. . . . But I got pretty fucking bored." He likened his enthusiasm for Joey to that he'd felt for the first Guy Lombardo record he heard. "The second time, the second record of his, made me want to smash the phonograph."[113] But he wasn't about to smash his own phonograph, not quite yet. Here came the New Year, here came Joey, traveling east to Maxwell with a cover letter explaining that this one "unwound itself in about an hour, so I tho't what the hell."[114]

O'Hara wasn't being as undisciplined or casual as "what the hell" might make it seem. He knew what he wanted from his bender-inspired brainstorm at the Pierre, and very soon after he'd finished the one-hour "what the hell" wonder, he wrote Richard Rodgers, asking if he and Lorenz Hart might be interested in making a musical "book show" about the gabby heel. "If they asked me, I could write a book." They asked; he wrote; one kind of worry was finished forever.

4. AT WAR AND ABOUT TOWN

Belle and John O'Hara returned to New York, where he wrote *Pal Joey*'s libretto—to be directed by George Abbott and to star Gene Kelly in the title role. They rented a long and narrow apartment on the ground floor of a brownstone on East 79th Street, between Fifth and Madison, and despite a lively social life, he steadied himself for hard work, letting Belle believe he didn't notice that she was watering his drinks. In addition to the libretto, O'Hara prepared the Pal Joey stories for publication in book form, and from July 1940 till February 1942 produced (for a thousand dollars each) a weekly column for *Newsweek*. "Entertainment Week" anticipated the vices of his later serial opinion pieces for *Collier's* and *Holiday,* for the *Trenton Times* and *Newsday*. They were cobbled together in often resentful haste, and showed the irritability of conversations on demand, and were used to drop names ("Jock" Whitney), settle scores (Edmund Wilson), prolong grudges (Clifton Fadiman), and to boast and bluster. Their effect on readers was ill-considered and unintended, for much of his self-aggrandizing was surely meant ironically, but such irony misfires without intimacy between the writer and reader, and O'Hara—to credit his consistency—would not snuggle up. As admiring a reader as Finis Farr recollected that "people who knew and liked O'Hara read his opening *Newsweek* columns, said to themselves, 'John is better than that,' and stopped reading."[1]

O'Hara wrote much of the *Pal Joey* libretto in Quogue, on Dune

Road, between interludes of golf and tennis. He was at ease there, felt appraised at a value that seemed just. He enjoyed contributing sketches to the country club's annual variety show, *Quogue Quips*. This was a good time for him, and it was an index of his confidence that he was shrewdly ruthless in translating the Joey material into a musical comedy that broke new ground with its unsentimental exploration of character. Independent of Rodgers, Hart, and Abbott, O'Hara decided to cannibalize parts from several different stories, developing an original plot wherein Joey haphazardly seduces a rich older dame (to be played by Vivienne Segal) who finances his schemes, which kindness is repaid by an even more haphazard scheme to blackmail her.

He was accustomed by his Hollywood experiences to the give and take of collaboration, and he recognized that Richard Rodgers and Lorenz Hart Jr. were not engaged in this enterprise merely to encourage a few short stories to burst into agreeable song. By O'Hara's accurate account, he trimmed and shaped, excising all topical references with an eye to giving the work a long shelf life, even as he honored what he termed its "argot and time spirit." According to Rodgers's autobiography, *Musical Stages* (1975), O'Hara went past his deadline in delivering the script and this tardiness inspired Hart's lyric "If They Asked Me, I Could Write a Book," right up there with "Bewitched, Bothered and Bewildered" among *Pal Joey*'s enduring numbers. At summer's end O'Hara handed in the book and assumed that he'd done his duty. But there was more. In any play there is always more; in a musical aiming for such tight, almost Brechtian integration of music and story, there was a great deal more. His view of the matter was simple: not wanting to play the fool or be played for one, "I had made up my mind not to be that perennial Broadway nuisance, The Author, so I stayed away from the theater."[2] George Abbott expected him to be on hand at rehearsals to rewrite on the fly, and when he wasn't, the courtly Rodgers—who found the writer "rather indifferent . . . to the creative aspects of the show"—cabled him, "SPEAK TO ME JOHN SPEAK TO ME."[3] An escalation of urgency was signaled by the appearance one morning at the O'Haras' apartment of Larry Hart, "all the way up from Duchess County" and announced— O'Hara reported in his memorial essay on Hart four years later—by "doorbells and the high-pitched voice of my Finnish maid." Before the master of the house had even enough presence of mind to lose his temper, "the door of my darkened bedroom was flung open and a voice was saying 'Get up, Baby. Come on, come on. You're hurting George's feelings.' "[4]

Hart, standing five feet tall before strapping on elevator shoes, was broodingly handsome, with a gloomy and dissolute face; he held strong opinions on matters musical and verbal, favoring wit over sentiment, and was well suited to O'Hara. They relished the customs and vernacular of lowlife characters, touts and con artists, petty gangsters and showgirls. Neither worked well with others. Both were rummies who played well with each other; their hangovers were legendary, nailing them to their beds, sending them to meetings with Rodgers or Abbott with faces powdered by emergency visits to the barber and eyes like pissholes in the snow. What was said of Thelonious Monk—that he didn't realize till middle age that there were two ten o'clocks in a single day—was true of O'Hara and Hart. Yet both were capable of heroically clearheaded bursts of concentrated work, Hart's lyrics unparalleled for their lucidity and assurance. At no time or place did they drink more avidly than during *Pal Joey*'s tryout in Philadelphia two weeks before Christmas of 1940. (Less than three years later, back in Philadelphia during the November opening of the revival of *A Connecticut Yankee,* Hart went on a bender—leaving his hat and coat in different bars, wandering from saloon to nightclub in the cold rain—that killed him.) Belle and John shared a suite with Budd Schulberg—supporting his friend during a nerve-racking time—at the Warwick Hotel, and at night O'Hara, Schulberg, and Hart gave the city's nightclubs and bars a workout that Joey himself might have found excessive. Frank MacShane tells of the hurly-burly of the final runup to opening night, the music and book rewrites, scenery rebuilds, rehearsals stretching from the forenoon till a couple of hours before dawn. Gene Kelly, then twenty-eight, fretted that playing such a nogoodnik as Joey would scuttle his acting career, but O'Hara consoled him with blarney: "Don't worry, kid. They'll like you." (Rodgers had settled on Kelly, whom he'd seen play a small part in William Saroyan's *The Time of Your Life* way back when he and Hart had agreed to O'Hara's proposal.) And Hart had a solution for everyone's woes: "Let me buy you a stimulant."[5]

On opening night, December 11 at Philadelphia's Forrest Theater, the O'Haras and their friends (among them Tom O'Hara and his wife, and the Pottsville Purity League's Ransloe Boone) waited for reviews in the nightclub of the Adelphi Hotel. This must have been a spectacularly crummy cabaret, because so appalling was its show that O'Hara and

Hart—thinking to have burlesqued a cheesy joint in their musical comedy—decided (as O'Hara remembered aloud to Lucius Beebe) that "instead of a violent caricature we had on our hands only a somewhat underexposed photograph."[6] Benumbed by off-key music and befouled by off-color jokes, benighted, begrimed, and bedeviled by the smoke of cheap cigars, O'Hara waited for the newspapers' verdicts with a stack of telegrams in front of him. "I bet he sent them to himself," MacShane quotes an onlooker as grousing.[7]

Richard Rodgers had anticipated that *Pal Joey* would be controversial. "Not only would the show be different from anything we had ever done before," he remembered in *Musical Stages*, "it would be different from anything anyone else had ever tried."[8] Rodgers understood from the beginning that it was a hazard having as a hero a "conniver and braggart who would do anything and sleep anywhere to get ahead." He also understood that such a character played well to Hart's knowledge and invention. Abbott, however, was anxious, and at the beginning of the collaboration seemed more preoccupied with cutting the costs to his reputation as a Broadway heavyweight than with mounting an uncompromising musical. Rodgers, seeing clear signs of the director's misgivings, suggested to him face to face and emphatically that he back out and make way for someone with greater enthusiasm, and from that confrontation forward, in Rodgers's account, the production "George staged was a beauty. Nothing was softened for the sake of making the characters more appealing. Joey was a heel at the beginning and he never reformed." At the end, rather than embracing "as the orchestra swelled with the strains of the main romantic duet," Joey and his erstwhile lover walked off the stage "in opposite directions. There wasn't one decent character in the entire play except for the girl who briefly fell for Joey—her trouble was simply that she was stupid."[9] In a 1951 piece for the *New York Times*—"'Pal Joey': History of a Heel"—Rodgers forgivingly accounted for the critical resistance to Joey as a function of his novelty:

> In the conventional sense, [Joey's] characteristics were those of a villain, and so long as there was an orchestra in the pit, the villain was supposed to wear a black mustache and be nasty all the way. Since that time, however, characters in musical plays have become more human, and the attitude of the public toward these characters has become more human, too.

> While Joey himself may have been fairly adolescent in his thinking
> and his morality, the show bearing his name certainly wore long pants,
> and in many respects forced the entire musical comedy theatre to wear
> long pants for the first time. We were all pretty proud of this fact.[10]

Long pants on long legs: *Pal Joey* had a run of three hundred seventy-four performances on Broadway at the Ethel Barrymore Theater, followed by a three-month national tour, followed by a 1952 revival* (produced by Jule Styne, with Harold Lang as Joey) inspired in part by the great popularity among crooners and jazz musicians of "Bewitched, Bothered and Bewildered." (Another New York revival, with Patti LuPone as Vera, followed in 1995.)

In Rodgers's memory, audience response was "mixed," as they say, with half the first-nighters applauding and the other long-faced, sitting still in "stony, stunned silence." In his taxi from the theater to an opening-night party at Hart's Central Park West apartment, to await reviews, O'Hara was so anxious he puked out the cab's window. The reviews following the Christmas opening were also mixed, with one of them, by the *Times*'s Brooks Atkinson, causing Hart to burst into tears after hearing it phoned in at his party, then to flee to his bedroom and refuse to come out. Perhaps he took too much to heart Atkinson's view of the "scabrous lyrics" of "Bewitched, Bothered and Bewildered" ("Romance—finis / Your chance—finis / Those ants that invaded my pants—finis— / Bewitched, bothered and bewildered no more!"), or perhaps he was wounded by his characterization of *Pal Joey*'s story as "odious," or bruised by Atkinson's final sentence: "Although *Pal Joey* is expertly done, can you draw sweet water from a foul well?"[11] Other notices were enthusiastic, some wildly. Richard Watts, in the *Herald-Tribune*, anticipating priggish objections to the work's unblinking portrayal of a scoundrel, remarked that it is "a novel fault in a musical show when a too strikingly drawn character is to be held against it,"[12] and Wolcott Gibbs, in the *New Yorker*, understood that the show was a turning point in the theater, that populating "a song-and-dance production with a few living, three-

*Marjorie Benchley, illustrating the caprice of O'Hara's peevishness, remembered having told him in 1952 during a celebratory dinner at "21" that she liked the revival of *Pal Joey* even better than the original, which the entire Benchley clan was on record as liberally adoring. "What was wrong with the original?" he demanded, brows beetling, ears reddening, slow burn about to ignite into a fine grudge.

dimensional figures, talking and behaving like human beings,"[13] would thereafter become a rational artistic enterprise.

With the success of *Pal Joey* O'Hara became a New York celebrity. He was interviewed by the *New York Times* and the *Herald-Tribune.* Both noted his new abode, a "colorful duplex next door to Cartier's and a stone's throw from his beloved '21' " (*Times*), "in the opulent shadow of Cartier's" (*Tribune*). His breakfast tastes were detailed—a noonish meal of lemon juice, tea, and cornbread—as well as (*Times* again) his literary distastes—novels of "social or ethical significance, such as *A Farewell to Arms* (which he had earlier claimed to have memorized) or *For Whom the Bell Tolls.*" (There would soon be a payback—of course—for those ill-selected examples, just as the selection itself might have been encouraged by Hemingway's suggestion, in response to a presentation copy of *Files on Parade,* urging O'Hara to combine the left jab of his perfected dialogue with the right hook of some literary purpose higher than mere accuracy.) O'Hara confessed, reasonably enough, that he wrote not for "posterity, but for the audience of his day and his nation."[14]

This would have seemed a perfect wedding of ambition and opportunity. O'Hara might have made a great second career as a playwright . . . if only he didn't express such disdain for actors. He never acknowledged or perhaps understood the extraordinary good fortune of having had Gene Kelly as Joey Evans, and in fact went out of his way to lampoon him in a short story ("Conversation at Lunch")* and other actors in dozens of unflattering vignettes. Paradoxically, in his *Newsweek* column he advised his readers not to go to *Pal Joey* after the cast was changed and Kelly left. Finis Farr writes that in the last years of his life O'Hara told Wylie of the pride he felt in "all the work he had provided for actors, electricians, stage carpenters" in theaters and on film soundstages.[15] What these artisans might have done for him was less on his mind.

It's odd, this scorn for actors. Certainly he seemed to have enjoyed chorines before Belle came along, and John Steinbeck's second wife, Elaine Scott, remembers him in those post–*Pal Joey* seasons as an avid

---

*In a 1955 "Appointment with O'Hara" column, he used the occasion of writing a few nice words in *Collier's* about Grace and Nancy Kelly to take yet another *ad hominem* swipe: "Gene Kelly got his big break in a musical show for which I wrote the libretto, but I never had any trouble restraining my enthusiasm for him."

theatergoer. Married until 1949 to the Western star Zachary Scott, she is forthcoming, a no-nonsense Texan who worked as a stage manager on Broadway musicals, beginning with Rodgers and Hammerstein's first collaboration, *Oklahoma!,* in 1943. She used to see much of O'Hara backstage, flirting with the chorus girls, and would shoo him away with what she and he took to be good-humored exasperation.

In 1995 she recalled those occasions vividly, certain that he felt sympathy for the theater, her own passion, and evoked him as a friend for whom she felt uncomplicated affection. She was insistent that I register how friendly she felt toward him, and was bewildered as well as angered by women who diminished him as coarse or physically offensive. She had found O'Hara appealing; she used the word "sexy," adding that she liked to flirt with him. He had, she wanted me to know, "weight" and gravity, a presence.

In a 1942 *Newsweek* column, O'Hara chose to memorialize what was to be one of the more inglorious anecdotes attached like a limpet to his history. As he reported the story, the war correspondents Vincent Sheean and James Lardner, together with Ernest Hemingway, were off together at the Spanish Civil War when they found themselves with some unexpected dividend of spare cash from a royalty or expense-account payment and wondered aloud how best to spend it, and Hemingway had said of this lagniappe, "Let's take the bloody money and start a bloody fund to send John O'Hara to Yale," about which remark O'Hara remarked, "It's a mean little story, but it shows what my friends think of me." In his biography of O'Hara, Matthew J. Bruccoli quotes a letter to him from Sheean that ameliorates the disdain a bit by subtracting "bloody," and goes on to explain that he excised Hemingway's snub from his own book to avoid one of O'Hara's "savage rages." And still later Don Schanche, the *Esquire* interviewer of O'Hara, told Bruccoli that O'Hara said of the sally that "it was the first time I knew Hemingway had any real envy of me."[16] It remains a puzzle why O'Hara retailed the story to his *Newsweek* readers, unless being known to know Hemingway was more pleasurable than the great man's opinion of him was painful.

Second in infamy only to this self-serving and spurious jape is the oft-told tale of Hemingway and O'Hara's blackthorn walking stick, and to this disgrace Elaine Scott was a witness. This happened in 1942, soon after O'Hara had published Hemingway's ridicule of him in *Newsweek*.

The setting was Costello's, a writers' favorite on Third Avenue where Elaine Scott was sitting in a back room with John Hersey and his wife, along with Sheean, Martha Gellhorn, and her husband, Ernest himself. O'Hara entered the bar, and in this version (told to Bruccoli by Hersey) he was drunk. Glimpsing the fun-sharing group in the back, and brooding that he wasn't among them, he hooked his walking stick on the bar and commenced to mutter darkly. Hemingway, walking past, paused and—Bruccoli writes—"pounded him hard on the back, with which he had been having trouble, and said, 'When did you start carrying a walking stick?' " O'Hara said, "That's the best piece of blackthorn in New York." Hemingway: "It is, is it? I'm going to break it with my bare hands." Oh, boy. So O'Hara says, "Fifty says you can't," so Hemingway sez he's going to break it over his own head. I remember my father's blackthorn stick—a brutal, prickly cob of a thing, resistance objectified. But Papa broke it over his head, and Tim Costello mounted the pieces over his bar, and Carlos Baker celebrated the episode in *Ernest Hemingway: A Life Story,* and O'Hara amended the legend with versions even less flattering than the truth—pointing out, for example, that Hemingway reneged on his pledge to replace the treacherous damned thing, and failing to point out whether the loser paid his bet.* And Elaine Steinbeck can provide an end to the story, because she was with her husband John when he bought their friend John an even more rigorous blackthorn walking stick in Ireland, on the occasion of O'Hara's fifty-first birthday.

What exacerbated the ache of these experiences of Hemingway's disdain—and who would claim they shouldn't hurt?—was the timing of them, in the heat of a world war following other wars in which the author of O'Hara's humiliation had distinguished himself as a wounded ambulance driver, a fearless correspondent, and a militant partisan. Consider-

---

*As late as 1959, responding to an account of the incident in a *Holiday* feature on Costello's, O'Hara offered "the true story about my shillelagh." In this variation the shaming took place on St. Patrick's Day, which would provide subtle grounding for the display in a saloon of a "shillelagh." But the plot, as plots will, thickens: "They stopped to say hello to me and Hemingway commented that my walking stick was not a real blackthorn. He bet me fifty dollars he could break it over his head. I didn't want him to try it, because I understand Ernest has a silver plate in his skull, but he went ahead and broke it." And here breaks in, by footnote, Matthew J. Bruccoli (in whose *Selected Letters of John O'Hara* the correspondence is published), with unequivocal assurance: "Hemingway had no such silver plate" (p. 316).

ing O'Hara's reverence for the totems of distinction—plaques, trophies, certificates, club rosettes, fraternity keys—imagine the most revered of all outward signs of selection: the photograph on the piano or sideboard of J. O'Hara, Flt. Cmdr., RAF Eagle Squadron, posed beside his Spitfire; or Lt. Cmdr. John O'Hara, USN, posed on the bridge of his destroyer making the Murmansk run, with a full North Sea gale unable to dislodge his salad-loaded cap; or beribboned Maj. O'Hara, John, 109th Airborne Rangers, pictured behind the front lines in Normandy. But, in wartime fact, he was destined to remain that most pitiable of blackballees, a youngish guy in the pink and in mufti. A civilian.

There was, to be exact, a uniform in O'Hara's closet, tailored by Brooks Brothers, but that's an object for later examination. When Germany invaded Poland, O'Hara was thirty-four; when the Japanese bombed Pearl Harbor, thirty-six. He was outwardly robust, active at tennis and golf. He knew how this looked—oh, did he ever! In the fall of 1939 he wrote with patriotic excitement to William Maxwell about listening to Neville Chamberlain's announcement from 10 Downing Street of a state of war between Britain and Germany. His first reaction was to write for the *New Yorker* a memoir of war fever in Pottsville twenty-five years earlier. The essay was rejected, and is not among his collected papers, but it is possible to guess some of what he might've reported: that Pottsville had sent more soldiers to France with the American Expeditionary Force, per capita, than any city in America, but also that its coal economy prospered from the wartime demand for energy. He loved the lavish parades that gave Pennsylvania's doughboys their send-off, but when they limped back the doctor's son would see up close what became of some of them over there. In 1919, he won a Schuylkill County essay contest on the subject of a Victory Loan drive, and his prize was a spike-topped German helmet. His classmates remembered him making drawings of soldiers in battle. O'Hara was, even then, on his toes with respect to manly honor.

Charles W. Bassett might generalize excessively when he writes that "in his fiction, O'Hara's heroes never quite make it to the war, to the furnace where manhood is really forged."[17] But not by much: John Berryman judged, shortly before he killed himself, that an American man during peacetime could grow old without ever having or "getting" to learn whether or not he was brave. This is the kind of poppycock that gives men a bad name. Every human being gets chances aplenty to learn what courage is, and death. But just because it's poppycock doesn't mean that Berryman didn't believe it, and so in his singular way did John O'Hara. Beginning in 1939 he dreamed explicitly not about "the furnace where manhood is really forged" but about "what will go with my uniform," as he put it facetiously to Joseph Bryan III. He wanted a suitable commission, preferably in the navy, the gentleman's service, and to this end he campaigned his friends Robert Lovett, assistant secretary of war for air, and James Forrestal.

Forrestal, a self-made American-Irish multimillionaire, had had lustrous success at Princeton, where he was a scrappy boxer and editor of the *Daily Princetonian,* only to withdraw, mysteriously, shortly before graduation. Born poor in upstate New York, on Wall Street he had accumulated a fortune, and tempered the ferocity of its harvest by cutting a figure in nightclubs, social clubs, and expensive restaurants. O'Hara had seen much of Forrestal at dinner parties in Manhattan and at "21." In 1940, Forrestal went to Washington to help Roosevelt walk a pro-Britain line along the boundaries of American neutrality; he soon became under secretary of the navy, and in 1944 secretary of the navy, and in 1947 the first secretary of defense. Before the war, it was neither unusual nor discreditable for well-placed Americans to use connections to get into a fight with Hitler. To lobby Forrestal for a commission was not to buy one's way out of the Civil War draft, nor to get oneself transferred in November of 1941 from the Aleutians to a cushy post in, say, Honolulu. That O'Hara's self-importance caused him to aim too high for a place in the service was not surprising, nor were his impulsive expressions of self-interest and sometimes comical generosity. Mere weeks after Pearl Harbor, he was troubling Forrestal with his personal preoccupations, complaining how useless he felt, suffering "a strong sense of guilt and futility, and on the fiscal side, impulsive, unplanned, and sometimes extravagant donations to various Causes."[18] In the same letter—mailed during American and British naval catastrophes at Rabaul and Singapore—he reminded Forrestal of the offer of his Duesenberg Speedster as a VIP car: "It is still in storage, still for sale to the Navy for one buck. What do you think I ought to do about it?" (There is no evidence that Forrestal put American counterattacks against Japanese bases on the back burner to deal with this urgent inquiry.)

It's easy enough to scorn O'Hara for his failure of common sense, his almost pathological monomania, his amateur climber's eye for a mountain's peaks to the exclusion of its approaches.* If he were so ardent to serve, why not enlist? He tried. His gastric ulcers weighed against him, as did high blood pressure and his terrible teeth. For a person so particular about appearances, the state of his choppers was bewildering, so ill-cared-for that a tooth plopped into his food at a dinner party. (He began losing them in his twenties, and his *Esquire* profiler Don A. Schanche quotes a friend who'd asked why he refused to go to a dentist even when suffering from toothaches: "Why spend money on my teeth when I'm going to die soon?")[19] He needed a special health waiver to join any military service, and wasn't shy about asking for it. When nothing came of his importunings, he managed to wangle an appointment without pay to the Office of the Coordinator of Inter-American Affairs, Motion Picture Division. He was Chief Story Editor, according to his own self-mocking account, on the staff of Nelson Rockefeller. His campaign was to commission propaganda for distribution in Latin America, to persuade our neighbors that Hitler was unfriendly to Catholicism. How this bush-league mission must have tormented O'Hara! And when John Hay Whitney—his friend and colleague at the propaganda office—quit to take a commission in Air Corps intelligence, he deserted his post on sick leave. He was bedridden with flu for a couple of weeks, and then got a sty in his eye, and then suffered a case of piles acute enough to require emergency surgery. While recuperating in Quogue (on war footing, owing to the arrest of saboteurs at nearby Amagansett: no one allowed on the beach at night, lights to be blacked out on cars and oceanside houses), he decided to take flying lessons to qualify for the Civil Pilot Training Course, and to have his teeth pulled and replaced by China clippers in a bid to qualify for some active service, or at least the Merchant Marine, even the Red Cross.

It was 1942, and in his July 13 letter from Quogue to the actor Gilbert Roland—a fellow hemorrhoid-survivor—he reviewed the agony of their shared affliction and its surgical cure, then confessed that "I feel like a jerk being out of uniform when I go to '21' and places like that, and at the

---

*A quarter-century after the war ended, O'Hara confided—with a straight face, to the very interviewer he had encouraged to write a profile that might be a resource for obituary writers—that he had "once thought of killing Hitler—thought about it quite seriously, in fact, in about 1935. I thought, 'Here I am; I'm a damned good shot; I'm a blue-eyed American type, and I could go over there and shoot him.' I gave that idea up. I wouldn't have written B*Utterfield 8* . . . if I hadn't" (Don A. Schanche, "John O'Hara Is Alive and Well in the First Half of the Twentieth Century [He Owns It]," *Esquire* (August 1969): 84–86, 142, 144–49.

250
THE ART OF BURNING BRIDGES

Field Club here the kids I used to play tennis and golf with are all gone—
or come home on leave." Friends such as Al Wright and John McClain
were winning medals. In an unmailed letter to an unidentified younger
friend nicknamed "Folkstone," he made no effort to disguise his pain and
shame, but felt he needed to say that it was his ulcer that barred him from
flying a Liberator or driving a tank—"If I didn't have milk I would die,"
he claimed, and perhaps believed—and the manifestation of his discomfort was precisely that: a manifestation. It always came for this master of
surfaces to the surface: feeling like "a jerk when I go to '21' and have a
toddy with Major Sy Bartlett, Major Rex Smith, Captain Bob Wylie [his
brother-in-law, like his other brothers-in-law in uniform] . . . all duked
out in their zoot suits."[20] The representation of election—uniforms and
decorations—might have been merely shorthand for an interior condition of grace in O'Hara's scheme, but I'm not so sure the show itself
didn't figure as the benediction. At a time when the dullest student of
manners and biography knew how to read the subtlest distinctions in military ribbons and ranks,* he wrote to William Maxwell asking him to have
New Yorker staffers research how to buy from "some consulate or lega-
tion" a foreign "medal, rosette, etc., and the right to wear it." That
O'Hara's declared motive was to mock the wearing of decorations only
thinly masks his preoccupation, and failed to console its thwarting.

In his "Folkstone" letter, O'Hara expressed his resentment of Lovett
and Forrestal, whom he had been "working on" for two years and more,
"so the only conclusion I can come to is that they just plain didn't want
me." Indignation didn't prevent him from writing Forrestal yet again,
two weeks after composing the above letter, asking now that he put him
up for the Racquet & Tennis Club in New York. He didn't get in.

With Forrestal's recommendation he did wangle a tryout at the Office
of Strategic Services, stiff name for the dashing OSS, a more exclusive
and suave association even than Park Avenue's Racquet & Tennis Club.
Under the charismatic leadership of General William ("Wild Bill")
Donovan, the espionage and subversive warfare agency that evolved into
the CIA began as a venture of Ivied Wall Street lawyers, Ivied history and
geography and French professors, Ivied crew strokes, Ivied remittance

---

*In "Summer's Day," an O'Hara story from this time, a character is introduced as "a tall young man
in a white uniform with the shoulder-board stripe-and-a-half of a lieutenant junior grade" (John
O'Hara, "Summer's Day," in *Pipe Night* [New York: Random House, 1945], pp. 56–62).

men and polo stars. Yale, *toujours,* with its brotherhoods of mumbo-jumbo, high-road-traveling secret societies, was the favorite breeding ground of World War II spies. Robin Winks calculates, in his *Cloak & Gown: Scholars in the Secret War, 1938–1961,* that Yale had sent more graduates than any other university to the OSS and the CIA. Master of Yale's Berkeley College at the time of *Cloak & Gown's* 1987 publication, Winks boasts that forty-two members of the class of 1943 were recruited by the OSS with the help of professors and crew coaches. Why Yale, especially? The secret service wanted young men with "a sense of grace . . . an ease with themselves . . . a certain healthy self-respect" and "independent means."* Scoffers nicknamed the OSS *Oh-So-Social,* noting the clubmen and Russian princes, bored Wall Street lawyers and yachtsmen who made up the small cadre institutionalized in 1942 under the wing of the Joint Chiefs of Staff. Not neglected either were young women, well-schooled debs like Gertrude Sanford Legendre, sister of the polo whiz "Laddie" Sanford. A big-game hunter, Gertrude Legendre died in March of 2000 at ninety-three, and her obituary's first sentence referred to her work in the OSS, which assigned her in 1944 to France, where she was captured by a German sniper, held prisoner in Germany for six months, and escaped into Switzerland pursued by armed border guards. This kind of derring-do—daredevil escapades by spook-crews with such team titles as Downes' Ducks, covert ops code-named Operation Banana or Operation Penny Farthing or Falling Sparrow—drew to the OSS the cream of the crop of men and women John O'Hara most prized. Blue bloods like Joseph Alsop, Allen Dulles, Richard Bissell, Paul Mellon, David Bruce, and Tracy Barnes—some callow, many smart and reckless and idealistic—recruited not only jejune playboys but also representatives of what would become Georgetown's dominant social class, the meritocracy, an establishment of intellectuals and artists with good manners.

Wild Bill Donovan—like Forrestal—was an overachieving Irish boy from upstate New York, the son of an immigrant railroad yardmaster. A football paladin at Columbia (where he came to know Franklin Delano Roosevelt at the law school), Donovan won a Medal of Honor during World War I at Ourq in 1918, battling with New York's 69th Regiment,

*Quoted by Jon Weiner, in his *Nation* review, September 5, 1987. Weiner ended his skeptical review of Winks's apologia with a mordant exhortation: "Historians of Harvard and Princeton now have an obligation to those institutions to show that Yale did not stand alone when the C.I.A. called" (Jon Weiner, "Book Review of Cloak & Gown," *Nation,* 5 September 1987, 204).

the Fighting Irish; a movie, *The Fighting 69th,* was made of his feats in combat. He was a shrewd lawyer, but with a romantic streak, influenced in his commando schemes by the exploits of Mosby's Raiders in the Civil War. A "silky charmer" in the eyes of an admirer, he married an heiress, and, like Forrestal, he admired literary writers, especially those who were celebrities.* One might expect, then, that in the two proud Irishmen—Donovan and O'Hara—ambition and resource would join fruitfully. In November of 1943 O'Hara arrived at the secret OSS training camp in Virginia, where he studied encryption and the art of disguise, grew a beard, and took his Purity League handle, "Doc," as a code name. Physical training was required, and O'Hara wasn't equal to it. In mid-December he washed out, or quit. Except for "Late, Late Show" (1966), a static story about a static marriage in which the husband raises with his wife the subject of his wartime service in the OSS and then churlishly refuses to answer her questions about what he did, this was one of his few life experiences he didn't write about, perhaps to honor confidentiality agreements, perhaps from compunction. That he had concluded he was not physically capable of taking responsibility for the lives of colleagues and subordinates—of holding up his end—was as much as he ever cared to reveal of the brief episode.† He did write from Quogue to Joseph Bryan III (at war in the Pacific), with whom he was notably unguarded, that he expected to finish World War II on his duff, among fellow civil-

---

*Perhaps inevitably, Ernest Hemingway was sucked in or sucked his way into the OSS. The journalist D. T. Max, writing in the *New York Times Magazine* (July 18, 1999), gives a tragicomic account of Hemingway's Hardy Boys spy-work in Cuba. Assigned to identify Spanish fascists who might be spying on U.S. ship movements, Hemingway was Agent 08 in what the OSS named the Crime Shop, which Hemingway renamed the Crook Shop. His cohort was made up of barflies, Basque jai-alai players, Long Island dandies, and layabouts. Headquarters was Hemingway's Finca Vigia, and intelligence conferences were raucous occasions to drink wine and throw food and chairs at one another. When the FBI's J. Edgar Hoover looked into the Crook Shop's antics, the OSS shut it down, turning Hemingway toward an anti-U-boat offensive conducted on his comfortable fishing boat, the *Pilar.* This was Hemingway at his most fatuous, playing solemnly at war games, taking aboard cronies such as seasick Winston Guest—yet another millionaire polo player—and training for the planned U-boat sinkings by lobbing grenades at "wooden targets with faces painted on them"; these dummies, bobbing unharmed in the greasy groundswell, Hemingway gave the name "Hitlers." His current wife, Martha Gellhorn, "berated his 'shaming and silly life,' which she saw as an excuse to go fishing with Government gasoline and avoid his typewriter."

†In 1949, shortly after Forrestal's suicide, O'Hara applied to join the CIA. Joseph Bryan III arranged a dinner party at which he could display his friend's grace and wit to the intelligence service's higher officers. Instead, O'Hara got drunk, and that was that.

ians whom he execrated for their reflexive grousing about shortages of gasoline and meat and Scotch: "I am so fucking sick of myself that it's a good thing I don't use a straight razor. Or live in a tall building."[21]

All that remained for O'Hara now was an assignment as a war correspondent, and all the better publications had long since been spoken for while he maneuvered among his connections for a suitable commission. He was reduced to wheedling an assignment from *Liberty,* a third-rate *Collier's, Saturday Evening Post,* and *Life* wannabe. He was sent to the Pacific Fleet, Task Force 38, but the real payoff before he left was a uniform, at last, with the sham rank of lieutenant commander.* He ordered it, of course, from Brooks Brothers, and—even without the insignia that identified an armed combatant in an armed service—it fit beautifully.

At the height of the Quogue Field Club's summer season O'Hara was flown to Honolulu, and after a few days and nights of getting to know Waikiki's better hotels and clubs he boarded the aircraft carrier *Intrepid,* later in the war to be at the center of the action at Leyte Gulf and storied island invasions. His time aboard began badly, when he visited Captain William Crozier's quarters and found that the skipper's bookshelf held none of his books. Frank MacShane reports O'Hara remarking "darkly, 'I should never have come on this ship.' "[22] He missed the Battle of Leyte Gulf by a month and, other than watching a Japanese bomber being shot down far in the distance, saw no action at all from the *Intrepid;* yet he admitted to his friend Frank Sullivan (and no shame on him) that "I was scared most of the time."[23] He found it difficult to climb and descend deck to deck, referred to his experience as "psychological warfare." Within a couple of days of the distant bomber's would-be attack, O'Hara—after "inventing an excuse to go home," in MacShane's account—was transferred by boatswain's chair to an empty tanker, the *Kaskasia,* disembarking in San Francisco two months after embarking for Honolulu. All that came of his tour, as he wrote Sullivan, was a squabble with *Liberty,* who got put on his "prick list" and for whom he produced a single piece of fluff, "Nothing From Joe?" about letters to and from the fighting men. The short essay's burden is that "every letter you don't write to the man you ought to be writing to is a slap in his face,

---

*Honorific ranks were given to war correspondents so that they would be safe from indictment as spies if they were taken by enemy forces.

or worse. . . . Loneliness is everywhere, and color-blind." To license his
sermon, O'Hara explains that his words are being written "aboard a
Naval vessel in the Pacific" and that it is also based "on observations I
have made of Army personnel." It is as stiff a run of words as he ever
published, and for the very reason of its discomfort—its anxious want of
authority, the absence of signature in its voice—it is worthy of notice.

"Nothing From Joe?" is documentary evidence of a grave failure of
confidence, a creative breakdown, perhaps even a nervous collapse, that
O'Hara's letters about his wartime mortification had been declaring for
years. By a sequence of transitions as forced as a jigsaw puzzle assembled
by the helter-skelter jamming of its pieces in incoherent order, the essay
moves from its banal putative subject to a bewildering and unprotected
meditation on doubt. Joe doesn't write home because he cannot endure
"the horror of subjecting himself to the ordeal of concentration on his
loneliness. . . . It gets so out here, anywhere, that a man counts on only
one person, his mother." Where did *this* come from? None of O'Hara's
remarks, before or after, about his mother—generally a wholesome
range from irritation to lively pride—prepares for or flows from this
addled declaration.* Not that he pauses long on Mom: the subject turns
at once to suspicion, mistrust, betrayal, and—central to O'Hara's darkest
fears—rejection.

> The most loved, the most trusted woman a man has ever known can
> become suspect under the conditions that prevail out here—and by out
> here I mean any place where a man is being kept from his woman. With
> some men, with most men, it is a simple suspicion: that awful thought of
> his woman in another man's arms, that look given to another man. . . .
> But with all men the awful thing is the fear of not being loved, of being
> dismissed, brushed off, forgotten. No man can stand that. There are
> men who have had all the time in the world for the self-torture of imag-
> ining their women making love to someone else. Some of these men
> have so expertly set the scene that they have expressed their apprecia-
> tion of their own artistry by the supreme accolade, suicide.[24]

---

*In our 1995 interview, Brendan Gill expanded on remarks he'd made earlier in the *New Yorker*,
where he theorized that Irish Catholic boys, like O'Hara, "brought up by nuns and priests, wished
that every woman, even every mother, could remain a virgin; the fact that women made love, and
especially that one's own mother made love, or had once made love, was intolerable" (September
15, 1975). Now, twenty years later, Gill returned with relish to the subject, announcing it by a
throwaway line, stunning in its offhandedness, All men, don't you know, hate all women.

While at sea, in place of letters home he kept a diary. Matthew J. Bruccoli quotes from an entry written on August 16, 1944, the tenth anniversary of *Appointment in Samarra*'s publication: "I am sometimes beset by the fear that when I finish this masochistic task [the writing of the diary?] my life will be over. That, however, is almost certainly up to Belle."[25] It would be impossible to exaggerate how loving was his reliance on her serenity, warmth, and acceptance. O'Hara's irrational jealousy—no sooner felt than expressed—might have been comic were not his vulnerability so exorbitant.

A happy outcome of this unhappy war experience was the therapeutic result of life aboard ship, with flavorless food and no alcohol. He lost twenty pounds during the two months he was apart from the wife he so dearly missed, and his physical vigor improved, and so too—by his own account—his ardor. For so private a man O'Hara was selectively and indecorously confessional, perhaps an unstartling quality in a writer determined to unsettle. He had confided to Adele Lovett that "Belle is upside down inside" and that "I'm sterile and I know it."[26] And writing to Frank Sullivan about his tour in the Pacific, he revealed that he had lost interest in having "progeny," and that Belle's brother had advised against a pregnancy because "her ticker is peculiar," but that she'd always wanted a baby and he was pleased and proud to give her what she wanted.[27] The child, he explained, would be named Wylie, "boy or girl," in honor of Belle's family. A girl it was, born June 14, named Wylie Delaney O'Hara, and she changed his life for the better, and her father knew it from the start.

Much change was needed, though it took O'Hara many years to articulate how desperate his situation was in 1945. More than two decades later he told an audience at London's Foyles Bookstore that during the war another kind of "creative sterility" beset him.* "Between the invasion of Poland and the Japanese surrender . . . I could not write anything longer than a short story."[28] Not quite *couldn't* write, in fact. His story production declined from one hundred and eighteen in the 1930s to seventy-five in the '40s (and only twenty in the middle of the war years, with novels down in the same period from three to one), though the critic

*O'Hara was even more giving and emphatic to an unidentified London newspaper interviewer the day of the Foyles talk: "I was dissipating all my energies in drink and high living. I was drinking a quart of whisky a day and that takes time—not just to drink, but to have your hangover and to get better from your hangover. It was a period when I couldn't write."

Steven Goldleaf, who did the math, rightly calculates that "this was an unproductive period *for John O'Hara*. For most writers, this period would have been considered productive and, for many, even a high-water mark of productivity."[29]

Being out of the action probably influenced O'Hara's shrift-like disclosure to Gilbert Roland in 1942: "It seems impossible for me to think in terms of another novel at this point. The best I can do is store up impressions for a novel to come later. It's a hell of a time to be a writer or at any rate a writer who is 37 years old and very likely 4-F."[30] Juxtaposed with a comment he made during a 1959 lecture at Rider College—"I love to write. When I am not writing I am really wasting my time, and when I no longer can write, I will soon die"—the self-hushed O'Hara must have found himself in a quagmire.[31]

In fact, 1945 was a year of conquest for his virtuosity and career. *Pipe Night,* his third story collection, published by Duell, Sloan and Pearce, induced the most influential critical response he ever received, a cover review in the *New York Times Book Review* by Lionel Trilling. Of the book's thirty-one stories, twenty had appeared in the *New Yorker,* but in a grudgingly admiring preface Wolcott Gibbs, that canny arbiter of the magazine's antipathies and enthusiasms, rightly noted the capacious reach of *Pipe Night*'s settings and characters: "His range of subject and treatment is too great for an editorial mind accustomed to writers, generally speaking, as rigidly typed as the seals in the circus."[32] Gibbs invokes cruel stories in which "every lady is a tramp and every man an enemy" (the reflexively Hobbesian slant that vexed Louis Auchincloss, among others), and sad stories in which "it is possible to be bored to death or break your heart in the most exclusive surroundings." Gibbs alludes also to *Pipe Night*'s Hollywood stories, one of which—"Fire!"—is as funny as anything O'Hara ever wrote.* Another, "Bread Alone" (about which more later), shows a black car-washer and his son at Yankee Stadium.

---

*A Hollywood star, Alta, has encouraged an ex–newspaper reporter and current studio-contract hack to write a play as a vehicle for her Broadway exaltation. He quits drinking and does so, then delivers it to her house, puffing up the modest elevation of her driveway while her dogs bark at him. She sends him away while she reads the play, and when he returns, "[Alta] let him close the door. He followed her to the library. She walked to the fireplace and stood with her back to him for a count of fifteen before she turned around. Then she threw back her head the way she did to denote gallantry on the screen.

" 'Paul,' she said. 'I am not—going—to do—your play. It'snotforme, Paul. I am not—going—todoit.' "

"Graven Image" is the dominant story in *Pipe Night*, one of half a dozen that fans of O'Hara's work are likely to praise. Only seven pages, an enactment of ambition and exclusion, of pecking order and resentment, it describes Charles Browning's trajectory from deference to candor to hubris to humiliation, and as if that weren't enough for "Graven Image" to achieve, it also describes a New Deal under secretary's transitions from humiliation to hauteur to noblesse oblige to inclemency. And all this during a lunch meeting at a Washington hotel dining room. The story's situation is uncomplicated, almost binary, but bristling with social and circumstantial perils: Charles Browning and the under secretary, Joe (no surname), were at Harvard together. Browning was in Porcellian, from which Joe was blackballed. The illustrious Harvard club is first alluded to by the under secretary's curiosity about the whereabouts of "a small golden pig" (Porcellian's emblem) that Browning keeps with infuriating insouciance attached to a bunch of his keys in his trouser rather than vest pocket. Browning has come to Washington as a supplicant: he all but begs for a job in the service of their country from the "little man" whom he accompanies to the dining-room table "making one step to two of the Under Secretary's, [bringing] up the rear." It is suggested, but unspecified, that Browning has influence on Wall Street, and that this is FDR's government ("The Boss" is invoked), and that Browning is angling for a post for reasons of patriotism rather than self-interest, "My country, 'tis of thee," as the under secretary sardonically puts it.

Priority of every degree is explored, beginning with the complex calculus as to where the under secretary's chauffeur should park. When the car pulls up, the hotel doorman commands the chauffeur to wait and asks the passenger, with offhand resonance, "Will the Under Secretary be here long?" The official then "said," rather than asked, "Why?" and in the response, its loaded nonchalance, are exquisitely calibrated grades of obsequiousness and presumption: "Because if you were going to be

---

Paul reflects on the eight months he has invested in this bespoke product. " 'Passed up some awfully good picture jobs. A guy'd kinda like to know what's wrong with it.'

"She clasped her hands behind her back and gave him her three-quarter face. 'I read it avidly, punct—conscientiously, fascinatedly. The doctor is fine, strong. The rabbi—you will kill intolerance wherever your play is shown. . . . The mother? I cried. I couldn't help it. The little midget? Beautiful, beautiful. He was beautifully done, Paul, and never too much of him.' "

In other words—as they say today in Hollywood—it's a piece of shit. Or, as Alta explains, " 'The fire isn't there! The fire!' " (John O'Hara, "Fire!" in *Pipe Night* [New York: Duell, Sloan and Pearce, 1945], pp. 154–61).

here, sir, only a short while, I'd let your man leave the car here, at the head of the rank."[33] Prevalence and transience, class and provisional authority, are in play here, as O'Hara inhabits both the envious and spiteful under secretary and the assured and graceful Charles Browning. Consider these details: the under secretary has caused the lunch reservation to be made, but the maître d'hôtel and Browning are "chatting" easily in French; the maître d'hôtel knows the out-of-town office-seeker better, and is more comfortable with him, than the high officeholder. But when the under secretary places his lunch order, Browning bends the knee: "I'll take whatever you're having." He has sufficient dignity and cunning not to kowtow when the under secretary baits him about "your Racquet Club pal" across the dining room: "You keep track of things like that?" Browning asks. With this question—at once impertinent and inquisitive, answered by "Certainly . . . I know every goddam club in this country, beginning back about twenty-three years ago. I had ample time to study them all then, you recall, objectively, from the outside"—Browning begins an ascendancy that climaxes with the under secretary's subtle promise of the very job Browning has sought and for which he is qualified. Browning is ecstatic, having negotiated the shoals; and he summons the waiter to impulsively order drinks—and here O'Hara's diction bristles with subtext: "The Under Secretary yielded and ordered a cordial." Expansive, Browning tells his new patron, "Joe, you're the best." He confides, looking at his half-finished Scotch, "You know, I was a little afraid. That other stuff, the club stuff." The under secretary says, "Yes." "Browning says, 'I don't know why fellows like you—you never would have made it in a thousand years, but'*—then, without looking up, he knew everything had collapsed—'but I've said

---

*Nelson W. Aldrich's mercilessly clear-eyed *Old Money: The Mythology of Wealth in America* elucidates the "snob's agony" in the "unprotected social space" of friendships—built on the charm or power or celebrity of the climber—with old money. The aristocrats "inadvertently, for the most part" (a delicate caveat there) made the climber "realize the tantalizing difference between friendship and belongingness. Scott Fitzgerald and Tommy Hitchcock might be friends, but there was no way, even if he had gone to Harvard, that Scott Fitzgerald could belong to the Porcellian Club. To belong to the Porcellian Club it was not enough—it still isn't—that one be friends with a member. One has to have been friends with him always, and in that elusive past perfect tense of the verb *to be* the socially ambitious read their sad fate" (Nelson W. Aldrich Jr., *Old Money: The Mythology of Wealth in America* [New York: Allworth Press, 1996], p. 52).

   (Of course Fitzgerald created from Tommy Hitchcock's bona fides the monstrous character of Tom Buchanan.)

exactly the wrong thing, haven't I?' " The under secretary says, "That's right."*

To read this story is akin to watching a match between a skilled boxer and a coarse bruiser, in which the boxer—certain he has won on points—drops his guard. But the story matters to readers because its stakes are higher than the question of who wins. The title reaches far, to a meditation on the price of violating the spirit of the Second Commandment. Which of these two characters, after all, has been blinded by reverence for the iconic pig? Perhaps both, and for O'Hara to probe so delicately this inquiry into the costs of idol-worship—matters of judgment and empathy touching on the democratic proportion of "my country 'tis of thee"—is to remind his readers of the depth of his wisdom about class, a wisdom too often trumped by his narcissism. (Of course it is also true that in many good writers' best work they understand and elucidate weaknesses that in their lives they are powerless to control.)

Lionel Trilling was explicit in his celebration of the book's and its author's peculiar comprehension of class and discrimination. In his first sentence Trilling places O'Hara alone among practicing writers to whom the American republic "presents itself as a social scene," in the way "the social scene" once stirred the intelligence of William Dean Howells and Edith Wharton, "or in the way that England presented itself to Henry James, or France to Proust."[34] He then exactly describes the true purpose of this fiction of manners:

> More than anyone now writing, O'Hara understands the complex, contradictory, asymmetrical society in which we live. He has the most precise knowledge of the content of our subtlest snobberies, of our points of social honor and idiosyncrasies of personal prestige. He knows, and persuades us to believe, that life's deepest intentions may be expressed

*George Plimpton hoped that O'Hara would agree to sit for a *Paris Review* interview in his magazine's commendable series "Writers At Work." To this end he wrote O'Hara during the 1950s and 1960s, inviting him. He got no response. Plimpton then had a Good Idea. Knowing of O'Hara's interest in exclusive clubs, he telephoned him in Princeton to repeat the invitation, and mentioned by way of persuasive detail that he, like Browning, had been a member of Porcellian. No response. It was an expertise they shared, Plimpton continued, this intimate knowledge of The Pork. Heavy breathing, then aggressive silence. "John? . . . Mr. O'Hara? . . ." The sound of a Princeton telephone being returned to its cradle. Later, asking a close friend of O'Hara's what might have gone wrong, the friend said, "Oh, Jesus, John! As sensitive as an unshucked oyster. He was sore that you interviewed Hemingway first" (George Plimpton, telephone conversation with author, June 6, 2000).

by the angle at which a hat is worn, the pattern of a necktie, the size of
a monogram, the pitch of a voice, the turn of a phrase of slang, a gesture
of courtesy and the way it is received. "Cigarettes, there in the white
pigskin box," says one of his cinema queens, and by that excess of specification we know the room and the mind and the culture in which the
box has its existence.

That particular "excess of specification" to which Trilling alludes appears
in "Fire!" and it is there, of course, to evoke vanity and spurious authority. It is there, that is, for a good fictional reason, akin to the mannered
and mannerly contests in "Graven Image." To appreciate O'Hara's
achievement—more important, to enjoy it—a reader should apprehend
the decorums and sensitivities being violated by one character and then
another. Louis XIV's guests at the theater at Versailles in 1677 were outraged at the performance of Racine's *Phèdre*, scandalized by a queen's
use of the second-person familiar in conversation with her stepson; such
emotional response to a pronoun required a strict education in syntax as
well as an appreciation of the nuances of seduction. It could once have
been argued that in a democratic republic—a would-be or reluctant
democracy, depending on one's perhaps temporary vantage—adjust-
ments of accent and dress, whether a man wore a hat on the street and
what kind of hat he wore and at which angle were crucial guides to one
person's judgment of another's standing, ambition, or insecurity. A peasant might have gone bareheaded because he couldn't afford a hat. A
boor might have gone bareheaded because he didn't know better. A gentleman—or middle-class aspirant—would wear a hat, of varying degrees
of fineness, which fineness might be determined by considerations of
style or of workmanship. And a member of what passed for nobility in a
young country without a nominal aristocracy might go hatless, to express
a social security beyond the reach of conventional condemnation. Of
course, at some time between the presidencies of Truman and Kennedy,
Americans began to profess and then even to experience a distaste for
such matters of discrimination. Whatever happy consequence this has
had for our society of brother and sister citizens, it has had a depleting
effect on the possibilities of fiction. Roughly ten years after the publication of *Pipe Night*, Flannery O'Connor—with her conspicuous indifference to regulated decorum—wrote that "manners are of such great
consequence to the novelist that any kind will do. Bad manners are better than no manners at all."[35]

It's no wonder that O'Connor referred specifically to "the novelist." The kind of authority O'Hara achieved in "Graven Image" was conventionally—this when the concept of "convention" still had vestigial muscle—expected to be the dominion of the novelist. Trilling made this plain in his review of *Pipe Night:* "The novel was invented, one might say, to deal with just the matter that O'Hara loves. Snobbery, vulgarity, the shades of social status and pretension, the addiction to objects of luxury, the innumerable social uncertainties, the comic juxtaposition of social assumptions—the novel thrives on them, and best knows how to deal with them."*

Decisively contemptuous of the "tiresome" short stories he saw as representative of these years—serial corruptions of the genre of "the great Chekhov" by Katherine Mansfield and like villains guilty of emotional abbreviation and chilly distance—Trilling was probably right that novels might register better than stories seismic social changes and provide, given their duration, a more literal experience of the exertions of social climbing; but he was ruinously wrong about what his advice would mean for O'Hara's future work. Though he excluded most of *Pipe Night*'s stories from the tied-neat-with-a-bow genre "we have all admired" while "secretly we have been bored with it," though he admired O'Hara's general immunity in this collection to narrative clichés by dint of his "passionate social curiosity and his remarkable social intelligence," something wasn't quite right: "O'Hara's stories are getting neater, tighter and more economical in their form, and this, I suppose, constitutes an increase in expertness. But I cannot observe the development with pleasure, not merely because the span, tempo and rhythm of the stories in *Pipe Night* need to be varied to avoid monotony, nor because I have a taste for a more relaxed kind of writer such as O'Hara himself gave us in 'The Doctor's Son,' but because this increasing virtuosity of brevity seems to tend away from the novel and it seems to me that for O'Hara's talents the novel is the proper form."

Odysseus had Circe to warn him against the lure of the Sirens' song, and he possessed the self-protective cunning to have his comrades tie him to the mast as he sailed abeam of their seductive call. O'Hara, on the

---

*Trilling's passion for the novel burned with an almost sacred heat; he believed it to be civilization's most refined expression of intellectual elevation and moral complexity. But the novelist who had his considered esteem was not an American realist—Dreiser or Steinbeck aroused his disdain—but Henry James. And O'Hara would not have seemed his inevitable choice for an heir to the Master's lacework of inferences and contingencies.

other hand, put his helm over hard and aimed straight for the reef. And why shouldn't he have? Trilling was daring him to be great, or at least to stretch out, to shine bright in an age of lesser lights.* Every short-story writer I've known, not excepting Raymond Carver, at some vulnerable moment believed, or was persuaded to seem to believe, that stories were wind sprints to prepare for the marathon. And most editors and publishers prefer to print novels, some because it is possible to make a small profit from them, others simply because they prefer to read them. And is it too reductive to invoke bigger is better? But the fiction writers I know almost universally cite—when applauding a life-changing piece of fiction, a piece of work from which they can quote, or want to read aloud after dinner—this or that short story. One of the O'Connors', say, Flannery's "Parker's Back" or Frank's "Guests of the Nation," maybe, Cheever's "Goodbye, My Brother" or Welty's "Powerhouse." Even so, what novelist—what Dickens-worshipping John Irving of a big-picture, big-screen fantabulizer—wants to be instructed by a reviewer, Think smaller, or, as Auden urged confessional writers, Be brief, be blunt, begone? And this particular career-counselor wasn't just a reviewer: this was Lionel Trilling!

O'Hara was not promiscuous in his gratitude for admiring reviews, but this time he laid his heart out for a stranger to see. He wrote Trilling three days after the review appeared, thanking him effusively, and thought to add, "Already I have had several letters; one, for instance, from the Secretary of the Navy, who happens to be an old friend of mine, but he's still Secretary of the Navy and did take the time to write."[36] It is astonishing that the inventor of "Graven Image," with its perfect pitch for the flats and sharps of social intercourse, could so clumsily namedrop to the very critic who three days earlier had praised to the heavens O'Hara's acute tuning to his characters' expressions of pomposity.

---

*Almost a decade earlier, Fitzgerald had written O'Hara from Asheville, urging toward "something more ambitious" than stories and *Appointment in Samarra*. He urged a long work, "Zolaesque," advised him to "buy a file" in which to collect notes for "a novel of your time enormous in scale." In this letter, the author of *The Great Gatsby* and *Tender Is the Night*—with "The Crack-Up" on his mind—decided that he himself had aimed too low. The difficulty of experiencing wholesome pride—forget pleasure—from the good work one has achieved is one of the sad poverties of too many writers' lives. It's as though the writer agrees with reviewers that his value is set by the least he has made (F. Scott Fitzgerald, *The Letters of F. Scott Fitzgerald*, ed. Andrew Turnbull [New York: Scribner, 1963], p. 539).

Singled out for Trilling's special praise in *Pipe Night,* "Bread Alone" tells the story of a Mr. Hart, a black father and car-washer who wins a gambling pool at work and uses the winnings—which he does not report to his wife—to take his son to the ballpark. Booker is a "strange boy of thirteen . . . a quiet boy, good in school, and took after his mother, who was quite a little lighter complected than Mr. Hart."[37] Mr. Hart broods from the fifth inning on about his rare good luck; his large family needs money and he is "not sure his son is even pleased" to be at Yankee Stadium, since Booker is attentive but silent. In the eighth inning, on a two-and-one count, DiMaggio pokes one into the stands, where the ball bounces off the seats a few rows back and disappears. After the Yankees win and the crowd begins to disperse, Booker brings forth the ball from his shirt, where he'd hidden it. " 'Present for you,' said Booker." Mr. Hart says, "I'll be god-damn holy son of a bitch. You got it? The ball?" Booker repeats, it's for his father. Mr. Hart "threw back his head again and slapped his knees. 'I'll be damn—boy, some Booker!' " It is probably churlish to object, at the story's end, to the "arm around his son's shoulders" and a valedictory hug that makes too flagrantly explicit this enactment of fondness after its previously border-patrolled reserve. It's Steven Goldleaf's enthusiastic judgment in *John O'Hara: A Study of the Short Fiction* that "Bread Alone" is perhaps *Pipe Night*'s finest story: "subtle," "fine and sad," and "uplifting at the end."[38] Trilling went further, declaring that after Gertrude Stein's "Melanctha" this story was "the best story that I knew about a Negro because the Negro is so precisely seen in all his particularity as a Negro that he wonderfully emerges, by one of the paradoxes of art, as a man and a father."[39] If I can't quite follow the resolution of that paradox—how can one have "particularity as a Negro"?—Richard Wright evidently could. Matthew J. Bruccoli reports that Wright told O'Hara that "Bread Alone" was the "only story about Negroes by a white author that he liked."[40]

Owing to the story's success and the affirming sentiments that it stirred, it is more destiny than wonder that "Bread Alone" was the occasion for yet another misunderstanding between O'Hara, the *New Yorker* (where it first appeared), and Harold Ross. The editor's questions, conveyed through William Maxwell, seemed fiddling literalisms to O'Hara: Why did Hart feel guilty about spending his winnings in the office pool? Was it likely he hadn't attended a game in fifteen years? If he hadn't, why did he care about baseball? Should O'Hara not provide greater detail as to the Jewishness of Mr. Hart's boss, Mr. Ginsburg, who pays out the winnings? Irked, O'Hara reared back and wrote to Maxwell: "That is the penalty of trying to write decently and with some respect for the possible reader, figuring, as I occasionally do, that anyone who can read can get what I'm saying." Justice so far, says Solomon, is on his side. Then, without even considering that the editor simply might not like the story, he throws a wild pitch: "I happen to know that Ross has an old hate on baseball, claiming that New Yorker readers don't know or care anything about it."[41] One *New Yorker* editor, namely Harold Ross, seems by a 1949 memo addressed to William Shawn to have had more than a passing curiosity about the game and its particulars:

> You said you would consider adding a thing or two to the Talk piece being prepared on the whisk broom that umpires use. At a ball game at the Yankee Stadium the other night, I noticed that the umpire seems to have a page boy at his call, a lad in a red coat (with some gilt on it, as I recall) who seemed to deliver messages to him and accept messages from him. These were oral, I believe, except in one instance possibly; I thought I saw the umpire write out a message. Nobody around me could explain the page boy; he is an innovation, evidently. Also, I think we could have something about how many baseballs an umpire's pockets will hold. They are apparently capacious. I have heard criticism of the fact that umpires are required to wear a coat all through the hot weather. Maybe they wear coats because they wouldn't have any place to keep the balls otherwise. Come to think of it, maybe that page boy delivered the new balls to the umpire, although I'm not sure; maybe it was the batboy. How many baseballs are used in a game, on the average? Is a ball ever used more than once, or, to state the question more comprehensively: When a ball is hit foul, another ball is immediately put in play by the umpire; the ball that went foul, if retrieved (as opposed to going over or into the stands) seems to go to the home team's dugout. Then, later, a quantity of balls are delivered to the umpire, who puts them in his pocket. Are these brand new balls, or are they balls that have been played with some, and been knocked foul?[42]

This bravura inquiry and meditation is an index of the magazine's and its founding editor's eccentric best, as sui generis as the nutty commitment to detail that O'Hara himself so proudly displayed. What I find remarkable in it, and temperamentally so at odds with O'Hara's cocksureness, is the way Ross's specificity is tempered by contingency, the declarative by the subjunctive. Red coat, with gilt, "as I recall." "Seemed," "I believe," "possibly," "I thought," "evidently," "apparently," "maybe," "if" . . . question within question, nesting Russian dolls of interrogation, postulation, second thought. And the whole matter—how do umpires get and store baseballs?—marginal, as in marginal queries, and sufficiently "capacious" to give marginality a good name.

It's routine for writers to describe their vocation as solitary, lonely, a one-worker shop. It's also routine for writers to grouch about the Vanishing Editor, the empty place left on earth when Maxwell Perkins—always Perkins—went to heaven. It's also routine for writers to bellyache about intrusive editors who small-change them with cavils, bluepenciling in the margins, *huh? . . . who he? . . . nah . . . pls untangle*—and maybe even suggesting that the narrative's tail would be more comely if worn on the head. Of course editors, like writers, have always come in every kind: smart and dumb, reckless and heroically engaged. There have always been acquisition editors, moved to puzzle out markets, and line editors mostly sensitive to language. Sometimes an editor can be both, but a writer's response to a good and sympathetic line editor—a good writer's ideal reader, if the writer is willing to regard *any* reader as ideal—can help sort out that writer's fundamental affection or hostility toward audience, whether to court them, boss 'em, or fuck 'em. A writer such as Vladimir Nabokov sets himself so deliberately apart from his readers that he scruples to remind them, even as they fall into the dream of his life in *Speak, Memory,* that they are forbidden to confuse their histories with his, much less themselves with him. Multilingual, a polymath, world-wise, with an appetite for learning and a love of tricks to trip an unwary reader, he must have been a nightmare to line-edit, but Ross and his colleagues managed. Whereas O'Hara became, in the mid-1940s, increasingly impossible to edit. If Ross's clumsy effort to regularize his sprung syntax emboldened O'Hara's resistance to questions of any kind about his compositions, it is also true—and it was O'Hara's loss at the *New Yorker* and later at Random House—that he was so determined to be solitary in his enterprise, only to speak and never to listen, that he robbed himself of all that he might have learned from a good many artful editors eager to be his ideal readers. It would have been nice to imagine a conversation, especially on the page, between Ross and O'Hara on the matter of baseball umpires, their tools, customs, servants, uniforms, and secret practices.

The editorial process of *A Rage to Live* ensured that no such exchange would ever develop. William Maxwell—to whom O'Hara felt comfortable railing at the magazine's "silly fucking God damn carping"[43]—had taken a sabbatical from the *New Yorker* to write, and O'Hara, beginning in 1945, was again being edited by Katharine White, who would convey to him Ross's "query sheets," along with her own prickly judgments.* He was told that his fictional drugstore had unacceptably odd closing hours and that he'd used improper punctuation. He responded sometimes to Ross through White, sometimes to her under cover of Ross, sometimes directly to her, mostly unable to know who was asking what. "When I present a fact like the closing of drug store, I know what I am talking about . . . I reject suggestion. I just won't have it. . . . Semi-colon stuff, no, nor sequence of tenses stuff, since after all I have my own ignorant style."[44] But he also allowed that if "the Editors" found a passage unclear, "you most certainly have a beef," the right to demand clarity, "a right which is implicit in the right to accept or reject."

In early 1948 O'Hara wrote White that a small check she'd sent him was likely to be the final "New Yorker draft I ever cash." He went on to complain that J. D. Salinger's "Perfect Day for Bananafish," recently published in the magazine, was a "reworking" of his own work, "a slight discourtesy."[45] It is difficult to imagine a less likely charge; except that Salinger's war veteran Seymour Glass shoots himself dead in his story, as O'Hara's characters frequently solved the problem of their fictional exits. But Salinger's delicate, withdrawing characters—with their acute nostalgia for innocence—are at the antipodes from O'Hara's thrusting cast of wanters and resenters.†

---

*White was not alone as a victim of O'Hara's editor-rage. Louis Forster, Ross's assistant, told Thomas Kunkel of O'Hara's meeting with Wolcott Gibbs—whom Mrs. White considered "the best editor of O'Hara there is"—in his *New Yorker* office: "their voices rising, then becoming more animated, until suddenly there was a veritable explosion: 'Gibbs, you're *fucking* my story!' With that, O'Hara stormed out" (Thomas Kunkel, *Genius in Disguise: Harold Ross of The New Yorker* [New York: Random House, 1995], p. 263).

†In early 1949 Mrs. White selected stories for an anthology of fifty-five *New Yorker* stories. O'Hara's "The Decision" was decided upon, together with stories by Salinger and Nabokov. When the anthology was published, Nabokov graded them: *A*'s for his own and for "A Perfect Day for Bananafish," a gent's *C*+ for O'Hara.

In this same letter, O'Hara offers a take-it-or-leave-it to the *New Yorker,* protecting his rights against their "right to accept or reject." He demanded a kill fee of $250 for every story the magazine returned. Three days later, Katharine White answered his complaints, one as petty as the system by which contributors got paid bonuses (according to whose fan mail outran whose), another as unreasonable as whining that he had no office at the magazine ("We gave you one when you asked for it and held it empty for months when you did not use it"). As to the kill fee: "Ross and the management will never pay anything for fiction submitted and not bought. We do not do business this way—never have, never will." Her final words in this letter were personal:

> I would take it as a friendly gesture if you would be willing to talk to me about the whole thing before you make any final decisions, or write any more letters of demand, abdication, or withdrawal. I have always thought of you as a friend and, as an editor, have always supported you. I care about your future. I also care about seeing your work in the magazine. I have put in a great deal of editorial life blood and actual physical life blood in your cause, so to speak, and I'm surprised that you are unwilling to see me. It might be that if we talked various difficulties and distresses could be ironed out, both emotional and financial. . . .
>
> If your conscience would be clear to decide before you even talked the matter over with me, my conscience would not. I very much doubt that yours would be either. Our association has been too long for such a parting of the ways. Mine would not be clear as an editor, because it is evident that you are under a misapprehension on a number of points, nor would it be clear in relation to you as a friend. If O'Hara and The New Yorker must part, let's at least wind things up on a basis of understanding and normal human relationship.[46]

This was not the only ultimatum O'Hara had been flinging in the face of editors during 1948. He went on the wagon to finish the marathon narrative of *A Rage to Live,* and he was all business. To Saxe Commins, his Random House editor after Bennett Cerf had wooed O'Hara from Duell, Sloan and Pearce, about the very long typescript coming his way: "You'd better get that surgical glint out of your eye, because far from my doing any ruthless cutting on the final MS, there will be ruthful additions."[47]* He told his Hollywood agent to tell Hollywood studios who wanted to buy his services, Get lost. *Collier's* asked to have a look at *A Rage to Live*. O'Hara's terms were self-confident: it would cost them $15,000 to steal a peek, and if they decided to buy, the price was $100,000, on top of the reading fee. In such a humor, he let Katharine White know he didn't care to meet with her to talk about his stipulations: "Quite frankly, I don't want to discuss my letter. . . . My statement of the terms gives me a perfectly good out: The New Yorker can accept them or reject them, and in the event of your rejecting them my conscience in regard to the long association will be quite clear; I didn't just quit. You, on your side, can say that the terms were anything from unsatisfactory to outrageous, and that you didn't want to do business, and that will be your out."

In the event, in the various showdowns he blinked: he gave up the kill fee for a higher per-story rate; he often returned to Hollywood to do piecework; *Collier's* didn't pay to read *A Rage to Live*, nor did they buy it, nor did *Good Housekeeping*, to whom Cerf tried to sell an excerpt without imposing a reading fee or preset price. *A Rage to Live* was not serialized nor well edited, and O'Hara very nearly drove Bennett Cerf and Random House from his camp during the nasty runup to publication.

With the death of Samuel Sloan a week after *Pipe Night* was published, O'Hara had been on the hunt for a different publisher. Newly a father and habitually certain that he would die young (whether the agent of his end was accident, disease, or terminal depression), mindful of his father's messy and meager estate and unwilling to rely on Belle's money, he was determined to do hard-nosed business with those to whom he had value. If such a determination could be considered prudent, it was also an efficient system for the translation of friends into enemies. To say *I love your work; let me publish it* and to be told *The better you like it the more I'll make you pay* is hardly an unprecedented call and response in the world of letters, but the pursuer might at least have earned the hope of being treated courteously when presented with the bill.

---

*Frank MacShane reports as settled fact that at the adjournment of a stormy visit to Random House—during which Commins expressed reservations about the frank and erotic language of *A Rage to Live* and implied that the Society for the Suppression of Vice might take an unwholesome interest in the novel—O'Hara "hurled" a glass paperweight at his editor before "storming out" (MacShane, *The Life of John O'Hara*, p. 145).

I'm skeptical, not least because MacShane reports that this "cleared the air" between the novelist and his publisher.

Beginning in 1947 with his collection *Hellbox* (named for a printing compositor's container in which discarded bits and pieces of metal type are gathered to be melted down and recast), Random House was O'Hara's publisher till his death, and well beyond. Especially at the beginning of the relationship, he routinely bullied Cerf and abused his affection. Cerf—a sturdy and genial man with an expertise in jokes and a sideline moonlighting on the television show *What's My Line?*—took it like a sport, usually. In drawing the contract for *A Rage to Live,* he assented to all of O'Hara's demands, and paid an advance against royalties of $10,000. (The novel would go through eight hard-cover printings, and when it passed one hundred thousand copies, at O'Hara's insistence, Random House presented to the author a cigarette box engraved with sentiments—". . . FROM HIS GRATEFUL PUBLISHERS AND THE FIRST HUNDRED THOUSAND PURCHASERS . . ."—he himself had dictated to them.)*

Nevertheless, only one book into this association, John O'Hara was bitter; he sulked, then took to the mails. Cerf had been negligent, hadn't taken him to lunch at the "Ritz, the Colony, Voisin, the Yale Club." He complained—"I am disappointed"—about the ads for *Hellbox;* they'd used the wrong blurbs, and there were too many (!), sapping the novelty of the coming novel. Moreover, before finishing *A Rage to Live* he wanted his advance doubled. Cerf, explaining that such a sum "simply is more than the traffic will bear," offered $2,500. And finally he blew his top:

> There really was no reason at all for the disagreeable and even threatening tone of your note of November 27th. . . . From the first day we talked about your coming with us, everybody in this office has done everything in his power to make you happy. You, on the other hand,

---

*O'Hara's fiscal sagacity was qualified. His decision to negotiate his own book and magazine contracts left him at the mercy of some cockeyed notions, the most consequential of which was to refuse to be anthologized, on the theory that the anthologies—skimming his cream—would cut into sales of his story collections. The unhappy outcome was that he effectively barred his fiction from school and college courses in American literature. And in 1949, acting through Belle, he directed the assistant treasurer of Random House—which then owed him $65,000 in royalties—"to provide for a yearly maximum payment $25,000" (Bennett Cerf, "Letter to John O'Hara," Correspondence [Columbia University Butler Library: Rare Books and Manuscripts, 1949], Bennett Cerf Papers [2 December]). Thus thumbing his nose at the tax man, he cut his nose off. Not too far in the future those pipsqueak yearly payments could be made on the interest earned on the interest from his accruing royalty account.

seem to take some kind of perverse delight in making us uncomfortable. Why? . . .

All we got for our pains was a note from you that read "I am disappointed." Twice I wrote to you to ask what you were disappointed about and you didn't even bother answering. How do you think that made us all feel? Or don't you care? . . .

I have started writing a letter of this sort to you several times before, but always decided not to go through with it. Now it seems to me all-important that we understand each other fully if we are to go on working together. . . . [W]e expect a certain amount of temperament from any author. We don't intend, however, to be whipping boys and I don't see what on earth you accomplish by putting us in that position.[48]

John O'Hara did seem to take a delight in creating and nursing grudges. It can't be ignored that he didn't seem to care that to receive a letter from him would often make you feel worse than you did before. To approach him with a kind word in a public place was a risky enterprise; to draw his attention was probably bad luck. Whatever he *was*, which is not for strangers to judge, he frequently behaved like a petulant bully. Although this is an answer to a question he never asked, sometimes I just can't like this man. I admire in his character that he was never disloyal, never shrewd in his own advancement, never two-faced. But whatever provocations can be debited to his enemies among editors, critics, night-club patrons, and unrequiting women, there is no excuse for his self-indulgent brutality, his sullen refusals to discuss with his antagonists the very grievances he brought to their uninvited attention. Like most bullies, his blood lust was excited especially by such amiable associates as Bennett Cerf, who might have seemed in their easygoing manners to take his amour propre, honor, importance, loftiness, and material fortunes too casually.

In any case, the exchange between author and publisher launched a less than promising start. Soon enough the "disappointed" author would ask his book publisher to help him out in an ugly dispute with his magazine editor—a favor that must have caused him to swallow a great amount of pride. And what provoked O'Hara on this occasion was a review—even given the *New Yorker*'s tendency to condescend in their book pages to their story writer's novels—shockingly indifferent to the human anguish of being belittled by a colleague.

5. THE TOMES

A Rage to Live has the virtues of ambition and tenacity. Set principally in Fort Penn, Pennsylvania, a stand-in for Harrisburg, with excursions to Philadelphia, New York, and the farm country near Fort Penn, its reach is generous, from before World War I until 1947. The cast of characters is populous: politicians, bankers, children, soldiers, grandparents, a contractor, newspaper people, farmers, cops, clubmen, scapegraces, a fop or two. It means to exhaust through exposition and dialogue the personal and family history of Grace Caldwell Tate by the accretion of details, an inventory of those customs and objects that certify her high social standing in the middle-sized pond of Fort Penn, and to expose without flinching the serial sexual indiscretions that bring her down. In its Modern Library edition of 1997—rightly classified "A Modern Library Giant"—it is seven hundred and thirteen pages. The length of O'Hara's jumbos—*Ten North Frederick, From the Terrace,* and *Ourselves to Know*—made easy sport for hostile reviewers equipped with such nouns as "doorstop" and "dumbbell" and "widow-maker." If his gigantism was a throwback to an age of greater leisure, modern reviewers—for whom time was money, say, twenty-five dollars a day—felt oppressed.

Just as Lionel Trilling seems to have been misguided in equating gravity with duration, so must a contemporary reader guard against confusing heft with mess. Despite the lessons of such long-reachers as Joyce, Faulkner, Elkin, Pynchon, and Mailer, it has become too unthinking to

judge a work massive *but* (can you believe it?) "disciplined" or "coherent" or—pregnant modifier—"engrossing." Whatever the limits of a
reader's stamina, the writer rightly persists if a piece of writing seems
better made long than short. Whether O'Hara was jaded, or spiteful, or
influenced by Fitzgerald's and Trilling's urgings, whether a vision came
to him in a dream—*Make Behemoths!*—or it simply seemed good business to strive for a grander payday than stories fetched, whether he
believed novels would win him prizes or merely was freed by financial
success to spend time however he pleased and was most pleased by writing long fiction, he was obliged to be the hostage of his hunches. If a
writer's hunches misguide him, readers will vote with their eyes and look
elsewhere. O'Hara didn't have to be stubborn to write what he wanted to
write; he had only to be honest or reckless, and he was both.

A Rage to Live begins with ample promise by assembling a crowd of
locals and visitors at a Red Cross festival at Riverside Farm, eleven miles
from Fort Penn, the impressive seat of Grace Caldwell's family, now
known familiarly as the "Tate Farm (old Caldwell place)."[1] The heroine
is married to Sidney Tate, of New York and Yale: Death's Head was his
secret society, meaning to compound the Rolls-Royceness of Skull and
Bones with the Bentleyness of its rival Wolf's Head. Despite these
impeccable credentials, Tate is an outsider in Fort Penn, which is why
the descriptive "old Caldwell place" is necessary—a nice touch, the kind
of smart detail O'Hara might've used as a grace note in a short story. But
the luxurious orchestration of the book's opening is nothing less than
symphonic:

> It would have been impossible for anyone on the Nesquehela Pike that
> day to miss the place, no matter what name he knew it by. The real
> farmers, of course, had not been deceived by the light rainfall of the
> morning, and they had begun arriving as early as ten o'clock . . . in
> spring wagons and hay wagons and truck wagons, some drawn by draft
> horses, some by teams of mules, some by mixed teams of horse-and-
> mule; and the next to arrive were farmers more prosperous than the
> earliest, and they came in buggies and buckboards and democrats and
> surreys and barouches and cut-unders. There was even a team of goats
> from a neighboring farm, a nice turn-out with real leather, not web, har-
> ness and a small-size truck wagon. Then a little later came the trucks

and automobiles: Ford cars and Maxwells and Chevrolets and Partin-Palmers and Buicks and Hahn trucks and Maccars and Garfords and Autocars and Vims, and a few Cadillacs, Franklins and one Locomobile and one Winton. And all this time there would be farm boys on horseback—some with English saddles, some with stock saddles, some with Kentucky saddles, some with a blanket-and-surcingle, and some bareback—and among these were a few fine saddle horses, but mostly they were work horses and mules, with one-piece ear-loop bridles and work-harness bridles with laundry rope for reins. And all day long too there were the farm boys with their bicycles, singly and in pairs, but more often in groups as large as twenty in number, causing their own particular sound, which was the hum of the wire wheels, and the sound of one bell quickly followed by twenty other bells. They were the grim ones, these boys, not quite of draft age, breaking the silence in their ranks to call out words in Pennsylvania Dutch, but ironically resembling the Belgian army cyclists, whose cousins the farm boys' cousins had beaten in war. The boys on horseback laughed; the boys on the bicycles had no laughter. Everything was clean and shining: the Dietz lamps on the wagons and trucks and buggies, and the nickel studding on the work harness, and the silver conchos on the stock saddles, and the automobile radiators, and the sprockets on the bicycles, and the snaffle bits and curb chains and the ferrules on the buggy-whips and the painted hooves of the horses and the yellow felloes on the wheels of the cut-unders and the black leather dashboards and the white painted canvas tops of the spring wagons and the brass-bound hose of the bulb horns and the three-by-six-inch windows in the barouches and the Prest-o-lite tanks and hub-caps of the automobiles, and the scrubbed faces and foreheads of the men and the women and the boys and the girls.[2]

The music swells, the repetitions and variations on *farm* and *work*, *saddle, truck*, and *wagon* conveying authority in a passage patient in its specification. This is high-density writing, avid and welcoming, that shows a vital picture busy with the details Breughel would have included. The passage sounds like a full-throated exhalation, with an audacious ease of movement, from the noise of a single bicycle bell to the reply of twenty to the guttural exclamations echoing in Pennsylvania Dutch cries heard in Flanders fields. Its nickel and silver gleams, as lovingly polished as the sentences.

If only *A Rage to Live* had sustained this exuberance, and its impulse to detail had remained committed to the artifacts O'Hara above all writers of his time knew how to distinguish, and it had exploited his understanding of farm life and small city commerce. . . . Instead he elected to lavish his attention on one character's odd and oddly crippling perversion of possibility, ambition, and beauty. In his long novels O'Hara was fatally attracted by case studies that were phenomenal rather than exemplary, thwartings and betrayals that stood for nothing larger than their individually peculiar sadness. Writing these words, I feel more than a little discomfort about subverting my conviction that a novelist is bound to honor only what provokes his or her interest. To hold that a writer owes the reader a damned thing (and vice versa), or to accuse him of creating characters who "stood for nothing larger" than their specific circumstances, is to traffic in Hallmark sentiment, to make a plea for moral fiction, for allegory, for vulgarity. But O'Hara, I believe, wanted Grace Caldwell Tate to "stand for" something, perhaps something as banal as Domestic Tragedy.

Brendan Gill's *New Yorker* review was a devastating assault on both O'Hara's intention and his execution. He opened with an urbane wisecrack that sex seemed to be on American minds these days, and placed *A Rage to Live* in the lineup with *The Kinsey Report* on sexual behavior: "Dr. Kinsey is perhaps the leading professional student of this subject and as such has had the advantage of having numerous assistants, as well as the financial backing of the Rockefeller Foundation. Dr. O'Hara, our leading amateur, has had to go it alone, at his own expense. On the other hand, O'Hara has long been one of the most prominent figures in the profession of letters, while Kinsey, an old gall-wasp man, is a taxonomist first and a literary craftsman second."[3]

He warms to his own stroke of wit: "Granted that Kinsey has the edge in statistics and O'Hara in style, the layman's immediate response to 'A Rage to Live,' as to [Kinsey's] earlier, pioneer work, is likely to be one of uncritical admiration for the amount of scholarly research involved." Now the reviewer makes the transition from snickering to sadism, and following a crocodile-teary lament for what might have been—a prototype of disdain—he aims to drive a stake through his colleague's heart:

> This feeling [of uncritical admiration] is soon displaced, however, by one of depression, and eventually of suffocation, for the reader who begins by being ashamed of having paid so little heed to the true nature

of the human condition ends by being convinced, half against his will, that the investigation of sexual practices had better be left, as it always used to be, not to the expert but to the young. It was predicted last year that the Kinsey Report would open our eyes and jolt us into a lively awareness of the complexity of our sexual problems; now it appears that the Report put more people to sleep than it awakened, and numbed our minds instead of jolting them. The recurrent passages of maudlin sexuality in "A Rage to Live," complete even to so worn a stencil as the prostitute with a loving heart and a high I.Q., may have the same effect. If so, it will be all the sadder, because the author has plainly intended to do more than out-Kinsey Kinsey; he has intended, indeed, to write nothing less than a great American novel. There was reason enough for this ambition. "A Rage to Live" is O'Hara's first novel in eleven years and comes exactly fifteen years after "Appointment in Samarra," which was, and is, an almost perfect book—taut, vivid, tough-minded, and compassionate . . . and five volumes of short stories, many of which are as good as anything in the language. Within the tight framework of these stories, apparently so small in compass but nearly always so explosive in force, O'Hara was able to take the measure of an astonishing variety of subjects, describing for us, with or without sex but with every appearance of authenticity, the customs of such dissimilar outposts of civilization as Hollywood, Stockbridge, Washington, D.C., and Hobe Sound, as well as half a dozen New Yorks—Wall Street, Jackson Heights, the Village, Fifty-second Street, Beekman Place, Riverside Drive. But it is an unbreakable convention of our time that a man who has written novels goes on writing novels, and perhaps partly for this reason, but surely for other deeper and more compelling reasons, O'Hara sat down and doggedly accumulated "A Rage to Live." . . .

A sprawling book, discursive and prolix, ranging in time from 1877 to 1947, and full of a multitude of semi-detached characters and subplots, what "A Rage to Live" does resemble is one of those "panoramic," three-or-four-generation novels that writers of the third and fourth magnitude turn out in such disheartening abundance. Dr. O'Hara's handy guide to healthy sex practices has been tucked inside the disarming wrapper of the formula family novel. . . .

In "Appointment in Samarra," there was nothing about Julian English that we did not know and want to know, but Grace Caldwell Tate is a fatally uninteresting woman, and her rage to live rarely amounts to

more than pique. It is hard to understand how one of our best writers
could have written this book, and it is because of O'Hara's distinction
that his failure here seems in the same nature of a catastrophe.

There is rough justice—too rough—in the specifics of Gill's accounting, and it is difficult to argue that Grace Caldwell Tate is *not* a "fatally
uninteresting woman." Her erotic compulsions might have been made
engaging as enactments of overpowering will, the feminine equivalent of
a rake's progress. Instead, O'Hara expresses her lust in an adolescent
wet-dream fantasy of the prim rich girl secretly wearing hot pants. Often
the diction—"sexual intercourse" and "menstrual periods"—is stilted,
having the effect of saltpeter. The Good Parts are at once flushed and
wooden, going for broke, aiming at about waist-level for the purple, fractured Language of Lust. Here are Grace and Sidney after the nuptials,
after the crossing of the threshold, after his discreet retirement to don
pajamas and bathrobe, after the adjustment of the lighting. They are
finally in bed: "The moment he touched her the rage began. 'Do everything! Kiss me? Kiss me here? Let me—no. No! Go in me. Quickly, Sidney, please. I'm going, I'm going. Don't do anything else, go in me. Oh,
you're in me and I'm all around you, just in time, time, time. Oh, such
wonderful, exquisite.' "[4]

A couple of pages later, during the penny-for-your-thoughts halftime
break, Grace muses: " 'Nothing *you* do shocks *me,* and nothing *I* do
shocks me. But you! Ah, Sidney, poor Sidney. Nobody'll ever know you
married a bad woman. But you're bad, too. I don't consider you a little
choirboy with rosy cheeks. Oh, I'm glad you married me.'

"In other years he often would think of what they had said that night,
and of what they had not said."[5]

It is common for the O'Hara of the tomes to break into such a
moment as Grace's confessions, to dash expository cold water on a character's fevered exclamations from narrative ambush: "in other years," in
some unspecified future, on some unspecified occasion, Sidney would
"often" think about what was not said on the night you just couldn't shut
Grace up.

Probably it is just as well that she didn't utter everything that night
which was on O'Hara's mind. It isn't till many hundreds of pages later
that the subject arises of "What's the word? It isn't incense, but almost
that." This coy allusion to incest is followed by an etymology lesson by

Grace's friend Betty on the root of *homo:* "*Homo* means *man.* But that is the Latin. In Greek it means *the same.* So when it happens between two men it's homosexual, and when it happens between two women it's homosexual too."*[6] Grace does "not resist" when guys who are not her husband or (even worse!) social equals put hands "inside her blouse and then under her skirt and inside her bloomers."[7] Why is this? That's just the way she is. Her adultery inspires a speech from ill-used Sidney that became a touchstone for O'Hara's contemporary reviewers:

> "You see in this world you learn a set of rules, *or* you *don't* learn them. But assuming you learn them, you stick by them. They may be no damn good, but you're who you are and what you are because they're your rules and you stick by them. And of course when it's easy to stick by them, that's no test. It's when it's hard to obey the rules, that's when they mean something. That's what I believe, and I always thought you did too. I'm the first, God knows, to grant that you, with your beauty, you had opportunities or invitations. But you obeyed the rules, the same rules I obeyed. But then you said the hell with them. What it amounts to is you said the hell with my rules, and the hell with me. So, Grace— the hell with you. I love you, but if I have any luck, that'll pass, in my new life."[8]

That's about as bad as it gets. Gill labels this declamation "something out of an old *Redbook,*" then the Skulled and Boned reviewer twists the knife by blaming Tate's matriculation at Yale for his homiletic probity. He also found occasion to regret the absence of O'Hara's previously "sure-fire, ice-cold" dialogue. In fact, less than a page after delivering his sermon and having "snapped off" the bedroom light, Sidney Tate hears Grace's plea:

---

*This was not the first time—and surely not the last—that he invoked lesbian love. The final novel published in his lifetime, *Lovey Childs: A Philadelphian's Story,* is a leering, voyeuristic exposé of the details of women seducing and enjoying women. There is no hint of priggish reproach of lesbian eroticism as such—O'Hara takes too much manifest pleasure in the details of his more lurid passages to create an occasion to condemn or to encourage—and so his fixation seems to have no subtext or supertext. Why he developed this fascination is beyond me. Writing for the *New Yorker* in 1975, Brendan Gill summarized O'Hara's obsession with sex as the fascination and shame of a "Jansenist, in spite of himself . . . loathing his body for committing sins that he no longer believed in but that cost him remorse. . . . He continued to believe, straight out of the penny catechism, that man was a fallen creature" (September 15, 1975). Well, I don't believe a word of it.

" 'Sidney, can't I come over? Please?'

"He laughed. 'Nope. Good night.' "[9]

Reviewers are frequently torn between the coherence of attack and the fitful stutter of justice. (I knew I was washed up as a book reviewer at *Esquire* when my supervising editor—looking over my shoulder at a party—charged me with being "too judicious.") Gill, however, made available neither space nor willingness to dull his rhetorical edge as he cut through the irregular mass of O'Hara's vices and virtues: he *was* wonderful; he *is* awful. On the one hand and on the other—that's all, if the writer is lucky, most reviewers have to give. But *A Rage to Live* needed a Vishnu. On one hand O'Hara resorted to interior monologues of stunning clumsiness. On a second hand his inflection was stunningly accurate ("You like him best?" a character asks Grace; "I like him the only," she answers). On a third he piles on senseless data. And on a fourth he nails the clothes and dressing-methods of a "meticulously civilian" and ambitious ex-officer.

Gill's review was shocking for where it appeared. Eleven years later O'Hara said of that editorial decision: "There are various degrees of treachery, and I consider *The New Yorker's* printing such a scurrilous review to be treachery of the lowest kind."[10] Harold Ross was hardly consistent in his policies regarding the reviewing of books by *New Yorker* writers, and a case could be made for loyalty-be-damned-we-call-'em-like-we-see-'em—a case Ross sometimes had made. But notwithstanding his magazine's treatment of O'Hara, he wrote E. B. White in 1938—apropos of a reference to Dorothy Parker in a Comment squib which, though friendly enough, might conceivably have irritated her—that "I don't think we ought ever, probably, to print anything slighting about her, or anything she might construe as slighting, because of the mountain of indebtedness the NYer is under to her."

A quarter century later, Gill saw fit to reprint his attack in full in *Here at The New Yorker*—"the review strikes me as sound"—and get in some new whacks: "O'Hara roared and howled with indignation, demanding of Ross that I be fired at once." In fact, he browbeat Bennett Cerf into writing Ross complaining about the review.* Gill reports this also (Cerf "howled and roared—or, rather, given Cerf's peculiar voice—squeaked

---

*This grievance has variations by the dozen. Cerf wrote in an account friendly to O'Hara that while his esteemed author held to a strict code of behavior, this presented difficulties to his friends, "since

and gibbered")[11] and that he, too, had demanded that Gill be fired at once. To no avail: Ross responded famously to Cerf, "You are incapable of ratiocination" and added that "you are my natural enemy."[12] Clearly there was sufficient ill will around to satisfy them all.

But it didn't end here, of course, not with O'Hara and Gill still alive to hound each other. Perhaps mistaking a scrupulous critic's measured praise for a cheerleader's credulous devotion, the smarting author of *A Rage to Live* wrote "Dear Lionel" that he was disappointed that Trilling hadn't reviewed the novel and that "the NYer fellow is, as I happen to know, in a bad way. . . . He is stuck on a pretty girl secretary in the office, who won't give him the time of day, and as a professional Catholic with a wife and a lot of kids he is in a mess."[13] In this letter he also takes a swipe at Wolcott Gibbs, remarking that Gill's use of "discursive" in his pan—a word O'Hara was confident Gill had never before used—stemmed in fact from Gibbs's reservations about *A Rage to Live,* which he'd shared with its author. If this plot seems as tangled and treacherous as the Nabokov-Wilson quarrel about who wrongfully gobbled whose brownies, wait till you hear Gill's version from *Here at The New Yorker:*

> Then something happened that doubled and redoubled O'Hara's wrath, and no wonder. Thurber, that incomparable mischief-maker, informed O'Hara that he had documentary proof of the fact that the review had been written not by me but by Wolcott Gibbs. Now, this was a master-stroke on Thurber's part; as [Gus] Lobrano once told me, Thurber was never so happy as when he could cause two old friends to have a falling-out. . . .
>
> With the invention of a single bold lie in respect to my review of *A Rage to Live,* Thurber had done two things: one, he had ensured that O'Hara would see me as a jackal, willing to let my name be used for a nefarious purpose and therefore a person permanently unworthy of forgiveness; and, two, he had ensured that Gibbs and O'Hara would quar-

there are some clauses in the code he has never bothered to explain." Thus, he complained, there was a period of three months during which O'Hara would not speak to him, "though to this day I have not the slightest idea what I did or said that angered him" (Bennett Cerf, "Portrait of a Pro," *Satuday Review* [11 January 1955]). Five years later and still bristling at Cerf's wonderment, O'Hara told a *Cosmopolitan* interviewer that there were *not either* any "secret clauses" or "complicated set of rules," and muttered darkly, he "knows damn well what he did." Interpreters agree that Cerf's offense was something either done or left undone in the feud with Gill.

rel.* Moreover, the most painful of O'Hara's paranoid fantasies would thus have been caused to come true—his oldest and dearest friend stood revealed as his worst enemy. Iago-Thurber took care to point out to O'Hara that my review contained the word "discursive," which O'Hara was surely aware was one of Gibbs' favorite words. . . . Desdemona's handkerchief wasn't in the same class with such evidence.[14]

So of course Gill never forgave Thurber.† But that grudge would have to wait. Meantime, fists threatened to fly. Of course there are competing versions, as ever with *sez you* and *sez who?* Having heard that O'Hara was going around town boasting that "he would knock my block off," Gill promised himself—"since I was a good many years younger and in much better physical condition"—that "I would do my best to knock *his* block off. In my mind's eye, I saw the big, fleshy head rolling unattached along the sidewalk, on the grey face a look of astonishment and dismay." The inevitable encounter came near the coatroom of "21." "O'Hara had been drinking, but then, he was always drinking in those days, and, besides, I had been drinking too."[15] The confessional clause, protected behind all those commas, is a crafty touch, cheaply bought evidence of a slanderer's blind sense of justice. "I walked across the room to him and said, 'Well, John, here I am. What are you going to do about it?' He stared at me dully, his lips working. At last there began to emerge from his lips a stream of vituperation . . . conventionally scatological." As the stream began "to peter out I said in a jeering tone, 'Is that the best you can do?' " He waited for O'Hara to swing first: "Fear conquered had done its work and adrenalin was racing through me like the headiest ice-cold champagne." Too bad his adversary didn't have a chance to review *that* sentence in the *New Yorker!* "In the way of the classic barroom bully," O'Hara "went on muttering imprecations" and Gill—high noon having passed—"shrugged and turned away."

In Bennett Cerf's *Saturday Review* account, "the *New Yorker* editors

---

*During an interview with the author, Marjorie Benchley mentioned as an illustration of O'Hara's grouchiness that having invited the O'Haras to dinner at this time, Belle had phoned to ask if Gibbs would be there. Assured that he was indeed invited, Belle said that she and John would not come. Mrs. Benchley, having thought that two dear friends might wish to share food, was mystified.

†*But wait!*—as they cry on the pre-dawn cable channels—*There's more!* During one of our conversations about O'Hara, Gill casually suggested that I might want to double-factcheck *his* version in *Here at The New Yorker* of the machinations. "I'm pretty sure I got that story wrong," Gill said. I do believe, though, that by the time he came clean he'd managed to forgive himself.

learned to rue that day" when they "seemed to take a malicious delight in singling out his *Rage to Live* for a vitriolic attack." He reported that Gill had approached O'Hara at a "Fifty-second Street restaurant . . . and proposed, 'This being the holiday season, John, what say we shake hands and forget our differences?' John's expression froze. 'I will give you,' he said, 'exactly thirty seconds to get out of my sight.' I never saw a critic disappear so quickly."[16] In Frank MacShane's version, Gill offered to buy O'Hara a drink. "O'Hara's eyes flashed, and he said, 'I wouldn't sit down with a son of a bitch like you for anything in the world.' "[17] Matthew J. Bruccoli has the most authoritative version, buttressed as it is by witness interviews. It seems there were *two* encounters, both at "21." In the first O'Hara "obscenely rejected Gill's friendly overtures" but "a brawl was averted." In the second, O'Hara was eating with Charles Addams, and Gill offered to stand them drinks, which inspired the remark: "You son-of-a-bitch, I wouldn't go to a dogfight with you."[18]

If you're hoping that's the end, tough luck. Later that same year, as Bruccoli tells it, O'Hara was at a dinner party in Princeton with John Hersey, who made the mistake of teasing him about his recent move to that college town, needling him about Yale and "addressing him as 'Professor.' "[19] As the guests prepared to leave, Hersey said, "Good night, Dr. O'Hara." To which O'Hara responded, "You son-of-a-bitch, you're a friend of Brendan Gill's." (For those who may have forgotten, in the offending review Gill had referred to "Dr. O'Hara's handy sex guide.") Still, Bruccoli was assured by Hersey that "there was no fistfight, though the report of one circulated."[20]

We're almost finished with this son of a bitching disputation, through no fault of Gill, who accounts for O'Hara's application to the Century Club: "I happened to be a member of the Admissions Committee. I urged his recommendation as a candidate on the grounds that he was a sour son of a bitch and a genius, and that a good club was one in which enemies as well as friends could find themselves at home; no sooner was O'Hara elected to the club than he wrote a stuffy letter to the House Committee, protesting the lack of a club tie."[21] For twenty years O'Hara cut the reviewer dead, in the Century Club, on the street, in the better restaurants. The last time Gill saw him was in Princeton, between halves of the Yale game, "coming out of the men's room under the concrete bleachers [looking] old and soft and pasty-faced. Again he cut me, without apparent effort, and again I felt the old, reluctant admiration rising in me. What a superlative grudge-bearer he was, and how Irish of him to be one."[22] But he wasn't a patch on Gill, Irish himself, who got the last word, literally, in a graceful obituary squib—fair-minded, more in pity than in sorrow, etcetera—written for the membership of the Century Club and memorializing his fallen foe.*

By the time *Ten North Frederick* was published in 1955 O'Hara, well settled in Princeton, had escaped the rough and tumble of both New York and the *New Yorker.* Comparative serenity—allowing for steady composition over unbroken stretches of time, so alien to O'Hara's earlier writing experiences in New York and Hollywood—was not necessarily the happiest circumstance for his fiction. Now he could stretch out and indulge evolutionary and inflationary and bloviationary instincts to his epic aspirations for the generations of Gibbsville.

Ten North Frederick takes for its title a street address there, home to the Chapin family, irreproachably respectable by the lights of that small city, secretly flawed by a hauteur and delusional ambition that reaches far beyond Pennsylvania precincts. " 'I would like to be President of the United States,' said Joe [Chapin],"[23] the novel's protagonist, in the middle of the three Chapin generations explored in *Ten North Frederick*. There is not the slightest empirical justification for the circumspect lawyer to entertain this pipe dream in the 1920s, no history of political or ideological fervor, no public encouragement, no instruction in Chapin Destiny, no mantle of dynastic inevitability handed down, Roosevelt-like, from his ancestors. The announcement's bravura freakishness is its novelistic appeal. The mischief and chaos promised by the expression of Joe Chapin's covert longing—the marvel of traveling by train for "five days and nights, from coast to coast at a high rate of speed and still be[ing] in the country that I'm president of"[24]—might carry a family story anywhere. That it doesn't—that *Ten North Frederick* instead chugs fitfully along, halting at sidings, steam-whistling relentlessly what it has beforehand efficiently announced, that families are not what they seem, and marriages even less so—results from a blurring of the tragic-comic vision that first led O'Hara to consider such a vaunting fantasy for his moderate, correct Yale-educated attorney at law.

*I'm sorry, I almost forgot a footnote. Years after O'Hara's death, his daughter Wylie was approached at a party and told that Brendan Gill would like very much to meet her. "Oh," she said, "I think not."

Ten North Frederick might have dramatized a cultural and psychological paradox: to find oneself at the summit of the Great Chain of Being in
even so modest a settlement as Gibbsville is to experience such elevation
above the groundlings that the very qualities essential to social distinction—propriety, decorum, modesty—are lost to altitude sickness. About
the chain itself, with all its finely graded links from the inert matter of
real estate to the *ens perfectissimum* of "*the* first citizen of Gibbsville,"
O'Hara is reliable. He knows ambition as well as smugness; he remembers how visitors to his grandfather's house in Lykens held their hats in
their hands as they walked up the path. He's intrigued once more with
locomotion, and of the 4:35 commuter train from Philadelphia he
observes that it "got the well-to-do home in time for dinner and the less
well-off home late for supper."[25] This is the train that carries Joe Chapin
to Gibbsville three days after a meeting with political bosses who have
led him along, milking him for cash while obliging him finally to confess
his secret dream, inasmuch as he couldn't puzzle out how to run for
president without anyone knowing. When he realizes he has been
gulled, he checks into a four-dollar-per-night hotel with two bottles of
eight-dollar-per-fifth Scotch and becomes an alcoholic.

If character is destiny in O'Hara's calculus, any story of flawed character is therefore a tragedy. The trouble with categorical imperatives,
though, is their contradiction of a reader's experience. Joe Chapin is as
blind as Oedipus, but Oedipus he's not, and it's better everyone agree on
that right off the bat. The material of *Ten North Frederick* is better
suited to Aristophanes than to Sophocles, but once O'Hara got his characters masked and on stilts, there was no bringing them back down to
earth. The most successful character in the novel—Mike Slattery—stays
firmly on the ground, and might even be said to crawl along it. O'Hara
introduces this political fixer with the narrative disclaimer that he is
"easy to define; too easy." He then proceeds to one of his most delicately
nuanced portraits of one ascending the upper-middle rungs of the ladder
to Olympus—or at least to the Lantenengo Country Club, newly
founded to relieve Gibbsville's unironical "sense of shame" for having
until the 1920s made do with a mere tennis club:

> He was Irish, second generation, and he had the pleasant unlined face
> of a well-fed, successful parish priest. He had the look of a man who
> spent a great deal of time with the barber, the manicurist, and the boot-

black. He had small, hairless hands, and small feet that in another time and land would have been expert in step-dancing. He was exquisitely tailored, always in dark blue, and always wore a black knitted necktie with a pearl stickpin. His Irishness was a secret weapon. He was frankly and proudly Irish, but the Irishness was actually a means of allowing the non-Irish to succumb to self-deception. He could tell a funny story, and he had a quick wit, and no one would ever have mistaken him for anything but what he was, racially. He was good company, not to be ignored. But where the non-Irish made their mistake was in assuming that that was all he was; a jovial man from the Emerald Isle. He didn't fool the Irish.[26]

But Mike Slattery fools Joe Chapin out of a hundred thousand dollars for party coffers, and he doesn't even bother to skim a layer off the top. He's got ambitions, Mike has, and among them is for his daughter to join—if she so desires—the sisterhood of the Sacred Heart, "an aristocratic order." So here is an honest crook, the most interesting kind, "above nervous larceny,"* a man more interesting than the predetermined Joe Chapin, marching to Yale in his father's worn path and then lock-stepping back to Gibbsville, his father's law firm and his family's house with its uninteresting address.

More oppressive than the shame of his secret ambition is the open fact of Joe Chapin's civilian status during the Great War. His law partner and friend Arthur McHenry, a Yale classmate who went to war, comes to realize that in missing service "Joe had been affected in much the same way as a classmate of theirs who had failed to make a senior society. At New Haven Joe and Arthur had tried to tell their friend the failure meant very little, and now Arthur tried (but only once) to convince Joe

---

*After law school, Slattery had been asked by local bosses to run for "chief burgess of Gibbsville, county clerk, sheriff, register of wills." He "laughingly" refused, "did not want to be marked with an early defeat for a minor office." In this he is the antipode of Joe Chapin, as he is in his self-effacing willingness to do work "that demanded the qualifications of a moderately industrious office boy, not a man with a law degree." But of course he knew just what he was doing; he was sometimes given envelopes to pass along. "It was only a venial political sin to pocket some of that money on its way from the committee to the ward leader: but when Mike was given $400 to deliver to a ward captain, the ward captain received $400, not $375. There would have been no comment and no disillusionment if Mike had paid himself a $25 delivery fee, but he early showed that he was not a $25 man. The $25 men are indispensable, but they invariably remain $25 men" (O'Hara, *Ten North Frederick* [New York: Random House, 1955], pp. 207, 208).

that there was no shadow over his patriotism or manliness."[27] What seems remarkable here—as elsewhere in O'Hara's many linkings of collegiate social disappointment and existential disgrace—is the want of irony. It is a mystery how loyally, with what blind faith, this shrewd skeptic accepted the conventional mandarin wisdoms. How could O'Hara have failed to hold to the fire the feet of a character who confuses membership in Skull and Bones with service at Verdun? In Chapin's Yale junior class, forty-five students were chosen for the brotherhoods of three tombs: Scroll and Key, Wolf's Head, and Skull and Bones.* While a socially aspirant fellow, feeling his shoulder go untouched on Tap Day, might say to himself that this was how it would feel to hear a doctor diagnose a malign tumor, how could a grown man have allowed himself to believe that a character hearing a cancer diagnosis would imagine as an equivalent curse how it would feel to go untapped by Wolf's Head? Such an unreliable table of equivalence is fatal to a novel of manners, whose narrator must demonstrate reliable judgment in order to seem a wise judge of his characters' misjudgment of weights and measures.

It's fathomable to be a snob or to be easily impressed by surfaces when one is young. Some lucky kids seem to be born "attractive" or "original" or both, with a strong chin or bushy eyebrows, with shrewd fashion sense or fearlessly open eyes or even with a coherent set of values. Sometimes this apparent grace is merely an accident of physiognomy, and in rare instances—from genes or by training—a kid can have from childhood the whole package: brains and courage and kindness. But most of us have to learn a day at a time—many days, a long time—what matters, what's decent or mean, what's authentic or bogus. After a while—after, say, a couple hundred short stories, half a dozen novels, and a half century of living—it becomes a vice to refuse to learn.

---

*Yale's version of discrimination—O'Hara's favorite—differed from Princeton's and Harvard's. Princeton's better eating clubs of the time (Ivy, Cottage, and Colonial) selected members according to unscientific principles of "attractiveness," a function of boyish decorum and understated haberdashery. Ivy might welcome a hockey player from a Montana high school as well as one from St. Paul's, if the high-schooler had the right haircut, so that in the annual club photo a stranger couldn't tell the young gents apart. As Nelson W. Aldrich Jr. has elsewhere explained, Harvard's better final clubs (Porcellian, and A.D.) insisted on "belongingness," a function of family name and schooling (Groton, St. Mark's, even Milton). Yale's secret societies selected gifted strivers according to their titled distinctions, so Tap Day was a contest between curricula vitae: captains of major teams (inclusive of hockey, squash, and rowing) were surely in the running, as was the editor of the *Yale Daily News* (unless he was or appeared "unattractive"), or a straight-arrow fundraiser.

Where was O'Hara's skeptical againster's reflex when he responded to the surfaces of conventional mandarin taste, those ubiquitous hunting prints in the entrance hall and poker-playing-dog prints in the downstairs can, those elephant's-foot umbrella stands, those boxy Brooks Brothers pinstripe suits and faux-regimental rep ties, those Church and Peal shoes, Dunhill lighters, the bay rum aftershave, the stuff assembled like props for a set design by Ralph Lauren, an inventory that any fool could accumulate with a starter set of wedding gifts? Corollary to this failure of skepticism in the tomes is O'Hara's inability to engage himself wholeheartedly with the properties of those cherished objects that compose his cultural universe. In a newspaper column mourning the "closure of my English bootmaker's Bespoke workshops" he grumbles that this deprives him of an extravagance, and concludes with sour fatalism that "good men and good things vanish."[28] But beyond the easy sentiment, *why* are these things good? Precisely *how* are they good? How are the hides selected? What skills are lavished upon their fabrication? How does the apprentice boot-maker master the craft of stitching? What's the best method of stitching and most durable thread? If the custom fitting of a pair of George Cleverley punched toe-cap semi-brogues cannot inspire the passionate detailing of Henry Adams's account of the erection of Chartres or John McPhee's of the shaping of a birchbark canoe, what difference does their *goodness* make to a writer? What good is this stuff? I have no doubt that behind and beneath his naming of the right cars, properest briefcase, or tiptop hat is knowledge, even love. But what's most sadly missing in this work is a dramatic imitation of objects in the process of being fashioned, taste in the process of being settled, manners in the process of being appreciated. I miss O'Hara's refined understanding of the things that define his characters and their longings. I miss the energy of ardor for calfskin, brass, linen, tulipwood, hand-rubbed Brewster green lacquer. Without the specificity of such longing, his long novels lack novelty.

O'Hara's bid for this quality in the portraits assembled for *Ten North Frederick* relies on his female characters. Mike Slattery's calculating wife, Peg, serves as his tactician. Joe's wife, Edith, is no less a conniver, but she is driven to her Lady Macbethness by a fury so general that O'Hara has to search high and mostly low in order to locate it. For one thing, she despises Joe for having married her—having settled for her—because she thinks of herself as plain. But finally, as in *A Rage to Live,* he relies on the Dirty Little Secret to explain all: Edith has hot pants. In their wedding bed Joe is such a gentleman that he misconstrues her moan and asks, "Do you want me to stop?" " 'No!' she said. . . . 'Do it to me, do it to me,' she said. 'Hurry.' She made it difficult for him to find her; she was already in the rhythm of the act and could not stop. 'For God's sake,' she said. 'For God's sake.' " Joe, doing his earnest darndest, answers, "I'm trying, dearest."[29]

Seven pages and many *dearests* later he is trying to reason with his now pregnant but still amorous wife. She invites him to make love to her, but he declines, explaining that sex "may affect the baby. I might hurt you." Telling him not to worry, she grows "unrestrained" and "noisy in her demands." When Edith says that other women have sex while they're pregnant, Joe replies that "their husbands are inconsiderate." (One thing for sure, this is not the making of a president.) Still, she keeps at it, asking if he believes that "miners and people like that don't have intercourse when the wife is pregnant." Joe recoils: "But we're not miners and people like that. I'm supposed to be a gentleman."[30] All that's stiff at 10 North Frederick is the diction, and it's lugubrious. The Chapins' daughter, Ann, is obliged to be educated "in the frightening mysteries of menstruation" by a teacher, and while she rarely considers "the act which, performed by her parents, had caused her existence . . . when she did she thought of her father visiting her mother in total darkness, without visual or tactile enjoyment or prolonged excitement."[31] Need I reveal that Ann is destined to elope, a dozen or so pages later, with Charley Bongiorno, a jazz pianist from Jersey City? In the same paragraph that the marriage is announced, "the process of nullification began immediately. The abortion was performed" . . . and so forth.[32] Mike Slattery arranges everything, and that's the last important favor Joe Chapin will be calling in. As for his relationship with Edith: "He would kiss her and touch her but the effect on her was no more exciting than a warm bath, and after his first attempts to force entrance into her, which were sufficient for him but inadequate for her, she would let him kiss her good night and no more."[33]

Inadequate for art but sufficient for the best-seller list (one hundred thousand copies plus sold in hardcover) and a censorship scandal. A couple of months following its publication, *Ten North Frederick* won the National Book Award, and while accepting the prize O'Hara gave in to emotion and couldn't finish his remarks; eight years later, given the

Award of Merit for the Novel by the American Academy of Arts and Letters,* O'Hara was so moved to receive the honor that he broke down completely while reminding the select audience that "at least some of the liberties that the younger writers enjoy today were paid for by me, in vilification of my work and abuse of my personal character."[34] In 1957 O'Hara had been elected to the National Institute of Arts and Letters (the Academy's cadet branch, a kind of waiting club), but within months he was squabbling with that august assembly for its seeming indifference to the suppression of the paperback version of *Ten North Frederick* on newsstands in Detroit, Cleveland, and Albany, deemed obscene by the uniformed and armed critics of those cities, unfit for public display, let alone study. As was becoming usual in such farces, the police got the worst of the publicity, and O'Hara's sales were boosted. But because he had believed that membership in the Institute would armor him against charges that he was a boudoir-padding panderer, he was so enraged by its refusal to publicly protest this censorship that in 1961 he quit. He'd come back in 1964, after he got his medal and redeemed his long-held wish to wear the Institute's rosette, but he never did make it into the Academy, a perceived slight that would never cease to rankle.

In 1958 Random House published *From the Terrace*, his longest novel—and is it ever! This monster occupies nearly nine hundred densely printed pages, uses more than half a million words, has the equivalent stretch of ten or a dozen short novels, with the whole nine hundred yards told in a single chapter.† The title's terrace refers to a location in southern California from which the family history of Alfred Eaton is languidly reviewed to his second wife, Natalie, during the "calm and peaceful autumn" of his premature old age (while, to use a title for a later story collection, *Waiting for Winter*). Eaton is an O'Hara "type," the wellborn Pennsylvania gentleman who would survive a sad childhood to prosper financially and socially after college, only to fold back slowly into

---

*He was justly proud of this recognition by his peers; the Merit Medal had previously been bestowed only on Theodore Dreiser, Thomas Mann, and Ernest Hemingway.

†Less than three years before his death, in an interview with Alden Whitman, obituary writer for the *New York Times*, O'Hara allowed that "it was a hell of a task writing it. . . . It bears more than one or two readings, because there's more to it than meets the eye the first time. But I've never reread it myself. I can't bear to. It would be a rather devastating experience" (*New York Times Book Review*, 26 November 1967, 5).

   Amen.

reserved sadness. ("Quiet and not glary. Rich brown, and gold.")[35] Eaton
is arguably the dullest of the stuffy, self-important specimens that began
with Sidney Tate and Joe Chapin and made way for Robert Millhouser
(*Ourselves to Know,* 1960) and George Bingham Lockwood (*The Lockwood Concern,* 1965). The latter sums up *his* family for his daughter:
"They were opportunists, but I will say for them that they stood off their
opposition for a whole century. They made no friends, but they did the
next best thing, which was to repel their enemies."[36]

George Lockwood falls, having earned his enemies one at a time, the
old-fashioned way, by being cold, conniving, criminal, and generally
awful. Alfred Eaton's fall is less dramatic (alas for *From the Terrace*): he
forgets to make friends. Born the second son of Samuel Eaton, a steel
mill owner in Port Johnson, Pennsylvania, a student at a third-rate
boarding school and at Princeton, navy officer during World War I, in
the airplane-manufacturing business and then a young partner in the
most prestigious investment bank on Wall Street between the wars,
finally assistant secretary of the navy in the Roosevelt administration
during World War II and all the time a clubman and partygoer, he has
somehow neglected to make friends. Lonely and idle, he is described on
page 893 by his closest business colleague when Natalie, weary of calm
and peaceful autumn, asks what the hell went wrong with Alfred.

> I don't know why he liked me, but he did, and I liked him very much,
> but I don't think he gave a damn for anyone else he saw, and I think
> that's the impression most men got. . . . I couldn't begin to go into the
> ways you can make an enemy in our business, and we all take enemies
> for granted. In any war, you have to have casualties. But Alfred didn't
> only make enemies. He failed to do the concomitant thing, which is to
> make a friend. When I speak of making a friend, I don't mean a pal or a
> chum, or a blood-brother. I only mean . . . a friendly connection. . . . In
> the money business you always need friendly connections, or friends,
> unless you're a genius, and Alfred isn't that. He's a very attractive man
> with an unattractive outlook on people.[37]

So that's it? At the close of a fifty-year family saga—ice-hearted father,
brother dead in childhood, drunk and lascivious mother, roistering college companion, uncounted clubmates, sexy and sex-driven first wife,
Mary, children including a son killed during flight training, manipulative

business partners, the gorgeous young Natalie for a mistress and second wife, the attention of a president of the United States, a world war to help manage—it comes down to having failed to make "a friendly connection"? Or did it come down to John O'Hara losing his way? Not irretrievably—rescue was always just a novella or short story away—but for the time being, certainly.

Alfred Eaton—insolent and with his self-respect "intact and possibly a little inflated," arrogant and condescending (like O'Hara regarding his hometown, reviewers, editors, and publisher)—had developed "an unattractive outlook on people." In character and author, what was most alarming about their dyspepsia was the relish they took in it. Alfred has cause for disappointment—his father prefers the memory of his dead son to the experience of the survivor, his wife betrays him, his business colleagues scheme, his mother is a loveless and unloved lush—but insufficient cause for misanthropy. O'Hara warms to the inventory of those who repulse Eaton: "Those he had learned not to trust, those who did not want to be known, the suspicious, the angry, the markedly cruel, the loud, the mean, the dirty, the self-pitying . . . the captain at "21," the traffic cop in Astor Place, the trainman on the Long Island, the septuagenarian brothers at the Racquet Club, the retired opera singer . . . the President of the United States."[38] For no one is his disdain more ungoverned than for those many sensualists whose erotic preferences differ from his own taste for the sight of "nipples show[ing] under the cashmere, revealing the nervous excitement [his son's girlfriend] was trying to cover," for breast-kissing, double entendres between the sheets, and "the lovemaking of highly experienced and adept persons."[39] A sideshow of not-quite-sufficiently-freakish freaks parade through *From the Terrace:* nymphos who can't "turn it off," "pansies" with "certain tendencies," war brides who "lapse into lesbian attachments," bisexuals (Alfred has utter contempt for "the cult of the bisexual woman"), and by now the almost inevitable perverted tutor. This time it's Dr. Jim Roper, the first Mrs. (Mary) Eaton's ex-fiancé, who corrupts her and several other central female characters by urging on them "two books, a translation from the Hindustani and another from the German, the first illustrated with line drawings."

Another alarming interest O'Hara had developed was a leering tropism for the border dividing sex from violence. During Alfred's bachelor days in New York he and Lex Porter have a party pad on Gramercy Park, where "neither of the young men always went to bed with the girl he had brought to the apartment, and they did not always stay with the same girl all night." The house policy was to "frig 'em young, treat 'em rough and tell 'em nothing."[40] More explicitly alarming was Alfred's memory of Lex from those postcollege years: "No woman who came to the Gramercy Park apartment was allowed to change her mind after she got there."[41] O'Hara's male characters since *Butterfield 8* were forever learning that knockdown battles in the bedroom—shouting, a bit of slapping, a forceful push onto the four-poster—would bring a hot blush to his mate's cheeks, with great sex ("modified rape") to follow. Gentlemen (Alfred Eaton and, in *Ourselves to Know,* Robert Millhouser) resisted the practical applications of this lesson; cads exploited the congruence.* For aversion therapy nothing serves like a session with this novel's erotic diction, in no way an advance on the language of *A Rage to Live.* The second Mrs. Eaton's first husband, a drunken lout who knows that Alfred's beating his time, challenges Natalie: "Does your thing twitch when you see his name in the *Times?*" (At a climax of *Ourselves to Know,* the shade of the hero's mother reveals to the novel's narrator through a report from the afterworld that many decades ago, sick with fever in her bedroom, she had been raped by the local preacher: "He had come to rape me. You must understand (she said) that I submitted to him rather than make a fuss. He pulled down the bedclothes and up with my nightgown and I lay there while he burned my insides with his thing."[42]

At moments like these, a reader must wonder how it can happen that a writer so alert to speech can traffic in such words as "insides" and "thing." Such failures of diction and tone are mostly confined to O'Hara's long novels, and a telling symptom of the self-indulgence encouraged by the long form is his habit in the tomes of including in telephone conversations and formal greetings the clutter of "hellos" and "very-pleased-to-meet-yous" that clot the aisles of dialogue. Alfred visits the New York apartment of his very rich Princeton classmate, Alex Porter, to meet Porter's family and eat lunch; he addresses Mrs. Porter:

---

*Even between a loving husband and wife—Devrow and Marian Budd—rough stuff is unexceptional, and in this instance inventively narrated: "He could hold her at arm's length with her feet not touching the floor; she could not span one of his biceps with two hands; he could exhaust her with his love-making, so that he was not ready when she was already spent, and his final charge into her was often an act of cruelty that she knew was unintentional and that she endured because it was his way. He was a god" (p. 126).

"How do you do?" said Alfred.

"I don't think you've met anyone, except the gentleman on my right."

"Hello, Alfred."

"Hello, Lex."

They shook hands, and it was the first time in their acquaintance that they had done so.

"This is my sister."

"How do you do?" said Alfred.

"How do you do?" said the sister.

A reader will get the idea well before Alfred is finally introduced to Lex's uncles. A master of inference in his short work, O'Hara steps all over punch lines in the tomes, explaining puns as well as anecdotes. At Princeton he spies an older girl he loves sitting on the Yale side at Palmer Stadium (a detail O'Hara got wrong, to his everlasting shame). Apart from breaking your hero's heart, how went the game, Mr. O'Hara? Glad you asked: "Yale, which had not been favored, won the game 13–7, thanks largely to Coach Shevlin and his Minnesota shift, a tricky bit of business that Shevlin had introduced at New Haven when he was brought in toward the end of the season."[43] He details which subway to ride, where it stops and which changes are to be made during a journey from Wall Street to the Racquet & Tennis Club. He gives Alfred preachy, banal, and homiletic speeches about the progress and outlook of World War II from the vantage of its middle years. (Germany will be beaten, but not without the sacrifice of men and treasure.)

He reports the state of the world and its inhabitants statistically. What percent of American women commit adultery? Learn it in *From the Terrace*. Another question, almost as burning: How many people "in the City of New York in the month of November in the year 1929" killed themselves? One hundred and nineteen, "only six more persons than had committed suicide in January of that year" of the Great Crash, "and the total for the year was 1,313."[44] Half a page of data follows, from "In 1930 there were 1,471 suicides" to "in 1934 there were 12,185 business failures" and 1,609 suicides, "the greatest number in the City's history, and the high point of a steady climb." The collage of uninflected facts is meant to show a daring narrative technique, in the experimental tradition of John Dos Passos's *U.S.A.* But the story these facts are intended to prove is an O'Hara warhorse: dial up sufficient pressure on a citizen or fictional character, and suicide is a plausible outcome.

If O'Hara's own statistics illustrate that suicide is in fact a freak outcome, his preoccupation with self-slaughter in the tomes—as an index of gravity or to punch up a plot or close a scene—had anticipated the utility of a computer macro program: key in CTRL-S and ENTER an apposite outcome. As in a dozen or so other instances, Julian English's suicide is invoked (Alfred Eaton, by farfetched coincidence, had accidentally wandered to Gibbsville and its country club the night Julian threw that drink in O'Reilly's face; Natalie's closest friend was Caroline English), diminishing its tragic weight in the Region's social history. Norma Budd, the beloved girl at the Princeton-Yale game and Alfred's first sexual partner, dies in a suicide pact with a "former Yale football star" and "outstanding polo player," a story grabbed from the headlines reporting the suicide in 1929 of Harry Crosby and Josephine Bigelow, also socially prominent. Under financial stress, a Port Johnson florist cuts his throat with his pocket knife. A hot young woman is introduced to sex by her brother, who then "hanged himself at prep school." In the tomes, many a suicide results from a failure of sexual restraint: a lover of Alfred's mother, rebuffed, "blew his brains out on a petulant impulse." Even Alfred's father, who dies of natural causes the day of his son's wedding, is press-ganged into service in the company: "It was the right and consistent moment for Samuel Eaton to die, a last protest against Alfred's going on living all those years. Samuel Eaton had not taken his own life by a suicidal act, but he had removed himself by his unwillingness to live."[45]

The revealing locution here is "the right and consistent moment" for a character—having exhausted his schematic purpose—"to die." Thus the preacher who rapes Zilph Millhouser in *Ourselves to Know* immediately hangs himself, concluding his crime with a pat punishment and solving the problem of anticlimax, of what his author could make of him next. In the same novel, a Latin teacher who is drawn sexually to Robert Millhouser hangs himself from a tree, evidently a rational if not inevitable response to temptation, let alone dishonor. And in the face of failure and the depletion of self-respect and esteem, the example who offers himself to Eaton is one Archie Busby, who throws himself in front of a subway train when his clubmates commence taking him for granted by calling on him for small favors. At the end of *From the Terrace* it is in just such a role that Alfred Eaton is left, a dead man walking.

When a novel breaks down in so many ways—fails in voice, pacing, proportion, energy of character, psychological credibility, and moral vision—it usually, as a literary work, fails utterly.* Yet, O'Hara considered *From the Terrace* his masterpiece, and there are passages in it so grand that for pages at a time it is possible to share his delusion. On hierarchies and the manifestations of deference he is observant and subtle. As a boy of eleven Alfred "had already noticed that some of the fathers and mothers of his friends would contradict themselves if they expressed views that conflicted with those of his own parents. ("Such a lovely day!" "A little too warm for my taste." "Well, yes, it is rather close.")[46] In turn, Mary's mother, Mrs. St. John, regarded from Wilmington the Eatons of Fort Johnson, or *Port* Johnson, whatever that little mill town was named: "They're nothing and nobody. The mother is a drunkard and other things beside, the father is a *nouveau-riche* war profiteer."[47]

The novel also offers several brief, almost impressionistically compressed descriptions of the consolations of long marriage, of adjustment and resignation. The sexual accommodations of Mrs. Budd to her husband have been quoted above; the settled affection between the daughter of James D. MacHardie (senior partner of Alfred Eaton's investment bank) and her husband, Creighton Duffy, is described with swift and sure daring: "She laughed a lot and smiled more. She was a jovial woman, and the quality had been brought out by Duffy in their perfect marriage. The MacHardie money had got her nothing but duty dances as a debutante, but Creighton Duffy wooed her with second helpings of ice cream and cake, and she had won him by devouring them. She became a Catholic (as she would have become a Mohammedan) because he asked her to. . . . They had each other, and it became increasingly unimportant that no one else wanted either one of them."[48]

This is a glimpse of the complex portraiture mostly missing from the tomes, the delicate willingness of O'Hara to seem surprised by his characters, a simulation of surprise credible only after a novelist's empathetic study of his inventions' quiddities. Creighton Duffy is Alfred Eaton's nemesis, a petulant and jealous man who brings Alfred low. He, too,

---

*These novels never failed commercially: *From the Terrace* sold out its first and only hardcover printing of one hundred thousand copies, and by 1966, Matthew J. Bruccoli reports, Bantam had sold two and a half million copies in paperback, together with thirteen million copies of O'Hara's other books.

exhibits sexual habits of potential interest to Havelock Ellis, but this time
O'Hara pulls back from the perverse in refusal to reduce and judge, as
he does so often elsewhere. He must, bless his soul, love Duffy's coarse
character, despite himself: "The slaps and ticklings that stimulated them
in their lovemaking had never gone past the danger point, and when
lovemaking had exhausted them they slept like enormous, untroubled
infants until time for their next feeding."

Writing about the sexual impulses and excesses of the characters of
Butterfield 8 and *Ourselves to Know,* Arthur Mizener rightly reproaches
O'Hara for his inclination always toward the extreme: "a tabloid newspaper's alternately sentimental and sensational view of life, a view that
characteristically takes extreme forms of behavior—especially of sexual
behavior—and unusual circumstances as typical."[49] A reader's confidence in O'Hara's judgment of individuals is frequently shaken; as
Mizener notes, "everything conceivable happens occasionally," but to
represent molestation and sexual violence and eccentricity of taste as
being inevitable—as if, behind closed doors, all is abuse and seduction—
is "the basic stuff of sexual fantasy, of pornography." Although Mizener
might have meant his dismay to have a moral component, my interest is
in the awful toll that O'Hara's indulgence of "unusual circumstance as
typical" exacted on his novels. Aristotle makes sense, I believe, in his
credo on this matter, that in make-believe a plausible impossibility is to
be preferred over an implausible possibility.

O'Hara owes no apology for his management of crowds, in contrast to
individuals. He does especially well in *From the Terrace* with the customs and economy of work in a mill town. The following passage prepares for the announcement of the birth on August 21 in the year 1894 of
Samuel Eaton's elder son:

> When the wind was right, that is to say when there was not much of it,
> and the day was clear and not too warm and not too cool, the whistle on
> the roof of the 18-inch mill at the Eaton Iron & Steel Company could
> easily be heard over a radius of two and a half miles. . . . Normally it was
> audible everywhere in the town of Port Johnson, a fact which was a
> cause of some annoyance to some of the citizens, but was no accident
> on the part of the owners of the Company or the borough council or the
> substantial men of the town. In installing their whistle the Company
> officials had had as their principal intent the summoning of the hands to

work in the morning and their release at the end of the working day, but in 1890, when the whistle was first being seriously considered, Port Johnson was without adequate fire warning. . . . A few citizens, who lived near the E. I. & S., objected to the whistle . . . but their objections were answered with the comment that it was for the common good, that they would get used to it, and to those who more persistently objected went the suggestion that they move elsewhere. . . .

As the whistle became a part of the daily-except-Sunday life of the community it was, as predicted, something the citizens got used to and in many cases depended upon. It was not advisable to use the whistle as a standard time signal where railroad-watch accuracy was essential, since the whistle had been known to be a full minute ahead of time in the morning and as much as two minutes off at the end of the working day. But for most citizens and their children in the public and parochial schools it was a convenience. The whistle was not always blown synchronously with the tolling of the Angelus by Henry Heilbrunner, sexton of St. John's German Catholic Church, who rang his bell in conformity with the time shown on his own silver pocket watch. It became a common saying among the citizens that "The Pope says it's six o'clock but Eaton says it's only five fifty eight."[50]

When the whistle blasted unexpectedly, "it was not a welcome sound," usually announcing fire or perhaps—if it was the colliery whistle over in Lyons or Gibbsville—a cave-in. Steel mill accidents were ugly enough, as Samuel Eaton discusses with a friend: "Did you ever see a man get his arm caught in the blooming-mill? Or *hear* him? I did. I got a couple of one-armed men on the payroll from that kind of an accident. And could I ever tell them that it happened through carelessness? Their own God damn carelessness? Huh. They'd lynch me."[51] But sometimes when the Eaton whistle sounded off, it was not to announce an accident, to call the weary to work, or to warn of fire. The E. I. & S. whistle also celebrates the beginning of the Peace concluding the Great War. This is one of the tomes' bravura productions, a gathering of the Port Johnson tribes on the order of the opening scene of *A Rage to Live* and, in *Ourselves to Know,* the homecoming to Lyons of the tattered Grand Army of the Republic. The Eaton whistle "made it official for Port Johnson. There were those in the crowd who believed that Eaton's had received word direct from Washington, if not from Foch's railway carriage."[52] The passages that follow use this joyful letting-go to dramatize crowd psychology, the dangerous edge of celebration, and this encourages an organic account of how the mill town has grown during the war years, pumping more money to "fast-spending men" unused to having it, attracting whores and swindlers, violence and institutional corruption. These scenes draw on O'Hara's experience as a newspaper reporter as well as his proven genius for the subtle social frictions of interdependent groups.

Ourselves to Know is principally about a scandal in a small town. Robert Millhouser, after a commitment to unwholesome solitude, meets, is seduced by, and marries a teenager, Hedda, one of O'Hara's most effective illustrations of sexual pathology. Mix the Bad Seed with Lolita and here's your cute little Hedda. She sleeps around, sneers, abuses the help, torments and publicly humiliates her fifty-one-year-old husband until he can no longer tolerate the shame and shoots her in her sleep. He goes to prison, is released, and in his old age hires a Princeton student and fellow townsman to write his sad story, which is tied off with an ugly bow: during World War II, the amanuensis, Gerald Higgins, dwells on Millhouser's death "to take my mind off Frances and the stories that got back to me."[53] But the passages from this novel I want to remember are the narrator's confessions of euphoria as he writes, of falling into the dreams of his characters, of scouting them like a detective and—more nobly—transporting himself into them. Higgins has come to love one of his subjects as "one can love a character in a novel who becomes a part of one's company of living acquaintance."[54] And to tell exactly what a biographer dreams will happen when he presumes to enter a subject's life, here's Higgins on Robert Millhouser: "Sometimes I could hardly wait to see what I would do next, and I believe that during those days I would have answered to his name."[55]

The tomes—the big four—are not successful. As a biographer longing to enter such a state that I would answer to John O'Hara's name, do I wish he'd not written them? Even one brash enough for the biographical enterprise knows better than to presume to dictate the dreams of another. Do I wish I'd never read them? Like everyone, I've walked out of stupid movies and noisy plays. I've shut many a novel at the half-hour mark. *From the Terrace* cost me a couple of weeks. There were times, reading its densely printed pages, when I was distracted by calculations of just how many weeks remain to someone in early old age. Nevertheless, for the Duffys' marriage and for Eaton's whistle, O'Hara's debt-free to me, not that he'd have reason to care.

6. A LOCAL HABITATION
AND A NAME

A year before he moved to Princeton, John O'Hara was invited to give a talk to the Elizabethan Club, Yale's undergraduate literary society. This occasion stimulated in him a frenzy of name-dropping and ass-kissing. Imagine *Ten North Frederick*'s Joseph Chapin one interview away from being named the Republican presidential candidate for 1934. Imagine John O'Hara within reach of an honorary degree. He offered his typescripts to the Yale library (excepting *Appointment in Samarra*'s, which, he assured interested persons, would be left to their university by Adele Lovett, "whose husband is one of Yale's most distinguished alumni, a member of this club").[1] To the speaking invitation from Herman Liebert of the Yale library, O'Hara responded that he had "just within the hour returned from Hobe Sound, Florida, where I was the guest of, I imagine, an old Elizabethan Club member, Philip Barry."

(The ambiguity of "I imagine" 's floating reference is a symptom of his disorienting ebullience.) He then alludes to his previous experience as a speaker at Exeter's Lantern Club (of which the president, as he specifies, was "young Michael Forrestal"; that would be the son of, I imagine, James), assures Liebert that "almost any time would be okay," and, in response to mention of an honorarium, he tut-tuts: "As to fee and expenses, if you know anything about me you know how I feel about Yale, and I certainly could not take any money from my friend Gilbert Troxell's club."[2] (Troxell was curator of American literature in Yale's library collections; O'Hara hoped he might engineer that honorary degree.)

The event was not a success. O'Hara had hoped to ad-lib charmingly, posed before a crackling fire. Instead he designed a breezy oration— "Writing, What's in It for Me?"—complete unto rehearsed hand and eye gestures. In it he referred to his income tax burden, his Duesenberg automobile, Lake Placid and Hobe Sound, Oxford,* an acquaintance "whose family really were up there in the chips. I don't mean *one* lousy million. I mean Big, Big. . . . He had TEN cigarette lighters. He had *thirty* pairs of shoes."[3] He referred to his friends Fitzgerald, Hemingway, Steinbeck, and Faulkner. He divulged that he hadn't gone to Yale and wished he had. He conceded that his father had not gone to Yale either, but to "Penn in the days when there was a Big Four." He allowed that he'd expected to win the 1934 Pulitzer Prize for *Appointment in Samarra* and knew which Monday to be out of town, for modesty's sake, when the prize was announced. (It went, O'Hara complained, to a novel about "an old lady who chewed tobacco and said God damn.")† He managed to allude to Cole Porter—"one of the founders of the Elizabethan Club," the "only man ever" to have "resigned from Skull and Bones"[4]— without naming him.

An index of O'Hara's peculiar interest in higher education was his enrollment the following autumn in Columbia's General School of Education, registering for a course in American history. He quit after a week,

---

*O'Hara was as promiscuous as Jay Gatsby with his references to Oggsford and less frequently to Cambridge, whose nonexistent concentration in Greats he confused with Oxford's (*literææ humaniores*), a first-class pass in which field was then calculated the highest honor attainable in the university's curriculum. I know, who cares? O'Hara would.

†Caroline Miller's *Lamb in His Bosom.*

but not before purchasing a Columbia University plaque that he then mounted on the wall of his Princeton study.

Princeton—generally the final two syllables in that Big Three word *harvardyale'n'princeton*—got O'Hara. He specified why to Gilbert and Jane Troxell, who had written to wonder whether husbands and wives really used the language of O'Hara's gamier recent novels:

> First of all, the name of my novel is A Rage to Live. A Rage for Living is the way Noel Coward would have taken liberties with Alexander Pope. . . . The news with us . . . is a kind of admission, a confession: we are forsaking New York and are going to live in Princeton. Yes, Princeton. It is not that Princeton has made me a better offer, but that Yale has made no offer at all. And after [Yale-connected] Dr. [Henry Seidel] Canby's remark at a Book of the Month Club meeting that he considered [*A Rage to Live*] "vulgar," I'm far from sure that I shall entrust the MS to Yale library. It's just possible that after all these years of blind devotion, I may be wrong about Yale,* or I may have been wrong about myself—secretly a Princeton admirer throughout.[5]

In fact, as O'Hara explained to the Troxells, he was drawn to a university town, and among such Princeton is as attractive as any, perched foliaceously midway between Philadelphia and New York, which he had decided—having experienced the quiet of Quogue—he was happier out of than in. "It is time I made '21' a restaurant instead of a career." More-

---

*Lili Pell Whitmer, a companion to Wylie O'Hara after Belle's death, asked Yale president Kingman Brewster at a Fairfield County fundraiser why Yale hadn't offered O'Hara an honorary degree. "Because he wanted it too much," Brewster said. He wouldn't quit wanting it. In a 1954 *Trenton Times-Advertiser* column, O'Hara admitted to bitterness and envy when Yale—"I had always spoken well of the place and of most of its alumni"—treated him like a New Haven "town girl . . . all right to play around with during the school year, but at Commencement the Yale Fellows always had a date with Thurber." Still: "If Yale wants me, it knows where to reach me." Bruccoli remarks that O'Hara was so "deeply hurt" by Yale's indifference that "he wrote a bitter letter to the *Yale Alumni Magazine*" in 1962, the year before Kingman Brewster—who'd known him since his New York courtship of Margaretta Archbald—became Yale's president. With that letter his ship, scuttled, sank. When I was an undergraduate at Princeton during the late 1950s and early 1960s it was a staple of sneering gossip among professors of the English department that O'Hara—who was nothing if not generous—was angling (unavailingly) for an honorary degree by piling typescripts on the stoop of Firestone Library. Even then I understood that the envious condescension of this gossip was a worse ignominy than O'Hara's avidity for trophies.

over, Wylie suffered from asthma, exacerbated by city dust. Five years after the move O'Hara told readers of his *Collier's* column that he lived in Princeton "because I like the sports" and because it is "comfortable" for a writer to have a research library at hand. "However, I've spent much more time in Palmer Stadium than in the book pit."

The O'Haras rented a comfortable house at 18 College Road West, across the street from the fairways of the Springdale Golf Club, a block and a bit distant from the "Dinky" depot (a railroad station built to harmonize with the adjoining campus's architectural pretensions), a tolerable walk from Nassau Street and downhill from the soaring, gothic Graduate College. In a neighborhood of grand federal and colonial houses, 18 College Road West—like its neighbor at number 20, into which the O'Haras moved a year later—was modest in scale and provenance, a gray prefab. The move, encouraged by Belle on behalf of John's work and serenity and health, was meant to be an expression of reserve. But of course the arrival of a celebrated writer in so tight a community was not destined to go unremarked.

Princeton University as an institution chose to respond to O'Hara's propinquity by its summa-level studious ignorance of him. He was never invited to teach a class or to read or lecture to students. It is a mark of his equanimity that despite such a frank insult to his pride he nonetheless treated as good friends several members of the university faculty and

---

That avidity was relentless. After Yale let him down, then Princeton, he schemed with Bennett Cerf to have Hiram Haydn, Cerf's Random House colleague, suggest to the provost of Rutgers (O'Hara's neighbor up Route 1) that the worthy author be given an honorary membership in Phi Beta Kappa. As O'Hara wrote Haydn, "I would love to have that key . . . if I had gone to college I probably would have made Phi Bete the hard way" (John O'Hara, "Letter to Hiram Haydn," Correspondence [Columbia University Butler Library: Rare Books and Manuscripts, 1956], Bennett Cerf Papers [17 January]). Ten days later Haydn wrote to Provost Mason Gross at Rutgers that during "a general desultory discussion . . . not too long ago, [John O'Hara] spoke with a quite surprising wistfulness about Phi Beta Kappa. To be sure, he did not attend college" (Hiram Haydn, "Letter to Mason Gross," Correspondence [Columbia University Butler Library: Rare Books and Manuscripts, 1956], Bennett Cerf Papers [27 January]). Evidently, for the State University of New Jersey this was a disqualifying impediment.

He gave his papers to Penn State, and then discovered that Penn State doesn't bestow honorary degrees. Finally, in 1964, American International College in Springfield, Massachusetts, tried to do the right thing. As he explained to the readers of one of his many columns whining like a Rodney Dangerfield bit—*no respect, I don't get no respect*—he chartered a plane to fly to the ceremony, but bad weather closed in and American International College "wanted me in person; no show, no degree in absentia." They gave the degree instead to Arlene Francis, of *What's My Line* (John O'Hara, *My Turn* [New York: Random House, 1966], p. 197).

administration, and kept to himself how bruised he must have felt. In an unpublished 1963 letter to John K. Hutchens, quoted by Frank Mac-Shane, O'Hara described a literary conference he had attended at Princeton soon after moving there. The professors "got to talking about Moll Flanders and James T. Farrell, et al., and after two hours of it I thought they sounded like a bunch of prep school boys talking about fucking. They knew all about it, and they knew absolutely nothing about it from experience. They were *dirty*, with their little chuckles and knowing allusions."

Neither, apparently, did he take out his contempt on students. John McPhee, in 1952 the undergraduate editor of the *Princeton Tiger*, found the nerve to ask O'Hara to contribute to the humor and literary magazine. Even recently—perhaps especially recently—McPhee was rueful as well as amused at his presumption in cadging from a celebrated professional a free piece, but that's what he got. The story, "The Favor," concerns an accident following a game at the Yale Bowl; encouraged by the writer's courtesy, McPhee said he'd like to change the venue to Princeton's Palmer Stadium, and telephoned O'Hara to ask whether this trifling change would be acceptable. "No," was the answer.

O'Hara got for his generosity a Revere silver bowl, inscribed *With thanks for The Favor.* McPhee delivered this gift to 20 College Road West, and O'Hara, clearly touched, asked whether McPhee might like to join him in a drink.

"I was only what? Twenty-one. I said sure I would."

O'Hara led his guest out to a terrace—*the* terrace, the one from which the big novel came*—excused himself, then returned with "an old-fashioned glass big enough to hold a softball. This was a *bucket* of booze."

The O'Haras were invited during their first year or so in Princeton to more dinner parties than they welcomed, and these often went badly. At J. Robert Oppenheimer's house O'Hara quarreled, about educational theory, with the nephew of Thorstein Veblen "who wrote," as O'Hara remembered later, "an overestimated book called *The Theory of the Leisure Class.*"[6] At another Princeton dinner party, Matthew J. Bruccoli

---

*On the other hand, McPhee has conceded that other terraces have been hallowed or blamed for *From the Terrace:* "Wherever there's a terrace, he wrote his novel on it."

reports that the wife of the *New York Times* bigwig Arthur Krock declared to O'Hara that *A Rage to Live* was a "fraud."[7] To such belligerence he would respond without forbearance, drinking till he was drunk, then glaring or snorting or turning his back—which often seemed to have a lurid target pinned to it. Soon he had a reputation for difficulty, though—as ever—not without exception. At a dinner at his house he had seated on his right a friend's new wife, a woman from the South who'd been warned to agree with whatever her host opined. Nervous, she drank too much, then opined her own self. "Mr. O'Hara, I have to tell you, your books are just trash. Whenever someone sends me one, I toss it right into the fireplace." A long silence commenced as guests stared at their salad. O'Hara made a noise, then a choking sound. He was laughing. "He knew a pugnacious drunk when he met one," in the recollection of Kate Bramwell.

Belle O'Hara undertook to monitor the cone of her husband's volcanic pride, vigilant to whatever—well-meant teasing or civil dispute—might provoke it to blow. Finis Farr tells of an instance when Kate, whom she'd known since St. Timothy's and who was her best friend in Princeton, had a "lively discussion" with O'Hara at her house one night before dinner, "to the point where he seemed to find it unwelcome." As they walked to the table, "Belle said to her old friend, in a low voice between clenched teeth, 'Kate—stop—baiting—John.' "[8] And Kate, assuredly, was not an enemy. Her fondness for this "kind" man was unreserved, and she explained to me in mortifying detail an episode when she had borrowed from him a pair of letters O'Hara and John Steinbeck had exchanged on the occasion of the Nobel Prize. These she took as show-and-tell to a reading-club meeting, and mislaid them. Retracing her steps to no avail, and unable to find them, distraught and terrified of her friend's peevishness ("and I don't scare easily"), she tried to enlist Random House to approach Steinbeck for a "replacement letter," though she couldn't imagine what words such a document might contain. Finally, she confessed to O'Hara what had happened.* "John was absolutely wonderful, superb, understood how awful I felt."

She also wanted to convey that she had been instrumental in seducing the O'Haras to Princeton, since it had been a weekend at her house that inspired them to look for a house of their own to rent. "They came as

---

*In fact she had folded the letters within a book, and long afterward discovered and returned them.

houseguests to our place on Stockton Street, where the guest rooms were small as closets. 'I see you don't encourage visitors to linger,' John said when he saw his and Belle's quarters."

Belle had always been drawn (like Pet before her) to the theater; she had acted at St. Timothy's, and it was one of her pleasures to go with Kate Bramwell to New York to attend plays and operas (she especially cherished Wagner). Owing to her congenital heart defect, Belle was meant not to exercise, but when Kate and other Princeton friends played tennis near the graduate college, she would venture onto the courts to hit a few balls, and her companions would rebuke her, "Get off the court! You know you shouldn't do this." Belle even trusted Kate with details of her condition that she hid from her husband.

O'Hara suffered his own disorder. During an August 1953 trip from Quogue to Pennsylvania he stopped in New York to change trains. He ordered lunch at "21" but was not up to eating it. Having enjoyed O'Hara-sized cocktails the previous night, he at first assumed that his malaise was a hangover. Riding in a taxi to Pennsylvania Station he decided to return to Quogue, then realized he was too ill to travel at all and asked to be taken to East 63rd Street, to Mrs. Wylie's apartment. The cab driver had reasoned that his fare was drunk (which he was not), and conveyed this to the doorman, for whom the sight of a stumbling O'Hara was a sight he had seen before. He left his enfeebled charge in the otherwise deserted apartment, where O'Hara would've died on the bathroom floor, forty-eight years old, had not Belle's sister Winnie come to the apartment and chanced upon him. O'Hara had vomited blood from a gastric ulcer and was ghost-white. His sister-in-law summoned a doctor, who in turn summoned an ambulance. On the way to the Harkness Pavilion of Columbia Presbyterian Hospital (the Knickerbocker Club of Manhattan's medical centers), O'Hara continued to vomit blood into a basin, and said to Winnie—who held the basin—"Aren't I the busy body?"*

---

*In one version—an extended and dramatized account sponsored by a fanciful family member—the doctor had arrived at the apartment, then removed O'Hara's vomit-fouled necktie to his office to analyze the stain, then concluded that the vomit contained blood, then—busy body indeed—rushed back to the Wylie apartment, and called for an ambulance.

O'Hara's youngest sibling, Kathleen O'Hara Fuldner, knows what caused the catastrophic malady: curry in a hamburger. This she might've concluded from the anti-curry-in-hamburger diet her brother practiced thereafter, an extreme version of what has come to be called "comfort food," creamed chicken and creamed corn and soft eggs and such.

His stomach lining was perforated. Having hemorrhaged grossly from a blood vessel eaten away by acid, he required liberal transfusions to return his blood pressure to a sufferable level. He understood what had become of him, and his doctors were happy to spell it out in blunt language: if he continued to drink he'd die. This he assuredly did not want to do. F. Scott Fitzgerald had drawn down his physical resources so low that his heart quit in 1940. Five years later—just before he died—Robert Benchley was asked about his health: "Except for an occasional heart attack, I feel as young as I ever did."[9] A few weeks later he bled to death, for O'Hara a stunning blow. (Forty friends and acquaintances assembled outside Benchley's hospital room offering to donate blood.) Many years later, in a *Newsweek* interview (June 3, 1963), O'Hara referred to that death in apocalyptic terms: "The party was over."

In keeping with the manners of his time—a compound of Benchley's reckless insouciance and Hemingway's grace under pressure—O'Hara faced his unsure future with casual throwaway lines. From the hospital he wrote to Joseph W. (Pat) Outerbridge, a Princeton neighbor who had become and remained his closest friend. Outerbridge had gone on the wagon, and in August of 1953 O'Hara climbed "up there on the cart" with him. "The only alternative is the glass-sided wagon with the six white horses. . . . A hell of a way for booze to treat me after I've been so kind to it."[10] Two weeks later, recuperating in Quogue, O'Hara got the news that Pet had died, lonely and unhappy, of complications subordinate to dipsomania.

Late that autumn Kate Bramwell detected that Belle's health was failing. They were at a lunch party with friends when she noticed that her friend's skirt was unzipped, an uncharacteristic negligence that Kate quietly drew to her attention. Belle confided that she was retaining fluid, an edema symptomatic of congestive heart failure; moreover, she was having difficulty breathing, and using rouge to camouflage her pallor. "My heart's not working." Her friend asked what her cardiologist advised, and Belle admitted that she hadn't made an appointment: she was busy taking care of John and attending to Wylie's school schedule. (After school Belle had often picked up her daughter and taken her to the movies, where she could rest her heart. They were agreed in their tastes, and utterly "ga-ga," in Wylie's memory, for *King Solomon's Mines* and its swashbuckling male lead, Stewart Granger.)* She hadn't told her husband what was happening—evidently he hadn't noticed, or perhaps hadn't known what to make of what he saw. It was decided that Belle would take refuge at the Gardiners' house while Wylie was at school and John was sleeping—according to his custom—till the crack of noon, and Kate would prop her up on pillows and help her relax. She knew she was dying, Belle told her. Her daughter was only eight, and how could she understand?

The crisis occurred during a New Year's party at a house on Nassau Street. Winter coats were to be put in a bedroom on the second floor. Belle insisted on hanging hers downstairs on the bannister, but when John wanted to leave the party her coat was nowhere to be found. Kate realized that she didn't want to "make a fuss" and so began "hauling herself upstairs," but this was more than she could manage. Halfway up she turned back, and O'Hara—seeing the anguish on her face—cried out, "My god!"

He took Belle immediately to Princeton Hospital, and her brother Robert came from New York to examine her. The gravity of her condition was not immediately clear, because after a few days her doctors assured O'Hara that she could soon come home. Kate Bramwell and her husband, Henry Gardiner, encouraged by this news, flew to Bermuda for a holiday. January 9, a week and a day after Belle's distress on the stairway, a Princeton family doctor phoned after dinner and told O'Hara that his wife had died. Witnesses agree that he let out a cry, what Frank MacShane characterizes as "a terrible noise,"[11] and called Wylie to him, and immediately told her the unspeakable news.

Memories have not been kind to the initial messenger. Kate Bramwell refers to that doctor—who was also her doctor—as "an idiot." He arrived at 20 College Road West carrying what one witness has described as "a ridiculous little parcel" of Belle's odds and ends. "It was pathetic." The energy of this scorn is puzzling: the doctor came in person, bearing what items his patient had left behind. What was the fault? Apart from the detail that a beloved woman died under his care, the avuncular physician

---

*A year and a half after Belle's death Wylie accompanied her father to California during a screenwriting stint, and dreamboat Stewart Granger was produced as a surprise guest at a Pacific Palisades party celebrating her tenth birthday. "I was mortified," she remembered, referring to the exquisite agony of being an object of scrutiny and conjecture.

evidently malpracticed condescension. He literally patted the sudden widower on the back and declared, "What you need is a good stiff drink." O'Hara said, "That's the last thing that I need." The doctor, feeling now a chilly draft, made ready to depart, but not before offering, fatuously, "Is there anything I can do to help?" O'Hara, capping his fury, said, Yes, why yes, there was. Wylie's toy poodle Straus seemed to have a cold; on his way out might the doctor be good enough to examine him?*

Grief's grip tightened the circle of the initiated, all outsiders and all visitors but a few blackballed. What was cruel to the doctor was useful, if not wholesome, for those abandoned by Belle's vanishing. Speaking through the voice of his alter ego Jim Malloy in the novella *We're Friends Again,* O'Hara hallows Belle, adhering to the dates and duration of their connection: "I met a fine girl, and in December of that year we were married and we stayed married for sixteen years, until she died. As the Irish would say, she died on me, and it was the only unkind thing she ever did to anyone."[12] This eulogy, dignified by musical and emotional precision, was composed five or six years after her death, but in the immediate aftermath such rhetorical consolations were unavailable. In 1969 O'Hara told Don A. Schanche (and *Esquire*'s readers) how it had been in January of 1954: "That was the one great tragedy of my life. If I'd been drinking then, I probably would have committed suicide. But I had a nine-year-old [sic] daughter, and I said to myself, 'Here I am. My wife has just died. I've had a near fatal illness. What shall I do about this child?' "[13]

What he did about, with, and for Wylie came as natural as heartbeat: he loved her and had let her know as much—without obliging her to be grateful, or even to acknowledge, that he relished her company. And he did this in the fondest way warmth can be expressed—daily, habitually, cumulatively. Her earliest memories are not of pain or bewilderment or fear but of her father's predictable tenderness. On her third birthday he had taken her to the circus, riding downtown on the upper deck of a Fifth Avenue bus. This was Flag Day, and her father assured her that the flags had been hoisted to celebrate her passage. At the circus they sat "of

---

*How can I help? A narrow border divides generosity from solipsism. In *An Unfinished Woman* Lillian Hellman tells that when Alan Campbell died, a woman asked the same of his widow, Dorothy Parker. "Get me a new husband," Parker answered. How vulgar, the altruist scolded. "I'm sorry," Parker said. "Then run down to the corner and get me a ham and cheese on rye."

course" in the front row, and when a gorilla or more probably a clown in a gorilla suit approached "I freaked." Wylie was so panicked that she had to be taken home to the New York apartment, where she fled to the bathroom to further escape danger. Her father came to her there, and sat on the bathtub. She remembers him taking a silver cigarette case from his jacket pocket and stuffing cigarettes in his ears and up his nose and a few in his mouth, making her laugh "till my fear was washed away."

Asked whether her father had ever seemed intimidating, she laughed, as though the question were as ridiculous as nostrils sprouting cigarettes.

"He was unscary, my baby boy."

This is a tender woman, ferociously angered by cruelty. Kate Bramwell has a vivid memory of Wylie, as a little girl in Princeton, visiting her house with a school friend. Mrs. Gardiner's son was dyslexic and he had written an essay on *Ethan Frome,* now framed and hung on a wall, that by his mother's lights was "very good but badly misspelled." The companion, noticing it, began mocking its phonetic approximations, until Wylie commanded, "Don't laugh! It's *very* good."

Sensitivity unaccompanied by vanity or self-importance encourages compassion and good character, but Wylie's skin—as thin as her father's—left her exposed to vicissitudes and vulnerable to bruises. As vigorously as she laughs, so effusively does she weep, and this reflex too—which she understands to be congenital—causes her to laugh. "Don't mind this. Don't pay any attention. Here go the waterworks," she said, weeping copiously as she remembered from her girlhood a charged family scene on the occasion of her mother assuring her that "I love you more than I love anyone in the whole, wide world." Wylie, competitive for affection, had pestered her mother to repeat this to her father, to Belle's husband, whereupon O'Hara "was devastated," so much so that he suggested perhaps they preferred him to leave them alone with each other.

Remembering this more than forty years later awakened pain referred from father to daughter. Wylie described herself, without excessive condemnation, as having been a "bad" little girl. No contemporary accounts support such a judgment, though others have described tantrums and her clinging—even jealous—attachment to her mother. She resisted with special fierceness Belle's final stay in the hospital, and it would not be the oddest belief if she had grown up convinced that she hadn't resisted fiercely enough. "Soft, vulnerable, and insecure" is the trinity of adjectives she uses to describe the susceptibilities of both her father and herself. Such shared exposure might have been an invitation for the cruelty sometimes fed by familiarity, a meanly lifted eyebrow or smirk of recognition; but between Wylie and John O'Hara it triggered latitude and acts of guardianship. The notorious grudge-nourisher became with her a quick forgiver. When, as a kid, she felt ashamed for having done something "bad," her father would pooh-pooh the offense, dismissing it as "water under the bridge."

Of course nothing in the world could possibly console a man for the death of his adored wife. And what must this have been like for an eight-year-old girl who'd been especially close to her mother? After her mother died, Wylie protected herself with ceremonies and customs. She wore a baseball cap at all times "to keep bad thoughts out," as she told Mary Leigh Pell (now Mrs. Robert F. Whitmer III), who left Smith College to become Wylie's companion.

Mary Leigh—"Lili"—had known the O'Haras in Quogue, where she summered with her family. Her father, the Reverend Walden Pell II, an Episcopal minister and the headmaster of St. Andrew's School in Delaware, had rowed at Princeton and Oxford, where he was a Rhodes scholar. (In 1933 O'Hara had boasted to F. Scott Fitzgerald that he had "some remote kinship" with the historic Pell family of New York, but this was surely wistful and probably fanciful.) In the winter of 1952, during a Princeton University dance weekend, Belle had asked Lili if there were anyone suitable in Quogue who might care for Wylie during the summer. Having searched and failed to find, Lili reported as much to Belle, then added, "Maybe I could do it," to which Belle responded, "Oh, I thought you'd never get the point."

That summer and the next worked out well for the summer sitter and her charge. (Lili has noted, self-mockingly, that O'Hara enjoyed the circumstance of having Walden Pell's daughter "as a slave.") This was not a hardship post. The house the O'Haras had bought on Dune Road, east of town (and where Wylie O'Hara Doughty, her children, and husband Scott spend summer vacations) is the Platonic form of a Beach Cottage. Long and low, the house is exquisitely simple, with rooms of generous dimensions and a fieldstone fireplace. There's a sunny deck fronting the Atlantic and the interior, of unpainted wood, is cool and dark.

Lili Pell dubbed Wylie "the Play Queen" for her regal shyness, and remembers with a smile the young girl's impishness. The author was not to be interrupted when he was working in a bedroom large enough to double as a study; the two would sometimes crouch beneath his window, singing one of Belle's favorites—"When I Fall in Love," or one of their own, "Glowworm"—increasing the volume until he stopped typing and peered out, wagging his finger, pretending not to see them and muttering menacingly, "I can hear you there."

Even then, Wylie remembers, she and her father were "silly and goofy together." But at Quogue he was also protective, especially at the edge of the ocean thirty or so yards from their front door. While Wylie swam, guarded by Lili, he would stand on the beach fully dressed, street shoes and all, with a megaphone such as crew coaches and cheerleaders use, and if, to torment him, his little girl ventured toward the deeps, he'd bellow through it, "Come back! Come . . . back . . . in!" His daughter remembers his gallantry when a beach ball, a favored toy, blew into the sea and he waded in—tricked out in plus-four golfing tweeds—to retrieve it.

The O'Haras' alloy of stubbornness and vulnerability attracted Lili, who was midway through her sophomore year at Smith when Belle died. After the funeral service organized by Kate Bramwell at Trinity Church on Stockton Street, Lili was with a small group at 20 College Road West when Wylie took her aside and said, "Something's got to happen here." Both the diction and the sentiment seem precocious for a child, but Wylie understood that her father needed help, and that she did. The following day the cortege traveled to Quogue, where Belle was buried; Kate consoled O'Hara that her friend would never have let herself die if he and Wylie weren't strong enough to make it on their own. This was a compassionate speculation, but Lili Pell felt obliged to lend a hand; she told her parents that she wanted to leave Smith to take care of Wylie, and to her surprise her father—a lifelong academic—agreed to support this magnanimous gesture, which might have seemed—even for an idealistic college student trained in Christian charity—compulsively quixotic.

Lili's mother arranged that she live a ten-minute walk away in a respectable widow's boarding house, which was near enough to Albert Einstein, her Mercer Street neighbor, to shout *Howdy*. O'Hara offered to pay her twenty-five dollars per week, and she began work at once. She'd arrive at the household early enough to join Wylie for breakfast, prepared by a live-in housekeeper and cook, then would drive Wylie less than a mile to school at Miss Fine's, the most brightly polished of Princeton's finishing schools, and return to 20 College Road West to order food and plan menus. O'Hara, once an enthusiast of lamb chops, was now the victim of his wretched teeth; he favored mushy food; and now—intimidated by his recent ulcer crisis—he was adamant that spinach be creamed, eggs be poached (firm whites but pliant yolks), toast be crustless, and top round be ground. His preferred entree was a hefty helping of buttered mashed potatoes, stimulated by a sprinkle of paprika.

He would rise in time for lunch and lounge about in his pajamas, reading several newspapers (New York and Trenton) before Lili picked up Wylie at Miss Fine's, often bringing her home with friends, of whom there was no dearth. The girls made a boisterous gang—self-styled "the Purples," as "it was necessary," in Lili's recollection, for members to wear articles of clothes "of that color." The kids would charge around, pretty much ignoring the father in his sleepwear, and he tolerated all this with amused resignation. One of Wylie's closest friends then was Patience Outerbridge, daughter of O'Hara's great friend Pat, and she recalls finding nothing remarkable about a man dressed at teatime in his pajamas; adults were enigmas, and one puzzle was as plausible as the next. She remembers that O'Hara often treated the girls as though they were campers, toasting marshmallows for them, and for himself, in the fireplace.

Lili attempted, hopelessly, to impose on the household a version of the discipline she'd learned at her father's boarding school. If she badgered Wylie to do her homework, O'Hara would instruct her to leave the child in peace, concerned that upsetting her near dinnertime would have a baneful influence on Wylie's digestive process. At dinner he would sometimes lecture, on whatever arcanum held his immediate attention. "Did you know," he might ask, "that the most toxic of all mammal bites is that of homo sapiens?"* After dinner the peculiar and ephemeral knowledge that was an O'Hara signature was put to use at Scrabble. The father feigned outrage at Wylie's resourceful use of tiles

---

*A witness to the solemnity with which O'Hara expostulated his certitudes remembers him from a Princeton dinner party at about this time. Visiting from Washington, she had not met him before but had heard much gossip and did not realize that he had quit drinking. So she assumed he was alcoholically stubborn, exhaustingly exhaustive, tiresomely tireless in his debate with a fellow guest *exactly* how long—expressed as a ratio of other racetrack distances, expressed also as an absolute unit of furlongs—the Triple Crown course at Belmont was. His antagonist, a retired CIA officer—dropping the name Vanderbilt, owner of Native Dancer—made a glancing reference to the distance

T-N-S-O to form a four-point colloquialism for a nasal excretion. Then the television would be lit, Steve Allen regarded, the gossip of the city exchanged, and at last Wylie would be tucked in, Lili sent home to Mercer Street and O'Hara back to work.

A couple of weeks before Belle died, he had accepted the offer of a Princeton friend, James Kerney, editor and publisher of the *Trenton Times-Advertiser,* to write a weekly book column, under the rubric "Sweet and Sour," for the Sunday edition. These little essays, for which he agreed to be paid only one hundred dollars apiece, were to be informal, on whatever topic he was pleased to address. He began the thirteenth of these columns by conceding the expansive latitude (and wandering course) of the previous pieces: "It's not the first time that has happened. What has happened? That I have begun a Sunday message with every intention of preaching on one topic, and almost immediately get diverted to something else. Heaven knows I am not at a loss for things to write about. Due to the tolerance of my boss—and a rather shabby trick I played in getting him to agree that I could write about authors, which means everybody—I'll never run out of things to say. My first aim is to entertain myself, thereby presumably entertaining you."[14]

He exercised this license with abandon, promising his readers in his first column to reward his friends and punish his enemies in the extended world of publishing, writing, and maybe—if it suited him—reading. Not that he troubled himself to read systematically for this column, in the way that some wretched reviewer might. As with "Appointment with O'Hara," his biweekly column for *Collier's,* and in anticipation of his disastrous "My Turn" in *Newsday,* which endured fifty-three weeks of the author's logical abuse, political cocksureness, rhetorical excess, and feral social appetite beginning in late 1964, this was John O'Hara at his dismissive and contemptuous worst. As Sheldon Grebstein, a sympathetic early biographer, wrote in 1966, reading these columns "one waits in dreadful anticipation of O'Hara's next blunder. . . . He is simultaneously embarrassing and infuriating in his vainglorious-

---

as eleven furlongs, a mile and three eighths. No, O'Hara correctly insisted: the Belmont Stakes was run on a course of twelve furlongs, a mile and one half. In fact, he added, till 1873 the punishing course was a mile and five eighths! The ex-CIA-man said this could not be so; he knew what he knew. Well then, O'Hara said, above the desultory clink of forks and knives signaling the awful death of a dinner party: "How many rods in a furlong?" The man didn't know—as you and I do—that the correct response was forty. "Oh, never mind," he finally decided.

ness, vindictiveness and general bellicosity."[15] Ten years earlier Harvey Breit, the influential *New York Times* essayist and interviewer, wrote specifically of the columns collected in *Sweet and Sour* (published by Random House in 1954) that the journalist "though appearing casual is careless; his facts go unchecked; his biases are so rampant that contradictory arguments under his nose are overlooked. By his decisive use of the word 'class' to denote his highest praise, Mr. O'Hara is on his way, if he persists in his course, to become the Toots Shor of Literature."[16]

The prose of these columns is at once strident and offhand, debasing the process of meditation, confusing argumentation with being argumentative; point of view becomes prejudice in a rhetoric better suited to the letters-to-the-editor sections of college alumni magazines* than to opinion columns composed by the author of *Appointment in Samarra*. His tastes are subjected to neither system nor self-investigation; he won't allow himself to surprise himself, nor budge from the first position he ever took on a person or an issue. Except his political position.

In the autumn of 1964, during the campaign of Barry Goldwater against LBJ, *Newsday* commissioned O'Hara to write a weekly opinion column. This was a business scheme: the pieces were to be syndicated, and it was hoped by both parties—editor/publisher Harry F. Guggenheim and the columnist, who shared equally the syndication fee paid by each newspaper that ran "My Turn"—that O'Hara, due to the column's popularity, would earn much more than his weekly guarantee of one thousand dollars.† It probably didn't help conversational goodwill, a columnist's bread and butter, that the first sentence of his first piece was "Let's get off to a really bad start."[17] The "straight-ticket Democrat" of a

---

*In a 1965 "My Turn" column in *Newsday* O'Hara, praising the "Yale type"—"likely to be at least fourth generation, of part-Yankee stock, financially well fixed, conservative in all his tastes, friendly and polite without making many new friends after college . . . tolerantly but unwaveringly Protestant, optimistic, patient, dependable and good"—he notes the grumbling of this True Blue gang about the awarding of honorary degrees to JFK and Martin Luther King Jr. The "patience of these [Yale] men" is "remarkable. . . . Especially as they see the university they loved being taken away from them." And then, with an empathy as bewildering as it is pathetic, he adds that it "is almost a handicap to have gone to Yale if you want to get your son into the freshman class." O'Hara, true to the convention of these alumni-mag gripes, recounts the tragic tale of an acquaintance, a "fifth-generation Yale man who had to send his son to another Ivy League university" (O'Hara, *My Turn*, pp. 57, 58).

†An ebbing, flowing, and alarmingly ebbing assortment of daily and weekly newspapers—as many as sixty-five and as few as thirty—contributed varying tributes that incurred an annual net loss to

1954 "Sweet and Sour" column became by 1964 a Goldwater booster, a
Kennedy scorner, and an especially nasty Martin Luther King derider.
(He was proud to describe himself as a "conservative grouch": he disap-
proved of James Baldwin, Abe Lincoln, and Pearl Bailey, not to mention
fans of ballet.) Announcing that his vote was going to Goldwater, he
wrote a couple of weeks before the 1964 election that he believed "it's
time the Lawrence Welk people had their say. The Lester Lanin and
Dizzy Gillespie people have been on too long."[18] He meant it about the
vote, but when he wrote that "when the country is in trouble, like war
kind of trouble, man, it is the Lawrence Welk people who can be
depended upon, all the way. Those men and women who voted for
Nixon . . ." Excepting the worst of his war correspondence, this is the
only piece of writing in which O'Hara panders, and it would be pitiful
were it not laughable to imagine him tapping his feet to "The Lonely
Goatherd" or "Ghost Riders in the Sky." It's credible that O'Hara had no
taste for Diz's "Salt Peanuts," but how could he pretend to turn his back
on such Society Dance Music as Lester Lanin's "Cheek to Cheek" in
favor of the Champagne Music of "High Life Polka"?

It's also credible, however, that Goldwater's bluff plain talk and rectitude did appeal to him, and he remained resolutely immune to the
Kennedys' Irish charm and grace;* but this rightward political lurch had
unforeseen consequences on his commentary. His columns in support of
Henry Cabot Lodge and Nixon suffered from their smug affiliation with
those unsung heroes driving their Silver Clouds, living in houses with
names and feeling the painful pinch of their erstwhile custom-lasted
shoes squeezed by welfare-state taxes. It wasn't that he was on the wrong
side, but that he'd crossed over so mindlessly. O'Hara was hugely more
provocative as a crash writer than as a boom writer. Security (excluding
false security) is the least interesting of social situations, and without setting the privileged up for a fall, without exploiting the consequences of
hubris, a protagonist's comfort behind the shield of class is of puny situa-
tional value. Seldom in his opinion columns does he explore beneath the

---

Newsday of $16,689. "Financially," Guggenheim wrote O'Hara at the end, "it has been highly remu-
nerative only to you." The newspaper's commercial disappointment wasn't the half of it. Letters to
the editor were appalling: "just about the most inane thing I've ever read in a daily newspaper" and
"I think that John O'Hara's secret in turning out so much fiction is that he does not think. I am sure
he can write a column faster than some of his ardent readers can read it."

*In a bizarre burst of candor, O'Hara brags that "Mr. Kennedy and I had the same therapist for a
while" (O'Hara, *My Turn*, p. 48).

superficially placid surface of status, and when he does (Churchill's "aristocratic ancestry served its only useful purpose: it made him absolutely sure of himself") it's so refreshing that the reader is irritated to be reminded of the pieces' general deprivation. And where did his irony go? Now he seemed to be pressing down on those below and giving the ascendant a free lift to Paradise Island. If it's not too late (and for my money it never is) to get in a delayed hit on Norman Podhoretz, O'Hara's fearless stand on behalf of the well-padded if not well-pleased provoked a critical response that anticipated the notorious reviews given a few years later to that *Commentary* editor's confessional suck-up to the rich, *Making It*.

That really bad start O'Hara had promoted came to a ghastly bad end. A week *before* his first column ran, the executive news editor of the *Minneapolis Star-Tribune* wrote that the first two submissions "are completely unacceptable to us," and said plainly that the newspaper would refuse to honor its agreement to run O'Hara's work if it didn't improve. The *St. Petersburg Times* refused to run the second column (on smoking), and the *Houston Post* considered the early submissions were "a great disappointment." The *Milwaukee Journal* greeted publication day of the first column with a required sixty-day notice to cancel its participation. "I suppose you have heard from all over the country that the . . . O'Hara columns were of unbelievably poor quality." Singled out for special comment was the lack of "humor, sense and style. It is hard for me to believe that a man who can write as well as John O'Hara would want such dribble published under his name. Naturally, we do not hold you responsible for the sloppy workmanship."

Harry Guggenheim, called the Captain, was happy to establish responsibility for this fiasco, writing a "Dear John" letter that began, "There is a Spanish saying: '*Mientras amigos más claros.*' To a new and highly valued friend I am going to be frank. You have written 'My Turn' with your left hand between a couple of cigarettes and as a consequence it has gone badly."*

In the months following Belle's death, this occasional journalism connected him to a noisy arena from which he was retiring, a cultural mar-

---

*Contrary to his throwaway practice with incoming rounds of correspondence, O'Hara saved a thick file of denigration by newspaper editors (who bought the license to censure him by the payment of as little as ten dollars per week) and newspaper readers (who paid a dime for the shot). These letters are among the O'Hara papers at the United States Trust Company, New York.

ket of hustle and aspiration, social flood and ebb. He was lonely, of course, and often disconsolate. At such times he might telephone Pat Outerbridge and ask him to come over. This would be late at night, past what might otherwise have been Outerbridge's bedtime, but in Lili's memory Pat "steered" his friend through the most difficult nights. One of this kind man's children likened his availability to that of a doctor or pastor; no doubt he took seriously the mission of a nondrinking alcoholic to minister to a similar soul, but less solemnly, by that mysterious chemical bonding between unlike people, their friendship deepened. As outsiders to others' affections and marriages we profess astonishment at the disproportion between one partner's giving and another's getting, even as we experience in our own bonds the immateriality of such double-entry bookkeeping. If O'Hara made use of—in the ungenerous locution, "used"—Outerbridge, to the occasional resentment of the man and his family, he also seemed to take his friend's generosity for granted, based on the assumption that Pat liked him as much as he liked Pat. Some of the chores his friend was asked to perform were menial. O'Hara had bought a bright red MG TC in which to scoot around Quogue and the back roads of Princeton;* from Hollywood, where he went to earn money the year after Belle's death, he called on Outerbridge to store the car on blocks. This sounds more high-handed than it was; in truth it's an imposition in line with cat feeding, flower watering, and mail forwarding.

In this friendship each had gifts or circumstances the other admired. If Outerbridge was happy to have his twenty-fifth Harvard reunion entry in his college alumni directory written by a world-famous novelist, O'Hara was happy to call on this graduate of St. Paul's for school customs, nicknames, and history to authenticate fictional references. Outerbridge owned a small and sometimes struggling manufacturing business (Homasote) in West Trenton, and O'Hara visited him at work, quizzed him on the machinations of industrial enterprise, and asked him to research such business processes as laws of incorporation. Outerbridge was a noted Olympic and ocean-racing sailor, and with this came certification of ingenuity and grace under pressure, cardinal virtues in his new friend's long-held code.

For his part, Outerbridge was flattered by the warm attention his neighbor lavished on him. Lavish was not the businessman's preferred

*Wylie and her second husband, Scott Doughty, still drive this car in Quogue.

style, so when O'Hara presented him with a Halcyon (St. Paul's School) Boat Club blazer, Outerbridge felt unable to reciprocate and was oppressed by the gift.* O'Hara never stinted in his affections, nor did it seem to occur to him that his attention might not always be welcome. Outerbridge's son David sometimes was asked to run small errands for him, such as delivering the Sunday newspaper to his house on snowy days, and he remembers vividly an evening when O'Hara showed up unexpectedly at their house during Thanksgiving dinner, unusual in itself inasmuch as Outerbridge was generally summoned to 20 College Road West or to Linebrook. He didn't join the family at the table—"I always thought [that] curious, but he sat immediately behind me on an old chest, and I felt the chill of propriety on my neck."

That chill of propriety was soon compounded by the presence of Sister Barnes, divorced from Joseph Bryan III a few months after Belle died. O'Hara had known and liked Katharine Barnes—nicknamed in childhood for having two adored brothers—for many years. She had been Belle's good friend, and like her was lean, quick, and stylishly self-assured. A bit more than six months into his suddenly solitary life, he was in love with his old friend's ex-wife, and Belle's funeral was the occasion that triggered that love. Writing Katharine Barnes Bryan in July of 1954, he told her that "from the time I saw you at Belle's funeral there never was anyone else but you. . . . I loved you because you loved Belle and were there."† And like his devotion to Belle, this ardor was excited not by practical and physical considerations—the wish to give Wylie a

---

*David Outerbridge, Pat's son, recollected to me in a letter that O'Hara had specified that he wished to be buried wearing a necktie given him by his best friend. This would have been a necktie made by Gieves & Hawkes of London in the colors of either of two exclusive clubs: the Kew-Teddington Observatory Society, founded by Outerbridge as an association with no other purpose than to enable him to invite his friends to join it; or the Hessian Relief Society, O'Hara's parody of Outerbridge's parody of clubs: no Building and Grounds Committee, no building, no grounds, no meetings, no membership list, a society so secret that only O'Hara and Outerbridge knew who belonged, and only the very tippy top elite of their world belonged. In his *Who's Who in America* entry O'Hara included both clubs—together with the Racquet (Philadelphia) and Nassau (Princeton). (John McPhee reckons it "about as exclusive as a taxicab." For a hard-boiled brawler O'Hara could fret like a softie: when he and his Rolls-Royce got a speeding ticket in Princeton he offered his resignation to the officers of the Nassau Club, lest the publicity bring shame upon their house. The offer was refused.)

†Quotations from O'Hara's letters to Katharine Barnes are from photocopies of transcriptions made available to the author by a family member.

mother and to ease his own solitude—but by a passion dignified by articulate emotional wisdom and by an infatuation stoked rather than dampened by scruple. In his courtship of Sister, O'Hara behaved with steady
consideration. "I *need* you. I started needing you, I went on loving you, I
proceed to needing you more than ever. Does it frighten you? Because if
it does, let me say, let me reassure you, that you are absolved of all
responsibility in the matter. . . . This—we—is too good to let go. Whatever I lack that you require I can correct or make up for in other ways. I
am not stopping anything now, but only letting myself fall more desper-
ately in love with you" (June 19, 1954).

At the same time he let his excitement rip, confessing that "I love you
as intensely and really deeply as any love I had when I was in my teens or
twenties. . . . It is a better love, no less passionate, by God" (November
2, 1954). As he had with Belle, he consigned his fate to a loved woman's
decision. While he was in the Pacific, soon before he and Belle conceived Wylie, he had expressed his notional kismet in melodramatic
terms: Belle, he declared, held his life in her hands; whether she shel-
tered him or broke him was her choice. The context then was a vulnerability that—had it been less adoring—might've been perverted to
neurotic covetousness. His jealousy, because it was so unwarranted, was
instead touching, a child's delusion of the imminent hazard of abandon-
ment. Rather than brood Othello-like in response to suspected betrayals
by people he loved, O'Hara went off like a cannon. C. D. B. (Courtland)
Bryan, one of Katharine and Joseph Bryan's three children, relates
fondly in *Esquire* an encounter between his mother and O'Hara shortly
after they were married. O'Hara had emerged from his Princeton study
to discover his wife "talking in the living room with a man he did not
know. O'Hara took one black look, stormed back into his study and
slammed the door. Afterward, when the man had left, my mother went
in to ask O'Hara what was wrong. 'It's quite obvious,' he replied stiffly,
'you are inviting your lover right into our house.' " The fellow was "an
upholsterer who had come to measure some chairs for slipcovers."*[19]

*Nine weeks before they were married, O'Hara mailed his wife-to-be a couple of declarations: one
a runic meditation about the corrosive action of silent brooding and the other a warning about adultery, the transgression that had animated and would disfigure many of his fictional portraits:

A resentment is poisonous, cancerous; a quarrel is, or should be, surgical, explosive, purgative. . . .
If you have a beef against me, express it. Why not? I have no way of punishing you that doesn't also

After pledging to Sister that "my love can be taken for granted; I feel free to say that," he hand-delivered to her mother a formal and heartfelt letter attesting to his honorable intentions:

This *letter* may come as a surprise to you, but my guess is that you will be surprised by very little, if any, of what I say in it.

Here, then, is what will not surprise you: I love Sister, and I want to marry her.

I thought, and I was reconciled to the thought, that that part of my life was ended. Or, to put it another way, I believed that love would not happen to me again, and I was prepared to go through the rest of my life without it; without giving it, without getting it. And even when I began to see Sister with fair regularity I had myself almost convinced that this was a good, continuing friendship between two people who were coincidentally bereaved and disillusioned, and that that friendship would be satisfactory and sufficient. But then I began to realize that there was more to it than the need to see Sister, and one day when she asked me why I had done something I said "Because I love you," and the spontaneous declaration (which I wasn't even sure she had heard— we were in a car) told *me* what was really going on inside me.

It *wasn't* going on inside her. She didn't want it, she avoided it and carefully rejected it, and just as carefully I refrained from further declarations. I was afraid to frighten her off, and I did have to see her, more and more. Then one night in New York it had us . . . and I could tell her, over and over, when I didn't have to tell her, because she knew. . . .

I don't know how long you've known. . . . In any case you know it now, and I've been wanting to tell you not only as a mark of respect, but in the interest of our friendship, yours and mine.

I will tell you a little about myself . . . [who his parents were, that he was too poor to go to college, that his mother, "a devout Catholic . . . now accepts my schism from Rome"]. I would not go so far as to say my life is an open book, but there's nothing undisclosed that will hurt Sister or embarrass you.

hurt me at least as grievously as it does you. As I have said many times, the only thing I could not take from you is physical infidelity, and you know that so well that you would have to hate me in order to decide to go through with an affair; and if you hated me you wouldn't want to live with me, and I would know *that*. Unfaithfulness to me by you would be a large or small gesture of hatred, regardless of how much or little you cared for the other man (November 23, 1954).

> I would say that my financial prospects are fair—to—good.* Most
> reassuring to you must be the fact that I love Sister, the most important
> fact to you, and the most important fact to me. My best friends know
> that I love her, and I think that as an interested party you should know
> it too. Now you do, and I hope you approve.

Everyone who mattered approved, and John and Sister were married at her New York apartment by a woman justice of the peace, on January 31, 1955, O'Hara's fiftieth birthday (his wife was forty-five). No one doubted that they were happy, and lucky, to have found their way to each other. Her son C.D.B.—eighteen, a freshman at Yale, with an inevitable reflex of regret that his mother hadn't found sufficient pleasure with his father, whose cabled congratulation was signed "Frying Pan"—experienced the ceremony as encouragingly intimate and informal. As a would-be novelist, he was awed by O'Hara, "a big man, powerful, physically intimidating, like a fighter." After serving as best man, he and his brother, St. George,† sang a calypso toast whose lyrics have "mercifully" been erased by time: "I remember [O'Hara's] surprisingly pleased and shy expression. As foolish as our song might have been, he *appreciated* our doing it, just as he appreciated the too damn few nice things anyone ever did for him."[20]

His marriage to Sister marked the beginning for O'Hara of sixteen years of prosperity, productivity, and domestic attention. He had always been indulgent of his appetites, and for him what had felt satisfying to do once felt at least doubly satisfying to do twice: drink, eat, sleep, talk, feud, pitch woo, show off. Thomas Hobbes, believing prudence to be "but

---

*In the same letter in which he declared that his love for Sister was as intense as any he had felt in his teens, he shared with her also "a premonition of good luck, of worldly success that will happen to me as soon as we are really together. . . . [I]t keeps coming back to me, this hunch, I guess is the word, that with you, and only with you, I am going to be rich and famous and that it is going to make us closer together. Not, of course, that my being rich and famous will be a reason for your loving me more, but that your being my wife will give me the strength and the good sense that I will have to have in order to *get* rich and famous, and that your being my wife will enable me to keep richness and fame in their proper perspective, which means that we use them to make a good life together. I see you being in on everything I do, and I see myself relying on you, on your judgment, your scepticism, your loyalty" (November 2, 1954).

†St. George later disappeared mysteriously while day-sailing off the coast of Hawaii.

experience," might have said that middle age had tamped O'Hara down or at least leveled him off. But if anything his appetite increased by the year, replacing drink and resentment with a will to dominate not only his work but his fellow citizens' opinion of it. Despite the pugnacity of his columns, the good opinion of others—seldom his betters or even his equals—mattered to him in ways that seemed either pathetic or farcical, depending on the beholder's point of view. Molière could have done justice to the scenes Squire O'Hara created to show off his prosperity in Princeton, especially after he and Sister moved in 1956 to Linebrook, a house they had built on woody land she'd bought from Princeton University, and whose interior she'd designed and decorated. One of Wylie's childhood friends remembers the move from College Road West to the junction of Province Line and Pretty Brook Roads as a registration of the distinction between Belle's easy grace and Sister's more conventional propriety. Katharine invited even the children among her circle to call her Sister, but for all her charm there was also a chill—her voice had a "velvety tone with a bite to it," in the words of an admirer—and French provincial Linebrook reflected her formal properties, with its "just-so" living and dining rooms.*

The protagonist of "The Flatted Saxophone" (1963), George Cushman, reveals—indeed revels in—a truculence that O'Hara didn't perfect until he quit drinking. Cushman has not quit drinking—he has lined up at a wedding reception "One, two, three, four, five, six, seven, eight, nine, ten, eleven, twelve, thirteen, fourteen, fifteen, *sixteen*, seventeen, eighteen, nineteen. Nineteen Scotches"—and he sits alone at a table for six and sourly tells fellow guests looking for a seat that the empty chairs are "all spoken for."[21]

A friend of mine whose wedding O'Hara attended around that time remembered him as sensationally disapproving, regarding her and those wedding guests unknown to him with baleful skepticism. His sour disposition was noted and retailed in a Philadelphia magazine on the occasion of his return in 1967 for a party at the Pottsville Club given by a childhood friend. The reporter, after grumbling that O'Hara four years earlier had accepted and then didn't honor an invitation to the centennial din-

*The house has no architectural pretensions, and its scale is modest. In a rural setting, set low and rambling on two and a half acres, it was sold seventeen years after the O'Haras built it in 1957 for the modest price of $154,000.

ner at the town library (so unrelenting in its hostility to his work), now reported that he failed to make passes at any of the local ladies: "he just sat around sort of grumpy." In fairness, O'Hara had seen a Pottsville woman's warning in print that the doctor's son wouldn't dare return to town "in daylight." Even so, from his vantage in a letter to Alfred Wright, it was a successful visit to a party for "the people I have known all my life, in a club where my father once lived, on the street where I was born. For the first time since 1927 . . . I had a good time there, recalling people's middle names and old sweethearts and so on." Driving home to Princeton he told Sister that he had "enjoyed the feeling of rediscovering my roots, indeed of rediscovering them for the first time. At twenty-two I was too young to have anything but roots; at sixty-two the tree that I had become (I fancy myself as a sturdy oak type) was something more than a stick pushed haphazardly into the ground."[22]

In fact O'Hara's perceived surliness at parties was often due to severe back pain. The late Joseph M. Fox, a Random House editor, accepted a forceful invitation to a small black-tie dinner dance at Linebrook.* Between O'Hara's ugly treatment of his first editor at Random House, his bullying of Cerf, his expressed contempt for publishing and all its devices from contract through editing to promotion and royalties, Fox had not expected to enjoy his Princeton evening, but did. O'Hara was charming to and charmed by Fox's wife, Jill, dancing often with her; she was struck by how supple a dancer he was, especially gifted at the fox-trot, but also mentioned to her husband—as though O'Hara's clock *must* strike thirteen—that their host wore a corset. This was assumed to be a vain prop, to reef in a belly, though in fact it was a back brace, worn to ameliorate O'Hara's pain.

It is also a fact that O'Hara's perceived surliness was due as well to disdain, snobbery, and indifference. A man who had tagged along as an out-of-town guest to lunch at Linebrook remembered that his host was aloof and incurious about him to the point of frank rudeness. O'Hara ignored

*Fox was pressed by Bennett Cerf into a service he refused to perform—removing from the New York Racquet & Tennis Club, of which he was a member, a supply of matchbooks that O'Hara wished to display in the public rooms of his house.

In later years, Fox grew irritated with himself for having refused this favor. He didn't like to be commanded by Cerf, and also had a distaste for social climbing, but in 1995 he told me, "For Christ's sake it was easy enough to do. I should have gotten him the damned matches. It would have made him happy, and what would it have cost me?"

the young man, talking through him in the direction of other guests, interrupting his efforts to make small talk. At the end of the day the good-bye was cold, so he was startled to receive within a few days an invitation to return next week for another lunch with the O'Haras. The sight that greeted him as he parked his sedan in Linebrook's circular drive was as striking as Brendan Gill's memory of O'Hara got up cap-a-pie in a cowboy outfit. There, leaning against his smoke-green Rolls-Royce Silver Cloud (interior hides in forest green, on which lamb's-wool rugs were scattered), was displayed a figure wearing a tweed hat and mirror-polished Peal boots, with a double-breasted tweed waistcoat beneath a tweed suit. This suit, in the appraising eye of the beholder, had been customized by Brooks Brothers, which condemned it to be a sad simulacrum of Savile Row foxhunting garb.

O'Hara invited the young gentleman—who, as you might've guessed, had confessed to his host after his first visit to having been attractively educated at Eton and Trinity College, Cambridge—into his study for a chat before lunch. The Linebrook study seemed as decorated as a museum exhibit: Famous Writer's Workplace. (In fact the study now *is* a library exhibit, faithfully transported plaque by celebrity nightclub candid by miner's lamp by *Who's Who* from Linebrook to Pattee Library at Penn State, where O'Hara's mementos, instruments of composition, and knickknacks are, with his words, in the permanent record.)

Serenity can be a writer's friend; familiarity is another writer's enemy. During his professional vagrancy, O'Hara had written in newsrooms, residential hotels, New York and southern California apartments whose details no visitor seems able to recall. Like so much else, this changed in Princeton; especially at Linebrook, where he set and dressed his stage. Here's the inevitable *credo,* Conrad's words carved into a plaque: "My task, which I am trying to achieve, is, by the power of the written word, to make you hear, to make you feel. It is, before all, to make you see." The reference books reveal more explicitly than this sentiment his fields of specialization: *Baird's Manual of College Fraternities* shelved near *Factors in the Sex Life of Twenty-two Hundred Women.* Here's the big gray Remington Noiseless, of course. A photo of him standing with Bennett Cerf and Cardinal Francis Spellman, whose archdiocese at 451 Madison Avenue shared the grand old Villard House courtyard—in which piazza O'Hara insisted on parking his Rolls-Royce—with Random House at 457 Madison. (Joe Fox, who would neither confirm nor deny that he had once placed a plastic dog turd on the automobile's supple leather driver's seat, related that Cerf—after squeezing a church contribution from O'Hara—had induced the neighborly Cardinal to bless JOH-1, the Silver Cloud.) The study shows O'Hara costumed as Hitler and Robert Benchley as an admiral (without trousers). Toy cars, a violin, and a banjo-mandolin (Benchley's). Walking sticks and canes. (His friend James Kerney, in a *Trenton Evening Times* profile, described O'Hara as an "accidental collector," and quoted him, " 'You buy a cane. Then you buy a second cane. Your friends say, *What can we give O'Hara for Christmas? Oh, he collects canes.*' ")[23] A blare of horns: coaching horn, foxhunting horn, a French automobile horn, a horn blown atop Mt. Everest. An odd piece of antique hardware has been identified by Matthew J. Bruccoli as a "mounted Stewart speedometer (set at 42983, the birthdate of Grace Tate of *A Rage to Live*). In his office he kept a Cape Cod lighter, cuspidors, an Astrolite miner's lamp, a horseshoe, and a framed winning hand—seven cards totaling nineteen—at blackjack. In other frames are O'Hara in a coonskin coat, posing for *Holiday* with a Stutz; and Pat Outerbridge sailing in the Bermuda Race; and O'Hara standing with Senator John F. Kennedy and W. H. Auden at the National Book Awards. Bruccoli waxes extravagant in his estimation of the room's studied affect, "neither a cluttered den nor a showplace. Everything was neat, but it was a working room. It was his safe place where thousands of good words were written every week. He referred to it as his laboratory, and it was also his church—*laborare est orare.*"

Reporters came from *Newsweek* and *Esquire* to profile O'Hara in his hideout. He would be photographed—authentically at ease—leaning back in a swiveling office chair, a cigarette at the ready. The total picture invites dismissive summary: gone knee-jerk conservative, the commercially successful and prolific scribbler bypasses all editorial restraints to crank out reflexive opinion pieces and melodramatic tomes prepackaged for Hollywood; smug, complacent, insular, and insolent, he misplaces or abandons the concentrated fury that inspired his best work: stories and *Appointment in Samarra*.

During an interview with the late William Maxwell I asked O'Hara's old friend and editor whether he suspected that O'Hara might have written short stories because alcohol made long work so difficult, whether he might have abandoned alcohol to replace it with an addiction to fecundity. Though I didn't say as much, what I none-too-subtly meant was,

What happened to John O'Hara? Maxwell stared at me, turned to his typewriter, and typed with bravura speed, "It would be indecent to speculate." This was chastening, on several counts. Even before he would discuss O'Hara with me, there was a brief interview in the austere writing room of his New York apartment. Why was I interested? Fair question.

When I began this inquiry I was puzzled by a recurring inconsistency between the summary judgments of his character by strangers and the affectionate testimonials of his friends. These latter tributes seemed— by their warmth—to spring from emotions deeper than loyalty. I had read Farr, Bruccoli, and MacShane because of my admiration for O'Hara's better work, and what I had found missing in their accounts— the specifics of why a cherished friend was cherished—I had the hubris to believe I could name. Most of O'Hara's closest friends were dead when I began my research, but some were kicking and willing to talk. I got right to work interviewing and—to beat the clock—left the transcription of my notes for later. As I talked and asked questions I was aware that a few chestnuts were getting reroasted—those anecdotes, quips, and fables that dog O'Hara (and every public person). I believed things were going well: blanks were being filled in, associations connected, dates recalled. I was certain by the expressions on their faces and in the emphatic delivery of their answers that those who claimed to have cared for O'Hara were speaking from the heart.

Then I began transcribing, and here is what I got. What follows is both representative of most of my conversations and a verbatim record of a particular conversation with a close O'Hara friend from Princeton, a university dean who had visited Linebrook as often as a couple of times a week. I have edited out only *uhs* and false starts.

"I loved the man."

"Why?"

"I dunno."

"How did you express your love?"

"The usual ways."

"What did you talk about?"

"You know."

"I don't know."

"We just shot the shit."

"About sports? Politics? Girls? Money? Books?"

"The usual. What you do when you talk to a friend. Shot the shit. You know."

Our dialogue lengthened but did not deepen. It was like most of the talks I had with O'Hara's friends. Was I asking the wrong questions? Maybe. Still I was sure I could do better than Farr, Bruccoli, and Mac-Shane, could find *reasons* buried in the continuing testimonials to O'Hara's friendship, their recollections of eating and bar hopping with him, watching television or a football game with him, sitting alone with him in his study. I just had to read more closely and listen more sharply. But what I sought I never found: just as O'Hara only rarely could or wished to tell why, *specifically*, hand-lasted shoes made his pulse quicken, his friends rarely specified why he made their hearts lift. This, for a biographer, was humbling. But to be humbled is not necessarily to be stupefied or silenced.

"Why are you interested?" William Maxwell had simply asked.

I might have said, "I dunno." Instead I declared my lack of interest in putting O'Hara on the couch or—worse—cobbling together some unified thesis solving the mystery of O'Hara's life and imagination.

"So those things don't interest you," he said. "What does?"

"I won't know till I'm finished," I said.

Maxwell cupped his ear and asked me to repeat what I'd just said, so I did.

"I thought you said that," Maxwell said. "I'm glad."[24]

We could proceed. His method was unusual, the most honorable response to a request for information that I have ever experienced. I would ask a question and he would listen, stare for a moment at the ceiling, and swivel his chair to a typing table just big enough to support a thirty-year-old electric Smith-Corona. "It would be indecent to speculate" reminded me—who needed reminding—that a writer's progress or trajectory is never so simple as climb, decline, or free fall. Michael J. Arlen once said of a writer friend of ours who was recently having a bad time with what had been a brilliant career, and having a bad time in part because she was writing about matters of interest to her and perhaps no one else, "Her only rocket launch that matters is the one that went highest; the highest stays up there forever."

Maxwell would type his response and give me the sheet of draft paper to keep, making no copy for his own records. He answered in this manner so that he said only and exactly what he meant to say, without fear of having been misheard. And what he said, again and again, was that while "Being a fiction editor at *The New Yorker* was like being an animal trainer," O'Hara had been direct and grown-up in their dealings.

By the late 1950s, subtle signals were being received at the *New Yorker* that O'Hara might be willing to come home. Ross had died in 1951, and before Wolcott Gibbs died, in 1958, he told the magazine's chief fiction editor that all that O'Hara required was Brendan Gill's execution and fifty thousand dollars or so in punitive damages. By 1960 Roger Angell was campaigning William Shawn to effect O'Hara's return, and Shawn was eager to oblige. Accordingly, Maxwell was delegated that summer to read, in Quogue, several novellas that O'Hara had recently completed.

Maxwell and his wife, Emily, were greeted and fed by Sister and welcomed by John, who retired after dinner to work, leaving his favored editor with three original typescripts (as usual, O'Hara had made no copies) and a violent stomachache, which Sister was called upon to soothe. Maxwell read one novella, and didn't much care for it, then he read another and began to realize the perilous position he'd put both of them in. Then he read "Imagine Kissing Pete," the Jim Malloy tale of coming back to Gibbsville to visit the old gang, and offered on the spot to buy it for ten thousand, and neither he nor O'Hara referred to the other novellas—"The Girl on the Baggage Truck" and the aptly titled "We're Friends Again"—that were later collected in *Sermons and Soda Water.*

This reunion with the *New Yorker* marked the beginning of a remarkable run of O'Hara's short fiction. The Vintage edition of Frank Mac-Shane's *Collected Stories of John O'Hara* is four hundred and eighteen pages. Everything in it after page 108 was written for or after *Sermons and Soda Water:* "In the Silence," "How Can I Tell You?" "The Flatted Saxophone," "Ninety Minutes Away," "Fatimas and Kisses," "Natica Jackson," "Can I Stay Here?" So at the very time the tomes were bloating and the columns were small-talking, O'Hara was writing—about many a thing under his and your sun—some of the best and best-finished of his fiction. Speculation, then, is not only indecent; it is futile and unnecessary.

O'Hara continued to be churlish, taking special offense at imperfect telephone manners. He scolded Bennett Cerf—threatening to leave Random House—if he ever again had his secretary phone and ask him to "hold for Mr. Cerf." Over this same custom he traded insults with Robert Montgomery—mentioning that "Bob Lovett" and "Jim Forrestal" made their own calls to him, "even when they were Secretary of Defense"—during negotiations in 1961 for a television production of "Imagine Kissing Pete." (Montgomery responded to O'Hara's reproachful letter "in which you take it upon yourself to lecture me on telephone etiquette. . . . I am somewhat surprised to find that you are offended by what is common practice among busy people. However, it is much too late for me to change my manners or for you to change yours. I am, of course, very much impressed by your statement that two of our more prominent public servants were on such intimate terms with you. But it does not give me any greater confidence in our security to know that they were so meticulous in not offending your sense of telephone propriety.")

O'Hara was seldom comfortable or open-hearted with any but a few among friends and family. Sister, who got along especially easily with O'Hara's mother, with whom she had a teasing relationship,* encouraged her husband to draw closer to his siblings, but except for Tom, his youngest sister, Kathleen, and sometimes Mary, they experienced their eldest brother's chill. When they visited Princeton he hid from them in his bathroom or at Palmer Stadium; and when he was finally urged in 1961 by Sister to share with them a bit of his estate, he bestowed on each of his nineteen nieces and nephews an educational trust of $1,000, but the accompanying letter was hedged with mandates and warnings, not to mention his farfetched reminder that—owing to his tax bracket—the $19,000 actually had cost him $80,000.

But there had been Belle, and now there was Sister, and a visitor to O'Hara's study could not miss the prominence in his pride and affection for his daughter. Because he was so alert to formal expressions of respect and regard—to an often unwholesome degree—it might be expected that his loyalty to kin and old friends would be fundamental, intrinsic, at least dutiful. Cut one O'Hara and all O'Haras bleed. Fact was, in *From the Terrace,* he had developed for Alfred Eaton a pseudo-rational and unsentimental theory about family duty and affection. This he referred to as "natural indifference." He is discussing with Natalie his mother and sisters:

---

*"Hello," she once answered the phone, "This is Sister O'Hara." "Well," responded the caller, "This is Mother Superior."

We belong to the same family, but we go our separate ways, by choice and because life is like that. Men and women my age may be members of a family as they would be members of a church or club, but a church or club they don't use much. And they're only *members* of a family. They can't be considered as inseparable parts of a family. People don't think that way. They think and behave as individuals first, and as units of a family second—and a bad second. . . . Parents have a natural protective instinct for their young children, but we've gone on for thousands of years thinking that it lasts, and it doesn't. At least it doesn't necessarily. It isn't an elemental instinct. The female parent in time takes her teats away from the child . . . and that *is* an elemental instinct.[25]

Earlier in the novel the narrator has clinically examined Alfred's waning care for his mother: "He loved her, but it was no more than a state of love, a continuing habit and of dwindling intensity. For quite a while he had been loving her as he loved the American flag; he loved her because he did not *not* love her."[26] Twelve pages later Alfred cancels out his father:

Alfred knew that thenceforth and forever their relationship was to be unencumbered, at least on his part, by any vestige of dutiful love or of active hatred. They were like two business men who had had a falling-out, and—again on his part—his feeling was of relief. He had not been able to love his father, and he did not want to hate him.[27]

O'Hara and Eaton are distinct characters, of course, but the author's evident indifference toward most of his brothers and sisters puts in more dramatic relief his insistent, elated care for his daughter. In his study he kept close photos of Wylie, childhood messages from her, a ceramic ashtray she'd fabricated in an elementary-school crafts class. (Bygone times indeed, and sorely missed: a schoolkid's ashtray-for-Dad project!) The letters between them began in childhood, and they will be recognizable thematically and stylistically to any father or mother who has written to a beloved child, to any child who has written back.*

At ten Wylie (and Sister) signed a contract promising to practice piano fifteen minutes daily, with O'Hara vowing to demonstrate "proper

---

*O'Hara's letters to Wylie have been published in Matthew J. Bruccoli's *Collected Letters*. Wylie's to her father are in her private collection, shared with the author.

respect" for their performances. He was required—with no respect promised in return—to play for them a single fiddle piece in response. Two years later, from camp, Wylie was writing to thank her father "for your advice on riflery. I already knew about breathing, because that's one of the first things they teach you here . . . and *puh-leeze* don't give me a lecture on [my report], even if it's atrocious."

The recoil against lectures and advice is usually playful, sometimes irritated, but almost always within the orthodox limits of fond pushing and pulling between a father and a daughter. O'Hara urges her to take greater care with finances, and she listens but will not grovel. When he instructs her how to manage a school crisis at St. Timothy's, she fires back that his advice is as unwelcome as it is misguided, and he concedes the point. Then, with Wylie approaching graduation and feeling—under the institutional pressure of a damned Prize Day—that she has let down the side, O'Hara responds immediately:

> My dear:
>   I wanted you to be head of school, captain of the Spiders, tennis champion, and to get your classmates in a crap game in the Sixes Room and win $18,000 so that you could buy me a Rolls-Royce for Christmas.
>   Seriously, if you think I am in any way disappointed in you, you are out of your little pink mind. I do not want you to be any of the things you are *not* at the sacrifice of the things that you *are:* a warm, human, honorable, decent, sensitive girl. Far from being the kind of person who makes a big splash in her, or his, teens, you are entering a future that is so exciting that I believe you sense it yourself, deep down. I believe you sense it because you are having a final struggle, wrenching yourself away from the past. It is almost like giving birth to yourself. Keep this letter and in ten years, or even five, see if the old man isn't right. I'll even put the date on this letter. And don't be *afraid* of the future. You'll get what you want, if it's what you want.[28]

O'Hara is warm, confiding, vulnerable. It is when his vulnerability turns extreme, or what seems to Wylie perverse, that she answers back in anger and pain. In 1965, when she was nineteen and he was suffering especially from the tooth and jaw ailments that plagued his last years, he complained that she didn't sympathize sufficiently with his distress. She wrote back immediately:

Dear Daddy

First of all, I love you. Second of all, the reason why I haven't asked you how you were is because I have always had this thing about you and Mummy when you are sick. I remember before Mummy died she used to cough sometimes, and I used to tell her to shut up. There is nothing I would rather do than sympathize but I just can't stand or accept the fact that you are sick. I am sure you don't believe me or understand what I am saying, but I don't understand it myself. Every time I have seen you touch your jaw I have wanted to scream.

I told Sister about this a few years ago, but I guess she didn't believe me or else thought it was silly.

Anyway, as silly and crazy as it may be it is true, and I really can't help it.

I know you think I am being melodramatic, but I think it is important that you believe me. You may remember that I didn't want to go to Mummy's funeral, and while you were at the burial ceremony I was laughing away with my cousin Jane. This wasn't because I was too young to conceive of death—I had pretty much learned about death when Mr. [Philip] Barry died—it was because I had to pretend to myself that it hadn't happened . . .

So I am sorry, Daddy, that you are in pain, but I just can't tell you to your face.

In September of 1966 Wylie married Dennis J. Holahan, whom O'Hara identified in letters to friends as Andover '61 and Yale '65 (Fence Club). He had finished officer candidate school in Newport, and after the wedding would be posted to Guam. This ceremony Wylie cheerfully describes as "Daddy's wedding," and it was a big deal, service at St. Vincent's and reception at New York's Colony Club, a guest list that included Claude Rains, Glenway Wescott, George F. Kennan, Dorothy Parker, and Truman Capote. The photos of O'Hara from that day show him beaming.

In fact, he was failing rapidly. From Guam Wylie scolded him for his intrusiveness ("Please don't ever tell me how this and that is in the Navy. We have adjusted to it in our own way"), but when she next saw him she was alarmed at his listlessness and distemper, despite the pleasure he took in the first of two grandchildren—Nicholas followed by Belle—born before he died, at sixty-five in his sleep, after a session of work, on April 11, 1970.

He was buried in Princeton Cemetery; Aaron Burr is buried there, as is President Grover Cleveland, mathematician John von Neumann, pollster George Gallup, and the unlucky parents—or what was left of them before cremation—of the murderous Menendez boys. Sister caused to have put on his gravestone what has become a notorious claim: "Better than anyone else, he told the truth about his time, the first half of the twentieth century. He was a professional," an epitaph he had patched together in response to a hypothetical question put by a reporter from the *Princeton Packet.* This is, as others have often and gleefully noted, a vainglorious and astonishing claim. Once again the pride that served John O'Hara so well in his work betrayed him miserably in his life, and then after his death. Because he deserves an honest memorial, let me offer an alternative, from his September 30, 1955, "Appointment with O'Hara":

"I was one of those lucky people who always knew what they wanted. And what I wanted is what I am: a nonstarving author who is allowed to do the best he can."

NOTES

PREFACE: THE ONE WHO DIDN'T WIN THE NOBEL PRIZE

1. John O'Hara, *Selected Letters of John O'Hara,* ed. Matthew J. Bruccoli (New York: Random House, 1978), p. 410.
2. Joel Sayre, "John O'Hara: A Reminiscence," *Washington Post Book World,* 18 March 1973.
3. Burton Bernstein, *Thurber: A Biography* (New York: Dodd, Mead, 1975), p. 258.
4. Fran Lebowitz, "A Humorist at Work," interview by James Linville and George Plimpton, *Paris Review* 127 (summer 1993): 185.
5. Janet Malcolm, *The Silent Woman: Sylvia Plath & Ted Hughes* (New York: Alfred A. Knopf, 1994), p. 154.
6. Ibid., pp. 154, 155.
7. Wolcott Gibbs, "Watch Out for Mr. O'Hara," *The Saturday Review,* 19 February 1938, 10–12.

1. THE REGION

1. Leo L. Ward, *A Collection of 20 Historical Musings,* written for *Pottsville Republican,* reprinted by Publications of the Historical Society of Schuylkill County (Pottsville, 1994), pp. 53, 55.
2. William Ecenbarger, "Forgetting John O'Hara: Pottsville's Revenge," *Philadelphia Inquirer,* 16 May 1984, 13–17.
3. Ibid., pp. 13–17.
4. Ibid., p. 13.
5. John O'Hara, *Selected Letters of John O'Hara,* ed. Matthew J. Bruccoli (New York: Random House, 1978), p. 106.

6. John O'Hara, "Ninety Minutes Away," in *Collected Stories of John O'Hara*, ed. Frank MacShane (New York: Vintage, 1986), p. 229.

7. O'Hara, *Letters*, pp. 438, 439.

8. Ibid., p. 436.

9. Ibid., p. 437.

10. Charles W. Bassett, "O'Hara's Roots: The Pottsville Years—1905–1927," *Pottsville Republican*, 27 March 1971.

11. William V. Shannon, *The American Irish: A Political and Social Portrait* (Amherst: University of Massachusetts Press, 1989), p. 17.

12. Thomas Flanagan, "The Molly Maguires: An American Story of Truth and Justice Denied," *Los Angeles Times Book Review*, 5 April 1998, pp. 3, 4.

13. Gavan Daws, *A Dream of Islands: Voyages of Discovery in the South Seas* (New York: Norton, 1980), p. 101.

14. Finis Farr, *O'Hara: A Biography* (Boston: Little, Brown, 1973), p. 34.

15. John O'Hara, *Ourselves to Know* (New York: Random House, 1960), p. 3.

16. John O'Hara, unpublished letter to Graham Watson, 19 July 1965.

17. Don A. Schanche, "John O'Hara Is Alive and Well in the First Half of the Twentieth Century (He Owns It)," *Esquire* (August 1969): 84–86, 142, 144–49.

18. John O'Hara, "Why Manchester Roots for Its Small-Town Doctor," *New York Daily Mirror*, 9 March 1950.

19. Anonymous, "Seventy-Five Years Ago (Reprinted from 1916)," *Pottsville Republican*, 21 August 1991.

20. O'Hara, *Letters*, p. 481.

21. Farr, *O'Hara*, p. 38.

22. O'Hara, *Letters*, p. 357.

23. Ernest Hemingway, "Indian Camp," in *The Short Stories of Ernest Hemingway* (New York: Charles Scribner, 1966), p. 94.

24. Matthew J. Bruccoli, quoting Walter Farquhar, quoting John O'Hara's mother, in *The O'Hara Concern: A Biography of John O'Hara* (New York: Random House, 1975), p. 11.

25. John O'Hara, "The Doctor's Son," in *Collected Stories of John O'Hara*, p. 3.

26. O'Hara, *Collected Stories*, p. 13.

27. Hemingway, "Indian Camp," p. 95.

28. O'Hara, *Collected Stories*, pp. 25, 26.

29. Bassett, "Pottsville Years," 22 May 1971.

30. John O'Hara, "Don't Say It Never Happened," in *"An Artist Is His Own Fault": John O'Hara on Writers and Writing*, ed. Matthew J. Bruccoli (Carbondale: Southern Illinois University Press, 1977), p. 213.

31. John O'Hara, *My Turn* (New York: Random House, 1966), p. 103.

32. Frank MacShane, *The Life of John O'Hara* (New York: E. P. Dutton, 1980), p. 13.

33. John O'Hara, "It Must Have Been Spring," in *Collected Stories of John O'Hara*, p. 27.

34. O'Hara, *Collected Stories*, p. 28.

35. Brendan Gill, *Here at The New Yorker* (New York: Random House, 1975), p. 269.
36. O'Hara, *My Turn*, p. 208.
37. Bassett, "Pottsville Years," 15 January 1972.
38. O'Hara, *My Turn*, p. 209.
39. Ione Geier, "O'Hara Era in Pottsville," *Pottsville Republican,* 14 October 1978.
40. Bruccoli, *The O'Hara Concern*, p. 20.
41. John O'Hara, "Dancing School," *New York Herald-Tribune,* 3 August 1930, p. 7.
42. MacShane, *The Life of John O'Hara*, p. 16.
43. Shannon, *The American Irish*, pp. 244, 245.
44. John O'Hara, *Butterfield 8* (New York: Random House, 1994), p. 50.
45. F. Scott Fitzgerald, "The Rich Boy," in *Babylon Revisited and Other Stories* (New York: Charles Scribner, 1960), p. 152.
46. O'Hara, *Butterfield 8*, p. 51.
47. O'Hara, *Letters*, p. 76.
48. F. Scott Fitzgerald, *The Letters of F. Scott Fitzgerald*, ed. Andrew Turnbull (New York: Charles Scribner, 1963), p. 503.
49. Beverly Gary, "A Post Portrait: John O'Hara: Part Two," *New York Post,* 19 May 1959.
50. Bassett, "Pottsville Years," 12 June 1972.
51. Farr, *O'Hara*, p. 69, quoting Pat Outerbridge.
52. Bassett, "Pottsville Years," 12 June 1972.
53. Alden Whitman, "O'Hara, in Rare Interview, Calls Literary Landscape Fairly Bleak," *New York Times,* 13 November 1967, p. 49.
54. O'Hara, *Letters*, p. 85.
55. Ibid., p. 9.
56. Ibid., p. 4.
57. Bruccoli, *The O'Hara Concern*, p. 27.
58. John O'Hara, "In the Silence," in *Collected Stories of John O'Hara*, p. 174.
59. O'Hara, *Letters*, p. 378.
60. Bruccoli, *The O'Hara Concern*, p. 28.
61. Bassett, "Pottsville Years," 17 July 1971.
62. Ibid.
63. O'Hara, *Letters*, p. 10.
64. Schanche, "O'Hara Alive and Well," p. 147.
65. Charles Child Walcutt, "John O'Hara: 1905-1970," in *American Writers: A Collection of Literary Biographies,* Vol. III: Archibald MacLeish to George Santayana, ed. Leonard Unger (New York: Charles Scribner, 1974), p. 364.
66. O'Hara, *Collected Stories*, p. 26.
67. John O'Hara, *A Cub Tells His Story* (Iowa City: Windover Press, 1974).
68. Ibid.
69. Farr, *O'Hara*, p. 79.

70. O'Hara, *Collected Stories*, p. 185.
71. Bassett, "Pottsville Years," 3 July 1971.
72. Farr, *O'Hara*, p. 98.
73. John O'Hara, "Appointment with O'Hara," *Collier's*, 23 December 1955.
74. Bassett, "Pottsville Years," 20 March 1971.
75. O'Hara, "Why Manchester Roots."
76. Ibid.
77. Farr, *O'Hara*, p. 82.
78. Bruccoli, *The O'Hara Concern*, p. 40.
79. O'Hara, *Letters*, p. 15.
80. O'Hara, "Why Manchester Roots."
81. John O'Hara, *Ourselves to Know* (New York: Random House, 1960), p. 185.
82. Bassett, "Pottsville Years," 20 March 1971.
83. Farr, *O'Hara*, pp. 84, 85.
84. John O'Hara, "Fatimas and Kisses," in *Collected Stories of John O'Hara*, p. 325.
85. Bassett, "Pottsville Years," 20 November 1971.
86. O'Hara, *Letters*, p. 481.
87. Walter S. Farquhar, "Musings," *Pottsville Journal*, 30 August 1949.
88. Bruccoli, *The O'Hara Concern*, p. 43.
89. John O'Hara, "The Girl from California," in *Collected Stories of John O'Hara*, p. 169.
90. O'Hara, *Letters*, p. 19.
91. Ibid., p. 25.
92. MacShane, *The Life of John O'Hara*, p. 37.

2. UPTOWN AND DOWN

1. John O'Hara, "These Stories Were Part of Me," in *"An Artist Is His Own Fault,"* ed. Matthew J. Bruccoli (Carbondale: Southern Illinois University Press, 1977), pp. 121, 122.
2. John O'Hara, *Selected Letters of John O'Hara*, ed. Matthew J. Bruccoli (New York: Random House, 1978), p. 31.
3. Meade, *Dorothy Parker: What Fresh Hell Is This?* (New York: Penguin Books, 1989), p. 84.
4. J. Bryan III, *Merry Gentlemen (And One Lady)* (New York: Atheneum, 1985), p. 92.
5. Kyle Crichton, *Total Recoil* (Garden City: Doubleday, 1960), p. 19.
6. O'Hara, *Letters*, pp. 28, 29.
7. Walter S. Farquhar, "Musings," *Pottsville Journal*, 30 August 1949.
8. Eric Alterman, "Monster With a Commitment," *Columbia Journalism Review* 32, I (May/June 1992): 65.
9. Frank MacShane, *The Life of John O'Hara* (New York: E. P. Dutton, 1980), p. 41.

10. Don Cook, "The Paper: The Life and Death of the Herald Tribune," *Los Angeles Times Book Review,* 23 November 1986, 2.

11. Martin F. Nolan, "Something's Missing—and Very Missed—in San Francisco," *Boston Globe,* 28 January 1998, A-19.

12. O'Hara, *Letters,* p. 31.

13. David Bird and Maurice Carroll, "A Journalists' Hangout Becomes a Gift Shop," *New York Times,* 29 May 1984, B3.

14. H. D. Quigg, "The Times Square That Was a Paean to an Era," *UPI,* 24 November 1984.

15. O'Hara, *Letters,* p. 37.

16. Beverly Gary, "A Post Portrait: John O'Hara: Part Three," *New York Post,* 21 May 1959.

17. Matthew J. Bruccoli, *The O'Hara Concern: A Biography of John O'Hara* (New York: Random House, 1975), p. 59.

18. Joel Sayre, "John O'Hara: A Reminiscence," *Washington Post Book World,* 18 March 1973.

19. MacShane, *The Life of John O'Hara,* p. 42.

20. O'Hara, *Letters,* p. 32.

21. Ibid., p. 37.

22. Ibid.

23. MacShane, *The Life of John O'Hara,* p. 43.

24. Finis Farr, *O'Hara: A Biography* (Boston: Little, Brown, 1973), p. 126.

25. Wolcott Gibbs, "Watch Out for Mr. O'Hara," *The Saturday Review,* 19 February 1938, 10–12.

26. O'Hara, *Letters,* p. 55.

27. Ibid., p. 33.

28. Harry Ferguson, "The Memory Machine," *The Atlantic Monthly,* March 1976, 72–76.

29. John O'Hara, "An Artist Is His Own Fault," in *John O'Hara on Writers and Writing: "An Artist Is His Own Fault,"* p. 57.

30. Anonymous, "A Rage to Write," *M.D. Medical Newsmagazine,* April 1971, 154–60.

31. John O'Hara, *Sweet and Sour: Comments on Books and People* (New York: Random House, 1954), pp. 4, 5.

32. John O'Hara, *Butterfield 8* (New York: Random House, 1994), p. 110.

33. John O'Hara, "Imagine Kissing Pete," in *Collected Stories of John O'Hara,* ed. Frank MacShane (New York: Vintage, 1986), p. 120.

34. O'Hara, "An Artist Is His Own Fault," p. 33.

35. Bruccoli, *The O'Hara Concern,* p. 71.

36. Farr, *O'Hara,* p. 129.

37. John K. Hutchens, "John O'Hara From Pottsville, Pa.," *New York Herald-Tribune,* 4 December 1955.

38. John O'Hara, *My Turn* (New York: Random House, 1966), pp. 159, 160.

39. Gibbs, "Watch Out for Mr. O'Hara," pp. 10–12.

40. Bruccoli, *The O'Hara Concern*, p. 63.

41. O'Hara, *Letters*, p. 63.

42. James Thurber, *The Years with Ross* (Boston: Atlantic Monthly Press, 1959), p. 13.

43. Gibbs, "Watch Out for Mr. O'Hara," pp. 10–12.

44. Farr, *O'Hara*, p. 122.

45. O'Hara, *Letters*, p. 43.

46. John O'Hara, "Letter," *New Yorker Correspondence* (New York Public Library).

47. O'Hara, "Letter," 27 January 1931.

48. Katharine Angell White, "Letter to John O'Hara," *New Yorker Correspondence* (New York Public Library), 10 April 1930.

49. O'Hara, *Letters*, p. 43.

50. Ibid., p. 71.

51. Farr, *O'Hara*, p. 134.

52. Kyle Crichton, "Letter to John O'Hara," Charles Scribner's Sons Archive (Princeton University), 11 October 1932.

53. O'Hara, *"An Artist Is His Own Fault,"* p. 18.

54. MacShane, *The Life of John O'Hara*, p. 57.

55. Bruccoli, *The O'Hara Concern*, p. 76.

56. O'Hara, *Letters*, p. 47.

57. Gary, "A Post Portrait: John O'Hara: Part Three."

58. Crichton, *Total Recoil*, p. 176.

59. O'Hara, *Letters*, p. 50.

60. Crichton, *Total Recoil*, p. 142.

61. Kyle Crichton, "Letter to John O'Hara," dated "March, 1930."

62. O'Hara, *Letters*, p. 52.

63. Kyle Crichton, "Letter to John O'Hara," 1 September 1931.

64. Bruccoli, *The O'Hara Concern*, p. 85.

65. Crichton, "Letter to John O'Hara," 1 September 1931.

66. O'Hara, *Letters*, pp. 55, 56.

67. Harold Ross, "Letter to John O'Hara," *New Yorker Correspondence*, 6 June 1933.

68. John Updike, "O'Hara's Messy Masterpiece," *The New Republic*, 2 May 1988, 38–41.

69. Farr, *O'Hara*, p. 139.

70. Thomas Kunkel, *Genius in Disguise: Harold Ross of The New Yorker* (New York: Random House, 1995), p. 196.

71. William Ecenbarger, "Forgetting John O'Hara: Pottsville's Revenge," *Philadelphia Inquirer*, 16 May 1984, 13–17.

72. Crichton, *Total Recoil*, p. 177.

73. O'Hara, *Letters*, p. 88.

74. John O'Hara, "Of Thee I Sing, Baby," in *The Doctor's Son* (New York: Harcourt, Brace, 1935), p. 150.

75. Burton Bernstein, *Thurber: A Biography* (New York: Dodd, Mead, 1975), p. 212.

76. Ibid., p. 213.

77. Ibid., p. 258.

78. O'Hara, *Letters*, p. 47.

79. Ibid., p. 64.

80. Ibid., p. 73.

81. Peter S. Prescott, "John O'Hara," *Newsweek*, 12 January 1981.

82. O'Hara, *Letters*, pp. 69, 70.

83. Ibid., p. 76.

84. Bruccoli, *The O'Hara Concern*, p. 88.

85. Anonymous, "Profile," *Pittsburgh Bulletin-Index*, 12 July 1933.

86. Kyle Crichton, "Letter to John O'Hara," Papers of John O'Hara (United States Trust Company, New York), 1 June 1960.

87. O'Hara, *Letters*, p. 337.

88. Ibid., pp. 77, 78.

89. Robert Van Gelder, "John O'Hara, Who Talks Like His Stories," *The New York Times Book Review*, 26 May 1940, 12.

90. O'Hara, *Letters*, pp. 80, 81.

91. Farr, *O'Hara*, p. 153.

92. Norman Mailer, "Dorothy Parker (1949)," in *The Time of Our Time* (New York: Random House, 1998), pp. 50, 51.

93. Beverly Gary, "A Post Portrait: John O'Hara: Part Two," *New York Post*, 19 May 1959.

94. Gibbs, "Watch Out for Mr. O'Hara," pp. 10–12.

95. O'Hara, *Letters*, p. 79.

96. Ibid., p. 429.

97. Ibid., p. 83.

98. Ibid., p. 82.

99. Ibid., pp. 92, 93.

100. John O'Hara, *Appointment in Samarra* (New York: Modern Library, 1994), p. xx.

101. Sinclair Lewis, "Review of Appointment in Samarra," *Saturday Review*, 6 July 1934.

102. O'Hara, *Appointment in Samarra*, p. 6.

103. Ibid., p. 11.

104. Ibid., pp. 4, 5.

105. F. Scott Fitzgerald, "Winter Dreams," in *Babylon Revisited and Other Stories* (New York: Charles Scribner, 1960), p. 114.

106. Ibid., p. 135.

107. F. Scott Fitzgerald, "Babylon Revisited," in *Babylon Revisited and Other Stories*, p. 214.

108. O'Hara, *Appointment in Samarra*, pp. 218, 219.

109. Ibid., p. 32.

110. Ibid., p. 198.
111. Ibid., pp. 246, 247.
112. Edmund Wilson, "The Boys in the Back Room: James M. Cain and John O'Hara," in *A Literary Chronicle: 1920–1950* (Garden City: Anchor, 1952).
113. John O'Hara, "Natica Jackson," in *Collected Stories of John O'Hara,* p. 370.
114. O'Hara, *Appointment in Samarra,* pp. 247, 248.
115. Ibid., p. 251.
116. O'Hara, "An Artist Is His Own Fault," p. 147.
117. Charles Child Walcutt, *John O'Hara,* University of Minnesota Pamphlets on American Writers, No. 80 (Minneapolis, 1969), p. 7.
118. O'Hara, *Letters,* pp. 344, 345.
119. Norman Podhoretz, "John O'Hara and Mary McCarthy," in *Doings and Undoings* (New York: Noonday Press, 1964), p. 78.
120. Bruccoli, *The O'Hara Concern,* p. 116.
121. O'Hara, "An Artist Is His Own Fault," p. 165.
122. Updike, "O'Hara's Messy Masterpiece," pp. 38–41.
123. Bruccoli, *The O'Hara Concern,* p. 109.

3. TWENTIETH CENTURY LIMITED

1. Finis Farr, *O'Hara: A Biography* (Boston: Little, Brown, 1973), p. 173.
2. John O'Hara, *Selected Letters of John O'Hara,* ed. Matthew J. Bruccoli (New York: Random House, 1978), p. 345.
3. Patricia Ward Biederman, "Literary Legends," *Los Angeles Times,* 24 February 1995, Valley Life, 8.
4. O'Hara, *Letters,* pp. 93, 94.
5. Farr, *O'Hara,* p. 182.
6. John O'Hara, "Hello Hollywood Good-Bye," *Holiday* (May 1968): 54, 55; 125–29.
7. O'Hara, *Letters,* p. 400.
8. Frank MacShane, *The Life of John O'Hara* (New York: E. P. Dutton, 1980), p. 72.
9. Matthew J. Bruccoli, *The O'Hara Concern: A Biography of John O'Hara* (New York: Random House, 1975), p. 112.
10. O'Hara, *Letters,* p. 106.
11. MacShane, *The Life of John O'Hara,* p. 68.
12. Anonymous, "John O'Hara's Pottsville," *Philadelphia Sunday Bulletin Magazine,* 25 October 1964.
13. O'Hara, *Letters,* p. 107.
14. Ibid., p. 402.
15. John O'Hara, *The Big Laugh* (New York: Random House, 1962), p. 101.
16. Ibid., pp. 100, 101.
17. John O'Hara, "Drawing Room B," in *Collected Stories of John O'Hara,* ed. Frank MacShane (New York: Vintage, 1986), p. 91.
18. Ibid., p. 92.

19. Ibid., p. 95.

20. John O'Hara, *The Doctor's Son and Other Stories* (New York: Harcourt, Brace, 1935), pp. 293, 294.

21. John O'Hara, "Ninety Minutes Away," in *Collected Stories of John O'Hara,* p. 235.

22. Brooke Allen, "Intimations of Mortality," *The New Criterion* (January 1995): 63.

23. O'Hara, *Collected Stories,* p. 229.

24. Ibid., pp. 246, 247.

25. Marion Meade, *Dorothy Parker: What Fresh Hell Is This?* (New York: Penguin Books, 1989), p. 261.

26. J. Bryan III, *Merry Gentlemen (And One Lady)* (New York: Atheneum, 1985), p. 116.

27. Farr, *O'Hara,* p. 177.

28. O'Hara, *Letters,* p. 101.

29. Ibid., p. 96.

30. Ibid., p. 107.

31. Ibid., p. 104.

32. John O'Hara, *Here's O'Hara* (New York: Random House, 1946), p. vii.

33. John O'Hara, *Butterfield 8* (New York: Random House, 1994), p. 99.

34. Ibid., p. 18.

35. O'Hara, *Letters,* p. 109.

36. Ibid., p. 108.

37. Louis Begley, "The Age of Vice," *Mirabella* (October 1994): 38.

38. O'Hara, *Butterfield 8,* p. 4.

39. John O'Hara, "Imagine Kissing Pete," in *Collected Stories of John O'Hara,* p. 123.

40. Herman Melville, *The Confidence-Man: His Masquerade* (Evanston: Northwestern University Press, 1982), p. 238.

41. O'Hara, *Butterfield 8,* p. 111.

42. O'Hara, "Imagine Kissing Pete," p. 120.

43. Ibid., p. 119.

44. Ibid., p. 120.

45. Ibid.

46. Ibid., p. 131.

47. O'Hara, *Butterfield 8,* pp. 25, 26.

48. Malcolm Cowley, "Hemingway Mixed with Hearst," in *Critical Essays on John O'Hara,* ed. Philip B. Eppard (New York: G. K. Hall, 1994), p. 33.

49. John O'Hara, "Remarks on the Novel," in *John O'Hara on Writers and Writing: "An Artist Is His Own Fault,"* ed. Matthew J. Bruccoli (Carbondale: Southern Illinois University Press, 1977), p. 100.

50. Heywood Broun, "On a Train Getting Away From It All," 31 October 1935: source of clip at Pennsylvania State University library unknown.

51. George Stevens, "Appointment in Park Avenue," *Saturday Review of Literature* (19 October 1935): 14.

52. Cowley, "Hemingway Mixed with Hearst," pp. 33, 34.
53. Bruccoli, *The O'Hara Concern,* p. 123.
54. O'Hara, "Hello Hollywood Good-Bye," p. 55.
55. O'Hara, *Letters,* p. 109.
56. Meade, *Dorothy Parker,* p. 186.
57. Ibid., p. 187.
58. Ibid., p. 196.
59. Ernest Hemingway, *True at First Light,* ed. Patrick Hemingway (New York: Scribner, 1999), p. 233.
60. O'Hara, *Letters,* p. 115.
61. Ibid., p. 116.
62. Meade, *Dorothy Parker,* p. 257.
63. Edmund Wilson, *The Thirties: From Notebooks and Diaries of the Period,* ed. Leon Edel (New York: Farrar, Straus & Giroux, 1980), p. 722.
64. MacShane, *The Life of John O'Hara,* p. 82.
65. Bruccoli, *The O'Hara Concern,* p. 134.
66. O'Hara, *Letters,* p. 120.
67. Ibid., p. 118.
68. Dorothy Parker, "Dorothy Parker," interview in *Writers at Work: The Paris Review Interviews,* ed. Malcolm Cowley, Writers at Work (New York: Viking, 1958), p. 81.
69. Sheilah Graham, *The Garden of Allah* (New York: Crown, 1970), p. 146.
70. MacShane, *The Life of John O'Hara,* p. 85.
71. Ibid., p. 87.
72. Bruccoli, *The O'Hara Concern,* p. 137.
73. John O'Hara, "The Follies of Broadway," *Holiday* (February 1967): 25.
74. O'Hara, "Hello Hollywood Good-Bye," pp. 54, 55, 125–29.
75. MacShane, *The Life of John O'Hara,* p. 87.
76. Farr, *O'Hara,* p. 188.
77. O'Hara, *The Big Laugh,* p. 239.
78. O'Hara, *Letters,* p. 61.
79. Farr, *O'Hara,* p. 187.
80. MacShane, *The Life of John O'Hara,* p. 92.
81. Harold Ross, "Letter to John O'Hara," The New Yorker archive in New York Public Library (11 August 1947).
82. MacShane, *The Life of John O'Hara,* p. 92.
83. O'Hara, *Letters,* p. 128.
84. Ibid.
85. John O'Hara, *Hope of Heaven,* in *Three of the Best* (London: Ravette, 1986), pp. 80, 81.
86. Bruccoli, *The O'Hara Concern,* p. 148.
87. O'Hara, *Letters,* p. 133.
88. Sterling North, "The Bright Young Drunks of American Literature," *Chicago Daily News,* 23 March 1938.
89. O'Hara, *Hope of Heaven,* p. 140.

90. John O'Hara, "Letter to Harold Ross," The New Yorker archive in New York Public Library (5 October 1939).

91. Brendan Gill, *Here at The New Yorker* (New York: Random House, 1975), pp. 159, 160.

92. Thomas Kunkel, *Genius in Disguise: Harold Ross of The New Yorker* (New York: Random House, 1995), p. 320.

93. John O'Hara, "Price's Always Open," in *Collected Stories of John O'Hara*, p. 36.

94. O'Hara, *Collected Stories*, p. 41.

95. Edmund Wilson, "The Boys in the Back Room: James M. Cain and John O'Hara," in *A Literary Chronicle: 1920–1950* (Garden City: Anchor, 1952), p. 220.

96. Louis Auchincloss, "The Novel of Manners Today: Marquand and O'Hara," in *Reflections of a Jacobite* (Boston: Houghton, Mifflin, 1961), p. 149.

97. Steven Goldleaf, *John O'Hara: A Study of the Short Fiction* (New York: Twayne, 1999), p. 28.

98. James Thurber, *The Years with Ross* (Boston: Atlantic Monthly Press, 1959), p. 13.

99. John O'Hara, "Do You Like It Here?" in *Collected Stories of John O'Hara*, pp. 64, 65.

100. O'Hara, *Letters*, p. 129.

101. Ibid., p. 134.

102. Ibid.

103. John O'Hara, "Appointment with O'Hara," *Collier's*, 19 August 1955.

104. MacShane, *The Life of John O'Hara*, p. 99.

105. Katharine Angell White, "Letter to John O'Hara," The New Yorker archive in New York Public Library (21 January 1932).

106. Katharine Angell White, "Letter to John O'Hara," The New Yorker archive in New York Public Library (15 December 1932).

107. Katharine Angell White, "Letter to John O'Hara," The New Yorker archive in New York Public Library (3 December 1937).

108. O'Hara, "Remarks on the Novel," p. 99.

109. O'Hara, *Letters*, p. 143.

110. Earl Wilson, "It Happened Last Night," *New York Post*, 28 March 1948.

111. O'Hara, *Letters*, p. 148.

112. Ibid., p. 145.

113. Ibid., pp. 153, 154.

114. Ibid., p. 156.

4. AT WAR AND ABOUT TOWN

1. Finis Farr, *O'Hara: A Biography* (Boston: Little, Brown, 1973), p. 193.

2. John O'Hara, "On Larry (Lorenzo) Hart," *New York Times*, 27 February 1944, II, 1.

3. Richard Rodgers, *Musical Stages* (New York: Da Capo Press, 1995), p. 199.

4. O'Hara, "On Larry (Lorenzo) Hart."

5. Ibid.

6. Lucius Beebe, "Stage Asides," *New York Herald-Tribune,* 12 January 1941.

7. Frank MacShane, *The Life of John O'Hara* (New York: E. P. Dutton, 1980), p. 113.

8. Rodgers, *Musical Stages,* p. 199.

9. Ibid., p. 200.

10. Richard Rodgers, " 'Pal Joey'—History of a Heel," *New York Times,* 30 December 1951.

11. Brooks Atkinson, "The Play: Christmas Night Adds 'Pal Joey,' " *New York Times,* 26 December 1940.

12. Richard Watts, Jr., "The Theatre: No Longer a Winter of Discontent," *New York Herald-Tribune,* 5 January 1941.

13. Wolcott Gibbs, "Upturn," *New Yorker,* 4 January 1941.

14. Benjamin Welles, "John O'Hara and His Pal Joey," *New York Times,* 26 January 1941.

15. Farr, *O'Hara,* p. 196.

16. Matthew J. Bruccoli, *The O'Hara Concern: A Biography of John O'Hara* (New York: Random House, 1975), p. 164.

17. Charles W. Bassett, "O'Hara's Roots: The Pottsville Years—1905–1927," *Pottsville Republican,* 15 May 1971.

18. John O'Hara, *Selected Letters of John O'Hara,* ed. Matthew J. Bruccoli (New York: Random House, 1978), p. 166.

19. Don A. Schanche, "John O'Hara Is Alive and Well in the First Half of the Twentieth Century (He Owns It)," *Esquire* (August 1969): 86.

20. O'Hara, *Letters,* p. 168.

21. John O'Hara, "Letter to Joseph Bryan III," John O'Hara Collection at Pennsylvania State University (25 April 1944).

22. MacShane, *The Life of John O'Hara,* p. 125.

23. O'Hara, *Letters,* p. 187.

24. John O'Hara, "Nothing From Joe?" *Liberty* (9 December 1944): 20, 21.

25. Bruccoli, *The O'Hara Concern,* p. 173.

26. MacShane, *The Life of John O'Hara,* p. 126.

27. O'Hara, *Letters,* p. 188.

28. John O'Hara, "An Artist Is His Own Fault," in *John O'Hara on Writers and Writing: "An Artist Is His Own Fault,"* ed. Matthew J. Bruccoli (Carbondale: Southern Illinois University Press, 1977), p. 113.

29. Steven Goldleaf, *John O'Hara: A Study of the Short Fiction* (New York: Twayne, 1999), pp. 39, 40, and 120.

30. O'Hara, *Letters,* p. 172.

31. O'Hara, "An Artist Is His Own Fault," p. 7.

32. Wolcott Gibbs, "Preface," in *Pipe Night* (New York: Duell, Sloan and Pearce, 1945), pp. ix–xii.

33. John O'Hara, "Graven Image," in *Pipe Night,* p. 125.

34. Lionel Trilling, "John O'Hara Observes Our Mores," *New York Times Book Review,* 18 March 1945, 1, 29.

35. Flannery O'Connor, "The Fiction Writer & His Country," in *Mystery and Manners: Occasional Prose,* ed. by Sally and Robert Fitzgerald (New York: Farrar, Straus & Giroux, 1969), p. 29.

36. John O'Hara, "Letter to Lionel Trilling," Correspondence at Columbia University Butler Library: Rare Books and Manuscripts, Lionel Trilling papers (21 March 1945).

37. John O'Hara, "Bread Alone," in *Pipe Night,* pp. 80–85.

38. Goldleaf, *John O'Hara: A Study of the Short Fiction,* p. 45.

39. Trilling, "John O'Hara Observes Our Mores," pp. 1, 29.

40. Bruccoli, *The O'Hara Concern,* p. 177.

41. O'Hara, *Letters,* pp. 151, 152.

42. Harold Ross, "Letters from the Editor," in *Letters from the Editor: The New Yorker's Harold Ross,* ed. Thomas Kunkel (New York: Modern Library, 2000), p. 364.

43. John O'Hara, "Letter to William Maxwell," New Yorker archive in New York Public Library (Undated, 1940).

44. O'Hara, *Letters,* p. 198.

45. John O'Hara, "Letter to Katharine White," New Yorker archive in New York Public Library (Undated, 1948).

46. Katharine Angell White, "Letter to John O'Hara," New Yorker archive in New York Public Library (10 February 1948).

47. O'Hara, *Letters,* p. 207.

48. Bennett Cerf, "Letter to John O'Hara," Correspondence at Columbia University Butler Library, Rare Books and Manuscripts, Bennett Cerf Papers (29 November 1948).

5. THE TOMES

1. John O'Hara, *A Rage to Live* (New York: Random House, 1997), p. 6.

2. Ibid.

3. Brendan Gill, *Critical Essays on John O'Hara,* ed. Phillip B. Eppard (New York: G. K. Hall, 1994), pp. 52–54.

4. O'Hara, *A Rage to Live,* p. 165.

5. Ibid., p. 167.

6. Ibid., p. 609.

7. Ibid., p. 575.

8. Ibid., p. 301.

9. Ibid., p. 302.

10. Jack Keating, "John O'Hara's World of Yale, Society, and Sex," *Cosmopolitan* (September 1960): 59–63.

11. Brendan Gill, *Here at The New Yorker* (New York: Random House, 1975), p. 272.

12. Thomas Kunkel, *Genius in Disguise: Harold Ross of The New Yorker* (New York: Random House, 1995), p. 284.

13. John O'Hara, "Letter to Lionel Trilling," Correspondence at Columbia University Butler Library, Rare Books and Manuscripts, Lionel Trilling papers (21 August 1949).

14. Brendan Gill, *Here at The New Yorker,* p. 273.

15. Ibid., p. 274.

16. Cerf, "Portrait of a Pro," from undated *Saturday Review* clip at Pennsylvania State University Library.

17. Frank MacShane, *The Life of John O'Hara* (New York: E. P. Dutton, 1980), p. 146.

18. Matthew J. Bruccoli, *The O'Hara Concern: A Biography of John O'Hara* (New York: Random House, 1975), p. 192.

19. Ibid., p. 203.

20. Ibid.

21. Gill, *Here at The New Yorker,* pp. 276, 277.

22. Ibid., p. 279.

23. John O'Hara, *Ten North Frederick* (New York: Random House, 1955), p. 259.

24. Ibid., p. 302.

25. Ibid., p. 355.

26. Ibid.

27. Ibid., p. 220.

28. John O'Hara, *My Turn* (New York: Random House, 1966), p. 82.

29. O'Hara, *Ten North Frederick,* p. 161.

30. Ibid., p. 168.

31. Ibid., p. 309.

32. Ibid., p. 324.

33. Ibid., p. 330.

34. John O'Hara, "An Artist Is His Own Fault," in *John O'Hara on Writers and Writing: "An Artist Is His Own Fault,"* ed. Matthew J. Bruccoli (Carbondale: Southern Illinois University Press, 1977), p. 102.

35. John O'Hara, *From the Terrace* (New York: Random House, 1958), p. 813.

36. John O'Hara, *The Lockwood Concern* (New York: Random House, 1965), p. 327.

37. O'Hara, *From the Terrace,* p. 893.

38. Ibid., pp. 591, 592.

39. Ibid., p. 495.

40. Ibid., p. 306.

41. Ibid., p. 776.

42. John O'Hara, *Ourselves to Know* (New York: Random House, 1960), p. 167.

43. O'Hara, *From the Terrace,* p. 160.

44. Ibid., p. 536.

45. Ibid., p. 348.

46. Ibid., p. 43.

47. Ibid., p. 301.
48. Ibid., p. 685.
49. Arthur Mizener, "Reconsideration," *New Republic,* 11 November 1972, 30.
50. O'Hara, *From the Terrace*, p. 6.
51. Ibid., p. 229.
52. Ibid., p. 220.
53. O'Hara, *Ourselves to Know*, p. 408.
54. Ibid., p. 165.
55. Ibid., p. 179.

6. A LOCAL HABITATION AND A NAME

1. John O'Hara, "An Artist Is His Own Fault," in *John O'Hara on Writers and Writing: "An Artist Is His Own Fault,"* ed. Matthew J. Bruccoli (Carbondale: Southern Illinois University Press, 1977), p. 63.
2. John O'Hara, *Selected Letters of John O'Hara,* ed. Matthew J. Bruccoli (New York: Random House, 1978), p. 203.
3. O'Hara, "An Artist Is His Own Fault," p. 59.
4. Ibid., p. 70.
5. O'Hara, *Letters*, pp. 228, 229.
6. John O'Hara, *My Turn* (New York: Random House, 1966), p. 97.
7. Matthew J. Bruccoli, *The O'Hara Concern: A Biography of John O'Hara* (New York: Random House, 1975), p. 203.
8. Finis Farr, *O'Hara: A Biography* (Boston: Little, Brown, 1973), p. 218.
9. J. Bryan III, *Merry Gentlemen (And One Lady)* (New York: Atheneum, 1985), p. 58.
10. O'Hara, *Letters*, p. 240.
11. MacShane, *The Life of John O'Hara* (New York: E. P. Dutton, 1980), p. 158.
12. John O'Hara, "We're Friends Again," in *Sermons and Soda Water* (New York: Random House, 1960), p. 64.
13. Don A. Schanche, "John O'Hara Is Alive and Well in the First Half of the Twentieth Century (He Owns It)," *Esquire* (August 1969): 149.
14. John O'Hara, *Sweet and Sour* (New York: Random House, 1954), p. 75.
15. Sheldon Norman Grebstein, *John O'Hara* (New York: Twayne, 1966), p. 141.
16. Harvey Breit, *The Writer Observed* (New York: World, 1956), p. 20.
17. O'Hara, *My Turn*, p. 3.
18. Ibid., p. 13.
19. C. D. B. Bryan, "My John O'Hara," *Esquire* (July 1985): 103.
20. Ibid.
21. John O'Hara, "The Flatted Saxophone," in *Collected Stories of John O'Hara,* ed. Frank MacShane (New York: Vintage, 1986), p. 203.
22. O'Hara, *Letters*, p. 508.
23. James Kerney Jr., "The Simple Life . . . But in Style," *Evening Times,* 23 May 1966.

24. William Maxwell, Interview with the author, New York, 6 January 1995.

25. John O'Hara, *From the Terrace* (New York: Random House, 1958), pp. 808, 809.

26. Ibid., p. 260.

27. Ibid., p. 272.

28. O'Hara, *Letters,* p. 431.

BIBLIOGRAPHY

Aldrich, Nelson W. Jr. *Old Money: The Mythology of Wealth in America.* New York: Allworth Press, 1996.

Allen, Brooke. "Intimations of Mortality." *The New Criterion* (January 1995): 62–67.

Alterman, Eric. "Monster With a Commitment." *Columbia Journalism Review* 32, 1 (May/June 1992).

Anonymous. "Brother Mart Says: Kind, Shy, Great Guy." *Pottsville Republican,* 15 January 1972.

———. "John O'Hara's Pottsville." *Philadelphia Sunday Bulletin Magazine,* 25 October 1964.

———. "Profile." *Pittsburgh Bulletin-Index,* 12 July 1933.

———. "A Rage to Write." *M.D. Medical Newsmagazine* (April 1971): 154–60.

———. "Seventy-Five Years Ago (reprinted from 1916)." *Pottsville Republican,* 21 August 1991.

Atkinson, Brooks. "The Play: Christmas Night Adds 'Pal Joey.' " *New York Times,* 26 December 1940.

Auchincloss, Louis. "The Novel of Manners Today: Marquand and O'Hara." In *Reflections of a Jacobite.* Boston: Houghton Mifflin, 1961.

Bassett, Charles W. "O'Hara's Roots: The Pottsville Years—1905–1927." *Pottsville Republican,* 1971.

Beebe, Lucius. "Stage Asides." *New York Herald-Tribune,* 12 January 1941.

Begley, Louis. "The Age of Vice." *Mirabella* (October 1994): 38.

Bernstein, Burton. *Thurber: A Biography.* New York: Dodd, Mead, 1975.

Biederman, Patricia Ward. "Literary Legends." *Los Angeles Times,* 24 February 1995, Valley Life, 8.

Bierce, Ambrose. *The Devil's Dictionary.* New York: Dover, 1993.

Bird, David, and Maurice Carroll. "A Journalists' Hangout Becomes a Gift Shop." *New York Times,* 29 May 1984, B-3.

Broun, Heywood. "On a Train Getting Away From It All." *Unknown,* 31 October 1935.

Brown, Anthony Cave. *The Last Hero: Wild Bill Donovan.* New York: New York Times Books, 1982.

Bruccoli, Matthew J. *The O'Hara Concern: A Biography of John O'Hara.* New York: Random House, 1975.

Bryan, J. III. *Merry Gentlemen (And One Lady).* New York: Atheneum, 1985.

Cerf, Bennett. Letter to John O'Hara. 29 November 1948. Correspondence, Bennett Cerf Papers. Columbia University Butler Library: Rare Books and Manuscripts.

Cook, Don. "The Paper: The Life and Death of the Herald Tribune." *Los Angeles Times Book Review,* 23 November 1986, 2.

Cowley, Malcolm. "Hemingway Mixed with Hearst." In *Critical Essays on John O'Hara.* Ed. Philip B. Eppard. New York: G. K. Hall, 1994.

Crichton, Kyle. Charles Scribner's Sons Archive, Letters to John O'Hara. Princeton University, Firestone Library.

———. *Total Recoil.* Garden City: Doubleday, 1960.

Daws, Gavan. *A Dream of Islands: Voyages of Discovery in the South Seas.* New York: Norton, 1980.

Ecenbarger, William. "Forgetting John O'Hara: Pottsville's Revenge." *Today (The Inquirer Magazine), Philadelphia Inquirer,* 16 May 1984, 13–17.

Faithfull, Starr. "Starr Faithfull to a Former Boyfriend." In *America 1900–1999: Letters of the Century.* Ed. Lisa Grunwald and Stephen J. Adler. New York: Dial Press, 1999.

Farquhar, Walter S. "Musings." *Pottsville Journal,* 30 August 1949.

Farr, Finis. *O'Hara: A Biography.* Boston: Little, Brown, 1973.

Ferguson, Harry. "The Memory Machine." *Atlantic Monthly* (March 1976): 72–76.

Fitzgerald, F. Scott. "Babylon Revisited." In *Babylon Revisited and Other Stories.* New York: Charles Scribner's Sons, 1960.

———. *The Letters of F. Scott Fitzgerald.* Ed. Andrew Turnbull. New York: Charles Scribner's Sons, 1963.

———. "The Rich Boy." In *Babylon Revisited and Other Stories.* New York: Charles Scribner's Sons, 1960.

———. "Winter Dreams." In *Babylon Revisited and Other Stories.* New York: Charles Scribner's Sons, 1960.

Flanagan, Thomas. "The Molly Maguires: An American Story of Truth and Justice Denied." *Los Angeles Times Book Review,* 5 April 1998, 3, 4.

Gary, Beverly. "A Post Portrait: John O'Hara: Part Three." *New York Post,* 21 May 1959.

———. "A Post Portrait: John O'Hara: Part Two." *New York Post,* 19 May 1959.

Geier, Ione. "O'Hara Era in Pottsville." *Pottsville Republican,* 14 October 1978.

Gibbs, Wolcott. "Preface." In *Pipe Night.* New York: Duell, Sloan and Pearce, 1945.

———. "Upturn." *New Yorker,* 4 January 1941.

———. "Watch Out for Mr. O'Hara." *Saturday Review,* 19 February 1938, 10–12.

Gill, Brendan. *Critical Essays on John O'Hara.* Ed. Phillip B. Eppard. New York: G. K. Hall, 1994.

———. *Here at The New Yorker.* New York: Random House, 1975.

Goldleaf, Steven. *John O'Hara: A Study of the Short Fiction.* New York: Twayne, 1999.

Graham, Sheilah. *The Garden of Allah.* New York: Crown, 1970.

Grosvenor, Peter. "John O'Hara . . . Two Blows He Had to Beat." *London Daily Express,* 4 May 1967, 6.

Hart, Stan. *Fumblefinger: A Life Out of Line.* New York: Abeel & Leet, 1999.

Hemingway, Ernest. "African Journal." *Sports Illustrated,* 10 January 1972, 27.

———. "Indian Camp." In *The Short Stories of Ernest Hemingway.* New York: Scribner, 1966.

Holmes, Charles S. *The Clocks of Columbus: The Literary Career of James Thurber.* New York: Atheneum, 1978.

Hutchens, John K. "John O'Hara From Pottsville, Pa." *New York Herald-Tribune,* 4 December 1955.

Just, Ward. *Honor, Power, Riches, Fame, and the Love of Women.* New York: E. P. Dutton, 1979.

Krim, Seymour. "Monumental Trivialist." *Harper's* (February 1981): 75–77.

Kunkel, Thomas. *Genius in Disguise: Harold Ross of The New Yorker.* New York: Random House, 1995.

Lebowitz, Fran. "A Humorist at Work." Interview by James Linville and George Plimpton. *Paris Review* 127 (summer 1993): 160–88.

Lewis, Sinclair. "Review of Appointment in Samarra." *Saturday Review,* 6 July 1934.

Long, Robert Emmet. *John O'Hara.* New York: Frederick Ungar, 1983.

Luce, Henry R. To John O'Hara. 6 April 1962. John O'Hara Papers, United States Trust Company.

MacShane, Frank. *The Life of John O'Hara.* New York: E. P. Dutton, 1980.

Mailer, Norman. "Dorothy Parker (1949)." In *The Time of Our Time.* New York: Random House, 1998.

Malcolm, Janet. *The Silent Woman: Sylvia Plath & Ted Hughes.* New York: Alfred A. Knopf, 1994.

Maxwell, William. Letter to John O'Hara. The New Yorker Archive. 20 June 1938. New York Public Library.

McFadden, Amy and Denise, et al. "CoalSpeak: Dictionary of the Coal Region." <http://www.coalregion.com/speak.htm>. 1998.

Meade, Marion. *Dorothy Parker: What Fresh Hell Is This?* New York: Penguin Books, 1989.

Melville, Herman. *The Confidence-Man: His Masquerade.* Evanston & Chicago: Northwestern University Press and the Newberry Library, 1982.

Mitgang, Herbert. "Obituary." *New York Times,* 12 May 1981, section D, 23.

Mizener, Arthur. "Reconsideration." *New Republic,* 11 November 1972, 30–32.

Nolan, Martin F. "Something's Missing—and Very Missed—in San Francisco." *Boston Globe,* 28 January 1998, A-19.

North, Sterling. "The Bright Young Drunks of American Literature." *Chicago Daily News,* 23 March 1938.

O'Connor, Flannery. "The Fiction Writer & His Country." In *Mystery and Manners: Occasional Prose.* Ed. Sally and Robert Fitzgerald. New York: Farrar, Straus & Giroux, 1969.

O'Hara, John. *Appointment in Samarra.* New York: Modern Library, 1994.

———. "Appointment with O'Hara." *Collier's,* 23 December 1955.

———. *The Big Laugh.* New York: Random House, 1962.

———. "Bread Alone." In *Pipe Night.* New York: Duell, Sloan and Pearce, 1945.

———. *Butterfield 8.* New York: Random House, 1994.

———. *A Cub Tells His Story.* Iowa City: Windover Press and Bruccoli Clark, 1974.

———. "Dancing School." *New York Herald-Tribune,* 3 August 1930, 7.

———. "Do You Like It Here?" In *Collected Stories of John O'Hara.* Ed. Frank MacShane. New York: Vintage, 1986.

———. *The Doctor's Son and Other Stories.* New York: Harcourt, Brace, 1935.

———. "The Doctor's Son." In *Collected Stories of John O'Hara.* Ed. Frank Mac-Shane. New York: Vintage, 1986.

———. "Don't Say It Never Happened." In *"An Artist Is His Own Fault": John O'Hara on Writers and Writing.* Ed. Matthew J. Bruccoli. Carbondale: Southern Illinois University Press, 1977.

———. "Drawing Room B." In *Collected Stories of John O'Hara.* Ed. Frank Mac-Shane. New York: Vintage, 1986.

———. "Fatimas and Kisses." In *Collected Stories of John O'Hara.* Ed. Frank Mac-Shane. New York: Vintage, 1986.

———. "The Flatted Saxophone." In *Collected Stories of John O'Hara.* Ed. Frank MacShane. New York: Vintage, 1986.

———. "The Follies of Broadway." *Holiday* (February 1967): 25.

———. *From the Terrace.* New York: Random House, 1958.

———. "The Girl from California." In *Collected Stories of John O'Hara.* Ed. Frank MacShane. New York: Vintage, 1986.

———. "Hello Hollywood Good-Bye." *Holiday* (May 1968): 54, 55, 125–29.

———. *Here's O'Hara.* New York: Duell, Sloan and Pearce, 1946.

———. "Hope of Heaven." In *Hope of Heaven.* London: Ravette, 1986.

———. "How Can I Tell You?" In *The Hat on the Bed.* New York: Random House, 1963.

———. *Imagine Kissing Pete.* In *Collected Stories of John O'Hara.* Ed. Frank Mac-Shane. New York: Vintage, 1986.

———. "In the Silence." In *Collected Stories of John O'Hara.* Ed. Frank Mac-Shane. New York: Vintage, 1986.

———. "It Must Have Been Spring." In *Collected Stories of John O'Hara.* Ed. Frank MacShane. New York: Vintage, 1986.

———. *The Lockwood Concern.* New York: Random House, 1965.

———. "Memoirs of a Sentimental Duffer." *Holiday* (May 1965).

————. *My Turn*. New York: Random House, 1966.

————. "Natica Jackson." In *Collected Stories of John O'Hara*. Ed. Frank Mac-Shane. New York: Vintage, 1986.

————. "Ninety Minutes Away." In *Collected Stories of John O'Hara*. Ed. Frank MacShane. New York: Vintage, 1986.

————. "Nothing From Joe?" *Liberty*, 9 December 1944, 20, 21.

————. "Of Thee I Sing, Baby." In *The Doctor's Son*. New York: Harcourt, Brace, 1935.

————. "On Cars and Snobbism." *Holiday* (August 1966): 52, 53.

————. "On Larry (Lorenzo) Hart." *New York Times*, 27 February 1944, II, 1.

————. *Ourselves to Know*. New York: Random House, 1960.

————. "Price's Always Open." In *Collected Stories of John O'Hara*. Ed. Frank MacShane. New York: Vintage, 1986.

————. *A Rage to Live*. New York: Modern Library, 1997.

————. "Remarks on the Novel." In *John O'Hara on Writers and Writing: "An Artist Is His Own Fault."* Ed. Matthew J. Bruccoli. Carbondale: Southern Illinois University Press, 1977.

————. *Selected Letters of John O'Hara*. Ed. Matthew J. Bruccoli. New York: Random House, 1978.

————. *Sweet and Sour: Comments on Books and People*. New York: Random House, 1954.

————. *Ten North Frederick*. New York: Random House, 1955.

————. "These Stories Were Part of Me." In *John O'Hara on Writers and Writing: "An Artist Is His Own Fault."* Ed. Matthew J. Bruccoli. Carbondale: Southern Illinois University Press, 1977.

————. "Untitled Letter." In Finis Farr, *O'Hara: A Biography*. Boston: Little, Brown, 1960.

————. "When Bands Were Big." *Holiday* (April 1967): 26.

————. "Why Manchester Roots for Its Small-Town Doctor." *New York Daily Mirror*, 9 March 1950.

————. "An Artist Is His Own Fault." In *John O'Hara on Writers and Writing: "An Artist Is His Own Fault."* Ed. Matthew J. Bruccoli. Carbondale: Southern Illinois University Press, 1977.

————. "Fire!" In *Pipe Night*. New York: Duell, Sloan and Pearce, 1945.

————. "Graven Image." In *Pipe Night*. New York: Duell, Sloan and Pearce, 1945.

————. "Summer's Day." In *Pipe Night*. New York: Duell, Sloan and Pearce, 1945.

O'Neill, Hugh. "Review of the Life and Times of Franklin Pierce Adams." *Los Angeles Times Book Review*, 9 November 1986.

Parker, Dorothy. "Dorothy Parker." Interview in *Writers at Work: The Paris Review Interviews*. Ed. Malcolm Cowley. New York: Viking Press, 1958.

Plimpton, George. Telephone conversation with author. 6 June 2000.

Podhoretz, Norman. "John O'Hara and Mary McCarthy." In *Doings and Undoings*. New York: Noonday Press, 1964.

Prescott, Peter S. "Appointment with O'Hara." *Newsweek*, 12 January 1981.

Quigg, H. D. "The Times Square That Was a Paean to an Era." *UPI*, 24 November 1984.

Roberts, Edwin A. Jr. "The Curtain Falls on O'Hara's Stage." *National Observer*, 30 November 1974, 26.

Rodgers, Richard. *Musical Stages*. New York: Da Capo Press, 1995.

———. " 'Pal Joey'—History of a Heel." *New York Times*, 30 December 1951.

Ross, Harold. *Letters from the Editor: The New Yorker's Harold Ross*. Ed. Thomas Kunkel. New York: Modern Library, 2000.

Roth, Philip. "Writing American Fiction." In *The American Novel Since World War II*. Ed. Marcus Klein. New York: Fawcett World Library, 1969.

Sayre, Joel. "John O'Hara: A Reminiscence." *Washington Post Book World*, 18 March 1973.

Schanche, Don A. "John O'Hara Is Alive and Well in the First Half of the Twentieth Century (He Owns It)." *Esquire* (August 1969): 84–86, 142, 144–49.

Shannon, L. R. and Betsy Wade. "Last Days of the Newspaper Saloon." *Columbia Journalism Review* 31, 2 (July 1992): 37.

Shannon, William V. *The American Irish: A Political and Social Portrait*. Amherst: University of Massachusetts Press, 1989.

Shaw, David. "Trials of the Trib." *New York Times Book Review*, 26 October 1986, 7.

Shoup, Mike. "Mining the Coal Country Anthracite Long Ago Abdicated in This Pennsylvania Region." *Philadelphia Inquirer*, 14 August 1994, Travel Section.

Steinbeck, John. *Steinbeck: A Life in Letters*. Ed. Elaine Steinbeck and Robert Wallsten. New York: Viking Press, 1975.

Stevens, George. "Appointment in Park Avenue." *Saturday Review of Literature*, 19 October 1935, 14.

Thurber, James. *The Years with Ross*. Boston: Atlantic Monthly Press, 1959.

Trilling, Lionel. "John O'Hara Observes Our Mores." *New York Times Book Review*, 18 March 1945, 1, 29.

Tuttleton, James W. *The Novel of Manners in America*. New York: W. W. Norton, 1974.

Updike, John. "O'Hara's Messy Masterpiece." *New Republic*, 2 May 1988, 38–41.

Van Gelder, Robert. "John O'Hara, Who Talks Like His Stories." *New York Times Book Review*, 26 May 1940, 12.

Walcutt, Charles Child. *John O'Hara*. University of Minnesota Pamphlets on American Writers, vol. 80. Minneapolis: University of Minnesota Press, 1969.

———. "John O'Hara: 1905–1970." In *American Writers: A Collection of Literary Biographies*. Vol. III: Archibald MacLeish to George Santayana. Ed. Leonard Unger. New York: Charles Scribner's Sons, 1974.

Walton, Edith H. "Mr. O'Hara's Stories." *New York Times Book Review*, 24 February 1935, 7.

Ward, Leo L. *A Collection of 20 Historical Musings*. Pottsville: Historical Society of Schuylkill County, 1994.

Watts, Richard, Jr. "The Theatre: No Longer a Winter of Discontent." *New York Herald-Tribune*, 5 January 1941.

Weiner, Jon. "Book Review of Cloak & Gown." *Nation*, 5 September 1987, 204.

Welles, Benjamin. "John O'Hara and His Pal Joey." *New York Times,* 26 January 1941.

Whitman, Alden. "O'Hara, in Rare Interview, Calls Literary Landscape Fairly Bleak." *New York Times,* 13 November 1967, 49.

Wilson, Earl. "It Happened Last Night." *New York Post,* 28 March 1948.

Wilson, Edmund. "The Boys in the Back Room: James M. Cain and John O'Hara." In *A Literary Chronicle: 1920–1950.* Garden City: Anchor, 1952.

————. *The Thirties: From Notebooks and Diaries of the Period.* Ed. Leon Edel. New York: Farrar, Straus & Giroux, 1980.

Winks, Robin. *Cloak & Gown: Scholars in the Secret War, 1938–1961.* New York: Morrow, 1987.

INDEX

physical appearance, 206
social life in Princeton, 304
O'Hara, Gen. Charles, 12
O'Hara, Eugene (brother), 22, 172,
199, 215
O'Hara, Helen Petit ("Pet") (first wife),
91, 126, 229, 231
abortion, 134–5
death of, 305
divorce, 136–7, 138, 140
Fitzgerald and, 145
honeymoon, 121–3
married life, 120–1, 128, 129–31,
132–3
personal qualities, 119
physical appearance, 119
post-marital relationship, 141, 184,
185
theatrical career, 119, 130
wedding, 119–20
O'Hara, Capt. James, 11
O'Hara, James (brother), 22, 69
O'Hara, James (uncle), 13
O'Hara, John
acting stint, 208
actors, contempt for, 130, 174, 244–5
alienation of friends, 185, 268
apartments, taste in, 213
automobile ownership, 167, 168–9,
182, 316
awards and honors, 287–8
back pain, 322
Bermuda trip, 121–3
birth of, 6
bootlegging experience, 75
bumming about, 75–9, 95
business-like approach to writing,
268, 269n
celebrities' attraction for, 88–9
celebrity status, 244
child born to, 255
childhood and youth, 6, 18–25,
28–31, 33–9, 41–8
class, ambivalence about, 35

clubmanship, interest in, 50–1, 317n
"confession" incident, 43–4
"cowboy outfit" incident, 33
"creative sterility" of 1940s, 255–6
critics' judgments, response to, 142
dancing classes, 37–8
death of, 331–2
drinking habit, xix, 30, 45, 53–4, 75,
76–7, 86–7, 90, 130–3, 135, 139,
141, 202, 203, 212, 213, 236, 241,
305
editors' advice, disregard of, 265–6
education, 33–6, 41–4, 45–7, 51–3,
299–300
epitaph for, 332
estrangement from family in
Pottsville, 215, 328
European visit (1939), 229–32
fashion-consciousness, 61–2
film-writing work, 166, 167, 168, 169,
176, 201, 209, 235
fistfighting, 29, 42, 47, 66, 130
"flight over New York" incident, xix
genealogical interests, 10–12
Hollywood stays, 164, 165–70, 174,
200–13, 235, 316
honorary degrees, longing for,
300–1n
horsemanship, 20, 22, 31
inquisitiveness of, 93
Irishness, attitude toward, 38–41
jealousy of, 318
journalism career, 55–61, 73–4,
83–91, 93, 94-6, 99–100, 137–8,
140, 141, 142, 163–4
low points of his life, 78–9, 105–8,
117–18
loyalty to kin and old friends, 328–9
lung cancer scare, 65, 66–7
marriages, see O'Hara, Belle Wylie;
O'Hara, Helen Petit ("Pet");
O'Hara, Katharine Barnes ("Sister")
medical career, rejection of, 28

TEXTUAL PERMISSIONS

PHOTOGRAPHIC CREDITS

A NOTE ON THE TYPE

This book was set in Caledonia, a face designed by William Addison Dwiggins (1880–1956) for the Mergenthaler Linotype Company in 1939. It belongs to the family of types referred to by printers as "modern," a term used to mark the change in type styles that occurred around 1800. Caledonia was inspired by the Scotch types cast by the Glasgow typefounders Alexander Wilson & Sons circa 1833. However, there is a calligraphic quality about Caledonia that is completely lacking in the Wilson types. Dwiggins referred to an even earlier typeface for this "liveliness of action"—one cut around 1790 by William Martin for the printer William Bulmer. Caledonia has more weight than the Martin letters, and the bottom finishing strokes of the letters are cut straight across, without brackets, to make sharp angles with the upright stems, thus giving a modern-face appearance.

W. A. Dwiggins began his association with the Mergenthaler Linotype Company in 1929, and over the next twenty-seven years he designed a number of book types, the most interesting of which are Metro, Electra, Caledonia, Eldorado, and Falcon.

Composed by North Market Street Graphics, Lancaster, Pennsylvania

Printed and bound by Berryville Graphics,
Berryville, Virginia

Designed by Iris Weinstein